高职高专"十二五"规划教材

化学化工基础英语

Fundamental English in Chemistry & Chemical Engineering

刘庆文　主编　马　竟　副主编
肖　扬　主审

·北京·

本书由三个部分20个单元构成，每个单元由课文、难点注释、词汇表、课后练习和阅读材料组成。课文主要内容有无机化合物、有机化合物、高分子聚合物的命名和性质，精细化工产品、分析检验仪器设备和化工生产设备的介绍，还包括相关企业和涉及化工产品的品名、性质、储存、包装和危险品等级等内容。书后附有练习答案、课文中文参考译文、总词汇表、化学化工常用构词、常见有机基团、常见有机化合物命名、元素名称及读法和常用化工产品英文缩写与中文名称对照表等可供查阅。

本书内容语言精炼、知识性强、覆盖面广、难度适中，可作为高职高专商务英语专业的补充教材，也可作为高职高专化学化工专业英语教材，还可作为从事化工商贸活动和化工生产、管理、经营、销售等专业人员的参考资料。

图书在版编目(CIP)数据

化学化工基础英语/刘庆文主编．—北京：化学工业出版社，2007.12（2021.2重印）
高职高专"十二五"规划教材
ISBN 978-7-122-01673-7

Ⅰ．化⋯ Ⅱ．刘⋯ Ⅲ．①化学-英语-高等学校：技术学院-教材②化学工业-英语-高等学校：技术学院-教材 Ⅳ．H31

中国版本图书馆CIP数据核字（2007）第192311号

责任编辑：旷英姿　　　　　　　　　　　装帧设计：关　飞
责任校对：洪雅姝

出版发行：化学工业出版社（北京市东城区青年湖南街13号　邮政编码100011）
印　　装：北京七彩京通数码快印有限公司
787mm×1092mm　1/16　印张15½　字数409千字　2021年2月北京第1版第7次印刷

购书咨询：010-64518888　　　　　　　　售后服务：010-64518899
网　　址：http://www.cip.com.cn
凡购买本书，如有缺损质量问题，本社销售中心负责调换。

定　　价：38.00元　　　　　　　　　　　　　　　　　　　　　　版权所有　违者必究

前　言

近年来，高职高专商务英语专业的毕业生进入化工企业工作时，最大的困难是缺乏化学化工知识、化学化工英语词汇、术语等，对仪器和设备的英文表达了解也不多。为了使学生毕业后能尽快胜任化学化工外贸工作，化学化工类高职院校商贸英语专业开设化学化工基础英语课程十分必要，为此化学工业出版社组织编写了本教材。

本书选材来源于原版英文书籍、杂志、英语化学化工网站、国内外知名企业仪器设备样本等资料。由三个部分20个单元构成，每个单元由课文、难点注释、词汇表、课后练习和阅读材料组成。课文主要内容有无机化合物、有机化合物、高分子聚合物的命名和性质，精细化工产品、分析检验仪器设备和化工生产设备的介绍，还包括相关企业和涉及化工产品的品名、性质、储存、包装和危险品等级等内容。书后附有练习答案、课文中文参考译文、总词汇表、化学化工常用构词、常见有机基团、常见有机化合物命名、元素名称及读法、常用化工产品英文缩写与中文名称对照表等可供查阅。

本书内容语言精炼、知识性强、覆盖面广、难度适中，可作为高职高专商务英语专业的补充教材，也可作为高职高专化学化工专业英语教材，还可作为从事化工商贸活动和化工生产、管理、经营、销售等专业人员的参考资料。为方便教学，本书配有电子课件。

本教材由天津渤海职业技术学院刘庆文担任主编，马竟担任副主编，天津渤海化工联合进出口公司肖扬主审。其中第1～6单元由马竟编写，第7～13、15单元由刘庆文编写，第14、16～20单元由湖南化工职业技术学院陈文娟编写，全书由刘庆文统稿。

在本书编写过程中得到了许多同志的鼎力支持和热情帮助，中国远大集团远大海外经济投资发展有限公司副总裁南泉、天津渤海化工集团公司教育培训中心常务副主任杨厚俊同志、天津渤海化工联合进出口公司李锡琴、王艳华和李嘉庆同志对本书的编写都给予了具体的建议和指导，天津渤海职业技术学院的范琳老师帮助录入了许多材料，在此一并表示衷心的感谢。

本书虽然经过多次补充和完善，但限于编者水平，书中不足之处在所难免，恳请广大读者指正。

编者
2007年9月16日

CONTENTS

PART ONE　BASIC KNOWLEDGE OF INORGANIC AND ORGANIC CHEMISTRY …… 1
　Unit 1　Basic Concepts of Inorganic Chemistry ……………………………………… 1
　Unit 2　Acids, Bases and Salts ……………………………………………………… 8
　Unit 3　Naming Inorganic Compounds …………………………………………… 14
　Unit 4　Naming Organic Compounds ……………………………………………… 23
　Unit 5　The Nature of Organic Compounds ……………………………………… 29
　Unit 6　Hydrocarbons ……………………………………………………………… 36
　Unit 7　Aromaticity and Naming Benzene ………………………………………… 44
　Unit 8　The Properties of polymers ………………………………………………… 51
　Unit 9　Rubber and Plastic ………………………………………………………… 60
　Unit 10　Fine Chemicals …………………………………………………………… 66

PART TWO　INTRODUCTION OF ANALYTICAL INSTRUMENTS …………… 75
　Unit 11　Ultraviolet and Visible Spectrophotometer ……………………………… 75
　Unit 12　Gas Chromatograph ……………………………………………………… 83
　Unit 13　Atomic Absorption Spectrometry ………………………………………… 91
　Unit 14　Infrared Spectrometer …………………………………………………… 96
　Unit 15　Mass Spectrometer ……………………………………………………… 104
　Unit 16　Nuclear Magnetic Resonance Spectrometry …………………………… 111

PART THREE　INTRODUCTION OF CHEMICAL EQUIPMENT ……………… 117
　Unit 17　Crystallization Equipment ……………………………………………… 117
　Unit 18　Distillation Equipment …………………………………………………… 124
　Unit 19　Drying Equipment ……………………………………………………… 132
　Unit 20　Reactors ………………………………………………………………… 140
　Key to the exercises ……………………………………………………………… 146
　Translation ………………………………………………………………………… 162
　第1部分　无机和有机化学基本知识 …………………………………………… 162
　第2部分　分析仪器介绍 ………………………………………………………… 181
　第3部分　化工设备介绍 ………………………………………………………… 194

Vocabulary ………………………………………………………………………… 202
　New Words ………………………………………………………………………… 202
　Phrases …………………………………………………………………………… 219

Appendixes ………………………………………………………………………… 230
　Ⅰ　化学化工常用构词 …………………………………………………………… 230
　Ⅱ　常见有机基团 ………………………………………………………………… 231
　Ⅲ　常见有机化合物命名 ………………………………………………………… 231
　Ⅳ　元素名称及读法 ……………………………………………………………… 235
　Ⅴ　常用化工产品英文缩写与中文名称对照表 ………………………………… 238

REFERENCES ……………………………………………………………………… 244

PART ONE BASIC KNOWLEDGE OF INORGANIC AND ORGANIC CHEMISTRY

Unit 1 Basic Concepts of Inorganic Chemistry

MATTER

Definition of Matter

Matter is defined as anything that occupies space and has mass. Mass is the quantity of matter which a substance possesses and, depending on the gravitational force acting on it, has a unit of weight assigned to it [1]. Although the weight then can vary, the mass of the body is a constant and can be measured by its resistance to a change of position or motion. This property of mass to resist a change of position or motion is called inertia. Since matter does occupy space, we can compare the masses of various substances that occupy a particular unit volume. This relationship of mass to a unit volume is called the density of the substance. It can be shown in a mathematical formula as $D=\dfrac{m}{V}$. The basic unit of mass (m) in chemistry is the gram (g), and of volume (V) is the cubic centimeter (cm^3) or milliliter (mL).

States of Matter

Matter occurs in three states: solid, liquid, and gas. A solid has both a definite size and shape. A liquid has a definite volume but takes the shape of the container and a gas has neither definite shape nor definite volume. These states of matter can often be changed by the addition of heat energy. An example of this is ice changing to liquid water and finally steam.

Composition of Matter

Matter can be subdivided into two general categories: distinct substances and mixtures. The distinct substances are either elements or compounds. If a substance is made up of only one kind of atom, it is called an element. If, however, it is composed of two or more kinds of atoms joined together in a definite grouping, it is classified as a compound [2]. That a compound then always occurs in a definite composition is called the Law of Definite Composition of Proportion. An example of this is water: it always occurs in two hydrogen atoms to one oxygen atom relationship to form the compound water. Mixtures, however, can vary in their composition.

Chemical and Physical Properties

Physical properties of matter are those properties of matter that can be usually observed with our senses. They include everything about a substance that can be noted when no change is occurring in the type of structure that makes up its smallest component[3]. Some common examples are physical state, color, odor, solubility in water, density, melting point, taste, boiling point, and hardness.

Chemical properties are those properties which can be observed in regard to whether or not a substance reacts with other substances[4]. Some common examples are: iron rusts in moist air, nitrogen does not burn, gold does not rust, sodium reacts with water, silver does not react with water, and water can be decomposed by an electric current.

Chemical and Physical Changes

The changes matter undergoes are classified as either physical or chemical. In general, a physical change alters physical properties but the composition remains constant. The most often altered properties are form and state. Some examples are: breaking glass, cutting wood, melting ice, and magnetizing a piece of metal. In some cases, the process that causes the change can be easily reversed and we again have the substance in its original form.

Chemical changes are always changes in the composition and structure of a substance. They are always accompanied by energy changes. If the energy released from the formation of a new structure exceeds the chemical energy in the original substances, energy will be given off usually in the form of heat or light or both[5]. This is called an exothermic reaction. If the new structure, however, needs to absorb more energy than is available from the reactants, we have an endothermic reaction[6]. This can be shown graphically.

Conservation of Mass

When ordinary chemical changes occur, the mass of the reactants equals the mass of the products. This can be stated another way; that is, in a chemical change, matter can neither be created nor destroyed, but only changed from one form to another. This is referred to as the Law of Conservation of Matter. This law is contradicted by the Einstein mass-energy relationship, which states that matter and energy are interchangeable.

ENERGY

Definition of Energy

Energy is usually defined as the ability to do work.

Forms of Energy

Energy may appear in a variety of form. Most commonly, energy in reactions is evolved as heat. Some other forms of energy are light, sound, mechanical energy, electrical energy, and chemical energy. Energy can be converted from one form to another. An example of this is the heat from burning fuel being used to vaporize water to steam. The energy of the steam is used to turn the turbine wheels to produce mechanical energy. The turbine turns the generator armature to produce electricity. The electricity is then available in homes for use as light, heat, or the operation of many modern appliances.

Two general classifications of energy are potential energy and kinetic energy. Potential energy is due to position; kinetic energy is energy of motion. The difference can be illustrated by a boulder sitting on the side of a mountain. It has a high potential energy due to its position above the valley floor. If it falls, however, its potential energy is converted to kinetic energy. This illustration is very similar to the situation of electrons cascading to lower energy levels in the atomic model.

Conservation of Energy

Experiments have shown that energy is neither gained nor lost in physical or chemical changes. This principle is known as the Law of Conservation of Energy and is often stated as follows: Energy is neither created nor destroyed in ordinary physical and chemical changes.

CONSERVATION OF MATTER AND ENERGY

With the introduction of atomic theory and a more complete understanding of the nature of both matter and energy, it was found that a relationship exists between these two concepts[7]. Einstein formulated the Law of Conservation of Mass and Energy. This states that matter and energy are interchangeable under special conditions. The conditions have been created in nuclear reactors and accelerators, and the law has been verified. This relationship can be expressed by Einstein's famous equation:

$$E = mc^2$$
$$\text{Energy} = \text{Mass} \times (\text{Velocity of light})^2$$

New Words and Phrases

accompany [əˈkʌmpəni] *vt.* 陪伴，伴奏
appliance [əˈplaiəns] *n.* 用具，器具
armature [ˈɑːmətjuə(r)] *n.* （电动机、发电机的）转子，电枢
assign [əˈsain] *vt.* 分配，指派
atomic [əˈtɔmik] *adj.* 原子的，原子能的
body [ˈbɔdi] *n.* 身体，人，主要部分，物体
boulder [ˈbəuldə] *n.* 大石头，漂石
cascade [kæsˈkeid] *n.* 小瀑布，喷流 *vi.* 成瀑布落下
category [ˈkætigəri] *n.* 种类，别
centimeter [ˈsentiˌmiːtər] *n.* 厘米
chemical [ˈkemikəl] *adj.* 化学的 *n.* 化学制品，化学药品
chemistry [ˈkemistri] *n.* 化学
classification [ˌklæsifiˈkeiʃən] *n.* 分类，分级
component [kəmˈpəunənt] *n.* 成分 *adj.* 组成的，构成的
composition [ˌkɔmpəˈziʃən] *n.* 作文，组成，成分，合成物
compound [ˈkɔmpaund] *n.* 混合物，化合物 *adj.* 复合的 *v.* 混合，配合
conservation [ˌkɔnsə(ː)ˈveiʃən] *n.* 保存，保持，守恒
constant [ˈkɔnstənt] *n.* 常数，恒量 *adj.* 不变的，持续的
container [kənˈteinə] *n.* 容器，集装箱
convert [kənˈvəːt] *vt.* 使转变，转换……
decompose [ˌdiːkəmˈpəuz] *v.* 分解，（使）腐烂
density [ˈdensiti] *n.* 密度
distinct [disˈtiŋkt] *adj.* 清楚的，明显的，截然不同的，独特的
element [ˈelimənt] *n.* 要素，元素，成分
endothermic [ˌendəuˈθəːmik] *adj.* 吸热（性）的

exothermic [ˌeksəuˈθɔːmik] *adj.* 发热的，放出热量的
experiment [iksˈperimənt] *n.* 实验，试验 *vi.* 进行实验，做试验
formula [ˈfɔːmjulə] *n.* 公式，规则
generator [ˈdʒenəreitə] *n.* 发电机，发生器
graphically [ˈɡræfikəl] *adj.* 绘成图画似的，绘画的
gravitational [ˌɡræviˈteiʃnl] *adj.* 重力的
grouping [ˈɡruːpiŋ] *n.* 分组
hardness [ˈhɑːdnis] *n.* 硬，硬度，艰难
hydrogen [ˈhaidrəudʒən] *n.* 氢
inertia [iˈnəːʃjə] *n.* 惯性，惯量
interchangeable [ˌintəˈtʃeindʒəb（ə）l] *adj.* 可互换的
iron [ˈaiən] *n.* 铁，熨斗 *vt.* 烫平，熨
kinetic [kaiˈnetik] *adj.* 动的，动力（学）的
magnetize [ˈmæɡnitaiz] *vt.* 使磁化，吸引 *vi.* 受磁
mass [mæs] *n.* 质量，群众 *adj.* 群众的 *vt.* 使集合 *vi.* 聚集
mathematical [ˌmæθiˈmætikəl] *adj.* 数学的，精确的
milliliter [ˈmililiːtə（r）] *n.* 千分之一公升，毫升
mixture [ˈmikstʃə] *n.* 混合，混合物，混合剂
nitrogen [ˈnaitrədʒən] *n.* 氮
oxygen [ˈɔksidʒən] *n.* 氧
physical [ˈfizikəl] *adj.* 身体的，物质的，自然的，物理的
potential [pəˈtenʃ（ə）l] *adj.* 潜在的，可能的，位的 *n.* 潜能，潜力，电压
principle [ˈprinsəpl] *n.* 法则，原则，原理
product [ˈprɔdəkt] *n.* 产品，产物，乘积
property [ˈprɔpəti] *n.* 财产，性质，特性
reactant [riːˈæktənt] *n.* 反应物
relationship [riˈleiʃnʃip] *n.* 关系，关联
resistance [riˈzistəns] *n.* 反抗，阻力，电阻
reverse [riˈvəːs] *n.* 相反，倒退 *adj.* 相反的，颠倒的 *vt.* 颠倒，倒转
sodium [ˈsəudjəm, -diəm] *n.* 钠
solubility [ˌsɔljuˈbiliti] *n.* 可解决性，可解释性，溶解性
state [steit] *n.* 情形，状态 *adj.* 国家的，州的 *vt.* 声明，陈述，规定
structure [ˈstrʌktʃə] *n.* 结构，构造，建筑物 *vt.* 建筑，构成，组织
subdivide [ˈsʌbdiˈvaid] *v.* 再分，细分
substance [ˈsʌbstəns] *n.* 物质，实质，主旨
turbine [ˈtəːbin, -bain] *n.* 涡轮
vaporize [ˈveipəraiz] *v.* （使）蒸发
assign to 分配
be classified as 分类为
be composed of 由……构成
be converted from one form to another 由一种形式转变为另一种形式
be defined as 定义为

be made up of 由……组成
be referred to as 被称为
be subdivided into 被划分为
boiling point 沸点
in/with regard to 关于
melting point 熔点
the Einstein mass-energy relationship 爱因斯坦的质量能量关系式
the Law of Conservation of Mass and Energy 质量和能量守恒定律
the Law of Conservation of Matter 物质守恒定律
the Law of Definite Composition of Proportion 定比定组成定律

Notes

1. Mass is the quantity of matter which a substance possesses and, depending on the gravitational force acting on it, has a unit of weight assigned to it.
   is 和 has 是 Mass 的并列谓语，which a substance possesses 作定语修饰 quantity, depending on the gravitational force acting on it 是现在分词短语作状语。

2. If, however, it is composed of two or more kinds of atoms joined together in a definite grouping, it is classified as a compound.
   joined together in a definite grouping 为过去分词短语作定语修饰 atoms。

3. They include everything about a substance that can be noted when no change is occurring in the type of structure that makes up its smallest component.
   that can be noted 作定语修饰 everything，而 that makes up its smallest component 作状语从句中 structure 的定语，这是从句也为复合句的结构。

4. Chemical properties are those properties which can be observed in regard to whether or not a substance reacts with other substances.
   which can be observed in regard to whether or not a substance reacts with other substances 作定语修饰 properties。

5. If the energy released from the formation of a new structure exceeds the chemical energy in the original substances, energy will be given off usually in the form of heat or light or both.
   released from the formation of a new structure 过去分词短语作定语修饰 energy。

6. If the new structure, however, needs to absorb more energy than is available from the reactants, we have an endothermic reaction.
   than is available from the reactants 看作由关系代词引导的定语从句。例如，You spent more money than was intended to be spent. 你花的钱比想花的钱多。

7. With the introduction of atomic theory and a more complete understanding of the nature of both matter and energy, it was found that a relationship exists between these two concepts.
   With 引导的介词短语作原因状语。例如，With such knowledge and experience, he is sure to succeed. 有了这样的知识和经验，他一定能够取得成功。

Exercises

Ⅰ. Understanding the text

1. What is matter?
2. How can the mass of a body be measured?
3. What are element, compound and mixture?
4. State the definitions of physical and chemical properties.
5. State the definitions of physical and chemical changes.
6. State the definitions of the Law of Conservation of Mass, the Law of Conservation of Energy and the Law of Conservation of Matter and Energy.

Ⅱ. Translate the following into English
1. 重力
2. 物体的质量
3. 数学公式
4. 物质的状态
5. 物质的结构和组成
6. 熔点
7. 沸点
8. 质量和能量守恒定律
9. 化学性质和物理性质
10. 动能和势能

Ⅲ. Translate the passage into Chinese

All matter has mass. Chemists are interested in the masses of materials, because they want to know how much material they need to use to prepare a certain amount of a product.

The mass of an object is the quantity that measures its resistance to change in its state of rest or motion.

The mass of an object also determines its weight. The weight of an object is only a measure of the force with which the object is attracted by the earth. This force depends upon the mass of the object, the mass of the earth, and the position of the object on the earth's surface, especially the distance of the object from the center of the earth. Since the earth is slightly flattened at its poles, the distance of its surface at the North Pole or South Pole from its center is less than that at the equator. In consequence the weight of an object as measured by a spring balance, which measures the force, is greater at the North Pole or South Pole than at the equator. For example, if your weight, measured by a spring balance, is 150.0 lbs at the equator, it would be 150.8 lbs at the North Pole, measured on the same spring balance—nearly a pound more. Your mass, however, is the same.

Reading Materials

Tianjin Bohai Chemical Industry Group Corporation

Ranking 131 among the state top 500 enterprises, Tianjin Bohai Chemical Industry Group Corporation is an oversize (特大型) Chinese enterprises' group, which keeps an annual marketing amount over RMB ten billion Yuan and annual import and export value over US＄0.5 billion. Its products involve almost 3000 varieties including such numerous fields as salt manufacture (制盐), soda ash (纯碱), caustic soda (烧碱), organic chemical industry, inorganic chemical industry, refined chemical industry, rubber and plastic processing industry, bio-chemical industry, etc.

The yield of such products produced by Tianjin Bohai Chemical Industry Group Corporation take the leading position in Chinese chemical industry as polyvinyl chloride (聚氯乙烯), caustic soda, crude salt (原盐), soda ash, maleic anhydride (顺酐), phthalic anhydride (苯酐), epoxy propane (环氧丙烷), epichlorohydrin (环氧氯丙烷), dyestuff, pigment, organic peroxides, carbon black, large off-road tyres (大型工程轮胎), radial tires (子午线轮胎), sodium metasilicate pentahydrate (五水偏硅酸钠), and so on. And lots of its products enjoy a good reputation both at home and abroad.

The chief purpose of improving self-worth rests with having you gain larger success that is our promise to all of our customers.

Tianjin Bohai Chemical Industries Imp. & Exp. Corp.

Tianjin Bohai Chemical Industries Import & Export Corporation (TBCIIEC), one of the earliest-founded corporation combing industry and trade since the reform and opening to the outside in China, was established on Jan. 1st, 1986. With the opening policy, TBCIIEC has become a member of the close enterprises subordinate to the Bohai Chemical Industry Group Corporation. Serving as a window to the outside, TBCIIEC engages in import and export business as well as projects of economic and technology cooperation for Bohai Group. Based on the principle of equality, mutual benefit, exchange of needed goods and collaboration, TBCIIEC will make full use of its advantages of industy-trade combination and technology-trade combination so as to enlarge foreign trade business scope by means of developing import and export, counter trade (对销贸易), barter trade (易货贸易), compensation trade (补偿贸易), processing with supplied materials, assembling with supplied spareparts, import and export of technology, export of complete sets of chemical industry equipments, labor service (劳务服务), and contracted projects abroad (国外工程承包), etc.

Bohai Chemical will be always ready to provide customers with various kinds of high-quality chemical products, complete set of equipment and technology for chloro-alkali (氯碱) industry and chemical industry.

Export business scope: Soda Ash, Caustic Soda, Liquid Caustic Soda, Sodium Bicarbonate (小苏打), Agricultural Ammonium Chloride (农用氯化铵), Industrial Ammonium Chloride (工业用氯化铵), Barium Chloride, Sodium Bicarbonate (碳酸氢钠), Agricultural DDT, Polyvinyl Chloride Resin (聚氯乙烯树脂), Methionine (蛋氨酸), Oxalic Acid (草酸), Lindane (林丹), Sodium Pentachlorophenate (五氯酚钠), Monochlorobenzene, Formic Acid, Dichlorobenzene, Trichlorobenzene, Calcium Hypochlorite (次氯酸钙), complete equipment and technology for chloro-alkali industry.

Import business scope: Raw Chemicals, Packing Materials, Materials for Special Uses, Apparatuses, Instruments and Technology.

TBCIIEC is keen to establish business relationship with trade partners abroad and will cooperate with them wholeheartedly.

Unit 2 Acids, Bases and Salts

Acids

There are some characteristic properties by which an acid may be defined[1]. The most important are as follows.

1. Water solutions of acids conduct electricity. This conduction depends on their degree of ionization. A few acids ionize almost completely, while others ionize only to a slight degree. The table below indicates some common acids and their degrees of ionization.

ACIDS		
Completely or Nearly Completely Ionized	Moderately Ionized	Slightly Ionized
Nitric Hydrochloric Sulfuric Hydriodic Hydrobromic	Oxalic Phosphoric Sulfurous	Hydrofluoric Acetic Carbonic Hydrosulfuric (Most others)

2. Acids will react with metals that are more active than hydrogen ions to liberate hydrogen[2]. (Some acids are also strong oxidizing agents and will not release hydrogen. Somewhat concentrated nitric acid is such an acid)
3. Acids have the ability to change the color of indicators. Some common indicators are litmus and phenolphthalein. Litmus is a dyestuff obtained from plant life. When litmus is added to an acidic solution or paper impregnated with litmus is dipped into an acid, the neutral purple color changes to a pink-red color. The phenolphthalein is red in a basic solution and becomes colorless in a neutral or acid solution.
4. Acids react with bases so that the properties of both are lost to form water and a salt. This is called neutralization. The general equation is: Acid + Base $\longrightarrow$ Salt + Water

    An example is: $Mg(OH)_2 + H_2SO_4 \longrightarrow MgSO_4 + 2H_2O$
5. If an acid is known to be a weak solution, you might taste it and note the sour taste.
6. Acids react with carbonates to release carbon dioxide. An example is:

$$CaCO_3 + 2HCl \longrightarrow CaCl_2 + H_2CO_3 \text{ (unstable and decomposes)}$$
$$ \hookrightarrow H_2O + CO_2$$

The most common theory used in first-year chemistry is the Arhennius Theory, which states that an acid is a substance that yields hydrogen ions in an aqueous solution[3]. Although we speak of these hydrogen ions in the solution, they are really not separate ions but become attached to the oxygen of the polar water molecule to form the H_3O^+ ion (the hydronium ion). So it is really this hydronium ion we are concerned with in an acid solution[4].

Bases

Bases may also be defined by some operational definitions that are based on experimental observations. Some of the important ones are as follows.

BASES	
Completely or Nearly Completely Ionized	Slightly Ionized
Potassium hydroxide Sodium hydroxide Barium hydroxide Strontium hydroxide Calcium hydroxide	Ammonium Hydroxide (All others)

1. Bases are conductors of electricity in an aqueous solution. Their degree of conduction depends on their degree of ionization. See the table of the common bases above and their degrees of ionization.
2. Bases cause a color change in indicators. Litums changes from red to blue in a basic solution and phenolphthalein becomes a pink color from its colorless state.
3. Bases react with acids to neutralize each other and form a salt and water.
4. Bases react with fats to form a class of compounds called soaps. The earlier generations used this method to make their own soap.
5. Aqueous solutions of bases feel slippery and the stronger bases are very caustic to the skin.

SALTS

A salt is an ionic compound containing positive ions other than hydrogen, and negative ions other than hydroxide ions[5]. The usual method of preparing a particular salt is by neutralizing the appropriate acid and base to form the salt and water.

Acid Concentration Expressed as pH

Frequently, acid and base concentrations are expressed in a system called the pH system. The pH can be defined as $-\lg[H^+]$, where $[H^+]$ is the concentration of hydrogen ions expressed in moles per liter. The logarithm is the exponent of 10 when the number is written in the base 10.

An example of a pH problem is:

Find the pH of a 0.1 molar solution of HCl.

1st step: Since HCl ionizes almost completely into H^+ and Cl^-, the $[H^+]=0.1$ mole/liter.

2nd step: By definition $pH=-\lg[H^+]$

$pH=-\lg 10^{-1}$

3rd step: The logarithm of 10^{-1} is -1

So pH＝－(－1)

4th step：The pH then is＝1.

Since water has a normal H^+ concentration of 10^{-7} mole/liter because of the slight ionization of water molecules, the water pH is 7 when it is neither acid nor base. The normal pH range is from 1 to 14.

New words and Phrases

acetic [ə'si:tik] *adj.* 醋的，乙酸的

acidic [ə'sidik] *adj.* 酸的，酸性的

agents ['eidʒənt] *n.* 手段，工具，剂

ammonium [ə'məunjəm] *n.* 铵

aqueous ['eikwiəs] *adj.* 水的，水成的

barium ['bɛəriəm] *n.* 钡

base [beis] *n.* 底部，基础，底数，碱

basic ['beisik] *adj.* 基本的，碱性的

calcium ['kælsiəm] *n.* 钙

carbon ['kɑ:bən] *n.* 碳，（一张）复写纸

carbonate ['kɑ:bəneit] *n.* 碳酸盐 *vt.* 使变成碳酸盐，使充满二氧化碳

carbonic [kɑ:'bɔnik] *adj.* 碳的，由碳得到的

caustic ['kɔ:stik] *adj.* 腐蚀性的，刻薄的

conduct ['kɔndʌkt, -dəkt] *n.* 行为，操行 *v.* 引导，管理，传导

conduction [kən'dʌkʃən] *n.* 传导

dioxide [dai'ɔksaid] *n.* 二氧化物

dyestuff ['daistʌf] *n.* 染料

exponent [eks'pəunənt] *n.* 说明者，代表者，典型，指数

hydriodic [,haidri'ɔdik] *adj.* 氢碘酸的

hydrobromic ['haidrəu'brəumik] *adj.* 氢溴酸的，溴化氢的

hydrochloric [,haidrəu'klɔ:rik] *adj.* 氯化氢的，盐酸的

hydrofluoric ['haidrəflu(:)'ɔrik] *adj.* 含氢和氟的，含氟化氢的，氢氟酸的

hydronium [hai'drəuniəm] *n.* 水合氢，离子

hydrosulfuric [hai'drəusʌl'fjuərik] *adj.* 含氢及硫的

hydroxide [hai'drɔksaid, -sid] *n.* 氢氧化物，羟化物

impregnate ['impregneit] *vt.* 使怀孕，使充满 *adj.* 怀孕的，充满的

indicator ['indikeitə] *n.* 指示器，指示剂

ion ['aiən] *n.* 离子

ionization [,aiənai'zeiʃən] *n.* 电离，离子化（作用）

ionize ['aiənaiz] *vt.* 使离子化 *vi.* 电离电离，离子化

litmus ['litməs] *n.* 石蕊

logarithm ['lɔgəriθm] *n.* 对数

molar ['məulə] *adj.* 质量的，摩尔的 *n.* 臼齿，磨牙

neutral ['njuːtrəl] n. 中立者，中立国 adj. 中立的，中立国的，中性的
neutralization [ˌnjuːtrəlaiˈzeiʃən] n. 中立化，中立状态，中和
nitric ['naitrik] adj. 氮的，含氮的，硝石的
operational [ˌɔpəˈreiʃənl] adj. 操作的，运作的
oxalic [ɔkˈsælik] adj. 草酸的，乙二酸的
oxidizing [ˈɔksiˌdaiz] v. （使）氧化
phenolphthalein [ˌfinɔlˈfθæliːn] n. 酚酞
phosphoric [fɔsˈfɔrik] adj. 磷的（尤指含五价磷的），含磷的
polar ['pəulə] adj. 两极的，极性的 n. 极线，极面
potassium [pəˈtæsjəm] n. 钾
purple ['pəːpl] adj. 紫色的 n. 紫色
solutions [səˈljuːʃən] n. 解答，溶解，溶液
somewhat ['sʌm(h)wɔt] adv. 稍微，有点，有些
strontium ['strɔnʃiəm] n. 锶
sulfuric [sʌlˈfjuərik] adj. 硫的，正硫的
sulfurous ['sʌlfərəs] adj. 硫的，含硫的，亚硫的
table ['teibl] n. 桌子，石板，表格
attached to 附着
be concerned with 关心……
dip into 把……浸入（液体）中

Notes

1. There are some characteristic properties by which an acid may be defined.
   by which an acid may be defined 作定语从句修饰 properties，例如，This is the house in which Lu Xun once lived. 这是鲁迅曾经住过的房子。
2. that are more active than hydrogen ions 作定语修饰 metals，to liberate hydrogen 作状语表示结果。
3. which states that an acid is a substance that yields hydrogen ions in an aqueous solution 作定语从句修饰 theory，而其中的定语从句 that yields hydrogen ions in an aqueous solution 修饰 substance。
4. So it is really this hydronium ion we are concerned with in an acid solution. it 是形式主语，we are concerned with in an acid solution 是真正的主语。
5. A salt is an ionic compound containing positive ions other than hydrogen, and negative ions other than hydroxide ions. 句中 other than 表示"除……以外"。例如：There's nobody here other than me. 除了我这里没别人。

Exercises

Ⅰ. Understanding the text
1. What main properties do acids have?
2. What properties do bases possess?

Ⅱ. Translate the following expressions into English
1. 水溶液

2. 电离程度
3. 硝酸、盐酸、硫酸和磷酸
4. 氧化剂
5. 改变指示剂的颜色
6. 石蕊和酚酞指示剂
7. 碱性溶液、酸性溶液和中性溶液
8. 酸碱中和
9. 氢氧化钾、氢氧化钠和氨水
10. 用 pH 表示酸的浓度

Ⅲ. Translate the passage into Chinese

Acids have the following general properties: They taste sour, change blue litmus paper to red, act with active metals, liberating hydrogen, act with carbonates, liberating carbon dioxide, and neutralize bases. These properties are those of hydrogen ions (H^+) in water solutions of acids.

A base has the properties of the hydroxyl ion in solution. It can neutralize an acid. A substance with marked basic properties is an alkali.

Salts may be prepared by neutralization; by metal plus acid; by metal oxide plus acid; by metal carbonate plus acid; and by special methods. The solubilities of salts are summarized in solubility rules.

Some reactions are reversible. In reversible reactions, an equilibrium of two opposite chemical reactions is set up, under a given set of conditions of concentration, temperature, and pressure.

The rate of a chemical reaction is influenced by temperature; by pressure, if a gas is among the reaction substances or products; by the presence of a catalyst; and by the concentration.

The principle of mass action is: A reversible equilibrium reaction can be made to approach a nearly complete reaction by increasing the concentration of one of the reacting substances or by decreasing the concentration of a product.

Reading Materials

Chemical Industry Area of Leuna

Chemistry for a Whole Century

The smart and forward-thinking（前瞻性）plans of the world-renowned chemist Carl Bosch（卡尔.博施 1874—1940，德国化学家，曾获 1931 年诺贝尔化学奖）quickly put Leuna（罗伊纳，德国的一个化工区。）on the international map.

After the introduction of commercial ammonia（氨）synthesis, methanol（甲醇）soon followed in 1923 on a world-scale facilitated（推动）by the high-pressure process.

At the end of the 1920's Leuna became a production site for the mineral oil industry when Matthias Pier developed a brown coal hydrogenation process for the manufacture of synthetic fuels.

The year 1938 became a milestone（里程碑）in history. Women around the world had a reason to celebrate: in that year the synthesis of caprolactam（已内酰胺）leading to Perlon（贝纶或聚酰胺纤维）succeeded in Leuna.

The series of successes from the introduction of large-scale industrial processes knew no end（没有止境）. Until the Second World War this stronghold（要塞）of technology evolved into the biggest company of the German chemical industry. A fine example of one of these successes is the world's first production plant for the manufacturing of synthetic surfactants（表面活性剂）which was commissioned（投产）in 1942.

Even after the war Leuna remained a synonym for "chemistry".

Today's investors on-site（厂区内）are still benefiting from production initiated under the East German flag. The excellent raw material supply network includes crude oil（原油）and natural gas（天然气）from Russia and ethylene（乙烯）from the Czech Republic.

Since German reunification（再统一）in 1990, a new chapter in the history of the chemical site Leuna began. Company partnerships, established during the Grunderzeit [1871～1895 The Founding Epoch（时代）] period, once again reestablished themselves here to mutual advantage（共同的利益）. Linde AG is an example of one of the many companies. In 1916, Linde already constructed the first air separation unit.

Chemistry for the New Millenium（一千年）

The development of the chemical site Leuna is a barometer（晴雨表）for the overall growth of the state of Saxony-Anhalt（萨克森．安哈尔特州）.

Public investment grants have played a considerable role in supporting the establishment of new facilities by potential investors. Here, state-of-the-art（艺术级的）infrastructure is available at sustainable and favourable conditions with the support of policy-makers and authorities. Working in the investors' favour-environment permits approval for new plants which are usually very short in comparison to European standards.

As a consequence of its chemical tradition, the region has an extensive potential of highly-qualified experts. At present, approximately 9000 people work at the Leuna site. Tomorrow's specialists are being educated at international standards at the renowned universities and colleges in Leipzig（莱比锡）, Halle（哈勒）and Merseburg（马格堡）. Together with experienced, skilled employees they ensure the innovation potential of their companies.

This is not the only aspect that guarantees the "Dynamic in chemistry"…the neighbouring city Leipzig is well-known for its cosmopolitanism（世界主义）.

Unit 3　Naming Inorganic Compounds

Writing Formulas

From the knowledge of oxidation numbers and valence and the understanding of atomic structure, it is now possible to write chemical formulas. Table 3-1 is a list of oxidation numbers often encountered in a first-year chemistry course.

Table 3-1　Table of oxidation numbers

categories	Monovalent (Ⅰ)	Bivalent (Ⅱ)	Trivalent (Ⅲ)	Tetravalent (Ⅳ)	Ⅴ
METALS Cations (+)	Hydrogen H Potassium K Sodium Na Silver Ag Mercury (mercurous)(Hg) Copper(cuprous) Cu Gold(aurous) Au ① Ammonium (NH₄)	Barium Ba Calcium Ca Cobalt Co Magnesium Mg Lead Pb Zinc Zn Mercury (mercuric) Hg Copper(cupric) Cu Iron(ferrous) Fe Manganses (manganous) Mn Tin(stannous) Sn	Aluminum Al Gold(auric) Au Arsenic(arsenious) As Chromium Cr Iron(ferric) Fe Phosphorus (phosphorous) P Antimony (antimonous) Sb Bismuth (bismuthous) Bi	Carbon C Silicon Si Manganese (manganic) Mn Tin(stannic) Sn Platinum Pt Sulfur S	Arsenic As Phosphorus (phosphoric) P Antimony (antimonic) Sb Bismuth (bismuthic) Bi
NONMETALS Anions (−)	Fluorine F Chlorine Cl Bromine Br Iodine I	Oxygen O Sulfur S	Nitrogen N Phosphorus P	Carbon C	
	Last syllable nonmetal is changed to-ide in binary compound.				
RADICALS(−)	Hydroxide (OH) Bicarbonate (HCO₃) Nitrite (NO₂) Nitrate (NO₃) Hypochlorite (ClO) Chlorate (ClO₃) Chlorite (ClO₂) Perchlorate (ClO₄) Acetate (C₂H₃O₂) Permanganate (MnO₄) Bisulfate (HSO₄)	Carbonate (CO₃) Sulfite (SO₃) Sulfate (SO₄) Tetraborate (B₄O₇) Silicate (SiO₃) Chromate (CrO₄) Oxalate (C₂O₄)	Borate (BO₃) Phosphate (PO₄) Phosphite (PO₃) Ferricyanide [Fe(CN)₆]	Ferrocyanide [Fe(CN)₆]	

Note：①Radical.

General Observations

The symbols of the metals have $+$ signs while those of the nonmetals and all the radicals except the ammonium radical have $-$ signs.

When an element exhibits two possible oxidation states, the lower state can be indicated with the suffix-ous and the higher one with-ic. Another method of indicating this difference is to use the Roman numeral of the oxidation state in parentheses after the name of the element. For example: Ferrous iron or iron (II) for the $+2$ oxidation state of iron.

A radical is a group of elements which act like a single atom in the formation of a compound. The bonds within these radicals are predominantly covalent, but the groups of atoms as a whole have an excess of electrons when combined, and thus are negative ions.

When you attempt to write a formula, it is important to know whether it actually exists. For example, one can easily write the formula of carbon nitrate but no chemist has ever prepared this compound. Here are the basic rules for writing formulas with three examples carried through each step:

1. Represent the symbols of the components using the positive part first, and then the negative part.

    Sodium chloride   Calcium oxide   Ammonium sulfate

       NaCl   CaO   (NH$_4$) SO$_4$

2. Indicate the respective oxidation numbers above and to the right of each symbol.

(Enclose radicals in parentheses for the time being)

       $Na^{1+} Cl^{1-}$ $Ca^{2+} O^{2-}$ $(NH_4)^{1+} SO_4^{2-}$

3. Write a subscript number equal to the oxidation number of the other element or radical. This is the same as the mechanical criss-cross method. Since the positive oxidation number shows the number of electrons that may be lost or shared and the negative oxidation number shows the number of electrons that may be gained or shared, you must have just as many electrons lost (or partially lost in sharing) as are gained (or partially gained in sharing)[1].

      $Na_1^{1+} Cl_1^{1-}$ $Ca_2^{2+} O_2^{2-}$ $(NH_4)_2^{1+} (SO_4)_1^{2-}$

4. Now rewrite the formulas, omitting the subscript 1, the parentheses of the radicals which have the subscript 1, and the plus and minus numbers[2].

5. As a general rule, the subscript numbers in the final formula are reduced to their lowest terms. There are, however, certain exceptions, such as hydrogen peroxide (H_2O_2), and acetylene (C_2H_2). For these exceptions, you must know more specific information about the compound.

The only way to become proficient at writing formulas is to memorize the oxidation numbers of common elements (or learn to use the period chart group numbers) and practice writing formulas.

Naming Compounds

Binary compounds consist of two elements. The name of the compound consists of the two elements, the second name having its ending changed to-ide, such as NaCl= sodium chloride; AgCl= silver chloride[3]. If the metal has two different oxidation numbers, this can be indicated by the use of the suffix -ous for the lower one and-ic for the higher one. The more modern way is to use a Roman numeral after the name to indicate the oxidation state.

Examples:

$FeCl_2$ = ferrous chloride or iron (II) chloride

$FeCl_3$ = ferric chloride or iron (III) chloride

If elements combine in varying proportions, thus forming two or more compounds of varying composition, the name of the second element may be preceded by a prefix, such as: mono-(one), tri-(three), pent-(five)[4]. Some examples are: carbon dioxide, CO_2; carbon monoxide, CO; phosphorous trioxide, P_2O_3; phosphorous pentoxide, P_2O_5. Notice that, when these prefixed are used, it is not necessary to indicate the oxidation state of the first element in the name since it is given indirectly by the prefixed second element[5].

Ternary compounds, consisting of three elements, are usually made up of an element and a radical. To name them, you merely name each in the order of positive first and negative second.

Binary acids use the prefix hydro- in front of the stem or full name of the nonmetallic element, and add the ending -ic. Examples are hydrochloric acid (HCl) and hydrosulfuric acid (H_2S).

Ternary acids usually contain hydrogen, a nonmetal, and oxygen. Since the amount of oxygen often varies, the most common form of the acid in the series consists of merely the stem of the nonmetal with the ending -ic. The acid containing one less atom of oxygen than the most common acid has the ending-ous[6].

The acid containing one more atom of oxygen than the most common acid has the prefix per- and the ending -ic. The acid containing one less atom of oxygen than the-ous acid has the prefix hypo- and the ending-ous.

You can remember the names of the common acids and their salts by learning the following simple rules.

Rule	Example
-ic acids form-ate salts.	Sulfuric acid forms sulfate salts.
-ous acids form-ite salts.	Sulfurous acid forms sulfite salts.
hydro- (stem) -ic acids form-ide salts.	Hydrochloric acid forms chloride salts.

Where the name of the ternary acid has the prefix hypo- or per-, that prefix is retained in the name of the salt (hypochlorous acid = sodium hypochlorite). Table 3-2 is the formulas of common acids and bases.

Table 3-2 Formulas of common acids and bases

ACIDS(BINARY)		ACIDS(TERNARY)	
Name	Formula	Name	Formula
Hydrofluoric	HF	Nitric	HNO_3
Hydrochloric	HCl	Nitrous	HNO_2
Hydrobromic	HBr	Hypochlorous	$HClO$
Hydriodic	HI	Chlorous	$HClO_2$
Hydrosulfuric	H_2S	Chloric	$HClO_3$
BASES		Perchloric	$HClO_4$
Name	Formula	Sulfuric	H_2SO_4
Sodium hydroxide	NaOH	Sulfurous	H_2SO_3
Potassium hydroxide	KOH	Phosphoric	H_3PO_4
Ammonium hydroxide	$NH_3 \cdot H_2O$	Phosphorous	H_3PO_3
Calcium hydroxide	$Ca(OH)_2$	Carbonic	H_2CO_3
Magnesium hydroxide	$Mg(OH)_2$	Acetic	$HC_2H_3O_2$
Barium hydroxide	$Ba(OH)_2$	Oxalic	$H_2C_2O_4$
Aluminum hydroxide	$Al(OH)_3$	Boric	H_3BO_3
Ferrous hydroxide	$Fe(OH)_2$	Silicon	H_2SiO_3
Ferric hydroxide	$Fe(OH)_3$		
Zinc hydroxide	$Zn(OH)_2$		
Lithium hydroxide	LiOH		

New Words and Phrases

acetate ['æsiˌteit] *n.* 醋酸盐，醋酸纤维素及其制成的产品

acetylene [əˈsetiliːn] *n.* 乙炔，电石气

aluminum [əˈljuːminəm] *n.* 铝

anions [ˈænaiən] *n.* 阴离子

antimonic [ˌæntiˈməunik] *adj.* 锑的，含锑的

antimonous [ˈæntiˌməunəs] *adj.* 有锑的，似锑的

antimony [ˈæntiməni] *n.* 锑

arsenic [ˈɑːsənik] *n.* 砷，砒霜

arsenious [ɑːˈsiːniəs] *adj.* 含砒素的，含砷的

auric [ˈɔːrik] *adj.* 金的，正金的，三价金的

aurous [ˈɔːrəs] *adj.* 亚金的，一价金的，金的，含金的

bicarbonate [baiˈkɑːbənit] *n.* 重碳酸盐

bismuth [ˈbizməθ] *n.* 铋

bismuthic [ˈbizməθik, bizˈmjuːθik] *adj.* 铋的，含五价铋的

bismuthous [ˈbizməθəs] *adj.* 亚铋的，含三价铋的

bisulfate [baiˈsʌlfeit] *n.* 硫酸氢盐

bivalent [ˈbaiˌveilənt] *adj.* 二价的

bond [bɔnd] *n.* 结合（物），胶黏（剂），债券，合同 *v.* 结合

borate [ˈbɔːreit] *n.* 硼酸盐 *vt.* 使与硼酸混合

boric [ˈbɔːrik] *adj.* 硼的

bromine [ˈbrəumiːn] *n.* 溴

cation [ˈkætaiən] *n.* 阳离子

chlorate [ˈklɔːrit] *n.* 氯酸盐
chloric [ˈklɔːrik] *adj.* 氯的，含氯的
chlorine [ˈklɔːriːn] *n.* 氯
chlorite [ˈklɔːrait] *n.* 亚氯酸盐，绿泥石
chlorous [ˈklɔːrəs] *adj.* 亚氯酸的，与氯化合的
chromate [ˈkrəumeit] *n.* 铬酸盐
chromium [ˈkrəumjəm] *n.* 铬
cobalt [kəˈbɔːlt，ˈkəubɔːlt] *n.* 钴
copper [ˈkɔpə] *n.* 铜，警察
covalent [kəuˈveilənt] *adj.* 共有原子价的，共价的
cupric [ˈkjuːprik] *adj.* 二价铜的
cuprous [ˈkjuːprəs] *adj.* 亚铜的，一价铜的
exception [ikˈsepʃən] *n.* 除外，例外，反对，异议
ferric [ˈferik] *adj.* （正）铁的，三价铁的
ferricyanide [ˌferiˈsaiənaid] *n.* 铁氰化物
ferrous [ˈferəs] *adj.* 铁的，含铁的，亚铁的
fluorine [ˈflu（ː）əriːn] *n.* 氟
hypochlorite [ˌhaipəuˈklɔːrait] *n.* 次氯酸盐
hypochlorous [ˌhaipəuˈklɔːrəs] *n.* 次氯酸
iodine [ˈaiədiːn；（US）ˈaiədain] *n.* 碘，碘酒
lead [liːd] *n.* 领导，铅，石墨
lithium [ˈliθiəm] *n.* 锂
magnesium [mægˈniːzjəm] *n.* 镁
manganese [ˌmæŋgəˈniːz，ˈmæŋgəniːz] *n.* 锰
manganic [mæŋˈgænik] *adj.* 锰的，得自锰的
manganous [ˈmæŋgənəs] *adj.* （亚）锰的，二价锰的
mercury [ˈməːkjuri] *n.* 水银，汞
mercuric [məːˈkjuərik] *adj.* 汞的，含二价汞的
mercurous [ˈməːkjurəs] *adj.* 亚汞的，含水银的，一价汞的
monovalent [ˌmɔnəuˈveilənt] *adj.* 单价的
nitrate [ˈnaitreit] *n.* 硝酸盐，硝酸钾
nitrite [ˈnaitrait] *n.* 亚硝酸盐
nitrous [ˈnaitrəs] *adj.* 含有三价氮的，亚硝（酸）的
oxalate [ˈɔksəleit] *n.* 盐
oxide [ˈɔksaid] *n.* 氧化物
parentheses [pəˈrenθisis] *n.* 圆括号，插入语，插曲
perchlorate [pəˈklɔːreit] *n.* 高氯酸盐（或酯）
perchloric [pəˈklɔːrik] *adj.* （含）高氯的
permanganate [pəːˈmæŋgənit，-neit] *n.* 高锰酸
peroxide [ˈɔksaid] *n.* 氧化物
phosphate [ˈfɔsfeit] *n.* 磷酸盐
phosphite [ˈfɔsfait] *n.* 亚磷酸盐

phosphorous ['fɔsfərəs] *adj.* 磷的
phosphorus ['fɔsfərəs] *n.* 磷
platinum ['plætinəm] *n.* 白金，铂
positive ['pɔzətiv] *adj.* 正的，阳的，正电的
predominantly [pri'dɔminənt] *adj.* 卓越的，支配的，主要的，突出的，有影响的
proficient [prə'fiʃənt] *n.* 精通
radical ['rædikəl] *adj.* 根本的，基本的，激进的
respective [ris'pektiv] *adj.* 分别的，各自的
silicate ['silikit] *n.* 硅酸盐
silicon ['silikən] *n.* 硅，硅元素
silver ['silvə] *n.* 银，银子 *vt.* 镀银
stannic ['stænik] *adj.* 锡的，四价锡的
stannous ['stænəs] *adj.* 锡的，含有锡的，含二价锡的
subscript ['sʌbskript] *adj.* 写在下方的
suffix ['sʌfiks] *n.* 后缀，下标 *vt.* 添后缀
sulfate ['sʌlfeit] *n.* 硫酸盐 *v.* 以硫酸或硫酸盐处理，使变为硫酸盐
sulfite ['sʌlfait] *n.* 亚硫酸盐
sulfur ['sʌlfə] *n.* 硫黄 *vt.* 用硫磺处理
symbol ['simbəl] *n.* 符号，记号，象征
tetraborate [ˌtetrə'bɔːreit] *n.* 四硼酸盐
tetravalent [ˌtetrə'veilənt] *adj.* 四价的
tin [tin] *n.* 锡，马口铁，罐
trivalent [trai'veilənt] *adj.* 三价的
valence ['veiləns] *n.* （化合）价，原子价
zinc [ziŋk] *n.* 锌 *vt.* 涂锌于
as a (general) rule   总体上，通常
as a whole   总的来说
become proficient at   精通
carry through   达到，完成，坚持，保存
criss-cross ['kriskrɔs] *n.* 十字形 *adj.* 十字形的 *adv.* 十字形地
for the time being   暂时，目前
oxidation number   氧化数

Notes

1. Since the positive oxidation number shows the number of electrons that may be lost or shared and the negative oxidation number shows the number of electrons that may be gained or shared, you must have just as many electrons lost (or partially lost in sharing) as are gained (or partially gained in sharing).
since...shared，原因状语从句，定语从句 that may be lost or...修饰 electrons，定语从句 that may be gained or shared 修饰 electrons，as many...as...和……一样。

2. Now rewrite the formulas, omitting the subscript 1, the parentheses of the radicals which have the subscript 1, and the plus and minus numbers.

omitting...现在分词短语作伴随状语，which have the subscript 1 作定语从句修饰 radicals。

3. The name of the compound consists of the two elements, the second name having its ending changed to-ide, such as NaCl= sodium chloride; AgCl=silver chloride.
   the second name having...chloride 带有逻辑主语的现在分词短语作状语，起说明作用。

4. If elements combine in varying proportions, thus forming two or more compounds of varying composition, the name of the second element may be preceded by a prefix, such as: mono-(one), tri-(three), pent-(five).
   varying proportions, thus forming two or more compounds of varying composition 动名词短语作介词 in 的宾语，它们组成介词短语做句子的状语。

5. Notice that, when these prefixed are used, it is not necessary to indicate the oxidation state of the first element in the name since it is given indirectly by the prefixed second element.
   That...element. 宾语从句，其中 it 作形式主语，to indicate the oxidation state of the first element in the name 动词不定式短语作宾语从句的真正主语。

6. The acid containing one less atom of oxygen than the most common acid has the ending-ous.
   containing one less atom of oxygen than the most common acid 现在分词短语作定语。

Exercises

Ⅰ. Understanding the text
1. What should you learn, if you want to write formulas correctly?
2. Briefly introduce the basic rules for writing correct formulas.
3. How do you name binary compounds?
4. How do you name ternary compounds?
5. By what rules can you remember the names of the common acids and their salts?

Ⅱ. Translate the following into English
1. 氢氯酸（HCl）
2. 氢溴酸（HBr）
3. 硝酸（HNO_3）
4. 次氯酸（HClO）
5. 亚氯酸（$HClO_2$）
6. 氯酸（$HClO_3$）
7. 高氯酸（$HClO_4$）
8. 硫酸（H_2SO_4）
9. 氢氧化亚铁［$Fe(OH)_2$］
10. 氢氧化铁［$Fe(OH)_3$］

Ⅲ. Translate the passage into Chinese

As we come to less common and more complex compounds, the use of trivial names gives way to a more systematic approach. If there are only two elements in the compound, it is customary to name the more metallic element first and the less metallic, or more electronegative element second, with the suffix "-ide". Some examples are:

KCl	potassium chloride	NaBr	sodium bromide	CaO	calcium oxide
HI	hydrogen iodide	BaS	barium sulphide		

For compounds containing still only two elements but more than two atoms, the prefixes "mono-," "di-", "tri-" etc., become necessary. Some examples of such compounds are the oxides of nitrogen. Another such series is that of the oxides of chlorine. Because chlorine, like nitrogen, is slightly less electronegative than oxygen, the word chlorine comes first:

Cl_2O	Dichlorine monoxide	ClO_3	Chlorine trioxide
ClO	Chlorine monoxide	Cl_2O_7	Dichlorine heptoxide
ClO_2	Chlorine dioxide	ClO_4	Chlorine tetroxide

If no confusion can result, the prefixes "mono-" and "di-" are sometimes dropped.

Reading Materials

Function of Chemicals (Ⅰ)

1. What benefits do chemicals bring? Do we really need so many?

Everything we see and touch is made from chemicals. Many occur naturally; some are man-made. The chemical industry produces chemicals that bring tremendous benefits to our everyday lives. Thanks to new drugs, we now live longer. Did you know that the average life expectancy (寿命) in 1900 was only 55 years, whereas a child born today can expect to live to 80 or that more than two-thirds of all humans who have ever lived beyond the age of 65 are alive today?

The benefits of chemicals are everywhere we look. Paints protect our homes and bring colour to our lives. Lightweight plastics are used in cars to reduce petrol consumption while still being strong enough to protect us in accidents. Sporting and leisure activities rely on innovative materials for performance and safety - whether in sails for windsurfing (冲浪) or safety helmets (安全帽) for climbing. Computers and mobile phones contain hundreds of chemical products and only work because of advances in chemistry.

2. What is the chemical industry doing to reduce the number of chemicals that are dangerous to our health and the environment?

The industry works extremely hard to ensure that all the chemicals it produces can be used safely. When a new chemical is invented, it is normally for a particular purpose and its properties (性能) are carefully investigated to provide information about its safety in use.

Very many man-made chemicals are perfectly safe and pose (造成，产生) no threat to health or the environment when used properly. Some man-made chemicals, however, do have hazardous characteristics (毒性) that need to be properly considered to ensure that they can be used safely. Out of the many thousands of chemicals that are made, less than 1,000 fall into this category.

Incidentally, some of the most poisonous chemicals of all occur naturally, such as aflatoxins (黄曲霉毒素) which come from fungi (真菌) and snake venom (毒液).

We should also remember that hazardous chemicals are not made for the sake of it. They are intended for specific purposes and bring enormous benefits. Think of medicines, pesticides (杀虫剂) and water purifying (净水) chemicals. The way to make life safer is not necessarily to ban such chemicals, but to reduce our exposure to them-in other words, to make sure they are used in ways that minimize or remove the possible dangers.

Ultimately, decisions on what action, if any, needs to be taken are made by regulators and authorities who evaluate (评估) the information generated by the industry. We recognize the need for better safety information on some chemicals which have been on the market for many years.

3. Should hazardous chemicals be banned and replaced with safer ones?

The industry believes that chemicals should not be removed from the market simply because they may be hazardous. Many hazardous chemicals can be handled and used safely and bring enormous benefits (just think of petrol). Banning a chemical simply because it causes concern could cause more problems than it solves.

Instead, we believe that chemicals should be regulated (控制,管理) by a process called risk assessment (风险评估). This takes an objective, scientific view of a product with hazardous properties in relation to how the chemical will be used and the degree to which we are exposed to it in our everyday lives. In this way, it allows meaningful decisions to be made.

(Continued on page 27)

Unit 4　Naming Organic Compounds

Modern systems for naming aliphatic compounds are based upon the names of the alkanes, so it seems logical to deal with the naming of these compounds first.

With the exception of the first four members of the series, methane, ethane, propane and butane, the number of carbon atoms in the molecule is indicated by the Greek prefix for that particular number followed by the letters "-ane".

Names of alkanes

Number of carbons	Name	Formula	Number of carbons	Name	Formula
1	Methane	CH_4	6	Hexane	C_6H_{14}
2	Ethane	C_2H_6	7	Heptane	C_7H_{16}
3	Propane	C_3H_8	8	Octane	C_8H_{18}
4	Butane	C_4H_{10}	9	Nonane	C_9H_{20}
5	Pentane	C_5H_{12}	10	Decane	$C_{10}H_{22}$

Different conventions utilize these names in different ways. The most universal and systematic method is that devised by a commission appointed by the International Union of Pure and Applied Chemistry, which is referred to as the IUPAC System[1]. It provides a convenient and relatively straightforward method for naming even the most complicated molecules, and has the advantage that the same basic principles are employed for each series of compounds[2].

Common (or semi-systematic) names are sometimes retained for the names of many of the more simple compounds of the various homologous series, but for more complicated molecules the more widely applicable IUPAC system is generally adopted.

Common (Semi-systematic) Names

Many of the simpler compounds are named from their function or their source, and despite attempts to persuade chemists to adopt the IUPAC system universally for all compounds, these common names are still widely used.

In some respects the common name does have certain advantages even for complex structures, for although the IUPAC name may generally define structure more clearly it can, in some instances, be much more clumsy to use, especially if it is having to be continually repeated. Conversely, of course, it can rightly be argued that in a great number of cases the common name gives no indication of structure whatsoever[3].

One might reasonably suppose that the chemist is more interested in how a compound reacts rather than how it is named, but nonetheless at the present time the problem of standardizing nomenclature for all types of compounds is still a long way from being fully resolved. The preferred names adopted in this book are in accordance with those recommended by The Association for Science Education in their publication, Chemical Nomenclature, Symbols and Terminology for Use in School Science.

The IUPAC (Geneva) System of Nomenclature

The following provides an outline of the systematic principles adopted.

(1) The longest continuous chain of carbon atoms is selected and named according to the parent alkane.

(2) The carbon atoms of the chain are numbered in order to indicate the positions of any substituents in the chain. The end of the chain from which the numbering starts is chosen so as to use the lowest values, e. g.

$$\overset{1}{CH_3}-\overset{2}{CH_2}-\overset{3}{CH_2}-\overset{4}{CH_2}-\overset{5}{CH_3}$$

(3) The names of the substituents prefix the name of the parent alkane alphabetically and the positions of substitution precede whole.

(4) The numbers assigned to the functional groups are chosen so as to be as small as possible. These are usually placed in front of the name. The functional group numbers are given precedence over those assigned to other substituents. For example, consider the naming of the following alcohols. Simple alcohols are named by dropping the "-e" from the end of the name of the parent alkane and adding the suffix "-ol".

$$CH_3CH_2OH \quad \text{Ethanol} \quad \text{(parent aklane, ethane)}$$

$$\overset{3}{CH_3}\overset{2}{CH}\overset{1}{CH_2}OH \quad \text{2-Methyl-1-propanol (parent alklane, proppane)}$$
$$\quad\quad | $$
$$\quad CH_3$$

The nomenclature of compounds possessing other functional groups is dealt with as they are introduced in subsequent chapters.

New Words and Phrases

alcohol [ˈælkəhɔl] *n.* 酒精,酒
alkanes [ˈælkein] *n.* 链烃,烷烃
aliphatic [ˌæliˈfætik] *adj.* 脂肪族的,脂肪质的
alphabetically [ˌælfəˈbetikəl] *adv.* 依字母顺序地,字母地
butane [ˈbjuːtein] *n.* 丁烷
clumsy [ˈklʌmzi] *adj.* 笨拙的
conventions [kənˈvenʃən] *n.* 大会,协定,习俗,惯例
decane [ˈdekein] *n.* 癸烷
ethane [ˈeθein] *n.* 乙烷
ethanol [ˈeθənɔːl, -nəul] *n.* 乙醇,酒精
Geneva [dʒiˈniːvə] *n.* 日内瓦城（瑞士西南部城市）
heptane [ˈheptein] *n.* 庚烷
hexane [hekˈsein] *n.* （正）己烷
methane [ˈmeθein] *n.* 甲烷,沼气
nomenclature [nəuˈmenklətʃə] *n.* 命名法,术语
nonane [ˈnɔnein] *n.* 壬烷

octane ['ɔktein]   *n.* 辛烷
pentane ['pentein]   *n.* 戊烷
preferred [pri'fə:d]   *adj.* 首选的
prefix ['pri:fiks]   *n.* 前缀
propane ['prəupein]   *n.* 丙烷
substituent [sʌb'stitjuənt]   *n.* 取代，取代基   *adj.* 取代的
substitution [ˌsʌbsti'tju:ʃən]   *n.* 代替
whatsoever [wɔtsəu'evə (r)]   *pron.* 无论什么
at the present time   目前
be based upon   基于
common (or semi-systematic) name   普通命名（或半系统命名）
functional group   官能团
homologous series   同系列
in accordance with   与……一致，依照
in some instances   在某些情况下
in some respects   在某些方面
2-Methyl-1-propanol   2-甲基-1-丙醇
parent alkane   母烃
refer to sb. as   称某人为
with the exception of   除……以外

Notes

1. The most universal and systematic method is that devised by a commission appointed by the International Union of Pure and Applied Chemistry, which is referred to as the IUPAC System.
   that 指"命名法"，devised by...Chemistry 为过去分词短语作定语修饰 that，which...System 为非限制性定语从句修饰 that。

2. It provides a convenient and relatively straightforward method for naming even the most complicated molecules, and has the advantage that the same basic principles are employed for each series of compounds.
   本句为简单句，并列谓语动词 provides 和 has，that...compounds 为定语从句修饰 advantage。

3. Conversely, of course, it can rightly be argued that in a great number of cases the common name gives no indication of structure whatsoever.
   it 为形式主语，真正主语为主与从句 that...whatsoever.

Exercises

Ⅰ. Give the IUPAC names for the following and translate them into Chinese

Ⅱ. Give the correct name for the structural formula and translate it into Chinese

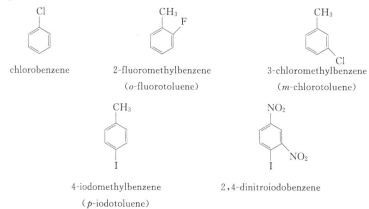

A. 1,1,4,4-tetramethylbutane
B. 2,2,4-trimethylpentane
C. 2,4,4-trimethylpentane
D. 2,2,4-trimethyloctane
E. 2,4,4-trimethyloctane

Ⅲ. Translate the passage into Chinese

Haloalkanes (Alkyl Halides)

Both common and IUPAC names are in general usage nowadays, although the international system, which considers the compounds as halo-substituted alkanes, is gradually becoming the more popular.

Formula	IUPAC name	Common name
CH_3Cl	chloromethane	methyl chloride
CH_3CH_2Br	bromoethane	ethyl bromide
CH_3CHICH_3	2-Iodopropane	Isopropyl iodide
$CH_3CF(CH_3)_2$	2-fluoro-2-methylpropane	tert-butyl fluoride
$C_6H_5CH_2Cl$	chloromethylbenzene	benzyl chloride

Aryl Halides

These are named in the usual way, using numbers to indicate the position of substituents in the ring.

chlorobenzene   2-fluoromethylbenzene   3-chloromethylbenzene
                 (o-fluorotoluene)   (m-chlorotoluene)

4-iodomethylbenzene   2,4-dinitroiodobenzene
(p-iodotoluene)

Aliphatic Amines

These are named by specifying the alkyl groups attached to the nitrogen atom followed by the ending "-amine".

Formula	Name
CH_3NH_2	methylamine
$CH_3CH_2NH_2$	ethylamine
$(CH_3)_2NH$	dimethylamine
$CH_3CH_2CH_2NH_2$	propylamine
$(CH_3)_2CHNH_2$	1-methylethylamine (Isopropylamine)
$CH_3CH_2NHCH_3$	ethylmethylamine
$(CH_3)_3N$	trimethylamine
$(CH_3)_3CNH_2$	1,1-dimethylethylamine (ter-butylamine)

More complex tertiary amines with different alkyl groups are named as derivatives of the longest chain, and an italic capital N is inserted before the name of each substituent.

$$CH_3CH_2CH_2N\begin{matrix}CH_2CH_3\\ \\CH_3\end{matrix}\quad \textit{N}\text{-ethyl-}\textit{N}\text{-methylpropylamine}$$

Compounds containing a tetravalent nitrogen are called QUATERNARY AMMONIUM COMPOUNDS and are named by changing the ending "-mine" to "-mmonium".

$(CH_3)_4N^+I^-$ Tetramethylammonium iodide

Aromatic Amines

The simplest of these is phenylamine (aniline), and most other simple compounds are named as derivatives of phenylamine.

Methylphenylamines are collectively called TOLUIDINES.

phenylamine (Aniline)

N-methylphenylamine

4-methylphenylamine (*p*-toluidine)

diphenylamine

Both aliphatic and aromatic amines can be named by inserting the ending "-amine" as a suffix to the name of the alkane or other appropriate hydrocarbon.

This method is rarely used for simple amines, but is widely adopted for compounds such as, 1,6-hexanediamine, $NH_2(CH_2)_6NH_2$, and 1,3-benzenesdiamine, $1,3\text{-}(NH_2)_2C_6H_4$.

Reading Materials
(Continued from page 22)

Function of Chemicals (Ⅱ)

4. Is it true that some man-made chemicals disrupt (扰乱) the endocrine systems (内分泌系统) of humans and wildlife?

There is no clear evidence to show that either natural or man-made hormones (激素，荷尔蒙) and hormonal-like substances cause health or reproductive problems. However, we recognize the concern and (European Chemical Industry Council，欧洲化学工业委员会), for a number of years, has been looking at understanding more about the so-called endocrine disruption effect (内分泌紊乱).

Since 1999, the chemical industry has undertaken a global research programme under the auspices (赞助，支持) of the International Council of Chemical Associations (ICCA) Long-range Research Initiative (LRI).

This programme is funding research by scientists intended to identify hazards, characterize risks and fill knowledge gaps in issues such as endocrine disruption.

5. What are chemical companies doing to make certain that their operations are safe?

Under its Responsible Care programme, the worldwide chemical industry is committed to improving all aspects of its health, safety and environmental performance and to sharing information on its activities and achievements by communicating with its employees and local communities.

A key part of Responsible Care is measuring performance in order to manage it better. During 2000, Cefic issued guidelines（准则，标准）to its members to encourage a consistent（一贯的）approach to the reporting of work-related illness. It is also urging its members to adopt integrated systems（完整的体系）for managing safety, health, environmental performance and quality.

We have seen continuous reductions in the number of accidents to our employees and significant falls in the industry emissions（散发）to air, water and land.

6. Does the chemical industry also have a programme to ensure that its products can be used safely?

Yes. This is called Product Stewardship（产品责任）-or Responsible Care applied to products. Product Stewardship covers more than just production and use; it also extends to other parts of the product chain such as transport, storage and eventual disposal. To be effective, Product Stewardship requires the close co-operation of everyone involved in the product life cycle.

7. Chemicals are transported by sea, road and rail. How does the industry ensure the safe distribution of its products?

Cefic makes constant efforts to improve the safety of goods in transit. Its Safety and Quality Assessment Systems (SQAS) are management systems implemented（实施，贯彻）in partnership with logistics（物流）companies to ensure the safe handling of chemicals between the plant and the customer.

In February 2000, Cefic and the International Union of Railways signed an agreement to develop a safety management system for chemicals transported by rail. Involving close partnership with the transport and logistics industries, SQAS have already proved effective for other forms of transport such as road and sea. Its extension to rail marks another advance in the industry Responsible Care programme.

8. What is the chemical industry doing about greenhouse gas emissions（温室气体排放）?

Cefic is working very hard to ensure that the chemical industry plays its full part in reducing the threat of global warming.

In response to the 1997 Kyoto Protocol（京都议定书）, European authorities are committed to reducing emissions of greenhouse gases by 8% between 1990 and 2012. To this end, the Commission is encouraging industrial sectors to enter long-term agreements at either national or EU level with the aim of showing demonstrable（明显的）progress by 2005.

Cefic believes that voluntary agreements on energy efficiency are more effective than energy taxes（征收能源税）in addressing global warming. Considerable advances have already been made over the last 30 years. Since 1990, the European chemical industry has already achieved a reduction of 96 million tones of carbon dioxide equivalents, almost one third of the EU's target（欧盟国家的排放目标）under the Kyoto Protocol.

Unit 5 The Nature of Organic Compounds

Introduction

Chemistry is a study of the elements and of how they react together to form compounds. ORGANIC CHEMISTRY relates solely to the chemistry of the compounds of carbon, which in the majority of cases also contain hydrogen. At first, it is difficult to realize the vast extent of this field of study until one appreciates that the number of compounds containing carbon and hydrogen is many times greater than the sum total of all the compounds of all the other elements and is increasing every year[1].

The term organic chemistry is rather misleading in as much as it is a relic of days when chemical compounds were categorized into only two classes, organic and inorganic, depending largely upon their source of origin[2]. Organic compounds were derived from living organisms such as vegetables and animal matter, whereas inorganic compounds were obtained from mineral sources.

Organic substances were known to man in prehistoric times and although nothing was known about them, other than their function and source of origin, they were utilized in a variety of ways[3]. Sugar in fruit was used for sweetening purposes and for making simple wines. Oils and fats from vegetables and animal matter were employed for making soap, and vegetable pigments, such as indigo and alizarin, were used for dyeing fabrics.

It was not until the sixteenth and seventeenth centuries that any really significant progress in isolating new organic substances was made[4]. During this period, compounds such as methanol, propanone (acetone) and ethanoic (acetic) acid were extracted from pyroligneous acid, which was obtained from the dry distillation of wood. Towards the end of the eighteenth century, with the wide application of solvent extraction to plant and animal matter, numerous new compounds were added to the list of those already known. It was during this era that a Swedish chemist, Scheele, succeeded in extracting 2-hydroxypropane-1,2,3-tricarboxylic (citric) acid from lemons, and later others isolated 2,3-dihydroxybutanedioic (tartaric) acid from grapes, 2-hydroxybutanedioic (malic) acid from apples, 2-hydroxypropanoic (lactic) acid from sour milk, uric acid from urine, 3,4,5-trihydroxybenzenecarboxylic (gallic) acid from nut galls and ethanedioic (oxalic) acid from wood sorrels[5]. Between 1772 and 1777, Lavoisier conducted a series of experiments on combustion, and it was during these experiments that he identified the presence of carbon and hydrogen in organic compounds, since they yielded carbon dioxide and water respectively as the products of combustion[6]. Furthermore, he was able to determine the amount of carbon dioxide evolved by dissolving it in a solution of potassium hydroxide.

Gradually the presence of other elements such as oxygen, nitrogen and sulphur, was found to be common to large groups of organic substances, and for the first time something was known about their chemical nature.

During the early nineteenth century, as more and more elements were being discovered, it became apparent that those elements associated with compounds derived from living organisms were limited to only a few and also that they tended to be readily combustible[7].

In 1828 the German chemist, Wohler, became the first person deliberately to synthesize an organic substance in the laboratory. After a chance observation that an aqueous solution of ammonium cyanate (NH_4CNO) evaporated, producing carbamide (urea), NH_2CONH_2, the then repeated the experiment several times to confirm his conclusion.

Nowadays preparative techniques and principles have become so lucid that organic compounds can be prepared with almost as much ease as most inorganic.

Characteristic Properties of Organic Compounds

Organic compounds are generally gases, volatile liquids or low melting-point solids, they tend to be insoluble in water unless they contain polar groups, such as —OH, —COOH, —SO_3H etc., but are usually soluble in organic, non-polar solvents, such as tetrachloromethane (carbon tetrachloride), ethoxyethane (diethyl ether), benzene etc. On burning in excess oxygen they yield carbon dioxide and water (except when the compound contains no hydrogen, which is comparatively rare), and the complete combustion of hydrocarbons (i.e. compounds containing only carbon and hydrogen) yields these as the only products.

Organic reactions are generally slow in comparison with many inorganic reactions and often require energy, usually in the form of heat. The reactions seldom proceed to completion, and consequently careful purification is necessary in order to isolate the desired product in a high state or purity. This contrasts quite markedly with many inorganic reactions which often proceed to completion instantaneously, especially those that take place in polar media.

The phenomenon known as isomerism is commonplace in organic chemistry. Isomerism is the ability of certain compounds, possessing the same molecular formula, to exist in different forms on account of their having different structural arrangements of atoms. For example, the formula C_2H_6O applies to two entirely different compounds, ethanol and methoxymethane, which possess distinctly different properties.

In order to understand and appreciate just how the molecules of compounds are formed from their constituent elements, it is essential to have at least a qualitative knowledge of the structure of the atoms of these elements, and then to consider the type of bonding involved in joining these atoms together.

New Words and Phrases

acetone [ˈæsitəun] *n.* 丙酮
alizarin [əˈlizərin] *n.* 茜素
benzene [ˈbenziːn, benˈziːn] *n.* 苯
benzenecarboxylic [ˈbenziːnˌkɑːbɔkˈsilik] *adj.* 苯羧基的
carbamide [ˈkɑːbəmaid] *n.* 尿素
citric [ˈsitrik] *adj.* 柠檬的，采自柠檬的

cyanate ['saiəneit] *n.* 氰酸盐
deliberately [di'libərətli] *adv.* 故意地
diethyl [dai'eθil] *adj.* 二乙基的
dihydroxybutanedioic [dihai'drɔksibju:tæni'daiəic] *adj.* 二羟基丁酸的
ethanedioic ['eθeindiəic] *n.* 乙二酸的
ethanoic ['i:θənic] *n.* 醋酸的
ether ['i:θə] *n.* 醚
ethoxyethane [e'θɔksi'eθein] *n.* 乙氧基乙烷
gallic ['gælik] *adj.* 五倍子的
grapes [greip] *n.* 葡萄，葡萄树
hydrocarbon ['haidrəu'kɑ:bən] *n.* 烃，碳氢化合物
hydroxybutanedioic [hai'drɔksibju:tæni'daiəic] *adj.* 羟基丁酸的
hydroxypropane [hai'drɔksi'prəupein] *n.* 羟基丙烷，丙醇
hydroxypropanoic [hai'drɔksi'prəupeinic] *adj.* 羟基丙酸的
indigo ['indigəu] *n.* 靛，靛青
instantaneously [ˌinstən'teinjəsli] *adv.* 瞬间地，即刻地，即时地
isomerism [ai'sɔmərizm] *n.* 同分异构现象
lactic ['læktik] *adj.* 乳的，乳汁的
Lavoisier [ˌlɑ:vwə'zjei] 拉瓦锡（1743—1794，法国化学家，氧发现者）
lucid ['lu:sid] *adj.* 明晰的
malic ['mælik，'mei-] *adj.* 苹果的，由苹果取得的
methanol ['meθənɔl，-nəul] *n.* 甲醇
methoxymethane [mə'θɔksi'meθein] *n.* 甲氧基甲烷
propanone ['prəupənəun] *n.* 丙酮
pyroligneous [ˌpaiərəu'ligniəs] *adj.* 焦木的，干馏木材而得
qualitative ['kwɔlitətiv] *adj.* 性质上的，定性的
Scheele 谢勒（1742—1786，瑞典化学家，第一个从尿结石里分离出来尿酸 $C_5H_4N_4O_3$）
tartaric [tɑ:'tærik] *adj.* 酒石的，似酒石的，含有酒石的
tetrachloromethane ['tetrəˌklɔ:rəu'mi:θein，-'me-] *n.* 四氯化碳
tricarboxylic [traiˌkɑ:bɔk'silik] *adj.* （分子中含有）三（个）羧基的
trihydroxy [traihai'drɔksi] *adj.* 三羟（基）的
urea ['juəriə] *n.* 尿素
uric ['juərik] *adj.* 尿的，取自尿中的
urine ['juərin] *n.* 尿
Wohler 维勒（1800—1882，德国化学家，第一个在实验室中从氰酸氨制备有机化合物尿素）
ammonium cyanate 氰酸铵
animal matter 动物质
be soluble in 溶于
be insoluble in 不溶于
carbon tetrachloride 四氯化碳
2,3-dihydroxybutanedioic (tartaric) acid 2,3-二羟基丁酸或酒石酸
dry distillation 干馏

dyeing fabrics 染色织物
ethanedioic (oxalic) acid 乙二酸或草酸
ethanoic (acetic) acid 乙酸或醋酸
2-hydroxybutanedioic (malic) acid 2-羟基丁酸或苹果酸
2-hydroxypropane-1,2,3-tricarboxylic (citric) acid 2-羟基丙烷-1,2,3-三甲酸
2-hydroxypropanoic (lactic) acid 2-羟基丙酸或乳酸
non-polar 非极化的
nut galls 核果瘤
polar groups 极性基
preparative techniques 制备技术
solvent extraction 溶剂萃取
sour milk 酸牛奶
3,4,5-trihydroxybenzenecarboxylic (gallic) acid 3,4,5-三羟基苯甲酸或五倍子酸
type of bonding 键型
uric acid 尿酸
volatile liquids 挥发性液体
wood sorrels 酢浆草

Notes

1. At first, it is difficult to realize the vast extent of this field of study until one appreciates that the number of compounds containing carbon and hydrogen is many times greater than the sum total of all the compounds of all the other elements and is increasing every year.
   it 是形式主语，to realize the vast extent of this field of study 是真正主语。Until ...every year 引导时间状语从句，其中 that...every year 为 appreciates 的宾语从句。

2. The term organic chemistry is rather misleading in as much as it is a relic of days when chemical compounds were categorized into only two classes, organic and inorganic, depending largely upon their source of origin.
   misleading ...organic and inorganic 为现在分词短语作表语，when ...origin 为时间定语从句。

3. Organic substances were known to man in prehistoric times and although nothing was known about them, other than their function and source of origin, they were utilized in a variety of ways.
   nothing...other than：除……之外，没有……例如：There's nobody here other than me.

4. It was not until the sixteenth and seventeenth centuries that any really significant progress in isolating new organic substances was made.
   It was not until...that...强调句型

5. It was during this era that a Swedish chemist, Scheele, succeeded in extracting 2-hydroxypropane-1,2,3-tricarboxylic (citric) acid from lemons, and later others isolated 2,3-dihydroxybutanedioic (tartaric) acid from grapes, 2-hydroxybutanedioic (malic) acid from apples, 2-hydroxypropanoic (lactic) acid from sour milk, uric acid from urine, 3,4,5-trihydroxybenzenecarboxylic (gallic) acid from nut galls and ethanedioic (oxalic) acid from wood sorrels.
   It was ...that...强调句型

6. Between 1772 and 1777, Lavoisier conducted a series of experiments on combustion, and it was during these experiments that he identified the presence of carbon and hydrogen in organic compounds, since they yielded carbon dioxide and water respectively as the products of combustion.

it was during these experiments that...organic compounds 强调句型

7. During the early nineteenth century, as more and more elements were being discovered, it became apparent that those elements associated with compounds derived from living organisms were limited to only a few and also that they tended to be readily combustible.

it 是形式主语，that...and also that...combustible 为并列的两个真正主语。

Exercises

Ⅰ. Understanding the text

1. What is organic chemistry defined as?
2. Are organic compounds derived from living organisms? Describe it.
3. What was identified by Lavoisier' experiment?
4. What is the great significance of Wohler's experiment?
5. Describe the characteristic properties of organic compounds.

Ⅱ. Translate the following into English

1. 2,3-二羟基丁酸或酒石酸
2. 2-羟基丁酸或苹果酸
3. 2-羟基丙烷-1,2,3-三甲酸
4. 2-羟基丙酸或乳酸
5. 3,4,5-三羟基苯甲酸或五倍子酸
6. 氰酸铵
7. 四氯化碳
8. 乙二酸或草酸
9. 乙酸或醋酸
10. 尿酸

Ⅲ. Translate the passage into Chinese

Alcohols

The IUPAC system is generally adopted for most alcohols, although common names, which are afforded by stating the name of the appropriate alkyl group followed by the word "alcohol", are still sometimes used for the simpler compounds, e.g. methyl alcohol, isopropyl alcohol, benzyl alcohol etc.

The IUPAC names are afforded by dropping the ending "-ane" of the corresponding alkane and replacing it with the suffix "-ol". The position of the hydroxyl group in the carbon chain is specified by inserting the appropriate number in the front of the name.

Formula	IUPAC name	Common name
CH_3OH	methanol	Methyl alcohol
CH_3CH_2OH	ethanol	Ethyl alcohol
$CH_3CH_2CH_2OH$	1-propanol	*n*-Propyl alcohol
$CH_3CHOHCH_3$	2-propanol	isopropyl alcohol

CH₃COH(CH₃)₂	2-methyl-2-propanol	tert-butyl alcohol
C₆H₅CH₂OH	phenylmethanol	benzyl alcohol
C₆H₅CH₂CH₂OH	2-phenylethanol	phenylethyl alcohol

Phenols

Phenols are compounds containing a hydroxyl group attached directly to an aromatic nucleus and have a general formula ArOH. Like alcohols they may be monohydric or polyhydric according to the number of hydroxyl groups that they contain. The simplest and most important member of this family of compounds is phenol itself.

phenol

4-methylphenol (p-cresol)

1-naphthalenol (1 or α-naphthol)

2-naphthalenol (2- or β-naphthol)

2-hydroxybenzenecarboxylic acid (2-hydroxybenzoic acid or salicylic acid)

1,4-dibenzeneol (hydroquinone)

Ether

The common system specifies the alkyl and/or aryl groups attached to the oxygen atom followed by the word "ether". Certain alkyl aryl ethers are afforded names which give no indication as to the structure, e.g. anisole (methoxybenzene) and phenetole (ethoxybenzene).

The IUPAC system regards them as alkoxy derivatives of alkanes or of the aryl nucleus.

e.g. CH₃CH₂CHCH₃ 2-methoxybutane
              |
             OCH₃

Formula	IUPAC name	Common name
CH₃OCH₃	methoxymethane	dimethyl ether
CH₃OCH₂CH₃	methoxyethane	ethyl methyl ether
CH₃CH₂OCH₂CH₃	ethoxyethane	diethyl ether (ether)
C₆H₅OCH₃	methoxybenzene	methyl phenyl ether or anisole
C₆H₅OCH₂CH₃	ethoxybenzene	ethyl phenyl ether or phenetole
C₆H₅OC₆H₅	phenoxybenzene	diphenyl ether

Reading Materials

Biodiesel

Biodiesel (生物柴油) made from rapeseed (油菜籽) could increase rather than reduce greenhouse emissions compared to conventional (传统) diesel fuels, reports a new study published in the journal Chemistry & Industry. Overall the researchers found that petroleum diesel and rapeseed biodiesel, presently the main biofuel (生物燃油) used across Europe, have a similar environmental impact. The results suggest that efforts to mitigate (缓和, 减轻) climate change through the adoption of rapeseed biodiesel may be of little use beyond energy security.

Comparing the full lifecycle emissions of greenhouse gases by the two fuels from production through combustion (燃烧) in cars, Eric Johnson, editor of Environmental Impact Assessment Review, and Russell Heinen, Vice President of SRI Consulting, found that "biodiesel derived from (提取) rapeseed grown on dedicated farmland emits (释放,散发) nearly the same amount of greenhouse gas emissions (defined as CO_2 equivalents) per km driven as does conventional diesel (传统燃料)."

They show that about two-thirds of greenhouse gas emissions from rapeseed biodiesel occur during the farming of rapeseed, when nitrous oxide (一氧化二氮) (N_2O), which is 200—300 times as potent (浓烈的) a greenhouse gas as CO_2 otherwise, is released into the atmosphere. In contrast, petroleum diesel releases roughly 85 percent of its greenhouse gas emissions during combustion in a vehi (机动车). The researchers say that the difference may be greater depending on land use.

"If the land used to grow rapeseed was instead used to grow trees, petroleum diesel would emit only a third of the CO_2 equivalent emissions as biodiesel," stated a release from the Society of Chemical Industry, publisher of Chemistry & Industry. Overall the study found that biodiesel and petroleum diesel have similar environmental impact.

What is asbestos and why should we be worried

Asbestos (石棉) is a naturally occurring mineral that is mined in various parts of the world including Canada, South Africa and Russia. It is resistant to heat, fire and chemicals, and it can easily be used in a wide range of products including building materials and fire-resistant materials (耐火材料).

Asbestos was widely used throughout most of the 20th century, particularly in the 1970s, and only stopped being widely used in the early 1980s when scientists realized how dangerous it could be. Because it has been so widely used, most homes in the UK built before the 1980s will probably have some asbestos in the building materials.

Asbestos is made up of lots of strands or fibres (纤维). These fibres easily break apart when they are damaged and are so light that they will float in the air. Some of those fibres can become so small that people breathe them in and they can get stuck in the lungs. This causes some types of cancer. The people most at risk of developing asbestos-related illness are those who have worked with the asbestos over a long time. It is very rare for asbestos-related diseases to be developed by people who have only occasionally come into contact with asbestos.

Unit 6 Hydrocarbons

Alkanes (Paraffins)

With the exception of the first four members of the series, methane, ethane, propane and butane, the straight-chain alkanes are named by taking the Greek prefix appropriate to the number of carbon atoms and adding the ending "-ane"[1].

For branched alkanes, the largest unbranched chain of carbon atoms is selected and named accordingly. The names of the alkyl substituents prefix the name of the main chain, the position of substitution being indicated by the appropriate number.

$$CH_3-CH_2-CH_2-CH_3$$
Butane

$$CH_3-CH_2-CH_2-CH_2-CH_3$$
Pentane

$$CH_3-CH(CH_3)-CH_2-CH_3$$
2-Methylbutane
(Isopentane)

$$CH_3-CH(CH_3)-CH_2-CH_2-CH_3$$
2-Methylpentane
(Isohexane)

$$CH_3-C(CH_3)_2-CH_3$$
2,2-Dimethylpropane
(Neopentane)

Alkenes (Olefins)

In accordance with the IUPAC system, an alkene is named by dropping the ending "-ane" from the name of the corresponding alkane and replacing it with the suffix "-ene"[2]. Where required, the position of the double bond is specified by placing the appropriate number in front of the name of alkenes. Ethene and propene are still sometimes referred to by their common names, ethylene and propylene respectively.

Formula	IUPAC name	Common name
$CH_2=CH_2$	Ethene	Ethylene
$CH_3-CH=CH_2$	Propene	Propylene
$CH_3-CH_2-CH=CH_2$	1-Butene	1-Butylene
$CH_3-CH=CH-CH_3$	2-Butene	2-Butylene
$CH_3-CH_2-CH(C_6H_5)-CH=CH_2$	3-Phenyl-pentene	—

Alkynes (Acetylenes)

The IUPAC names of alkynes are afforded by taking the stem of the name of the corresponding alkane and replacing the ending "-ane" of the alkane with the suffix "-yne"[3]. The position of the triple bond is indicated by putting the appropriate number in front of the alkynes.

Formula	IUPAC name	Common name
CH≡CH	Ethyne	Acetylene
$CH_3C\equiv CH$	Propyne	Methylacetylens
$CH_3CH_2C\equiv CH$	1-Butyne	Ethylacetylene
$CH_3C\equiv CCH_3$	2-Butyne	Dimethylacetylene
$CH_3CH_2CHC\equiv CH$ | C_6H_5	3-Phenyl-1-pentyne	—

Fractional Distillation of Petroleum

The crude petroleum is fractionally distilled, and the fractions are collected over a range of boiling point.

The carbon content of the alkanes in each fraction corresponds approximately to a definite range, with the simpler, more volatile homologues distilling over first. However, the carbon content of lighter fractions is enhanced by a certain proportion of the more volatile branched compounds of higher relative molecular mass. In practice, this is of little consequence, as the uses to which each fraction is applied depend almost essentially upon their volatility and viscosity rather than upon their respective constituents.

Fraction	Distillation temperature Range/℃	Approximate carbon content
Gas	Below 20	C_1—C_4
Light petroleum	20—60	C_5—C_6
(petroleum ether)	60—100	C_6—C_7
Petrol (gasoline)	40—205	C_5—C_{12} (cycloalkanes)
Paraffin (kerosene)	175—325	C_{12}—C_{18} (aromatics)
Gas oil	275—400	C_{12}—C_{25}
Lubricating oil	Non-volatile liquids	—
Asphalt (bitumen)	Residue	—

Uses of the Fractions

The more volatile fractions are used mainly as fuel.

Fraction	Uses
Gas	Heating
Light petroleum	Organic solvent
(petroleum ether)	Organic solvent
Petrol (gasoline)	Fuel for internal-combustion engines requiring volatile liquids
Paraffin (kerosene)	Heating fuel and for engines requiring less volatile liquids, e.g., tractors, jet engines
Gas oil	Heating fuel and for Diesel engines
Lubricating oil	Lubricant
Asphalt (bitumen)	Road construction and roofing

The lubricating oil fraction often contains long-chain alkanes (C_{20} ~ C_{34}) of high melting point which may form solid waxes when cold. If these were allowed to remain in the fraction, they would tend to block the oil pipes in the refinery, particularly in cold weather. Instead, they are separated out by cooling the fraction and filtering. The solid is sold as PARAFFIN WAX (m. p. 50~55℃) or used to make PETROLEUM JELLY (VASELINE).

Petroleum fractions also provide useful compounds for preparing other chemicals, and the more volatile ones, containing up to five carbons, provide probably the most important source of raw materials for large-scale preparations of aliphatic compounds.

New Words and Phrases

alkyl ['ælkil] *n.* 烷基，烃基 *adj.* 烷基的，烃基的
aromatic [ˌærəu'mætik] *adj.* 芳香族的
asphalt ['æsfælt] *n.* 沥青
bitumen ['bitjumin] *n.* 沥青
butene ['bju:ti:n] *n.* 丁烯
butylene ['bju:tili:n] *n.* 丁烯
butyne ['bjutain] *n.* 丁炔
dimethyl [ˌdai'meθil] *adj.* 二甲基的
dimethylpropane [ˌdai'meθil'prəupein] *n.* 二甲基丙烷
cycloalkane [ˌsaiklǝu'ælkein] *n.* 环烷烃
ethene ['eθi:n] *n.* 乙烯
ethyl ['eθil, 'i:θail] *n.* 乙烷基
ethylene ['eθili:n] *n.* 乙烯，乙烯基
ethyne ['eθain] *n.* 乙炔
gasoline ['gæsəli:n] *n.* 汽油
hydrocarbon ['haidrəu'kɑ:bən] *n.* 烃，碳氢化合物
isohexane [ˌaisə'heksein] *n.* 异己烷
isopentane [aisəu'pentein] *n.* 异戊烷，2-甲基丁烷
kerosene ['kerəsi:n] *n.* 煤油，火油
lubricant ['lu:brikənt] *n.* 滑润剂
methylacetylene ['meθilə'setili:n] *n.* 甲基乙炔
2-methylbutane ['meθil'bju:tein] *n.* 2-甲基丁烷
2-methylpentane ['meθil'pentein] *n.* 2-甲基戊烷
neopentane [ˌni:əu'pentein] *n.* 新戊烷，季戊烷
olefins ['əuləfin] *n.* 石蜡
paraffins ['pærəfin, -fi:n] *n.* 石蜡
pentane ['pentein] *n.* 戊烷
petrol ['petrəl] *n.* （英）汽油 [=（美）gasoline]
petroleum [pi'trəuliəm] *n.* 石油
propene ['prəupi:n] *n.* 丙烯
propylene ['prəupili:n] *n.* 丙烯
propyne ['prəupain] *n.* 丙炔
stem [stem] *n.* 茎，干
viscosity [vis'kɔsiti] *n.* 黏质，黏性

volatility [ˌvɒləˈtiliti] *n.* 挥发性
aliphatic compound　脂肪族化合物
alkyl substituent　烷基（烃基）取代基
branched alkane　支链烷烃
common name　普通命名法
crude petroleum　原油
double bond　双键
internal-combustion engine　内燃机
IUPAC name　IUPAC 命名法
organic solvent　有机溶剂
petroleum ether　石油醚
petroleum jelly　凡士林，矿油
3-Phenyl-1-pentene [ˈfenəl][pentiːn] *n.* 3-苯基-1-戊烯
3-Phenyl-1-pentyne [ˈfenəl][pentain] *n.* 3-苯基-1-戊炔
straight-chain alkane　直链烷烃
triple bond　三键

Notes

1. With the exception of the first four members of the series, methane, ethane, propane and butane, the straight-chain alkanes are named by taking the Greek prefix appropriate to the number of carbon atoms and adding the ending "-ane".
本句为简单句，taking...and adding...引导了并列的动名词短语作 by 的介词宾语。

2. In accordance with the IUPAC system, an alkene is named by dropping the ending "-ane" from the name of the corresponding alkane and replacing it with the suffix "-ene".
本句为简单句，dropping...and replacing...引导了并列的动名词短语作 by 的介词宾语。

3. The IUPAC names of alkynes are afforded by taking the stem of the name of the corresponding alkane and replacing the ending "-ane" of the alkane with the suffix "-yne".
本句为简单句，taking...and replacing...引导了并列的动名词短语作 by 的介词宾语。

Exercises

Ⅰ. Understanding the text

1. Give the IUPAC name for alkanes

　A. 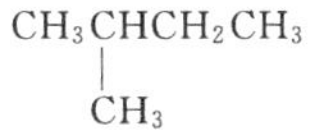　$CH_3CHCH_2CH_3$
　　　　　|
　　　　　CH_3

　B. 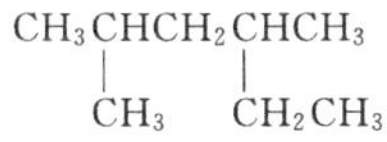　$CH_3CHCH_2CHCH_3$
　　　　　|　　　　|
　　　　　CH_3　CH_2CH_3
　　　　　　　　　$CH_2CH_2CH_3$

　C. 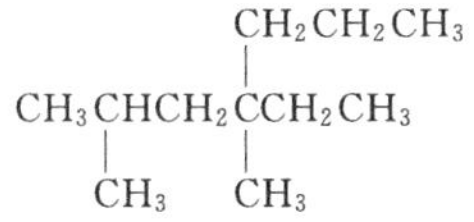　$CH_3CHCH_2CCH_2CH_3$
　　　　　|　　　|
　　　　　CH_3　CH_3

2. Give the IUPAC name for alkenes

　A. 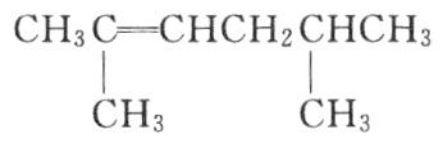　$CH_3C\!=\!CHCH_2CHCH_3$
　　　　　|　　　　　|
　　　　　CH_3　　　CH_3

B. 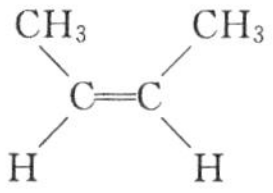 $\begin{array}{c}CH_3\\ \diagdown\\ H\end{array}C=C\begin{array}{c}CH_3\\ \diagup\\ H\end{array}$

C. $CH_3\underset{\underset{CH_3}{|}}{\overset{\overset{Cl}{|}}{C}}CH=CH_2$

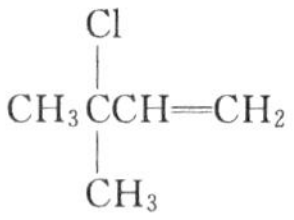

D. 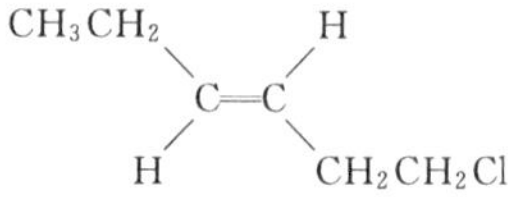 $\begin{array}{c}CH_3CH_2\\ \diagdown\\ H\end{array}C=C\begin{array}{c}H\\ \diagup\\ CH_2CH_2Cl\end{array}$

3. Give the IUPAC name for alkynes

A. $CH\equiv CCH_2CH_2Cl$

B. 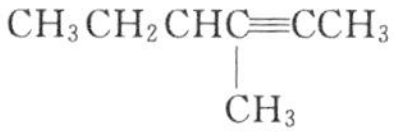 $CH_3CH_2\underset{\underset{CH_3}{|}}{C}HC\equiv CCH_3$

C. $CH_3C\equiv CCH_2\underset{\underset{CH_3}{|}}{C}HC\equiv CH$

D. 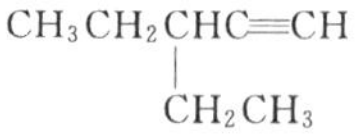 $CH_3CH_2\underset{\underset{CH_2CH_3}{|}}{C}HC\equiv CH$

Ⅱ. Write down the following formulas

1. A. 2,4-dimethylpentane

   B. 1,3-trimethylcyclopentane

   C. 2,5-dimethyl-5-ethylheptane

   D. 2,2,4-trimethylpentane

2. A. 4-bromo-1-pentene

   B. 3-ethyl-1-pentene

   C. 2,2-dimethyl-3-hexene

   D. *trans*-2-methyl-3-heptene

3. A. 1-propyne

   B. 3-methyl-1-butyne

   C. 2-methyl-3-hexyne

   D. 3-phenyl-1-pentyne

Ⅲ. Translate the passage into Chinese

Aldehydes

The name ALDEHYDE originates from the fact that the compounds are obtainable by dehydrogenating alcohols (alcohols dehydrogenated).

Common names are derived by replacing the ending "-ic" of the corresponding carboxylic acid with the suffix "-aldehyde".

IUPAC names are obtained by dropping the ending "-e" of the corresponding alkane and replacing it with suffix "-al".

Since the carbonyl group can carry only one alkyl group, it is by necessity always at the end of the carbon chain.

Formula	IUPAC name	Common name
HCHO	methanal	formaldehyde

CH_3CHO	ethanal	acetaldehyde
CH_3CH_2CHO	propanal	propionaldehyde
$CH_3(CH_2)_2CHO$	butanal	n-butyraldehyde
$C_6H_5CH_2CHO$	phenylethanal	phenylacetaldehyde

The simplest of the aromatic aldehydes is benzaldehyde, C_6H_5CHO.

Ketones

Common names are designated by specifying each of the hydrocarbon groups attached to the carbonyl group followed by the word "ketone".

IUPAC names are derived by taking the stem of the name of the corresponding alkane and replacing the ending "-e" with the suffix "one". The position of the carbonyl group is specified in the usual way, the carbonyl carbon being included in the numbering of the straight chain.

Formula	IUPAC name	Common name
CH_3COCH_3	propanone	acetone (dimethyl ketone)
$CH_3COCH_2CH_3$	butanone	methyl ethyl ketone
$CH_3CO(CH_2)_2CH_3$	2-pentanone	methyl propyl ketone
$CH_3CH_2COCH_2CH_3$	3-pentanone	diethyl ketone

Ketones in which the carbonyl group is attached directly to a benzene ring are named as phenyl derivatives of the appropriate aliphatic carbonyl compound. These compounds were formerly referred to collectively as phenones.

phenylethanone (acetophenone)   diphenylmethanone (benzophenone)

Carboxylic Acids

Common names are generally derived from the Latin or Greek name of their source of origin.

FORMIC ACID derives its name from the fact that it is obtainable by distilling crushed ants (Lat. formica, ant), although it is also present in stinging nettles and certain other plants.

On exposure to the atmosphere, wines, notably sweet ones with a fairly low alcohol content, often become sour and turn to vinegar (French vinaigre, sour wine) owing to attack by a bacterium, commonly referred to as the "vinegar fly". This micro-organism, instead of allowing the sugar to be converted into alcohol, turns it into acetic (ethanoic) acid (Lat. Acetum, vinegar).

Derivation of some other common names:

Name	Source	Derivation
proplonic acid	plant and animal products	Gr. proto (first) pion (fat)
butyric acid	rancid butter	Lat. butyrum, butter
caproic acid	goat's milk	Lat. Caper, goat

Positions of substitution in the hydrocarbon chain are denoted by the Greek letters α, β, γ, etc.

e. g. $\overset{\gamma}{CH_3}\overset{\beta}{CH}\overset{\alpha}{CH_2}COOH$ β-methylvaleric acid
   　　　|
   　　CH_3

IUPAC names are afforded by taking the name of the appropriate alkane and replacing the ending "-e" with the suffix "-oic" acid. Positions of substitution are denoted in the usual way by numbering the longest unbranched chain containing the carboxyl group.

Formula	IUPAC name	Common name
HCOOH	methanoic acid	formic acid
CH_3COOH	ethanoic acid	acetic acid
CH_3CH_2COOH	propanoic acid	propionic acid
$CH_3(CH_2)_2COOH$	butanoic acid	n-butyric acid
$(CH_3)_2CHCOOH$	2-methylpropanoic acid	isobutyric acid
$CH_3(CH_2)_3COOH$	pentanoic acid	n-valeric acid
$CH_3(CH_2)_{14}COOH$	hexadecanoic acid	palmitic acid
$CH_3(CH_2)_{16}COOH$	octadecanoic acid	stearic acid
$C_6H_5CH_2COOH$	2-phenylethanoic acid	phenylacetic acid

Names of aromatic acids are often related to the appropriate hydrocarbon, e. g. benzenecarboxylic (benzoic) and methylbenzenecarboxylic (toluic) acids, or, like the aliphatic compounds, derived from the name of one of their natural sources.

benzenecarboxylic acid
(benzoic acid)

3-methylbenzenecarboxylic acid
(m-toluic acid)

Reading Materials

Hazardous Chemicals

The chemicals encountered in the laboratory have a broad spectrum of physical, chemical, and toxicological (毒物学) properties and physiological (生理学) effects. The risks associated with the use of laboratory chemicals must be well understood prior to their use in an experiment. The chemicals used in the laboratory can be grouped among several different hazard classes. Many chemicals display more than one type of hazard. Highly hazardous chemicals require special written procedures to ensure safe use in the laboratory.

Toxic（有毒的）Chemicals

Toxicity is the potential of a substance to produce adverse reaction (有害反应) on the health or well-being (健康) of an individual. Whether or not any ill effects occur depends on: the properties of the chemical; the route by which the substance enters the body; the dose (the amount of the chemical acting on the body); and the susceptibility (易感性) of the exposed individual (接触者).

Organic Solvents

Organic solvents are one of the most commonly encountered groups of toxic chemicals and constitute one of the major hazards in a laboratory. Most are highly volatile (挥发) or flammable (易燃), such as ethers (乙醚), alcohols (乙醇), and hydrocarbons (碳氢化

合物).

Chlorinated（含氯的）solvents such as chloroform（氯仿）are often non-flammable but, when exposed to heat or flame, may produce carbon monoxide（一氧化碳）, chlorine（氯气）, phosgene（光气）, or other highly toxic gases（剧毒性气体）.

Inhalation（吸入）of solvent vapors may cause bronchial irritation（支气管炎）, dizziness（头昏眼花）, central nervous system depression（中枢神经衰弱）, nausea（恶心）, headache, or coma（昏迷）. Prolonged exposure to high concentrations of solvent vapors may result in liver（肝）or kidney（肾）damage. Skin contact may produce defatting（脱脂）and drying. Ingestion（摄入）of a solvent could result in severe physiological effects. In case of ingestion, call the Poison Control Center (589-8222), or seek medical aid immediately.

With the following chemicals, the odor threshold（极限）is higher than the acceptable exposure limit, such as chloroform; benzene（苯）; carbon tetrachloride（四氯化碳）; and methylene chloride（二氯甲烷）.

Certain solvents are known or suspected to be carcinogenic（致癌的）following prolonged exposure. See the section on Highly Hazardous Chemicals for special requirements for carcinogens（致癌物）. Examples of solvents that are known or suspected carcinogens include: chloroform; benzene; carbon tetrachloride; chlorinated ethers（氯乙醚）; methylene chloride; and polyhalogenated hydrocarbons（多卤代烃）.

All volatile and flammable solvents should be used in a properly functioning chemical hood（罩）. Never use ether or other highly flammable solvents in a room with an open flame or other ignition source present. The safe handling of flammable materials is discussed in the section on physical hazards of chemicals later in this chapter.

Unit 7 Aromaticity and Naming Benzene

It is convenient to classify organic compounds according to one of two general classes: ALIPHATIC (fatty) compounds and AROMATIC (fragrant) compounds[1]. The literal meaning of these terms have little or no significance nowadays, as compounds are categorized much more precisely by consideration of their molecular structure and properties.

Aliphatic compounds are those possessing open chains of carbon atoms or, alternatively, cyclic compounds whose structure and properties resemble such open-chain compounds[2].

Aromatic compounds are those possessing the ring structure of benzene or other molecular structures that resemble benzene in electronic configuration and chemical behaviour[3]. There are many compounds that, at first appearance, bear little resemblance to benzene, but have a basic similarity in electronic configuration.

However, at this stage, it is convenient to interpret aromatic character in terms of the benzene ring structure, since this definition incorporates most of the commonly encountered aromatic substances.

Historical Development of the Structure of the Benzene Molecule

The tetravalency of carbon was first recognized by Kekule in 1858, and numerous attempts at formulating the structure of the benzene molecule have since been made[4]. The comparatively large carbon content of aromatic compounds made the structures difficult to formulate, and early attempts produced unacceptable linear structures such as those shown below.

$$CH_3-C\equiv C-C\equiv C-CH_3$$
$$CH_2=CH-C\equiv C-CH=CH_2$$
$$CH\equiv C-CH_2-CH_2-C\equiv CH$$

Such compounds would be expected to readily undergo addition reactions across the unsaturated bonds, whereas benzene shows little tendency to undergo this type of reaction[5]. Furthermore, a linear molecule of this type would be expected to have several isomers, but benzene in fact has no isomers.

The realization that there were no structural isomers of the monosubstituted derivative, C_6H_5Y, implied the possible existence of a cyclic arrangement of carbon atoms, with all atoms being equivalent.

The fact that three structural isomers of disubstituted derivatives of benzene had been detected provided further evidence in favour of a cyclic structure[6].

In 1865 Kekule produced the first reasonably acceptable cyclic structure for benzene:

which is more conveniently written as:

Naming Substituted Benzene Derivatives

A benzene molecule in which one hydrogen atom has been replaced by an atom or group is referred to as a MONOSUBSTITUTED DERIVATIVE.

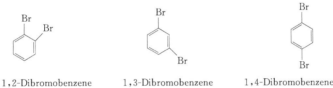

For each DISUBSTITUTED DERIVATIVE there are three different isomers, depending upon the positions of substitution in the ring. When the two substituents are attached to adjacent carbons in the ring, the isomer is referred to as the 1,2- or ortho (*o*) derivative; when they are in the next-but-one position, the isomer is referred to as the 1,3- or meta (*m*) derivative, and when they are diametrically opposite, it is referred to as the 1,4- or para (*p*) derivative. The positions of substitution are indicated by numbering the carbon atoms in the ring and choosing unity so as to give the lowest possible combination of numbers.

For example, consider the three isomers of dibromobenzene.

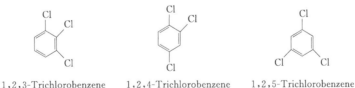

Three isomers exist for each TRISUBSTITUTED DERIVATIVE of benzene.

1,2,3-Trichlorobenzene   1,2,4-Trichlorobenzene   1,2,5-Trichlorobenzene

If one of the groups present gives rise to a compound with a special name, then only two positions of substitution are mentioned.

Dinitrobenzenecarboxylic acid   2-Chloro-4-nitrophenol
(2,6-Dinitrobenzoic acid)

The C_6H_5-part of a monosubstituted benzene derivative is called a PHENYL GROUP or RADICAL, which is analogous to the alkyl group in aliphatic systems. For convenience, especially when writing complicated structural formulae, the phenyl group is often abbreviated to "Ph".

Phenyl groups and substituted phenyl groups alike are collectively termed ARYL

GROUPS or RADICALS, and may be abbreviated to "Ar".

It is usual to refer to a system as an aryl group when its exact nature, apart from its general aromatic character, is of no specific importance to a particular reaction.

C_6H_5- Phenyl group or radical

$\left.\begin{array}{l} C_6H_5- \\ C_6H_4Y- \\ C_6H_3YZ- \\ \text{etc.} \end{array}\right\}$ Collectively termed aryl groups or radicals

New Words and Phrases

aromaticity [ˌærəməˈtisiti] *n.* 芳香族化合物的结构（特性）
chlorobenzene [ˌklɔːrəˈbenziːn] *n.* 氯苯
collectively [kəˈlektivli] *adv.* 全体地，共同地
derivative [diˈrivətiv] *n.* 衍生物
dibromobenzene [daiˈbrəuməuˈbenziːn] *n.* 二溴苯
disubstituted [daiˈsʌbstitjuːtid] *adj.* 二基取代的
fatty [ˈfæti] *adj.* 脂肪的，含脂肪的
fragrant [ˈfreigrənt] *adj.* 芬芳的，香的
Kekulé 凯库勒（1829—1896，德国化学家，有机结构理论奠基人）
meta [ˈmetə] *adj.* 间位的
methylbenzene [ˌmeθilˈbenziːn, -benˈziːn] *n.* 甲苯
monosubstituted [ˈmɔnəˈsʌbstitjuːtid] *adj.* 一元取代的
nitrobenzene [ˌnaitrəuˈbenziːn] *n.* 硝基苯
ortho [ˈɔːθəu] *adj.* 邻位的
para [ˈpɑːrə] *adj.* 对位的
tetravalency [ˈtetrəˈveilənsi] *n.* 四价
toluene [ˈtɔljuiːn] *n.* 甲苯
trichlorobenzene [ˌtraiklɔːrəˈbeziːn] *n.* 三氯（代）苯
trisubstituted [traiˈsʌbstiˈtjuːtid, -ˈtuːtid] *adj.* 三元取代的
addition reactions 加成反应
alkyl group 烷基
aromatic character 芳香性
aromatic compound 芳香族化合物
aryl groups or radical 芳香基，芳基
at this stage 眼下，暂时
be analogous to 类似于……，与……相似
be attached to 附属于，喜爱
be expected to 应该……
bear resemblance to 与……相同
chemical behaviour 化学作用
2-chloro-4-nitrophenol [ˈklɔːrə] [ˌnaitrəˈfiːnəul] 2-氯-4-硝基苯酚
cyclic compounds 环化合物

diametrically opposite 直对的
dinitrobenzenecarboxylic acid ［dainaitrəu'benziːnˌkɑːbk'silik'æsid］ 二硝基苯甲酸
2,6-dinitrobenzoic acid ［dai'naitrəuben'zəuik'æsid］ 2,6-二硝基苯甲酸
disubstituted derivatives 二取代衍生物
electronic configuration 电子构型，电子排布
gives rise to 引起，使发生
in favour of 参加支持……的活动
in terms of 根据，按照，在……方面
linear molecule 线性分子
literal meaning 字面意义
meta (m) derivative 间位衍生物
monosubstituted derivative 一元取代衍生物
next-but-one 间位的
open-chain compounds 开链化合物
ortho (o) derivative 邻位衍生物
para (p) derivative 对位衍生物
phenyl group or radical 苯基
substituted benzene derivatives 取代苯衍生物
unsaturated bond 不饱和键

Notes

1. It is convenient to classify organic compounds according to one of two general classes: ALIPHATIC (fatty) compounds and AROMATIC (fragrant) compounds.
   It 形式主语，to classify organic compounds… 动词不定式短语作真正主语。

2. Aliphatic compounds are those possessing open chains of carbon atoms or, alternatively, cyclic compounds whose structure and properties resemble such open-chain compounds.
   possessing open chains of…现在分词短语作定语修饰 those，whose structure and properties…定语从句修饰 cyclic compounds。

3. Aromatic compounds are those possessing the ring structure of benzene or other molecular structures that resemble benzene in electronic configuration and chemical behaviour.
   that resemble benzene…定语从句修饰 molecular structures。

4. The tetravalency of carbon was first recognized by Kekule in 1858, and numerous attempts at formulating the structure of the benzene molecule have since been made.
   since adv. "以后" 表示自1858年凯库勒发现四价碳原子之后。

5. Such compounds would be expected to readily undergo addition reactions across the unsaturated bonds, whereas benzene shows little tendency to undergo this type of reaction.
   would be expected to readily undergo addition reactions 虚拟语气，表示实际上未发生的加成反应。

6. The fact that three structural isomers of disubstituted derivatives of benzene had been detected provided further evidence in favour of a cyclic structure.
   that three structural isomers of disubstituted derivatives of benzene had been detected 同位语从句用来说明 fact。

Exercises

Ⅰ. Understanding the text

Give the IUPAC name for

[Structure 1: benzene ring with CH₃ and COOH in meta positions] [Structure 2: phenol with Br at ortho and Br at para] [Structure 3: 1,3-dinitrobenzene] [Structure 4: 1,3,5-trinitrobenzene]

Ⅱ. Write down the following formulas

methylbenzene   1,3-dinitrobenzene   3-chloro-benzenecarboxylic acid   2,4-dinitrophenol

Ⅲ. Translate the following passage into Chinese

Acid Chlorides

Each aliphatic compound is named by dropping the ending "-ic" from either the IUPAC or the common name of the corresponding carboxylic acid and adding the suffix "-yl" followed by the word "chloride".

Formula	IUPAC name	Common name
CH_3COCl	Ethanoyl chloride	Acetyl chloride
CH_3CH_2COCl	Propanoyl chloride	Propionyl chloride

Aromatic acyl chlorides may be considered as chlorides of the aromatic carbonyl, or named, like the aliphatic compounds, by replacing the ending "-ic" of the systematic or common name by "-yl", and adding the word chloride.

e.g. C_6H_5COCl Benzenecarbonyl chloride or Benzoyl chloride

Anhydride

Simple compounds are named by taking either the IUPAC or common name of the carboxylic acid containing the same acyl group and replacing the word acid with "anhydride". For mixed anhydrides, each acyl group is named separately.

Formula	IUPAC name	Common name
$(CH_3CO)_2O$	ethanoic anhydride	acetic anhydride
$(CH_3CO)O(COCH_2CH_3)$	ethanoic propanoic anhydride	aectic propionic anhydride

Aromatic anhydrides are similarly named as derivatives of their parent acid e.g. $(C_6H_5CO)_2O$ — Benzenecarboxylic anhydride or Benzoic anhydride.

Amides

Amides are monoacyl derivatives of ammonia, and may be classified as primary ($RCONH_2$), secondary ($RCONHR'$) or tertiary ($RCONR'_2$) according to the number of alkyl or aryl groups attached to the nitrogen atom.

Each compound is named by replacing the ending "-oic acid" (IUPAC) or "-ic acid" (common) of the corresponding carboxylic acid with the suffix "-amide".

Formula	IUPAC name	Common name
CH_3CONH_2	ethanamide	acetamide
$CH_3CONHCH_3$	N-methylethanamide	N-methylacetamide

The simplest amide formed from benzenecarboxylic (benzoic) acid is BENZENECARBOXAMIDE (BENZAMIDE), $C_6H_5CONH_2$.

Reading Materials

Incompatible（无法共存的）Chemical Mixtures

Avoid Dangerous Situations

Some chemicals shouldn't be mixed together. In fact, these chemicals shouldn't even be stored near each other on the chance that an accident could occur and the chemicals could react. Be sure to keep incompatibilities in mind when reusing containers to store other chemicals. Here are some examples of mixtures to avoid.

◇ Acids with cyanide（氰化物）salts or cyanide solution. Generates highly toxic hydrogen cyanide（氢氰酸）gas.

◇ Acids with sulfide（硫化物）salts or sulfide solutions. Generates highly toxic hydrogen sulfide（硫化氢）gas.

◇ Acids with bleach（漂白剂）. Generates highly toxic chlorine（氯）gas.

◇ Oxidizing acids [e.g., nitric acid（硝酸）, perchloric acid（高氯酸）] with combustible materials [e.g., paper, alchohols（乙醇）, other common solvents]. May result in fire.

◇ Solid oxidizers（氧化剂）[e.g., permanganates（高锰酸盐）, iodates（碘酸盐）, nitrates（硝酸盐）] with combustible materials (e.g., paper, alchohols, other common solvents). May result in fire.

◇ Hydrides（氢化物）[e.g., sodium hydride（氢化钠）] with water. May form flammable hydrogen gas.

◇ Phosphides（磷化物）[e.g., sodium phosphide（磷化钠）] with water. May form highly toxic phosphine（磷化氢）gas.

◇ Silver salts with ammonia in the presence of a strong base. May generate an explosively unstable solid.

◇ Alkali metals（碱金属）[e.g., sodium, potassium（钾）] with water. May form flammable hydrogen gas.

◇ Oxidizing agents（氧化剂）[e.g., nitric acid（硝酸）] with reducing agents（还原剂）[e.g., hydrazine（肼，联氨）]. May cause fires or explosions.

◇ Unsaturated compounds（不饱和化合物）[e.g., substances containing carbonyls（羰基）or double bonds（双键）] in the presence of acids or bases. May polymerize（聚合）violently.

◇ Hydrogen peroxide（过氧化氢）/acetone（酮）mixtures when heated in the presence of an acid. May cause explosions.

◇ Hydrogen peroxide/acetic acid（醋酸）mixtures. May explode upon heating.

◇ Hydrogen peroxide/sulfuric acid（硫酸）mixtures. May spontaneously detonate（引爆）.

What is the Most Poisonous Chemical Compound?

When you get right down to（开始认真考虑）it, everything is poisonous. Water will kill you if you drink too much of it. Oxygen is a deadly poison, yet we need it to live. However, there are some chemicals that we are better off not encountering. Here's a list of the most poisonous chemicals known. Keep in mind, toxicity varies from one species to another (i. e., what may be poisonous for a mouse may be more/less poisonous to a human) and within a species [i. e., age, sex, genetics all affect susceptibility (易受感染的情况) to a toxin]. I've listed the name of the toxin, its source, approximate average lethal dose (平均致命剂量) per kilogram of body weight, and the species.

 tetanus (破伤风): 1 nanogram (毫微克)/kg mouse, human

 botulinal neurotoxin (肉毒杆菌神经毒素) (bacteria): 1 nanogram/kg mouse, human

 shigella (志贺氏细菌性痢疾) (bacteria): 1 nanogram/kg monkey, human

 palytoxin (水螅毒素) (coral): 60 nanogram/kg dog

 diphtheria (白喉) (bacteria): 100 nanogram/kg human

 ricin (篦麻毒素) [from castor beans (蓖麻豆)]: 1 microgram/kg human

 aflatoxins (黄曲霉毒素) [mold (真菌) which grows on nuts, legumes (豆荚), seeds]: 1~784 micrograms, depending on type of aflatoxin duckling (oral)

 saxitoxin (贝类毒素) (shellfish): 3~5 micrograms mouse

 tetrodotoxin (河豚毒素) [fugu (河豚)]: 10 micrograms mouse

Unit 8 The Properties of polymers

The term polymer is generally reserved to describe compounds composed of at least several hundred repeating units and possessing relative molecular masses in excess of 5000, although in its broadest sense, polymerization is often used to refer to comparatively simple processes (as has already been seen) such as the cyclization of ethyne, methanal and ethanal[1].

Different texts group polymers in various ways, two of the more popular systems being to categorize them in terms of either their chemical mode of formation or by their physical properties and form[2].

The term ELASTOMER is usually applied to rubbers or rubber-like materials which possess definite elastic properties, i. e. the ability to undergo deformation on the application of a force and then to regain the original shape on removing the force. Polyethene, although it may be stretched, does not regain its original shape and therefore cannot be placed in this category.

Polymers classified as FIBRES can usually be drawn out as threads and then spun and woven.

PLASTICS are solid compounds which are capable of being moulded, whereas RESINS are solids or semisolids, usually transparent or translucent and possessing a characteristic luster, which are incapable of being moulded[3].

The classification of polymers according to these definitions is not strictly adhered to since the terms are often interchangeable. It is mainly for this reason, and to help avoid unnecessary ambiguity, that polymers in this chapter have been classified according to the type of chemical process by which they are formed.

Chemically, there are fundamentally two modes of polymerization: ADDITION POLYMERIZATION in which the product is theoretically an integral multiple of the monomeric reactant molecule(s) and consequently has the same percentage composition, e. g. polyethene polyphenylethene, (polystyrene); and CONDENSATION POLYMERIZATION which occurs between two different types of monomers, both of which are usually at least bifunctional in the same group, i. e. each reactant molecule contains a minimum of at least two of the same functional groups, usually in the terminal positions, e. g. Nylon 66, and polyesters such as Terylene[4]. If one of the reactants is more than bifunctional, polymerization occurs in three dimensions forming a massively cross-linked structure.

Condensation processes always result in the formation of a copolymer.

Organosilicon polymers (silicones) provide a different, but nonetheless important, type of condensation polymer and are discussed towards the end of this chapter.

Types of Linkages in Polymers

~~~A—A—A—A—A—A—A~~~   Linear polymer, e. g. polyethene

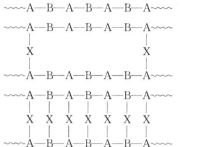

~~~A—B—A—B—A—B—A~~~ Linear alternating copolymer, e. g. Nylon

Minor cross-linked polymer
e. g. vulcanized rubber

Massively cross-linked polymer
e. g. carbamide-methanal (urea-formaldehyde) resin

In the above cross-linked polymers, the adjacent groups A, B and X, may be the same or different. Furthermore, the number of units that X represents can vary, and may be numerous.

In addition to forming linear alternating copolymers, copolymerization sometimes occurs to form random copolymers and block polymers.

~~~A—B—A—A—B—B—A~~~   Random copolymer

~~~A—A—A—A—B—B—B~~~   Block polymer

Copolymers may be formed as a result of either an addition process, e. g. SBR rubber, or a condensation process, e. g. Nylon 66.

Copolymerization between two different types of monomers, both of which are capable of forming an addition polymer in their own tight, very often leads to the formation of a material that exhibits the beneficial properties of the polymers of both individual monomers, e. g. Vinyon, which is a copolymer of chloroethene (vinyl chloride) and ethenyl ethanoate (vinyl acetate).

Effects of Cross-Linking on Physical Properties

Linear polymers and copolymers contain no linkages between the individual chains, although they may possess many branches, and therefore on heating the distance between each chain may increase markedly, causing the polymer to soften and become more flexible. Since the only binding forces between the polymeric chains are weak intermolecular attractions, it requires only a very small change in temperature to overcome them and bring about softening. On cooling, the process is reversed. Polymers of this type are called thermoplastics, e. g. polyethene and polychloroethene (polyvinyl chloride, PVC).

Cross-linked polymers are not softened so easily, since the individual chains are actually bound to each other, and usually by the time that sufficient heat has been provided to enable the cross-linkages to be broken the whole polymeric molecule has decomposed. Compounds of this type are described as thermosetting plastics, e. g. carbamide-methanol (urea-formaldehyde) and phenolmethanal resins, which require very strong heating in order to bring about any form of chemical change.

Polymers with massively cross-linked structures are virtually incapable of softening, although those with only minor cross-linking often exhibit thermoproperties which are intermediate between those of linear and massively cross-inked structures.

Natural and Synthetic Polymers

Nowadays, vast numbers of different types of polymers are made synthetically, although certain natural products such as rubber, wool, cotton and silk are used in what is virtually their raw form, and a great many more can be regenerated from cotton-wool, wood, straw, bagasse etc., by treating with Schweitzer's reagent, an ammoniacal solution of copper (II) hydroxide (Cuprammonium process). The alkaline solution of cellulose is squirted through fine jets into dilute sulphuric (VI) acid to destroy the tetramminecopper (II) complex; the cellulose is precipitated, and can be withdrawn as a thread and spun into a rayon fibre.

Treatment of the above cellulose product with ethanoic (acetic) acid causes hydroxyl groups in the cellulose to be replaced by ethanoate (acetate) groups (Acetate process), and forms a non-flammable material which has a shiny appearance and low water-absorption properties. Different forms of this polymer include cine film and Tricel.

A more favoured technique than the use of the tetramminecopper (II) complex in the U. K. and U. S. A. is the Viscose process in which the sodium salt of cellulose is treated with carbon disulphide to form a xanthate, which forms a viscous, colloidal solution in dilute alkali. After some time, during which several complex reactions occur, the cellulose is regenerated by treating with dilute acid. This polymer can be obtained as a rayon yarn or in the form of sheets (Cellophane) which can be made soft and pliable by passing them through a solution of 1, 2, 3-tri propaneol (glycerol).

A great many more synthetic fibres, artificial silks, lacquers, plastics etc., can be obtained from cellulose. Its derivatives include cellulose nitrate lacquers, cellulose mixed esters, cellulose nitrate plastics and cellulose ethers.

Conditions for Polymerization

The exact conditions used producing a number of materials commercially are often a closely guarded secret known only to the manufacturers, especially with regard to details as to the nature of the catalyst employed, so that precise information cannot always be stated for every process.

Certain techniques, although basically simple in principle, require extreme conditions, e. g. low-density polyethene requires pressures of up to 3000 atmospheres, and as a result are difficult therefore to simulate in the laboratory. However, many other processes are comparatively simple, both in principle and to perform, and can be carried out under normal or fairly moderate conditions of temperature and pressure, e. g. making Nylon 66, Nylon 610, phenol-methanal and carbamide-methanal (urea-formaldehyde) resins.

In order to govern the number of repeating units, the degree of branching, or the extent of cross-linking between the chains, the conditions under which a process takes place can often be controlled to "tailor-make" polymers to suit the purpose for which they are to be applied. For example, the various forms of Nylon can be manufactured as either a fibre or as a solid block, and polyethene can be obtained as a high-density, rigid, crystalline plastic or as a less dense and more flexible material.

There are now so many different polymers available that it would be impossible to discuss more than just a few of them. This chapter attempts to outline the techniques for preparing some of the more important and commonly encountered materials.

New Words and Phrases

ambiguity [ˌæmbiˈgjuːiti] *n.* 含糊，不明确
ammoniacal [əˈməuniækəl] *adj.* 氨的，氨性的
bifunctional [ˌbaiˈfʌŋkʃənl] *adj.* 有双功能基团或结合点的
cellophane [ˈseləfein] *n.* 玻璃纸
cellulose [ˈseljuləus] *n.* 纤维素
chloroethene [ˌklɔːrəuˈeθiːn] *n.* 氯乙烯
cine [ˈsini] *n.* 电影，电影院
copolymer [kəuˈpɔlimə] *n.* 共聚物
copolymerization [kəuˌpɔliməraiˈzeiʃən] *n.* 共聚合（作用）
crystalline [ˈkristəlain] *adj.* 水晶的，晶体的
cuprammonium [ˌkjuːprəˈməunjəm] *n.* 铜铵
cyclization [ˌsaikliˈzeiʃən] *n.* 环化（作用）
elastomer [iˈlæstəmə (r)] *n.* 弹性体，人造橡胶
ethanal [ˈeθənæl] *n.* 乙醛
ethenyl [ˈeθinil] *n.* 乙烯基
fiber [ˈfaibə] *n.* 纤维（=fiber）
fundamentally [ˌfʌndəˈmentəli] *adv.* 基础地，根本地
glycerol [ˈglisəˌrɔl] *n.* 甘油，丙三醇
lacquer [ˈlækə] *n.* 漆，漆器
linkage [ˈliŋkidʒ] *n.* 连接
luster [ˈlʌstə] *n.* 光彩，光泽
methanal [ˈmeθənæl] *n.* 甲醛
monomer [ˈmɔnəmə] *n.* 单体
monomeric [ˌmɔnəˈmerik] *adj.* 单节显性的
non-flammable [nɔnˈflæməbl] *adj.* 不易燃的
nylon [ˈnailən] *n.* 尼龙
organosilicon [ˌɔːgənəuˈsilikən] *adj.* 有机硅（化合物）的
phenolmethanal [ˈfiːnəlˈmeθənæl] *n.* 酚醛
phenylethene [ˌfenəlˈeθiːl] *n.* 苯乙基
pliable [ˈplaiəbl] *adj.* 易曲折的，柔软的，圆滑的，柔韧的
polyethene [ˌpɔliˈeθiːn] *n.* 聚乙烯
polyester [ˈpɔliestə] *n.* 聚酯
polymer [ˈpɔlimə] *n.* 聚合体
polymerization [ˌpɔliməraiˈzeiʃən] *n.* 聚合
polystyrene [ˌpɔliˈstaiəriːn] *n.* 聚苯乙烯

polyvinyl [ˌpɔliˈvainil] adj. 乙烯聚合物的
resin [ˈrezin] n. 树脂
rayon [ˈreiɔn] n. 人造丝，人造纤维
silicone [ˈsilikəun] n. 硅树脂
squirt [skwəːt] v. 喷出
terylene [ˈteriˌliːn] n. 涤纶
thermoplastics [ˌθəːməˈplæstiks] n. 热塑性塑料
translucent [trænzˈljuːsnt] adj. 半透明的，透明的
transparent [trænsˈpɛərənt] adj. 透明的，显然的，明晰的
tricel [ˈtrisl] n. 特列赛尔（三醋酯纤维织物，商标名）
1,2,3-tripropaneol [traiˈprəupeinəl] n. 1,2,3-丙三醇
vinyl [ˈvainil，ˈvinil] n. 乙烯基
vinyon [ˈvinjɔn] n. 维荣
virtually [ˈvəːtjuəli] adv. 事实上，实质上
xanthate [ˈzænθeit] n. 磺酸盐
yarn [jɑːn] n. 纱，纱线
acetate process   醋酸纤维法
addition polymerization   加聚反应
adhere to   黏着
be reserved to   保留用……
block polymer   嵌段共聚物，成块聚合物
carbamide-methanal (urea-formaldehyde) resin   脲醛树脂
chemical mode   化学模式
composed of   由……组成
condensation polymerization   缩聚合（作用）
cuprammonium process   铜铵法
dilute sulphuric (Ⅵ) acid   稀硫酸
draw out   抽出，拉长
ethenyl ethanoate (vinyl acetate)   醋酸乙烯酯
in a sense   在某种意义上
in excess of   超过，较……为多
linear alternating copolymers   线性交替共聚物
low water-absorption properties   低吸水性
massively cross-linked polymer   大型交联聚合物
massively cross-linked structure   大型交联结构
minor cross-linked polymer   小型交联聚合物
on the application of   ……方面的应用
organosilicon polymers   有机硅聚合物
phenolmethanal resin   酚醛树脂
polyvinyl chloride (PVC)   聚氯乙烯
rayon fibre   人造纤维
regenerate from   由……重建

relative molecular mass 相对分子质量
SBR rubber（Styrene Butadiene Rubber） 丁苯橡胶
Schweitzer's reagent 许维测试剂（铜氨溶液试剂）
tailor-make polymer 特制聚合物
tetramminecopper（Ⅱ）complex 四氨合铜络合物
thermosetting plastics 热固性塑料
vinyl chloride 氯乙烯
vulcanized rubber 硫化橡胶

Notes

1. The term polymer is generally reserved to describe compounds composed of at least several hundred repeating units and possessing relative molecular masses in excess of 5000, although in its broadest sense, polymerization is often used to refer to comparatively simple processes (as has already been seen) such as the cyclization of ethyne, methanal and ethanal.

   although …引导让步状语从句, composed of…and possessing…过去分词短语和现在分词短语做定语修饰 compounds。

2. Different texts group polymers in various ways, two of the more popular systems being to categorize them in terms of either their chemical mode of formation or by their physical properties and form.

   two of the more popular systems being to…现在分词短语做状语说明 in various ways。

3. PLASTICS are solid compounds which are capable of being moulded, whereas RESINS are solids or semisolids, usually transparent or translucent and possessing a characteristic luster, which are incapable of being moulded.

   Whereas 并列连词, which are capable of being moulded 限制性定语从句, possessing 前身略了系动词 possessing, which are incapable of being moulded 为非限制性定语从句。

4. Chemically, there are fundamentally two modes of polymerization: ADDITION POLYMERIZATION in which the product is theoretically an integral multiple of the monomeric reactant molecule (s) and consequently has the same percentage composition, e. g. polyethene polyphenylethene (polystyrene); and CONDENSATION POLYMERIZATION which occurs between two different types of monomers, both of which are usually at least bifunctional in the same group, i. e. each reactant molecule contains a minimum of at least two of the same functional groups, usually in the terminal positions, e. g. Nylon 6.6, and polyesters such as Terylene.

   ADDITION POLYMERIZATION 和 CONDENSATION POLYMERIZATION 均为同位语。而 in which… (polystyrene), which…monomers 和 both of which…group 均为定语从句。

Exercises

Ⅰ. Translate them into Chinese

   A. Polyethene

   B. Polychloroethene (polychloroethylene) (PVC)

C. Polyphenylethene (polystyrene)

D. Polytetrafluoroethene (PTFE, Teflon, Fluon)

E. Nylon 66

Ⅱ. Give them IUPAC names

A. 聚-2-甲基-1,3-丁二烯

B. 聚-2-氯-1,3-丁二烯

C. 聚丙烯

D. 酚醛树脂

E. 脲醛树脂

Ⅲ. Translate the passage into Chinese

Esters

Esters are named by taking either the IUPAC or common name of the parent carboxylic acid and replacing the ending "-ic" with the suffix "-ate", preceding this with the name of the alkyl or aryl group of the appropriate alcohol or phenol.

Formula	IUPAC name	Common name
HCOOCH$_3$	methyl methanoate	methyl formate
CH$_3$COOCH$_2$CH$_3$	ethyl ethanoate	ethyl acetate
CH$_3$COOC$_6$H$_5$	phenyl ethanoate	phenyl acetate

The simplest ester derived from benzenecarboxylic (benzoic) acid is METHYL BENZENECARBOXYLATE (BENZOATE), C$_6$H$_5$COOCH$_3$.

Sulphonic Acids

AROMATIC SULPHONIC ACIDS, which are of considerably greater importance than their aliphatic counterparts, are polar compounds in which the sulphur atom of the sulphonic acid group, —SO$_3$H, is attached directly to the benzene ring.

Names are afforded by attaching the ending "sulphonic acid" to the name of the compound to which the acid group is substituted.

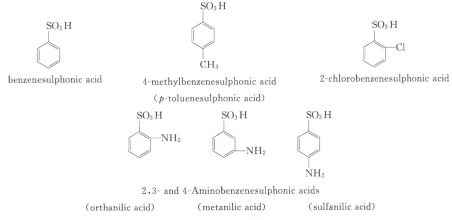

benzenesulphonic acid　　4-methylbenzenesulphonic acid　　2-chlorobenzenesulphonic acid
　　　　　　　　　　　　(*p*-toluenesulphonic acid)

2,3- and 4-Aminobenzenesulphonic acids
(orthanilic acid)　　(metanilic acid)　　(sulfanilic acid)

Amino acids

Amino acids are named systematically by considering them as amino derivatives of carboxylic acids, However, many are still referred to by their original names, which generally give no indication of their acidic properties, but refer rather to their relationship with amines. These names have the ending "-ine".

$$NH_2CH_2COOH \qquad \text{aminoethanoic acid (glycine)}$$

$$CH_3\underset{\underset{NH_2}{|}}{CH}COOH \qquad \text{2-aminopropanoic acid (alanine)}$$

Exceptions to this general rule with regard to common nomenclature occur amongst the acidic amino acids.

$$HOOCCH_2\underset{\underset{NH_2}{|}}{CH}COOH \qquad HOOC(CH_2)_2\underset{\underset{NH_2}{|}}{CH}COOH$$

aminobutanedioic acid (aspartic acid) 　　　　2-aminopentanedioic acid (glutamic acid)

Reading Materials

Classes of dangerous goods

The United Nations has published a book collecting the work of the Committee of Experts: Recommendations on the Transport of Dangerous Goods. These recommendations aim to present a basic, practical scheme of provisions that will allow national and international regulations governing various modes of transport to develop in a certain uniformity. The aim is to enable effective and successive transport and to ensure the safety of people, property, and the environment.

In these recommendations the goods are given an identification number (识别码) and are divided into the following classes describing the inherent hazards.

Explosive (炸药)

Substances and articles which have a mass explosion hazard

Substances and articles which have a projection (发射) hazard but not a mass explosion hazard

Substances and articles which have a fire hazard and either a minor blast (轻微爆炸) hazard or a minor projection hazard but not a mass explosion hazard

Substances and articles which present no significant hazard

Very insensitive substances which have a mass explosion hazard

Extremely insensitive articles which do not have a mass explosion hazard

Gases

Flammable gases

Non-flammable, non-toxic gases

Toxic gases

Flammable Liquids

Flammable Solids

Flammable solids

Substances liable to spontaneous combustion

Substances which in contact with water emit flammable gases

Oxidizing Substances; Organic Peroxides (过氧化物)

Oxidizing substances

Organic peroxides

Poisonous (=Toxic) **Substances**

Toxic substances
Infectious substances
Radioactive Material
Corrosive Substances
Miscellaneous（混杂的）Dangerous Substances

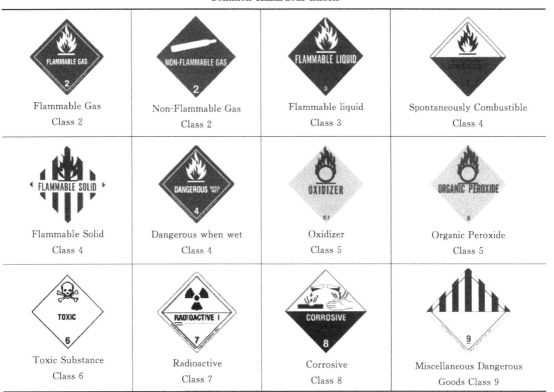

Common Hazardous Labels

Unit 9 Rubber and Plastic

Natural Rubber

Raw rubber is obtained from LATEX, which is extensively distributed in nature and occurs as a colloidal solution in a white fluid, from which it can be coagulated by simply adding ethanoic (acetic) acid[1]. The vast majority of all latex used commercially is obtained from the rubber tree, Hevea brasiliensis, which is a native of the Amazon region of Brazil but is nowadays grown on plantations in different parts of the world, e. g. Ceylon and Malaya.

Natural rubber is a type of hydrocarbon known as a polyterpene, $(C_5H_8)_n$, and exists in two isomeric forms. The cis isomer has considerable elastic properties whereas the trans isomer form, known as gutta-percha [trans-poly (methyl-1,3-butadiene)], is non-elastic and when heated above 100℃, softens to a plastic-like material. Uses of gutta-percha include the coverings for underwater cables and golf balls.

In its raw form, natural rubber contains only a limited number of cross-linkages between each polymeric chain and, as such, exhibits thermoplastic properties, i. e. it softens and becomes sticky on heating. On cooling, it becomes hard and brittle.

These problems can be largely overcome by vulcanizing. This technique was first discovered and introduced by Charles Goodyear (1838), and requires heating the raw rubber with up to 8 per cent sulphur, which forms cross-linkages between the polymeric chains[2]. The Cold Cure process of vulcanizing uses a 2.5 per cent solution of disulphur dichloride and carbon disulphide.

Accelerators for vulcanizing, which may be organic or inorganic, are used to increase the rate of combination and to allow the process to take place at lower temperatures.

Vulcanized rubber has greater tensile strength, durability and elastic properties over a wide range of temperatures.

The life of rubber articles can be considerably prolonged by the presence of another type of additive, known as anti-oxidants, which retard the process of autoxidation. Certain aldehyde-phenylamine (aniline) condensation products are used for this purpose and have an added advantage in that they also possess an accelerating action.

Synthetic Rubbers

The first synthetic rubber to be marketed (U. S. A. , 1932) was poly (2-chloro-1,3-butadiene) (neoprene). Unfortunately, this suffers from the disadvantage that, even today, it is still much more expensive to produce than natural rubber, and is therefore not generally suitable for manufacturing articles such as tyres etc. , although since it possesses a high resistance to chemicals and autoxidation it does have certain specialized uses[3]. The polymer is obtained from ethyne.

The cheapest commercial source of 1,3-butadiene is the vapour-phase catalytic dehydrogenation of butane, 1-butene and 2-butene.

1,3-Butadiene forms a number of useful copolymers, two of which are outlined below.

BUNA RUBBER was developed in Germany during the period 1927—1933 and was the first high relative molecular mass 1, 3-butadiene rubber to be manufactured. The process utilizes sodium as a polymerization catalyst, and in fact the name is contracted from the names of the monomer and the catalyst, 1, 3-butadiene and natrium (sodium).

SBR (GRS, Buna S or Cold Rubber) is without doubt one of the most universally important and useful synthetic all-purpose rubbers. It is obtained by the free-radical copolymerization of 1, 3-butadiene (70 per cent) and phenyl-ethene (styrene) (30 per cent), and was developed during World War II in order to replace unavailable natural rubber.

This product, which can be vulcanized in the same way as natural rubber, has a greater durability than most other synthetic rubbers and is used commercially for manufacturing tyres.

Harder rubbers can be obtained by increasing the percentage composition of styrene.

Plastics

Simple alkenes polymerize to form a family of long-chain addition polymers. These are strong, flexible solids which may adopt many forms and have a seemingly infinite number of domestic and commercial applications.

Polyethene is produced by a number of different techniques, each one producing a polymer with slightly different characteristics. Earlier processes all utilized extremely high pressures, ranging from 1000 to 3000 atmospheres, and temperatures of 200—400℃.

The ICI High Pressure Process requires ethane, containing a trace of oxygen, which serves as a free-radical initiator, to be subjected to a pressure in excess of 1500 atmospheres and a temperature of about 200℃. The thermal decomposition of organic peroxides may also be used to initiate the reaction.

The material produced by this process contains a comparatively large number of branched methyl groups, and is described as low-density polyethenes (0.92g/cm^3).

The Ziegler Process requires much more moderate conditions of 50—75℃ and 2—7 atmospheres. Ethene is passed into a hydrocarbon medium containing a suspension of titanium (IV) chloride and triethyl-aluminium (III) which functions as a catalyst. On completion of the reaction, the catalyst is decomposed by dilute acid and the polymer separated by filtration.

The Phillips Process again utilizes a hydrocarbon medium, but in this case the catalyst is chromium (III) oxide promoted by a mixture of silicon (IV) oxide (90 per cent) and aluminium (III) oxide (10 per cent). The conditions of 150—180℃ and 30—35 atmospheres are somewhat more stringent than those employed for the Zeigler process, and the polymeric chains contain rather more branched methyl groups, although still considerably less than those formed by the high pressure technique.

The Zeigler and Phillips products are referred to as high-density polyethenes (0.945—0.96g/cm^3), and have the polymeric molecules packed more regularly and more closely together to give a more rigid and highly crystalline material, possessing greater tensile strength. In addition, both of these materials have higher softening temperatures than low-density polyethenes, the softening range of Zeigler polymer being 120—128℃ and that of the Phillips polymer being 130—136℃.

Tetrafluoroethene is obtained commercially by the pyrolysis of chlorodifluoromethane, which, like certain other chlorofluoro-derivatives of methane and ethane, is a valuable refrigerant and is known as Freon-22.

Polymerization of tetrafluoroethene requires the presence of peroxide initiators and a pressure of 45—50 atmospheres.

Although Teflon is a thermoplastic it has a high softening point of 327℃, and is comparatively stable at temperatures in excess of 400℃. Furthermore, the polymer is also highly resistant to chemicals and possesses an extremely low coefficient of friction, making it especially suitable for manufacturing non-stick cooking utensils.

Benzene provides a useful raw material for commercially obtaining phenylethene (styrene). It undergoes a Friedel-Crafts alkylation reaction with ethane to yield ethylbenzene, which is then cracked to phenylethene.

Free-radical polymerization of phenylethene (styrene) is brought about by a dibenzenecarboxy peroxide (dibenzoylperoxide) initiator at a temperature of 85—100℃.

This produces a thermoplastic which is soluble in benzene. However, the presence of a trace amount of diethenylbenzene (divinylbenzene), $CH_2=CHC_6H_4CH=CH_2$, causes a high degree of cross-linking to occur and form a material that is no longer a thermoplastic nor soluble in benzene.

New Words and Phrases

aniline [ˈænili:n]　*n.* 苯胺　*adj.* 苯胺的

autoxidation [ɔːtɔksiˈdeiʃən]　*n.* 自然氧化

Ceylon [siˈlɔn]　*n.* 锡兰（Srilanka，首都为科伦坡 Colombo）

Charles Goodyear [tʃɑːlzˈgudjiə]　查尔斯·古德伊尔（1800—1860，发明硬橡皮制造法的美国人）

chlorodifluoromethane [ˈklɔːrəuˈdaiˌflu:ərəˈmeθein]　*n.* 氯二氟甲烷

condensation [kɔndenˈseiʃən]　*n.* 浓缩

dibenzenecarboxy [ˈdaiˈbenzi:nkɑːˈbɔksi]　*n.* 二苯羧基

dibenzoyl [daiˈbenzəuil]　*n.* 联苯甲酰

diethenylbenzene [daiˈeθinilˈbenzi:n]　*n.* 二乙烯基苯

divinylbenzene [daiˈvainilˈbenzi:n]　*n.* 二乙烯基苯

ethylbenzene [ˌeθilˈbenzi:n]　*n.* 乙苯

hevea [ˈhi:viə]　*n.* 三叶胶树（大戟科树木）

initiator [iˈniʃieitə]　*n.* 引发剂

neoprene [ˈni(ː)əupri:n]　*n.* 氯丁（二烯）橡胶

peroxide [pəˈrɔksaid]　*n.* 过氧化物，过氧化氢

plantation [plænˈteiʃən]　*n.* 种植园

pyrolysis [paiəˈrɔlisis, ˌpi-]　*n.* 高温分解

refrigerant [riˈfridʒərənt]　*adj.* 制冷的　*n.* 制冷剂
stringent [ˈstrindʒənt]　*adj.* 收缩的，变紧的
teflon [ˈteflɔn]　*n.* 特氟纶，聚四氟乙烯
tetrafluoroethene [ˈtetrəˈfluːrəˈeθiːn]　*n.* 四氟乙烯
titanium [taiˈteinjəm, ti-]　*n.* 钛
aldehyde-phenylamine (aniline) condensation products　乙醛苯胺浓缩产品
Ziegler　齐格勒（1898—1973，德国化学家，曾获得1963年诺贝尔化学奖）
all-purpose　通用的，多用途的
as such　同样地，同量地
buna rubber [ˈbjuːnəˈrʌbə]　丁钠橡胶
by the presence of　由于……的存在
chlorofluoro-derivatives　氯氟衍生物
Cold Cure process　冷硫化过程
colloidal solution　胶体溶液
elastic properties　弹性
free-radical　自由基，游离基
freon-22 [ˈfriːɔn]　氟里昂，二氟二氯（氟三氯）甲烷
Friedel-Crafts alkylation reaction　弗里德克尔-克拉夫茨烷基化反应
ICI (Imperial Chemical Industries Ltd)　英国化学工业公司
non-stick　东西不粘上的
plastic-like　塑料似的
poly (2-chloro-1,3-butadiene)　聚-2-氯-1,3-丁二烯
polymerization catalyst　聚合催化剂
tensile strength　张力
triethyl-aluminium [traiˈeθəlˌæljuːˈminjəm]　三乙（烷）基铝
without doubt　毫无疑问地

Notes

1. Raw rubber is obtained from LATEX, which is extensively distributed in nature and occurs as a colloidal solution in a white fluid, from which it can be coagulated by simply adding ethanoic (acetic) acid.
   which…in a white fluid 非限制性定语从句修饰 LATEX，from which…ethanoic (acetic) acid 非限制性定语从句修饰 fluid，from which 在定语从句中作状语。

2. This technique was first discovered and introduced by Charles Goodyear (1838), and requires heating the raw rubber with up to 8 per cent sulphur, which forms cross-linkages between the polymeric chains.
   and 后面省略了主语 this technique，which…polymeric chains 非限制性定语从句修饰 sulphur。

3. Unfortunately, this suffers from the disadvantage that, even today, it is still much more expensive to produce than natural rubber, and is therefore not generally suitable for manufacturing articles such as tyres etc., although since it possesses a high resistance to chemicals and autoxidation it does have certain specialized uses.
   that, even today, …certain specialized uses 同位语从句说明 disadvantage，although

since it possesses a high resistance to chemicals and autoxidation…specialized uses 为同位语从句中的让步状语从句，其中 since…autoxidation 为让步状语从句中的原因状语从句。

Exercises

Ⅰ. Understand the text

1. How do people get the raw rubber?
2. Who marketed the synthetic rubber in the first place? What are its advantage and disadvantage?
3. Compare and contrast the modes of formation and physical properties of high- and low-density polyethenes.

Ⅱ. Translate the following into Chinese by checking up the dictionary

1. monosaccharide [ˌmɔnəuˈsækəraid]
2. disaccharide [daiˈsækəraid]
3. polysaccharide [pɔliˈsækəraid]
4. glucose [ˈɡluːkəus]
5. fructose [ˈfrʌktəus]
6. maltose [ˈmɔːltəus](亦作 maltobiose)
7. lactose [ˈlæktəus]
8. starch [stɑːtʃ]
9. cellulose [ˈseljuləus]
10. sucrose [ˈsjuːkrəus]

Ⅲ. Translate the passage into Chinese

A polymer is a substance of high molecular weight, well above the size of the compounds considered so far. There is no agreement as to the minimum molecular weight of a substance in order for it to be classified as a polymer; however, a practical figure would be about 1,000. Many commercial polymers are found in the range of 10,000 to 50,000 although some of them have much higher molecular weights. A polymer is formed by the reaction of many low-molecular-weight molecules combining into a high-molecular-weight compound. A compound capable of conversion into a polymer, as ethylene is into polyethylene, is called a monomer (mono, one; mer, unit). A polymer then is a molecule of many units, and the process involved in the formation of one is termed polymerization.

An addition polymer results from the self-combination of many monomer units into a substance with a molecular weight above about one thousand. However, condensation process results in condensation polymer, in which there is an elimination of by-product, but self-addition is not involved.

Reading Materials

Transport and Storage

What happens during the transport of chemicals

Large amounts of chemicals and other products which can cause hazards to human health and harm to the environment are used at places of work.

Industrial production takes place, and raw materials are located, all over the world. Transport is necessary for products to reach consumers. The transport and storage of dangerous chemicals and goods has increased with technical development and production development.

An accident occurring during the transport of dangerous goods can lead to catastrophic (灾难性的) consequences, therefore laws and recommendations (建议) have been established to protect the society and the environment. But they can not be effective if you, whether you are an employer, worker, transporter or inspecting authority (检查机构), do not share the responsibility and follow existing recommendations and guidelines (指导) of transport and storage, in order to avoid unnecessary risks.

The hazardous properties of products or chemicals should be clearly stated so that people of all stages of the transport chain are aware of them. This information should always follow the goods so that people can recognize the risks, avoid accidental mishandling (违反运行规程) and have the right kind of the personal protection at their disposal in case of leakage.

Dangerous goods can be transported without causing unnecessary hazards if handled properly and with care.

What are dangerous goods?

Dangerous goods can be explosive, flammable, toxic, radioactive, corrosive (腐蚀的) or harmful in some other way to humans, animals or the environment. The environment includes other goods in transport, the transport vehicle, buildings, soil, roads, air, waterways and nature in general.

The empty containers and packages (包装) of dangerous goods can present the same hazards as the chemical substance or product they contained and should also be regarded as dangerous goods. 50 per cent of transported goods are dangerous. United Nations statistics show that half of all goods transported belong to the category (种类) of dangerous goods. Petroleum products transported by tankers (油轮) form a large proportion of all transported goods, but road and railway transport is also significant.

For example, 85% of chlorine, which is one of the very dangerous chemicals (剧毒化学品), is transported by rail. Large amounts of other highly dangerous goods, such as hydrochloric acid (盐酸), sulphuric acid (硫酸), sulphuric dioxide (二氧化硫), nitric acid (硝酸), phenol (石炭酸) and methanol (甲醇) are transported regularly.

Small drains (排水) make a river cause extensive damage, but we forget easily that small amounts of oil, gasoline, battery acids and refrigerator fluids are released to environment daily. Even small but frequent wastes from ships, households (家庭), cars or agriculture increase the load to the environment. For example one litre of oil can, under unfavorable circumstances, spoil 100,000 litres of drinking water. A spill of hydraulic fluid from a truck can lead to environmental damages.

Recommendations and instructions for the handling, storage and transport of dangerous goods must be clear and unambiguous (准确的) to avoid harmful or dangerous circumstances. Transport of dangerous goods does not pose under normal conditions a greater danger than any other transported goods if the responsible persons in the transport chain respect the existing recommendations and laws and are beware of (小心) the type of the hazards of the cargo.

Unit 10 Fine Chemicals

The fine chemical industry is an industry to produce fine chemical products. Fine chemical products and special chemical products are both called fine chemicals. Fine chemicals are divided into 11 categories of pesticides, dyestuffs, coatings (including paints and inks), pigments, reagents and high-purity chemicals, information chemicals (including photosensitive materials and magnetic recording materials), food and feed additives, adhesives, catalysts and auxiliaries, chemical drugs and chemicals for daily use.

Pesticide

Pesticide is biological, physical, or chemical agent used to kill plants or animals that are harmful to people; in practice, the term pesticide is often applied only to chemical agents. Various pesticides are known as insecticides, nematicides, fungicides, herbicides, and rodenticides, i. e. , agents primarily effective against insects, nematodes (or roundworms), fungi, weeds, and rodents, respectively.

Pesticides can be derived from plants (e. g. , pyrethrin, neem) or minerals, or they can be chemically manufactured (e. g. , DDT, dich loro-diphenyltrichloroethane). Natural predators and other biological methods are also used. Among the biological agents, parasites and predators feed on pests, pathogens sicken them, and pheromones interfere with insect mating. There are also genetically engineered pesticides, such as the toxin-producing Bacillus strain used against moth larvae.

Chemical pesticides are usually contact, stomach, or fumigant poisons. Contact poisons may have immediate or delayed effects after physical contact with a pest. Fumigants, which may initially have the form of a solid, liquid, or gas, kill pests while in a gaseous state.

Some insecticides and fungicides are systemic, i. e. , they are translocated by a plant from the area of application to other plant parts, where they affect only pests that feed on the crop[1]. Nonselective pesticides can affect both the targeted pest and other organisms; selective pesticides affect only the target pest. Persistent pesticides are those that remain in the environment for a long time.

Dye

Dye is any substance, natural or synthetic, used to color various materials, especially textiles, leather, and food. Natural dyes are so called because they are obtained from plants (e. g. , alizarin, catechu, indigo, and logwood), from animals (e. g. , cochineal, kermes, and Tyrian purple), and from certain naturally occurring minerals (e. g. , ocher and Prussian blue). They have been almost entirely replaced in modern dyeing by synthetic dyes. Most of these are prepared from coal tar, being formed from an aromatic hydrocarbon such as benzene, from which indigo is derived, or anthracene, which yields alizarin[2]. Although some materials, e. g. , silk and wool, can be colored simply by being dipped in the dye (the dyes so used are consequently called direct dyes), others, including cotton, commonly require the use of a mordant. Alizarin is a mordant dye and the color it gives depends upon the mordant used. Dyes are classified also as acidic or basic according to the medium required in the dyeing process. A vat dye, e. g. , indigo, is so called from the method of its application; it is first treated chemically so that it becomes soluble and is then used for coloring materials bathed in a vat. When the materials become impregnated with the dye, they are removed and dried in air, the indigo reverting to its original, insoluble form. The process by which a dye becomes "attached" to the material it colors is not definitely known[3]. One theory holds that a chemical reaction takes place between the dye and the treated fiber; another proposes that the dye is absorbed by the fiber.

Pigment

Pigment is a substance that imparts color to other materials. In paint, the pigment is a powdered substance which, when mixed in the liquid vehicle, imparts color to a painted surface. The pigments used in paints are nearly all metallic compounds, but organic compounds are also used. Most black pigments are organic, e. g. , bone black (animal black or charcoal) and lampblack. Some of the metallic pigments occur naturally. The brilliant and beautiful coloring of the rock and soil in some parts of the world. Yellow ocher, sienna, and umber are oxides of iron. Litharge is a yellow oxide of lead. Red lead is also an oxide of this metal. Lead chromate, or chrome yellow, is an important yellow pigment. White lead, or basic lead carbonate, is a pigment long in use; it is rendered more durable by mixture with zinc oxide. Cadmium yellow is a sulfide of cadmium. Ultramarine is an important blue pigment, as is Prussian blue (ferric ferrocyanide). Green pigment is produced by mixing Prussian blue and chrome yellow. Vermilion (mercuric sulfide) is red. Pigments occur in plant and animal bodies. The bright colors of plants, for example, are the result of the presence of such substances as chlorophyll (green) and xanthophyll (yellow), both of which are also found in some animals. Among others are carotene, the yellow of carrots and certain other vegetables, and anthocyanin, which imparts blue, red, and purple to flowers[4]. Blood receives its color from the hemoglobin in the red corpuscles. Coloration of human skin is caused by the presence of pigments.

Reagent

A reagent or reactant is a material used to start a chemical reaction. For example hydrochloric acid is the chemical reagent that would cause calcium carbonate to release carbon dioxide. Similarly, but less obvious, hydrochloric acid is the chemical reagent that reacts with zinc to produce hydrogen, even though in this case the hydrogen comes from the acid and not the metal. To classify any of the chemicals involved in a chemical reaction as the "reagent" is thus largely a matter of convention or perspective.

In another use of the term, when purchasing or preparing chemicals, "reagent" describes chemical substances of sufficient purity for use in chemical analysis, chemical reactions or physical testing. Purity standards for reagents are set by organizations such as ASTM International. For instance, reagent-quality water must have very low levels of impurities like sodium and chloride ions, silica, and bacteria, as well as a very high electrical resistivity.

Adhesive

Adhesive is substance capable of sticking to surfaces of other substances and bonding them to one another. The term adhesive cement is sometimes used in place of adhesive, especially when referring to a synthetic adhesive. Animal glue, a gelatin made from hides, hooves, or bones, was probably known in prehistoric times; it remained the leading adhesive until the 20th cent. It is now used especially in cabinetmaking. Animal glue is sold both as a solid (either ground or in sheets, to be melted in a water-jacketed glue pot and applied while hot) and as liquid glue (an acidic solution). Adhesives from vegetable sources are also important; they include natural gums and resins, mucilage, and starch and starch derivatives. They are commonly used for sizing paper and textiles and for labeling, sealing, and manufacturing paper goods. Other adhesives derived from animal and vegetable sources include blood glue, casein glue, fish glue, rubber adhesives, and cellulose derivatives. Adhesives having special properties are prepared from synthetic resins. Some synthetic adhesives, such as the epoxy resins, are strong enough to be used in construction in place of welding or riveting. Adhesive tapes have a coating of pressure-sensitive adhesive.

Catalyst

Catalyst is substance that can cause a change in the rate of a chemical reaction without itself being consumed in the reaction. Substances that increase the rate of reaction are called positive catalysts or, simply, catalysts, while substances that decrease the rate of reaction are called negative catalysts or inhibitors.

Enzymes are the commonest and most efficient of the catalysts found in nature. Most of the chemical reactions that occur in the human body and in other living things are high-energy reactions that would occur slowly, if at all, without the catalysis provided by enzymes. For example, in the absence of catalysis, it takes several weeks for starch to hydrolyze to glucose; a trace of the enzyme ptyalin, found in human saliva, accelerates the reaction so that starches can be digested. Some enzymes increase reaction rates by a factor of one billion or more. Enzymes are generally specific catalysts; that is, they catalyze only one reaction of one particular reactant (called its substrate). Usually the enzyme and its substrate have complementary structures and can bond together to form a complex that is more reactive due to the presence of functional groups in the enzyme, which stabilize the transition state of the reaction or lower the activation energy. The toxicity of certain substances (e.g., carbon monoxide and the nerve gases) is due to their inhibition of life-sustaining catalytic reactions in the body.

Catalysis is also important in chemical laboratories and in industry. Some reactions occur faster in the presence of a small amount of an acid or base and are said to be acid catalyzed or base catalyzed[5]. For example, the hydrolysis of esters is catalyzed by the presence of a small amount of base. In this reaction, it is the hydroxide ion, OH^-, that reacts with the ester, and the concentration of the hydroxide ion is greatly increased over that of pure water by the presence of the base. Although some of the hydroxide ions provided by the base are used up in the first part of the reaction, they are regenerated in a later step from water molecules; the net amount of hydroxide ion present is the same at the beginning and end of the reaction, so the base is thought of as a catalyst and not as a reactant.

Finely divided metals are often used as catalysts; they adsorb the reactants onto their surfaces, where the reaction can occur more readily. For example, hydrogen and oxygen gases can be mixed without reacting to form water, but if a small amount of powdered platinum is added to the gas mixture, the gases react rapidly. Hydrogenation reactions, e. g., the formation of hard cooking fats from vegetable oils, are catalyzed by finely divided metals or metal oxides. The commercial preparation of sulfuric acid and nitric acid also depends on such surface catalysis. Other commonly used surface catalysts, in addition to platinum, are copper, iron, nickel, palladium, rhodium, ruthenium, silica gel (silicon dioxide), and vanadium oxide.

New Words and Phrases

additive [ˈæditiv]　*n.* 添加剂
adhesive [ədˈhiːsiv]　*n.* 胶黏剂
anthocyanin [ˌænθəˈsaiənin]　*n.* 花青素，花色醣苷
anthracene [ˈænθrəsiːn]　*n.* 蒽
auxiliary [ɔːgˈziljəri]　*n.* 助剂
bacillus [bəˈsiləs]　*n.* 杆状菌，细菌
cabinetmaking [ˈkæbinitˌmeikiŋ]　*n.* 细木工艺
cadmium [ˈkædmiəm]　*n.* 镉
carotene [ˈkærətiːn]　*n.* 胡萝卜素
casein [ˈkeisiːin]　*n.* 干酪素，酪蛋白
catechu [ˈkætitʃuː]　*n.* 儿茶
cement [siˈment]　*n.* 水泥，接合剂
charcoal [ˈtʃɑːkəul]　*n.* 木炭
chlorophyll [ˈklɔːrəfil]　*n.* 叶绿素
chrome [krəum]　*n.* 铬，铬合金
coating [ˈkəutiŋ]　*n.* 被覆，衣料
cochineal [ˈkɔtʃiniːl]　*n.* 胭脂虫（由胭脂虫制成的）洋红
corpuscle [ˈkɔːpʌs(ə)l]　*n.* 血球，微粒
epoxy [eˈpɔksi]　*adj.* 环氧的
ferrocyanide [ˌferəuˈsaiənaid, -nid]　*n.* 氰亚铁酸盐，亚铁氰化物
fumigant [ˈfjuːmigənt]　*n.* 熏剂
fungi [ˈfʌndʒai, ˈfʌŋgai]　*n.* 真菌类

fungicides [ˈfʌndʒisaid] *n.* 杀真菌剂
gel [dʒel] *n.* 凝胶体
gelatin [ˈdʒelətin, ˈdʒeləˈtiːn] *n.* 凝胶，白明胶
glue [gluː] *n.* 胶，胶水
hemoglobin [ˌhiːməuˈgləubin] *n.* 血色素
herbicide [ˈhəːbisaid] *n.* 除草剂
hides [haid] *n.* 兽皮，皮革
hoof [huːf] 复数 hooves *n.* 蹄
hydrogenation [ˌhaidrədʒəˈneiʃən] *n.* 加氢，氢化（作用）
impart [imˈpɑːt] *vt.* 分给，授予
inhibitor [inˈhibitə(r)] *n.* 抑制剂
insecticide [inˈsektisaid] *n.* 杀虫剂
kermes [ˈkəːmiz] *n.* 胭脂，干燥雌体（取出作胭脂染料）
lampblack *n.* 灯烟，灯黑
larvae [ˈlɑːvə] *n.* 幼虫
litharge [ˈliθɑːdʒ，liˈθɑːdʒ] *n.* 一氧化铅，铅黄
logwood [ˈlɔgwud] *n.* 洋苏木树，洋苏木的心材（供作染料用）
mordant [ˈmɔːdənt] *n.* 媒染，媒染剂，金属腐蚀剂，金属箔黏合剂
moth [mɔθ] *n.* 蛾，蛀虫
mucilage [ˈmjuːsilidʒ] *n.* （植物的）黏液，胶水
nematicide [niˈmætisaid] *n.* 杀线虫剂（＝nematocide）
nematode [ˈnemətəud] *n.* 线虫类
ocher [ˈəukə(r)] *n.* 黄土，赭土
palladium [pəˈleidiəm] *n.* 钯
parasite [ˈpærəsait] *n.* 寄生虫，食客
pathogen [ˈpæθədʒ(ə)n] *n.* 病菌，病原体
pest [pest] *n.* 有害物
pesticide [ˈpestisaid] *n.* 杀虫剂
pheromone [ˈferəməun] *n.* ［生化］信息素
photosensitive [ˈfəutəuˈsensitiv] *adj.* 光敏的
pigment [ˈpigmənt] *n.* 色素，颜料
predator [ˈpredətə] *n.* 掠夺者，食肉动物
ptyalin [ˈtaiəlin] *n.* 唾液淀粉酶
pyrethrin [paiˈriːθrin] *n.* 除虫菊酯
reagent [ri(ː)ˈeidʒənt] *n.* 反应力，反应物，试剂
render [ˈrendə] *vt.* 熔解，精炼，通过加热减少
rhodium [ˈrəudiəm, -djəm] *n.* 铑
riveting [ˈrivitiŋ] *n.* 铆接（法）
rodent [ˈrəudənt] *adj.* 咬的，嚼的 *n.* 啮齿动物
rodenticide [rəuˈdentiˌsaid] *n.* 灭鼠剂
roundworm [ˈraundwəːm] *n.* 蛔虫
ruthenium [ruːˈθiːniəm] *n.* 钌

sienna [si'enə]　n. （富铁）黄土（用作颜料），赭色
strain [strein]　n. 同类，同族
substrate ['sʌbstreit]　n. 培养基
systemic [sis'temik]　adj. 系统的，全身的，（农药）散发的，内吸的
tar [tɑː]　n. 焦油，柏油
toxin ['tɔksin]　n. 毒素
translocate [trænsləu'keit]　vt. 改变……的位置
Tyrian ['tiriən]　n. 提尔人
Ultramarine [ˌʌltrəmə'riːn]　n. 深蓝色，天青石做成的蓝色颜料
umber ['ʌmbə]　n. 棕土，焦茶色
vanadium [və'neidiəm，-djəm]　n. 钒，铅矿
vat [væt]　n. （装液体的）大桶，大缸（尤指染缸）
vehicle ['viːikl]　n. 媒介物
vermilion [və'miljən]　n. 朱砂，朱红色
xanthophyll ['zænθəˌfil]　n. 黄色色素，叶黄质
a factor of one billion or more　十亿倍以上
activation energy　活化能
adhesive cement　胶浆，胶水
animal black　兽炭黑，骨炭
ASTM International　美国材料实验协会
basic lead carbonate　碱性碳酸铅
become impregnated with　充满……
bone black　骨炭
chrome yellow　铬黄
coal tar　煤焦油
complementary structure　补充结构
DDT [ˌdiːdiː'tiː]　（dichloro-diphenyl-trichloroethane）二氯二苯三氯乙烷（杀虫剂的一种）
feed additives　饲料添加剂
ferric ferrocyanide　铁氰化铁
finely divided　细碎粒（粒状）的
hydrogenation reaction　氢化反应
in place of　代替
lead chromate　铬酸铅
life-sustaining　一生的
magnetic recording materials　磁性记录材料
mercuric sulfide　硫化银
moth larvae　蛾幼虫
photosensitive material　光敏材料
Prussian blue　普鲁士蓝
Tyrian purple　提尔紫

Notes

1. Some insecticides and fungicides are systemic, i. e., they are translocated by a plant from the area of application to other plant parts, where they affect only pests that feed on the crop.
    i. e.＝that is to say，引导的句子起补充说明的作用。where…crop 非限制性定语从句修饰 plant parts。

2. Most of these are prepared from coal tar, being formed from an aromatic hydrocarbon such as benzene, from which indigo is derived, or anthracene, which yields alizarin.
    being…benzene 现在分词短语作定语修饰 coal tar，from which…anthracene 非限制性定语从句修饰 benzene，which yields alizarin 非限制性定语从句修饰 anthracene。

3. The process by which a dye becomes "attached" to the material it colors is not definitely known.
    by which…material 限制性定语从句修饰 process，it colors 为定语从句中的定语从句修饰 material，其中"it"代表 dye。

4. Among others are carotene, the yellow of carrots and certain other vegetables, and anthocyanin, which imparts blue, red, and purple to flowers.
    本句为倒装句，主语是 carotene 和 anthocyanin，the yellow…vegetables 是 carotene 补语，which…flowers 非限制性定语从句修饰 anthocyanin。

5. Some reactions occur faster in the presence of a small amount of an acid or base and are said to be acid catalyzed or base catalyzed.
    本句为简单句，主语为 Some reactions，并列谓语分别 occur 和 are said。

Exercises

Ⅰ. Understand the text
1. How many categories are fine chemicals divided into? What are they?
2. What are pesticides? What do they include?
3. What is dye? What are they come from?
4. What is pigment? What are used in paints?
5. What is a reagent?
6. What is adhesive? What do they derive from?
7. What is catalyst? How are they divided into two categories?

Ⅱ. Translate the following into Chinese
1. activation energy
2. adhesive cement
3. chemical drugs and chemicals for daily use
4. ferric ferrocyanide
5. fine chemicals
6. food and feed additives
7. high-purity chemicals
8. information chemicals
9. Prussian blue

10. vanadium oxide

Ⅲ. Translate the passage into Chinese

Surface active agents or surfactants are chemical compounds that when dissolved in water or another solvent, orient themselves at the interface between the liquid and a solid, liquid, or gaseous phase and modify the properties of the interface. The modification may be accompanied by frothing or foaming and by formation of colloids, emulsions, suspensions, aerosole, or foams.

This definition makes surfactants sound academic, in fact the manufacture of soap, a major surfactant, is the oldest branch of the chemical industry. Further more a recent survey of industrial processes showed that surfactants were the most widely applied group of compounds in the chemical and allied products industries. Surfactants are not only important as the active constituent of cleaning agents (soaps, detergents, etc.), which is their main use, but are also vital in the stabilization of emulsions (e. g., in foods and cosmetics), as mold release agents in the plastics industry, in flotation, in oil well drilling, and in a host of other applications.

Surfactants are classified chemically according to their hydrophilic group as anionic, cationic, nonionic, or amphoteric. Surfactants when used in cleaning agents are normally mixed with various additives to improve their performance and such formulations are known as detergents. Soap is an anionic surfactant but because of its long history is categorized separately from the so-called synthetic detergents. Hence we speak of soap and detergents.

Reading Materials

Chemical and Petroleum（石油）Storage

Tanks storing petroleum and hazardous（危险的）chemicals must meet minimum standards established by the United States Environmental Protection Agency (EPA) and the New York State Department of Environmental Conservation (DEC). New York's Hazardous Substances Bulk（大量）Storage Program provides guidelines and controls for the storage of many different hazardous chemicals.

The problem improper handling and storage of petroleum and hazardous chemicals can result in leaks and spills and pose a serious threat to the quality of the environment in New York State. Petroleum, additives（添加剂）and a variety of industrial chemicals have been discovered in many of the State's groundwater supplies（地下水供应系统）. In some wells, only trace quantities have been discovered; in others, levels have exceeded federal and state drinking water standards. Hundreds of drinking water supplies have been closed because of excessive chemical contamination（污染）.

Water contamination is only one consequence of poor handling practices. Mismanagement of some substances may pose occupational hazards（职业病）, present a fire or explosion risk or result in a release of odors or fumes with serious public health（公共卫生）and environmental consequences（环境影响）to the neighboring community.

Gasoline（汽油）, which fuels the millions of automobiles we all drive each day, is highly flammable and can flash violently when ignited. Gasoline and many other hazardous chemicals when inhaled （吸入） can cause drowsiness （睡意）, nausea （恶心） and other adverse health effects.

Once a chemical soaks （浸泡） into the ground, it disperses （分散） and may dissolve （溶解） and contaminate （污染） a water supply for many years. Cleanup is often difficult and it is usually expensive.

New York State has approximately 52,000 storage facilities which involve an estimated 125,000 bulk storage tanks. Leaks and spills occur as a result of poor housekeeping （库存管理）, overfilling （过量罐装） of tanks, loading and unloading mistakes, and poor maintenance （保养） and inspection （检查）.

When it comes to handling hazardous materials, there is truth in the old saying （谚语） - "an ounce of prevention is worth a pound of cure." For every dollar spent on preventing a spill, many dollars are saved in cleanup cost and damages.

New York State (NYS) prevents leaks and spills at petroleum and chemical storage facilities through the Bulk Storage Program operated by the NYS Department of Environmental Conservation (DEC). The Bulk Storage Program is based on four laws enacted over the past 20 years. Three are state laws requiring the DEC to develop and enforce standards for storage and handling of petroleum and chemical products and to regulate aboveground and underground tanks storing these products. For more information on these state regulatory programs, choose from the following topics.

Regulation （规章） of Petroleum Tanks

Regulation of Chemical Tanks

Regulation of Major Oil Storage Facilities

PART TWO INTRODUCTION OF ANALYTICAL INSTRUMENTS

Unit 11   Ultraviolet and Visible Spectrophotometer

Photometric methods are perhaps the most frequently used of all spectroscopic methods, and are important in quantitative analysis. The amount of visible light or other radiant energy absorbed by a solution is measured; since it depends on the concentration of the absorbing substance, it is possible to determine quantitatively the amount present.

Colorimetry involves the determination of a substance from its ability to absorb visible light. Visual colorimetric methods are based on the comparison of a colored solution of unknown concentration with one or more colored solutions of known concentration. In spectrophotometric methods, the ratio of the intensities of the incident and the transmitted beams of light is measured at a specific wavelength by means of a detector such as a photocell.

The absorption spectrum also provides a 'fingerprint' for qualitatively identifying the absorbing substance.

Components of a Spectrophotometer

There are several light sources available for use in the ultraviolet-visible region. Mercury-vapor lamps have been used but, owing to the heat evolved by these lamps, thermal insulation or cooling is required. More commonly used for the visible and near-infrared regions are tungsten-filament 'incandescent' lamps[1]. These are thermal or 'blackbody' sources in which the radiation is the result of high temperature of the solid filament material, with only a small dependence on its actual chemical nature. These sources provide continuous radiation from about 320 to 3000 nm—most of it, unfortunately, in the near-infrared. At the usual operating temperature of about 3000 K, only approximately 15% of the total radiant energy falls in the visible region, and at 2000K, only 1%. Increasing the operating temperature above 3000 K greatly increases the total energy output and shifts the wavelength of maximum intensity to shorter wavelengths, but the lifetime of the lamp is drastically shortened[4]. Inconveniently high temperatures are required for the production of much radiation in the ultraviolet region. The lifetime of a tungsten-filament lamp can be greatly increased by the presence of a low pressure of iodine or bromine vapor within the lamp; with the addition of a fused-silica lamp envelope, these are now called quartz-halogen lamps—a popular source at present. Most work in the ultraviolet region is done with hydrogen or deuterium electrical-discharge lamps typically operated under low-pressure D C conditions (about 40 V with 5 mm gas pressure). These lamps provide a continuum emission down to about 160 nm, but the window material generally limits the transmission at short wavelengths (about 200nm with quartz and 185nm with fused silica). Above about 360nm, hydrogen emission lines are superimposed on the continuum, so incandescent sources are generally used for measurements at longer wavelengths. Deuterium lamps are more expensive but have about two to five times greater spectral intensity and lifetime than a hydrogen lamp of comparable design and wattage.

The continuous radiation from the sources is dispersed by means of monochromators.

There are three main types of detectors presently in use. The barrier-layer or photovoltaic type is illustrated in Figure 11-1. This device measures the intensity of photons by means of the voltage developed across the semiconductor layer. Electrons, ejected by photons from the semiconductor, are collected by the silver layer. The potential depends on the number of photons hitting the detector. A second type is the photodetector or phototube shown in Figure 11-2. This detector is a vacuum tube with a cesium-coated photocathode. Photons of sufficiently high energy hitting the cathode can dislodge electrons, which are collected at the anode. Photon flux is measured by the current flow in the system. The vacuum phototube type of detector needs further (external) amplification to function properly. The last type of commonly used detector is schematically illustrated in Figure 11-3. This detector consists of a photoemissive cathode coupled with a series of electron-multiplying dynode stages, and is usually called a photomultiplies. The primary electrons ejected from the photocathode are accelerated by an electric field so as to strike a small area on the first dynode. The impinging electrons strike with enough energy to eject two to five secondary electrons, which are accelerated to the second dynode to eject still more electrons. This cascading effect takes place until the electrons are collected at the anode. Typically, a photomultiplier may have 9 to 16 stages, and overall gain of 10^6 to perhaps 10^9 electrons per incident photon.

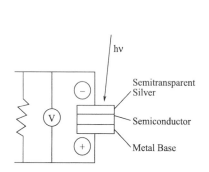

Figure 11-1 Barrier-layer or photovoltaic cell

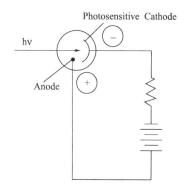

Figure 11-2 Vacuum phototube

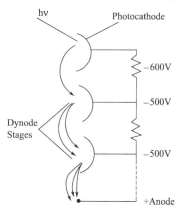

Figure 11-3 Vacuum photomultiplier

Single-and Double-Beam Spectrometers

The measurement of absorption of ultraviolet-visible radiation is of a relative nature. One must continually compare the absorption of the sample with that of an analytical reference or blank to ensure the reliability of the measurement. The rate at which the sample and reference are compared depends on the design of the instrument. In single-beam instruments, there is only one light beam or optical path from the source through to the detector. This usually means that one must remove the sample from the light beam and replace it with the reference after each reading. Thus, there is usually an interval of several seconds between measurements.

Alternatively, the sample and reference may be compared many times a second, as in double-beam instruments. The light from the source, after passing through the monochromator, is split into two separate beams—one for the sample and the other for the reference. Figure 11-4 shows two types of double-beam spectrophotometers. The measurement of sample and reference absorption may be separated in space, as in Figure 11-4A; this, however, requires two detectors that must be perfectly matched. Or, the sample and reference measurement may be separated in time, as in Figure 11-4B; this technique makes use of a rapidly rotating mirror or 'chopper' to switch the beam that comes from sample and reference very rapidly. The latter method requires only one detector and is probably the better of the two methods.

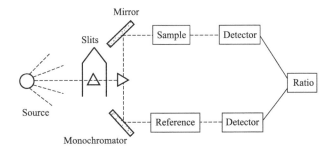

Figure 11-4A Double-beam-in-space configuration

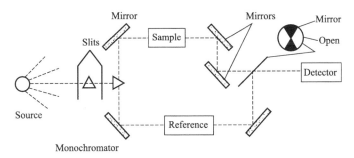

Figure 11-4B Double-beam-in-time configuration

Figure 11-4 Schematic diagram of two types of double-beam spectrophotometers

There are two main advantages of double-beam operation over single-beam operation. Very rapid monitoring of sample and reference helps to eliminate errors due to drift in source intensity, electronic instability, and any changes in the optical system. Also, double-beam operation lends itself to automation: The spectra can be recorded by a strip-chart recorder.

New Words and Phrases

anode ['ænəud] *n.* 阳极，正极
cathode ['kæθəud] *n.* 阴极
cesium ['si:zjəm] *n.* 铯
chopper ['tʃɔpə] *n.* 断路器，斩光器
colorimetry [ˌkʌlə'rimitri] *n.* 比色法
concentration [ˌkɔnsen'treiʃən] *n.* 浓缩，浓度
continuum [kən'tinjuəm] *n.* 连续统一体，连续光谱
cuvette [kju:'vet] *n.* 小玻璃管，透明小容器，试管
detector [di'tektə] *n.* 检测器
deuterium [dju:'tiəriəm] *n.* 氘
dislodge [dis'lɔdʒ] *vt.* -lodged, -lodging 驱逐，移出，移走
dynode ['dainəud] *n.* 倍增器电极
flux [flʌks] *n.* 流量，通量，助溶剂，焊接
impinging [im'pindʒiŋ] *n.* 碰撞
incandescent [ˌinkæn'desnt] *adj.* 遇热发光的，白炽的
monochromator [mɔnəu'krəumeitə] *n.* 单色器，单色仪，单色光镜
photocathode [ˌfəutəu'kæθəud] *n.* 光电阴极
photocell ['fəutəsel] *n.* 光电池
photodetector [ˌfəutəudi'tektə] *n.* 光电探测器
photoemissive [ˌfəutəui'misiv] *adj.* 光电发射的
photomultiply [ˌfəutəu'mʌltipli] *adj.* 光电倍增的
photon ['fəutɔn] *n.* 光子
phototube ['fəutəutju:b] *n.* 光电器
photovoltaic [ˌfəutəuvɔl'teiik] *adj.* 光电的
quartz [kwɔ:ts] *n.* 石英
schematically [ski'mætikli] *adv.* 图解地，图表地
spectra ['spektrə] 复数 spectrum ['spektrəm] *n.* 范围，光谱
spectral ['spektrəl] *adj.* 光谱的
spectrophotometer [ˌspektrəufə'tɔmitə] *n.* 分光光度计
tungsten ['tʌŋstən] *n.* 钨
ultraviolet ['ʌltrə'vaiəlit] *adj.* 紫外线的，紫外的
wattage ['wɔtidʒ] *n.* 瓦特数
barrier-layer 阻挡层，势垒
cesium-coated photocathode 涂铯光电阴极
deuterium electrical-discharge lamps 氘放电灯
fused-silica lamp envelope 熔融适应灯封套
mercury-vapor lamp 汞蒸气灯
photoemissive cathode 光电发射阴极
photometric methods 光度测定法
photon flux 光子通量

quantitative analysis　定量分析
quartz-halogen lamp　石英卤素灯
spectral intensity　光谱强度
spectrophotometric methods　分光光度法
spectroscopic methods　光谱分析法
strip-chart recorder　带状纸记录仪
tungsten-filament "incandescent" lamp　钨丝白炽灯
ultraviolet-visible region　紫外可见光区

Notes

1. More commonly used for the visible and near-infrared regions are tungsten-filament "incandescent" lamps.
   本句为倒装句，主语为tungsten-filament "incandescent" lamps，倒装部分为过去分词短语作表语部分。

Exercises

Ⅰ. Translate the following technical terms into English
① 斩光器
② 比色皿
③ 氘放电灯
④ 汞蒸气灯
⑤ 单色器
⑥ 发光阴极
⑦ 光电倍增器
⑧ 石英卤素灯
⑨ 钨丝白炽灯

Ⅱ. Translate the paragraph into Chinese

Shimadzu is one of the few manufacturers who incorporate the Microsoft Windows program into each software product. Working in the user-friendly Windows environment empowers you with instant control. You can walk right up to the instrument during your busy day and start being productive immediately, even if you are not a frequent user of spectrophotometers. Operation in Windows is quick and intuitive; it easily integrates with your lab's networks and supports hundred of peripherals. For the experienced spectroscopist, Shimadzu personal spectroscopy software offers more flexibility and a broader space of analysis than you may have thought possible.

Ⅲ. Translate the passage into Chinese

Model 723 Visible Spectrophotometer

This low-priced but high performance visible range spectrophotometer was designed to meet most of the rigid demands in quantitative as well as qualitative analysis daily. Incorporated with a monolithic microprocessor, Model 723 Visible Spectrophotometer possesses with many function that only can be found in much more sophisticated instruments. It has been extensively employed in the fields of medicinal and hygienic services, clinical inspections, biochemistry, petrol chemistry, environmental protection and quality control in various production lines.

Features

1. Coupled with advanced micro-processor control technique. Model 723 provides unique "0" and "100" autoadjusting function, directly eliminate the unmatching errors of the cells.

2. Outstanding measurement accuracy, reproducibility and stability.

3. Direct concentration readout, linearity regression, timed plotting, and wavelength scanning functions. Special functions can be expanded at user's demand.

4. A wide range of optional accessories is available to expand the system, such as conventional and semi-micro cuvettes, micro constant temperature autosampling attachment, integration sphere attachment, etc.

5. Easy handing, high degree of automation, reliable operation.

Construction

1. Plotter: Four colors (black, blue, green and red) can be chosen. The spectral curve and the rectangular coordinates can be printed clearly, and all kinds of parameters and determined data can also be printed.

2. LED Digital Display: Four place LED can display the determined data and the wavelength of the instrument.

3. LED State Display: Display the working mode and the four cell holder position.

4. Sample Compartment: Enough space for accommodating all accessories.

5. Monochromater: controlled by micro-computer, manual operations are not needed except sample compartment.

6. Keyboard: Many function keys and numeric keys. All functions can be operated through the soft touch keyboard. PVC film operation panel protects the instrument from dust encroaching.

Specifications

Wavelength Range	330—800nm
Wavelength Readout	4 place LED digital display
Wavelength Readability	0.1nm
Wavelength Accuracy	±0.1nm
Wavelength Reproducibility	0.5nm
Monochromator	Single Beam, Littrow Mount Grating 1200g/mm
Bandwidth	6nm
Stray Light	≤1% (T) at 360 nm
Light Source	Halogen Tungsten Lamp 12V 35W
Photometric Range	0—100% (T) 0—2A
Photometric Accuracy	±0.5% (T)
Photometric Reproducibility	0.4% (T)
Plotter	4 Colors Plotter
T-A Conversion Accuracy	≤±0.002 A at 0.5A
	≤±0.004 A at 1A
Stability	≤±0.004 A/1h
Power Consumption	80W

Power Requirement   220V±10%, 50—60Hz
Dimensions   560mm×400mm×260mm
Weight   25kg

Standard Setup

Model 723 Visible Spectrophotometer	1 unit
Power Cord	1 pc
10 mm glass cuvette	4 pcs
10 mm cuvette holder	1 pc
50 mm sell holder	1 pc
Holmium filter (For Wavelength Calibration)	1 pc
Halogen Tungsten Lamp 12V 30W	1 pc (spare)
Special wrench for replacing the lamp	1 pc
Fuse 2A	1 pc (spare)
Plotter Paper	1 roll (spare)
Plotter Pen 4 colors	1 set (spare)
Dust Cover	1 pc
Operational Manual	1 book

Optional Accessories

Semi-micro Fused Silica Cuvette

7521 Automatic Sampling Unit

7522 Constant Temperature Cuvette Holder

7524 φ60 mm Integrating Sphere Attachment

7523 Micro Auto Sampling Unit

7221 Micro Auto Sampling Unit

10 mm Fused Silica Cuvette

10 mm Air-tight Fused Silica Cuvette

10 mm Glass Cuvette

20 mm Glass Cuvette

30 mm Glass Cuvette

50 mm Glass Cuvette

Import & Export Dept. of Shanghai No. 3 Analytical Instrument Factory

Add: 77 Fen Yang Road, Shanghai P. R. China

Post Code: 200031

Tel: (021) 43754601

Fax: (021) 47187721

Cable: 5157 (SHANGHAI)

Reading Materials

General Knowledge of the Handling of Dangerous Materials

How to use hazardous (有害的), dangerous and inflammable (可燃的, 易燃的) materials safely

1. Identify and interpret standard hazard signage (标志) and documentation (说明).

2. Identify hazardous, dangerous and inflammable materials used within the enterprise.

3. Handle and use hazardous, dangerous and inflammable materials correctly according to Material Safety Data Sheets, legislative requirements and enterprise procedures（操作程序，步骤）.

4. Use personal protective clothing and equipment where appropriate.

5. Follow required emergency procedures（应急操作程序）related to hazardous, dangerous and inflammable materials.

How to store hazardous, dangerous and inflammable materials safely

1. Store materials safely and correctly in appropriate containers, according to legislative requirements（对危险品储存的法律规定）and enterprise procedures.

2. Clearly label（用标签注明）materials in accordance with regulatory（按规定的）and enterprise requirements.

3. Return materials being used to the correct storage place to minimize danger.

4. Complete any required documentation（说明，标明）about use and storage of hazardous, dangerous and inflammable materials.

How to reduce risk of poisoning（污染）

1. Read labels on containers carefully and follow instructions for use（使用说明）.

2. Identify poisonous substances and their particular characteristics and dangers.

3. Store poisonous substances appropriately, out of reach of children, pets and others.

4. Identify and follow procedures for handling poisoning or any suspected poisoning（怀疑有毒的）.

How to reduce the risk of fire from inflammable materials

1. Identify inflammable materials used in the enterprise.

2. Store inflammable materials in accordance with regulations and use them away from sources of heat and ignition（火源）.

3. Carry out high-risk activities involving inflammable materials, correctly and safely.

Learn to use fire extinguishers（灭火器）and other fire equipment

1. Note location of fire extinguishers and other fire equipment within the workplace.

2. Identify and operate extinguishers and other equipment for different fire situations（不同火势）correctly.

3. Use appropriate methods of fire extinguishment（灭火）for different fire situations.

4. Follow enterprise procedures for dealing with fire.

Handle LPG（liquefied petroleum gas）safely

1. Handle and use LPG in accordance with regulatory requirements, standards and enterprise procedures.

2. Use and maintain approved decanting equipment［（液化气）灌装设备］.

3. Decant LPG in a safe manner according to legislative requirements, enterprise procedures and Material Data Safety Sheets for LPG.

Unit 12　Gas Chromatograph

Gas-Chromatographic Instrumentation

Gas-chromatographic instrumentation differs very little from that used for other forms (see Figure 12-1) of column chromatography. A gas chromatograph consists of a source of carrier gas, the flow rate of which can be fixed at a desired magnitude within the range provided; an inlet that can be heated (25 to 500℃); a column in a thermostatted air bath (25 to 400℃); and a detector suitable for vapor-phase samples. The high temperatures are needed to vaporize the solutes of interest and maintain them in the gas phase. Because the distribution coefficient depends on the temperature, the latter is controlled to between ±0.1 and ±0.01℃ (depending on the precision desired in the measured retention times). The inlet and detector are generally maintained at a temperature approximately 10% (in ℃) above that of the column (in any case, above 100℃ for flame-ionization detectors; see later) to ensure rapid volatilization of the sample and to prevent condensation. The temperature of the column is usually set at least 25℃ higher than the boiling point of the solute (This is not, of course, an absolute requirement, since it is only necessary that a substance have a reasonably high vapor pressure at the operating temperature).

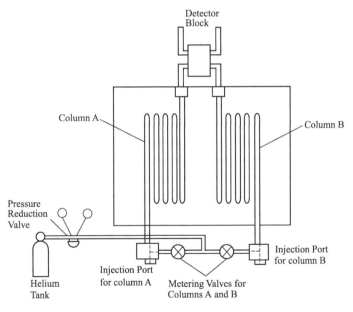

Figure 12-1　Block diagram of a dual-column gas chromatograph

Columns for Gas Chromatography

The most commonly used gas-chromatographic column consists of a tube filled with solid particles of fairly uniform size; the particles are coated with the liquid stationary phase. Perhaps the most commonly used support is marine diatomite (e. g., Johns-Manville Chromosorb). The choice of tubing material depends on the experiment. Aluminum and copper are commonly used, but may have chromatographically and catalytically active oxide films that make them undesirable for sensitive compounds (e. g., steroids); in such cases, stainless steel or glass is used (the latter is more inert, but is less conveniently manipulated).

Open tubular columns consist of 25—100m lengths of 0. 3—0. 6mm-i. d. steel, glass, or quartz (fused silica) tubing coated on the inside wall with a film of stationary phase. These are called wall-coated open tubular (WCOT) columns. The fused-silica types have become fairly popular because of the relative inertness of the inner surface, which results in reduced tailing of more polar solutes, and because of the high mechanical flexibility of such columns, although this contributes nothing to the chromatographic characteristics of the column[1]. The flexibility is the result of the polymer coating on the outside of the silica tubing, which excludes moisture and prevents hydration and cracking of the otherwise thin wall[2]. There are problems with coating polar stationary-phase films onto silica columns, but coatings can be prepared by forming a "bonded phase" in place using chemistries analogous to those used for preparation of "bulk" bonded phases for liquid chromatography[3].

Capillary gas chromatography was proposed and demonstrated in the first decade of gas chromatography. It was then virtually ignored until the 1970s, when a combination of patent maturation and the need to separate more and more complex mixtures (especially for environmental and biomedical studies) spurred commercial exploitation[3]. The improvement in commercial instrumentation followed the research of the earlier workers and little or no fundamental advances were involved. Most of the changes centered on (a) reduction of dead volumes in inlet and detector designs; and (b) better, more uniform, temperature-control ovens and improved linearity in temperature programming. The vast majority of capillary applications are temperature programmed with injection of the sample onto a relatively cold column. Injection onto a cold column tends to focus the injection band at the column head and reduces the apparent inlet contribution to band broadening.

Capillary columns have limited capacity compared to packed columns, that is, less stationary phase and therefore less absolute retention. As a result, many examples of capillary gas chromatography involve the determination of minor-level, rather than trace-level, components in the solutions injected (Through sample-preparation procedures, trace components in the actual analytical sample can still be determined by appropriate extraction and concentration methods, but the components are in relatively high concentration in the injected solution). Because of the low capacity of WCOT columns, and for other reasons, surface-coated open tubular (SCOT) columns have been introduced. These columns are internally coated with finely divided metal oxide, graphite, or alumino-silicate before the stationary phase is applied. As a result, they have somewhat increased capacity because of the larger surface area presented.

The major advantage of capillary columns is not in plate height, which is generally larger than with well-packed columns, but in the number of plates achievable with a relatively small pressure drop. For example, if 20,000 theoretical plates is a good upper limit for packed columns, then open tubular columns can have 75,000 to 150,000 plates. Capillary gas chromatography is a technique complementary to the use of packed columns. The latter are to be preferred when available resolution is adequate and the highest quantitative is desired.

Chromatographic Support Materials

The function of a chromatographic support is to hold the stationary phase. One useful type of support is provided by the marine diatomites, which are the skeletons of tiny unicellular algae (diatoms) and consist chiefly of amorphous hydrated silica with traces of metal-oxide impurities. This material has the advantages of high porosity and large surface area. Some properties of a variety of diatomite supports are given in Table 12-1. Chromosorb P, for example, is prepared from one particular grade of firebrick and is a pink (hence P), calcined diatomite that is relatively hard and not easily friable. It is used mainly with solutes of low to moderate polarity (e.g., hydrocarbons). It is a relatively good adsorbent, a quality that can be an interference. If there were no liquid phase at all, the support would act as an adsorbent, and gas-solid chromatography could be carried out. The effect of placing a thin film of liquid on an active adsorbent is to moderate the gas-solid activity, but not to eliminate it. It has been shown that even 20% by weight liquid loading does not eliminate this activity. Several techniques are used to reduce the activity—for instance, acid washing, and "silanizing" the active silica sites with dimethyldichlorosilane to displace the hydrogen. The choice of support for a given analysis is as important as the choice of a stationary phase; for instance, if retention is partly due to solution in the stationary phase and partly to adsorption on the support, then the retention time will vary with the size of the sample. Some compounds (e.g., sterols) may actually decompose on the column if a poor choice of support has been made.

Table 12-1 Properties of some diatomite supports

Properties	Chromosorb			
	A	G	P	W
Color	Pink,	Oyster White,	Pink,	White,
Type	Flux-Calcined	Flux-Calcined	Flux-Calcined	Calcined
Density, g/cm^3				
① Loose weight	0.40	0.47	0.38	0.18
② Packed weight	0.48	0.58	0.47	0.24
Surface area, m^2/g	2.7	0.5	4.0	1.0
Surface area, m^2/cm^3	1.3	0.29	1.88	0.29
Maximum liquidphase loading	25%	5%	30%	15%
pH	7.1	8.5	6.5	8.5
Handling characteristics	Good	Good	Good	Slightly Friable

New Words and Phrases

achievable [əˈtʃiːvəbl] *adj.* 做得成的，可完成的，可有成就的
adsorbent [ædˈsɔːbənt] *adj.* 吸附的 *n.* 吸附剂
algae [ˈældʒiː] *n.* 藻类，海藻

alumino-silicate [əˌljuːmənəuˈsilikeit] n. 铝硅酸盐
amorphous [əˈmɔːfəs] adj. 无定形的，无组织的
biomedical [ˌbaiəuˈmedikəl] adj. 生物（学和）医学的
calcine [ˈkælsain] v. 烧成石灰，煅烧
capillary [kəˈpiləri] n. 毛细管 adj. 毛状的，毛细作用的
carrier [ˈkæriə] n. 载体，吸收剂
chromatograph [krəuˈmætəɡrɑːf] n. 色谱仪，用色谱（法）分析
chromatographic [ˌkrəumætəˈɡræfik] adj. 色谱（分析）的，色谱法的
chromatography [ˌkrəuməˈtəɡrəfi] n. 色谱法
chromosorb [ˈkrəuməsɔːb] n. 红色硅藻土色谱载体
coefficient [kəuiˈfiʃənt] n. 系数
diatomite [daiˈætəmait] n. 硅藻土
diatoms [ˈdaiətəm] n. 硅藻属
dimethyldichlorosilane [daiˈmeθi ˌdaiklɔːrəl ˌdaiklɔːrə] n. 二甲基二氯硅烷
exploitation [ˌeksplɔiˈteiʃən] n. 开发，开采，剥削
firebrick [faiəbrik] n. 耐火砖
friable [ˈfraiəbl] adj. 易碎的，脆的
hydrated [ˈhaidreitid] adj. 含水的，与水结合的
i. d. = inside dimensions 内尺寸
inertness [iˈnəːtnis] n. 不活泼
inlet [ˈinlet] n. 进口，入口
maturation [ˌmætjuˈreiʃən] n. 成熟
oyster [ˈɔistə] n. 牡蛎，蚝
retention [riˈtenʃən] n. 保留值
silanize [ˈsilənaiz] vt. 使硅烷化
solute [ˈsɔljuːt] n. 溶解物，溶质
spur [spəː] vt. (spurred; spurring) 刺激，鼓舞，鞭策
steroid [ˈstiərɔid] n. 类固醇
support [səˈpɔːt] n. 载体
unicellular [ˈjuːniˈseljulə] adj. 单细胞的
absolute retention 绝对保留值
amorphous hydrated silica 无定形含水硅
bonded phase 键合固定相
capillary column 毛细管柱
capillary gas chromatography 毛细管气相色谱法
carrier gas 载气
column chromatography 柱色谱法
column head 柱头
dead volume 死体积
distribution coefficient 分配系数
flame-ionization detector 火焰离子化检测器
flow rate 流量

flux-calcined　熔融煅烧
gas chromatograph　气相色谱
gas-chromatographic column　气相色谱柱
gas-chromatographic instrumentation　气相色谱仪
handling characteristics　操作特性
liquid chromatography　液相色谱法
liquid stationary phase　液体固定相
marine diatomite　海藻土
minor-level　少量的
open tubular column　空心色谱柱
oyster White　牡蛎白
packed column　填充柱
plate height　塔板高度
polar solute　极性溶质
pressure drop　压力降
surface-coated open tubular (SCOT) columns　表面涂层空心色谱柱
thermostatted air bath　自动调温气浴
trace-level　痕量的
unicellular algae　单细胞海藻
wall-coated open tubular (WCOT) columns　涂壁空心色谱柱
well-packed　填充好的

Notes

1. The fused-silica types have become fairly popular because of the relative inertness of the inner surface, which results in reduced tailing of more polar solutes, and because of the high mechanical flexibility of such columns, although this contributes nothing to the chromatographic characteristics of the column.
   本句为复合句,although…column 引导让步状语从句,which…solutes 引导非限制性定语从句修饰主句中的 inertness。

2. The flexibility is the result of the polymer coating on the outside of the silica tubing, which excludes moisture and prevents hydration and cracking of the otherwise thin wall.
   本句为复合句,which…wall 为非限制性定语从句修饰 polymer coating。

3. There are problems with coating polar stationary-phase films onto silica columns, but coatings can be prepared by forming a "bonded phase" in place using chemistries analogous to those used for preparation of "bulk" bonded phases for liquid chromatography.
   in place　*adv.* 适当地,using…chromatography 现在分词短语作方式状语,其中 used…chromatography 为过去分词短语作定语修饰 those。

Exercises

Ⅰ. Translate the following technical expression into English
1. 无定形水合硅土
2. 毛细管柱

3. 载气

4. 柱色谱法

5. 死体积

6. 分配系数

7. 火焰离子化检测器

8. 液体固定相

9. 海藻土

10. 表面涂层空心管

Ⅱ. Translate the passage into Chinese

Shimadzu GC-14B Series

A GC-14B series gas chromatograph consists of a high-performance column oven, a flexible sample injection system, a separate flow control unit, high-sensitivity detector (s), detector control unit (s), a removable handy-type keyboard unit, and other units. Each unit is simply designed but ensures high performance.

1. Flow Control Unit

Various flow controllers, such as for single column flow line, dual column flow line, split/splitless sample injection, are available to suit the application.

2. Detector Control Unit

Up to three controllers, selected out of those for TCD, FID, ECD, FPD, and FTD, can be housed together. Addition of an optional controller case allows four controllers to be installed simultaneously.

3. Column Oven

The column oven has curved inner walls (same as the performance-proven oven of the GC-15A and GC-16A) to ensure exceptional repeatability of retention times. This type of column oven is best suited to capillary column GC. The oven is an upright type, which minimizes the influence of the heat radiated from the injection ports and the detector oven. A computer-controlled flap is provided at the rear to allow exchange of air in the cooling stage of a temperature programmed run.

4. Flexible Sample Injection Port System

(Each sample injection port unit is separately temperature-controlled.)

The sample injection port units are of a cartridge type, and up to four units selected out of the following can be installed together.

(1) Split/splitless unit

(2) Glass-insert system unit for single column

(3) Glass-insert system unit for dual colums

(4) Cool, on-column system unit

(5) Moving needle system unit

5. Detectors

Up to four detectors can be installed together.

(1) FID (Highly sensitive, flame ionization detector)

(2) C-ECD (Highly sensitive, constant-current electron capture detector with protected radiation source)

(3) ECD (Highly sensitive, constant-current electron capture detector)
(4) FTD (Highly sensitive flame thermionic detector)
(5) FPD (Highly sensitive and highly stable flame photometric detector)
(6) TCD (Easy-to-operate thermal conductivity detector)

6. Keyboard Unit

The control system is designed to ensure unmatched ease of operation. When this keyboard unit is disconnected, the GC-14B series can operate according to preset instrument parameters.

This keyboard unit is unnecessary when the GC-14B series is controlled by an external computer such as another GC, a data processor, a personal computer, or a host computer. This feature makes the GC-14B series especially suitable to LA (laboratory automation) applications.

(The keyboard unit has the same familiar key arrangement as the keyboard of the Shimadzu GC-9A series GCs.)

Reading Materials

What is Global Warming?

The term Global Warming refers to the observation that the atmosphere (大气, 大气层) near the Earth's surface is warming. This warming is one of many kinds of climate change that the Earth has gone through in the past and will continue to go through in the future. The increased amounts of carbon dioxide (CO_2) and other greenhouse gases (GHGs) are the primary causes of global warming.

Why is Global Warming important?

Temperature increases will have significant impacts (影响) on human activities, including: where we can live, what food we can grow, how and where we can grow food, and where organisms (生物) we consider pests (害虫) can thrive (泛滥). To be prepared for the effects of these potential impacts we need to know how much the Earth is warming, how long the Earth has been warming, and what has caused the warming. Answers to these questions provide us with a better basis for making decisions related to issues such as water resources and agricultural planning.

What is the Greenhouse Effect (温室效应)?

Our planet absorbs radiant energy (辐射能) from the sun and emits (散发) some of that energy back to space. The term (术语) greenhouse effect describes how water vapor, carbon dioxide, and other "greenhouse" gases in the atmosphere alter (改变) the return of energy to space, and in turn, change the temperature at the Earth's surface. These greenhouse gases absorb some of the energy that is emitted from the Earth's surface, preventing this energy from being lost to space. As a result, the lower atmosphere warms and sends some of this energy back to the Earth's surface. When the energy is "recycled (循环)" in this way, the Earth's surface warms.

Life on Earth would be very different without the greenhouse effect. The greenhouse effect keeps the long term annual average temperature of the Earth's surface approximately

32℃ (or about 58°F) higher than it would be otherwise.

How is the Greenhouse Effect related to Global Warming?

Greenhouse gases occur naturally in the Earth's atmosphere, but are also being added by human activities. This happens primarily through the burning of fossil fuels (化石燃料), such as coal, oil and natural gas, which releases carbon dioxide to the atmosphere. Over the past century, atmospheric carbon dioxide has increased due to human activities from 300 to 380 parts per million (ppm) (百万分之), and the average Earth temperature has increased approximately (大约) 0.7℃ (or about 1.3°F).

Given what we know about the ability of greenhouse gases to warm the Earth's surface, it is reasonable to expect that as concentrations of greenhouse gases (温室气体浓度) in the atmosphere rise above natural levels, the Earth's surface will become increasingly warm. Many scientists have now concluded that global warming can be explained by a human-caused enhancement (加强,加重) of the greenhouse effect. It is important to remember both that the greenhouse effect occurs naturally, and that it has been intensified (加强) by humankind's input (释放) of greenhouse gases into the atmosphere.

Are Ozone Holes (臭氧空洞) related to Global Warming or the Greenhouse Effect?

The formation of ozone holes is related to these scientific issues, yet is still distinct. Ozone plays a very important, natural role in the upper atmosphere [called the stratosphere (平流层,同温层)], where 90% of it exists. Stratospheric ozone acts as a shield (保护层) against harmful ultraviolet (UV) radiation (紫外线辐射) from the sun. This ozone can be destroyed by human-produced chemical compounds called chlorofluorocarbons (含氯氟烃), or CFCs. When these CFCs are combined with extremely cold stratospheric temperatures over the poles, solar radiation, and particular patterns of atmospheric circulation (气流), chemical reactions occur that cause "Ozone Holes" over Antarctica and the Arctic.

The formation of ozone holes is related to global warming and the greenhouse effect in two ways. First, CFCs are greenhouse gases. Thus, the release of these compounds into the atmosphere will have two separate effects: to destroy ozone and to add to the greenhouse effect. Second, if stratospheric temperatures or patterns of atmospheric circulation change as part of global warming, this will affect the chemical reactions that destroy ozone and cause the ozone holes to either grow or shrink (缩小).

Unit 13 Atomic Absorption Spectrometry

Among the most common techniques for elemental analysis are flame emission, atomic absorption, and atomic fluorescence spectrometry[1]. All these techniques are based on the radiant emission, absorption, and fluorescence of atomic vapor. The key component of any atomic spectrometric method is the system for generating the atomic vapor (gaseous free atoms or ions) from a sample, that is, the source. Numerous sources have been used to generate atomic vapor, among them, flames, direct-current arcs, alternating-current sparks, electrothermal atomizers, microwave plasmas, radiofrequency plasmas, and lasers. The most widely used sources are the flame and electrothermal atomizers, and it is these sources that will be discussed in this chapter[2].

Atomic absorption spectrometry (AAS) is one of the most important techniques for the analysis and characterization of the elemental composition of materials and samples. It was first proposed as a general-purpose analytical method in 1955 by Walsh in a landmark paper entitled "The Application of Atomic Absorption Spectra to Chemical Analysis."[3] In a more recent paper, Walsh indicated that the concept of atomic absorption was slowed over the decades before 1955 by such factors as a lack of photoelectric detection, a misinterpretation of Kirchoff's law, thinking only of continuum sources, and a failure to "avoid being stupid." The key contribution of Walsh was the use of the hollow-cathode lamp as the source. This put the required spectral resolution in the source, and allowed very simple measurement systems to be used. A block diagram of an atomic absorption spectrometer is shown in Figure 13-1.

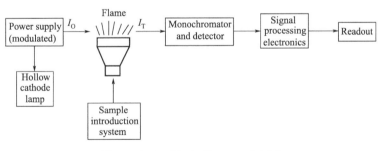

Figure 13-1 Block diagram of AAS

The choice and development of an appropriate source for an atomic absorption measurement was the key step in the emergence of atomic absorption spectrometry as an analytical method. The requirement perhaps seems simple; as with any absorption measurement, a source of radiation that can be absorbed by the sample is required. For the vast majority of molecular spectrometry absorption measurements, this is readily achieved using the combination of a broad-band source (continuum source) and a monochromator. However, the problem with the atomic absorption measurement is the very narrow (in the range 0.001 to 0.005 nm) absorption profile of atomic species in flames. Thus, starting with a continuum source, a very high resolution and costly monochromator is required to achieve such a bandpass, and then the resulting through-put is likely to be so low that little light is left with which to make the absorption measurement[4]. Walsh's suggestion in 1955 that an element-specific line source be used for the measurement gave birth to atomic absorption spectrometry as a general-purpose analytical technique. The primary source that he suggested be used was the hollow-cathode lamp.

A schematic diagram of a hollow-cathode lamp is shown in Figure 13-2. The cathode of the lamp is normally constructed from a single element (or an alloy of the element of interest), and the spectrum emitted by the lamp is the spectrum of the element and the filler gas, most often neon. See the paper by Pillow for a description of the hollow-cathode discharge. If an important line of the element is overlapped by a Ne filler-line, argon can be used as an alternative. The lamps are typically run at a current of a few milliamperes, and this requires an applied voltage of 100 to 300 V in series with a 5—10kΩ resistor. When the lamp is run at relatively low currents—approximately 3 mA—the line width of the atomic emission is about the same as (or narrower than) the atomic absorption profile of the free atoms in the flame. Thus, the hollow-cathode lamp provides an almost ideal source for the atomic absorption measurement, its wavelength exactly matched to that of the analyte and the bandwidth essentially ideal for the atoms in the flame.

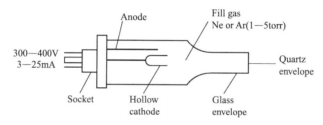

Figure 13-2 Schematic diagram a hollow-cathode lamp

It should be mentioned, however, that with a high-resolution echelle spectrometer and an intense continuum source, excellent atomic absorption determinations can be carried out.

New Words and Phrases

argon ['ɑːgɔn]   n. 氩
atomizer ['ætəmaizə]   n. 雾化器，原子化器
bandpass [bændpɑːs]   n（光谱）通带
characterization [ˌkæriktərai'zeiʃən]   n. 特性
echelle [ei'ʃel]   n. 阶梯（分级）光栅
filler ['filə]   n. 填充剂，漏斗
fluorescence [fluə'resns]   n. 荧光，荧光性
landmark ['lændmɑːk]   n. （航海）陆标，里程碑，划时代的事
milliampere [ˌmili'æmpɛə]   n. 毫安培
misinterpretation ['misinˌtəːpri'teiʃən]   n. 误译，曲解
multielement ['mʌltiˌelimənt]   n. 多元素，多元件
neon ['niːən]   n. 氖
overlap ['əuvə'læp]   vt. （与……）交迭

pillow [ˈpiləu] n. 枕头，枕垫
plasma [ˈplæzmə] n. 等离子体，等离子区
profile [ˈprəufail] n. 外形，轮廓
radiofrequency [ˈreidiəuˈfriːkwənsi] n. 射频
resistor [riˈzistə] n. 电阻，电阻器
resolution [ˌrezəˈljuːʃən] n. 分辨率，解析度
species [ˈspiːʃiz] n. 种类，（原）核素，物种
Walsh [wɔːlʃ] n. 沃尔什（姓氏）
alternating-current sparks 交流电火花
atomic absorption spectrometer 原子吸收分光光度计
atomic absorption spectrometry 原子吸收光谱测定法
atomic fluorescence spectrometry 原子荧光光谱法
atomic spectrometric method 原子光谱法
broad-band 带（频）宽
direct-current arc 直流电弧
electrothermal atomizer 电热原子化器
element-specific line source 特定元素线性光源
filler gas 填充气体
for the purpose of 为了，因……起见
give birth to 产生
general-purpose 多种用途的，多方面的
high-resolution echelle 高分辨率光栅
hollow-cathode lamp 空心阴极灯
in the emergence of 出现
Kirchoff's law 基尔霍夫定律
microwave plasma 微波等离子体
narrow absorption profile 窄吸收谱线轮廓
photoelectric detection 光电检测
radiofrequency plasma 射频等离子体
schematic diagram 示意图
slow over 慢下来，减缓，减速
spectral resolution 光谱分辨率
through-put 产量，通过量

Notes

1. Among the most common techniques for elemental analysis are flame emission, atomic absorption, and atomic fluorescence spectrometry.
   本句为倒装句，强调表语 Among...analysis，主语为 flame emission...spectrometry.

2. The most widely used sources are the flame and electrothermal atomizers, and it is these sources that will be discussed in this chapter.
   本句为并列句，and 连接的并列分句是强调句型，强调主语 these sources。

3. It was first proposed as a general-purpose analytical method in 1955 by Walsh in a landmark pa-

per entitled "The Application of Atomic Absorption Spectra to Chemical Analysis."
过去分词短语 entitled…Chemical Analysis 作定语修饰 paper。

4. Thus, starting with a continuum source, a very high resolution and costly monochromator is required to achieve such a bandpass, and then the resulting through-put is likely to be so low that little light is left with which to make the absorption measurement.
本句结构为并列复合句,现在分词短语 starting with a continuum source 为第一个并列分句的时间状语,第二分句含有 so…that 结构,with which…measurement 作定语修饰 little light。

Exercises

Ⅰ. Translate the following technical terms into English
1. 交流电火花
2. 宽带
3. 直流电弧
4. 电热原子化器
5. 高分辨率光栅
6. 空心阴极灯
7. 光电检测
8. 射频等离子体
9. 光谱分辨率

Ⅱ. Translate the passage into Chinese

Beijing Rayleigh Analytical Instrument Corporation (BRAIC) (the past name is Beijing Second Optical Instrument Factory) is the biggest spectroscopic instruments manufacturer appointed by the Ministry of Machinery Industry in China. Its fixed assets reach to RMB 32000000. Its area is about 60000 square meters, 900 employees including over 200 engineers and 30 specialists worked in BRAIC.

BRAIC, with over 25 years experience in manufacturing the spectroscopy instruments, has been ready for offering six series over 20 models products, they are: series of Atomic Absorption Spectrophotometers, series of Optical Emission Spectrometer, series of UV/VIS Spectrophotometers, series of Fourier Transform Infrared Spectrometers, series of Biochemical Analysers and series of Plane Grating Monochromators. The market of Atomic Absorption Spectrophotometers manufactured by BRAIC occupies over 50% of domestic marketing.

BRAIC had successfully imported the advanced technology from some countries of France, Japan, Switzerland and the United States on the projects of Atomic Absorption Spectrophotometer, UV/VIS Spectrophotometer and FTIR Spectrophotometer, etc. So the quality and performance of the instruments have been reached to the world level. The success made BRAIC's products not only won the international bid many times, but also exported to foreign countries, such as USA, Korea, Southeast Asia, Europe, etc.

BRAIC possesses imported automatic machining equipments such as Machining Center, numerically controlled Punching machine, numerically controlled press brake, etc. We have the testing room of high, low temperature, anti-high voltage, vibration for examining the instruments. And we have skilled engineers for advanced technology of optical processing, grating ruling and grating duplicating.

Beijing Rayleigh Analytical Instrument Corporation, the pride of China Spectroscopy instruments manufacturer!

Reading Materials

Type and Sources of Air Pollutants（污染物）

What is air pollution（污染）? Air pollution is normally defined as air that contains one or more chemicals in high enough concentrations to harm humans, other animals, vegetation（植物）or materials. There are two major types of air pollutants. A primary air pollutant is a chemical added directly to the air that occurs in a harmful concentration. It can be a natural air component, such as carbon dioxide, that rises above its normal concentration, or something not usually found in the air, such as a lead compound emitted by cars burning leaded gasoline. A secondary air pollutant is a harmful chemical formed in the atmosphere through a chemical reaction among air components. Serious air pollution usually results over a city or other area that is emitting high levels of pollutants during a period of air stagnation（停滞）. The geographic location of some heavily populated cities, such as Los Angeles and Mexico City, makes them particularly susceptible（易受影响）to frequent air stagnation and pollution buildup（增加）.

We must be careful about depending solely on concentration values in determining the severity air pollutants. By themselves, measured concentrations tell us nothing about the danger caused by pollutants, because threshold levels（临界浓度）, synergy（协同作用）, and biological magnification（生物放大效应）are also determining factors. In addition, we run into（遇到）the issue of conflicting views of what constitutes harm.

Major air pollutants following are the 11 major types of air pollutants.

1. Carbon oxides: carbon monoxide (CO), carbon dioxide (CO_2).
2. Sulfur oxides: sulfur dioxide (SO_2), sulfur trioxide (SO_3).
3. Nitrogen oxides: nitrous oxide (N_2O), nitric oxide (NO), nitrogen dioxide (NO_2).
4. Hydrocarbons（烃）(organic compounds containing carbon and hydrogen): methane (CH_4), butane (C_4H_{10}), benzene (C_6H_6).
5. Photochemical oxidants（光化学氧化剂）: ozone（臭氧）(O_3), PAN [a group of peroxyacylnitrates（硝酸过氧化乙酰类）], and various aldehydes（醛）.
6. Particulates（微粒）(solid particles or liquid droplets suspended in air): smoke, dust, soot（煤灰）, asbestos（石棉）, metallic particles [such as lead, beryllium（铍）, cadmium（镉）], oil, salt spray, sulfate salts（硫酸盐）.
7. Other inorganic compounds: asbestos, hydrogen fluoride (HF), hydrogen sulfide (H_2S), ammonia (NH_3), sulfur acid (H_2SO_4), nitric acid (HNO_3).
8. Other organic (carbon-containing) compounds: pesticides（杀虫剂）, herbicides（除草剂）, various alcohols, acids, and other chemicals.
9. Radioactive substances: tritium（氚）, radon（氡）, emissions from fossil fuel and nuclear power plants.
10. Heat.
11. Noise.

Unit 14　Infrared Spectrometer

Instrumentation for Infrared Spectroscopy

Infrared spectroscopy is a type of absorption spectroscopy. Therefore, a dispersive-type infrared spectrophotometer will have the same basic components as the instruments used for the study of absorption of visible and ultraviolet radiation, although the sources, detectors, and materials used for the fabrication of optical elements will be different. Although high-quality dispersive instruments are now in use and will continue to be produced, the most important development in instrumentation for infrared spectroscopy has been increased accessibility of dedicated high-speed computers, which has led to the proliferation of Fourier transform infrared spectrometers[1].

Sources

Infrared sources are insert solids that are electrically heated to approximately 2000K and produce intensity-versus-wavelength curves characteristic of blackbody radiation sources. Intensity is highest at 5000 cm^{-1} and decreases gradually to only 1% of the maximum at 500 cm^{-1}.

The Nernst glower is probably the most widely used infrared source. It is usually a cylinder composed of rare-earth oxides that has a diameter of about 2 mm and length of approximately 20mm. The operating temperature can be as high as 1800K. It has a negative temperature coefficient of resistance, and thus it is necessary to initially heat this source externally in order to pass sufficient current to maintain a desired temperature. This same property requires that the electrical current be limited in some manner so that the source will not become so hot that it is ruined.

Another source, the Globar, is a silicon carbide rod about 5mm in diameter and 50mm in length. It is operated at lower temperatures (around 1600K) than the Nernst glower in order to avoid air oxidation. The globar provides a greater output than the Nernst glower in the region below 1500 cm^{-1}.

A third infrared source is a tightly wound coil of nichrome wire which is electrically heated to incandescence. This source is of lower intensity in the infrared region than the previous two, but has a longer life.

Detectors

Because the available infrared sources are generally of low intensity and the energy of an infrared photon is relatively low, the detection of infrared radiation is more difficult than is the case in the ultraviolet and visible regions. The common phototubes are not useful in the infrared region because the photons are not sufficiently energetic to cause photoemission of electrons.

The two general classes of infrared detectors now in use are: (a) photon detectors, which are based on the photoconductive effect that occurs in certain semiconductor materials; and (b) thermal detectors, in which absorption of infrared radiation produces a heating effect, which in turn alters a physical property of the detector, such as its resistance[2].

Photon detectors consist of a thin film of semiconductor material, such as lead sulfide, lead telluride, indium antimonide, or germanium doped with copper or mercury, deposited onto a nonconducting glass and sealed into an evacuated envelope to protect the semiconductor from reaction with the atmosphere. Absorption of photon of sufficient energy by the semiconductor material promotes some of the electrons in the bound nonconducting state to the conducting state, resulting in a decrease in the resistance of the material. The excitation of these bound electrons requires a photon having an energy above a certain minimum value. These detectors therefore have definite cutoff points toward the far-infrared. Lead sulfide detectors are sensitive to radiation between 1 and 3 μm in wavelength and have a response time of about 10 μs. Detectors based on other materials, when cooled to liquid nitrogen or liquid helium temperatures, extend sensitivity to considerable longer wavelengths and have response times as fast as 20 ns.

Thermal detectors may be classified into four types based on the properties of the material. The thermocouple, the most widely used infrared detector, is composed of a small piece of blackened gold foil (the surface for absorbing the incident radiation) welded to two fine wires made of dissimilar metals[3]. A small voltage develops between the two thermocouple junctions. One of the junctions (the reference junction) is bonded to a heat sink and carefully shielded from the incident radiation, and thus remains at a relatively stable temperature. Because the incident radiation is chopped, only the temperature change of the thermocouple is important. To minimize conductive heat loss, the entire assembly is sealed in an evacuated housing having an infrared-transmitting window. A thermopile is the name given to a detector comprising several thermocouples connected in series so that their outputs are additive. These detectors have response times of about 100 ms and a relatively flat frequency response.

The second type of detector, the thermistor or bolometer, exhibits a change in resistance when illuminated by infrared radiation. Two matched sensing elements are used as two arms of a Wheatstone bridge, one of which is shielded from the infrared radiation, the other directly exposed and the surface coated to increase absorption. A temperature difference between the two elements produces a proportional voltage difference. A thermistor is constructed with oxides of metals such as cobalt or nickel that have high temperature coefficients of resistance of about 0.4% per ℃.

The Golay or "pneumatic" detector is based on the increase in pressure with temperature of a confined inert gas. Infrared radiation is absorbed by a rigid blackened metal plate sealed to one end of a small metallic cylinder. The heat is transmitted to the gas, which expands and causes a flexible silvered diaphragm affixed to the other end of the tube to bulge outward[4]. The distortion of the thin diaphragm can be measured either by making it part of an optical system in which a light beam reflects from it to a phototube, or by making it one plate of a dynamic parallel-plate capacitor: The distortion of the flexible diaphragm relative to fixed plate changes the average plate separation and thus the capacitance. The Golay detector has a sensitivity approximately equal to that of a thermocouple for near- and middle-infrared radiation and is not often used for this region. It is superior for the region below 200 cm^{-1} and is useful for instruments designed for the far-infrared region.

The most recently developed infrared detector is the pyroelectric detector. Certain crystals such as triglycine sulfate (TGS), deuterated triglycine sulfate (DTGS), lithium tantalite, and some others, possess an internal electric polarization along an axis resulting from alignment of electric dipole moments. Thermal alteration of the lattice spacing caused by absorption of infrared radiation results in a change of the electric polarization. If placed between electrodes consisting of metal plates connected through an external circuit, current will flow in the circuit to balance this charge redistribution. The pyroelectric effect depends on the rate of change of temperature and not on the absolute value. It therefore responds only to modulated radiation and not to slowly varying background radiation. Thus, the pyroelectric detector also operates with a much faster response time and is widely used for Fouried transform infrared spectroscopy.

Dispersive Infrared Spectrometers

By far the most common use of infrared spectroscopy is for qualitative identification of compounds. Thus, because of the complexity of infrared spectra, most commercial instruments are of the double-beam recording type which cancels background absorption caused by atmospheric gases such as CO_2 and H_2O.

The radiation from the source is split into two beams, one passing through the sample compartment and the other through the reference compartment. The rotating sector mirror alternately reflects the sample beam or transmits the reference beam onto mirror and, via mirror, through the entrance slit into the monochromator. Thus, the sample beam and the reference beam travel through the monochromator in alternate pulses. Each pulse is dispersed by grating, transmitted through exit slit and focused on the detector.

New Words and Phrases

accessibility [ˌæksesiˈbiliti] *n.* 易接近，可到达的
alignment [əˈlainmənt] *n.* 列队，成直线
antimonide [ˈæntiimənaid] *n.* 锑化物
bolometer [bəuˈlɔmitə] *n.* 测辐射热仪
cutoff [ˈkʌtɔːf] *n.* 切（断）开，关（闭，停）车，停电
dedicated [ˈdedikeitid] *adj.* 专用的
deposite [diˈpɔzit] *vt.* 沉积
deuterated [ˈdjuːtəreitid] *adj.* 含重氢的
diaphragm [ˈdaiəfræm] *n.* 膈，隔膜，隔板
dope [dəup] *vt.* 向……内掺入
evacuate [iˈvækjueit] *vt.* 抽真空

excitation [ˌeksi'teiʃən] n. 刺激，激发
germanium [dʒə'meiniəm] n. 锗
Globar ['gləu'bɑː] n. 格罗巴碳化硅电阻加热元件，碳硅棒
glower ['gləuə] n. 炽热体，灯丝
grating ['greiti] n. 光栅
illuminate [i'ljuːmineit] vt. 照明，照亮 vi. 照亮
incandescence [ˌinkæn'desəns] n. 白热，炽热
indium ['indiəm] n. 铟
infrared ['infrə'red] a. 红外线的
junction ['dʒʌnkʃən] n. 接头
mercury ['məːkjuri] n. 水银，汞
nichrome ['nikrəum] n. 镍铬铁合金，镍铬耐热合金
nickel ['nikl] n. 镍
nonconducting ['nɔnkən'dʌktiŋ] adj. 不传导的
pneumatic [njuː'mætik] adj. 汽动的
proliferation [prəulifəreiʃən] n. 增殖，扩散
proportional [prə'pɔːʃənl] adj. 比例的，成比例的
pyroelectric [ˌpaiərəuilektrik, ˌpi-] adj. 热电的
semiconductor ['semikən'dʌktə] n. 半导体
tantalite ['tæntəlait] n. 钽铁矿
telluride ['teljuraid] n. 碲化物
thermistor [θəː'mistə] n. 热敏电阻
thermocouple ['θəːməuˌkʌpl] n. 热电偶
thermopile ['θəːməupail] n. 热电堆
triglycine ['triglisain] n. 次氨基三乙酸
background absorption 背景吸收
blackbody radiation sources 黑体辐射源
deuterated triglycine sulfate（DTGS） 重氢硫酸三甘氨酸
dispersive-type infrared spectrophotometer 色散型红外光谱仪
double-beam 双光束
electric dipole moment 电偶极矩
entrance slit 进口狭缝
exit slit 出口狭缝
far-infrared 远红外
Fourier transform infrared spectrometers 傅里叶变换红外光谱仪
incident radiation 入射的辐射线
indium antimonide 锗化铟
infrared spectrometer 红外光谱仪
lead sulfide 硫化铅
lead telluride 碲化铅
lithium tantalite 锂钽铁矿
Nernst glower 能斯特灯

rare-earth oxides 稀土金属氧化物
reference compartment 参考比色皿
rotating sector mirror 旋转扇形反射镜
temperature coefficients of resistance 电阻温度系数
triglycine sulfate（TGS） 硫酸三甘氨酸
sample compartment 样品比色皿
silicon carbide rod 碳化硅棒
Wheatstone bridge 惠斯登电桥

Notes

1. Although high-quality dispersive instruments are now in use and will continue to be produced, the most important development in instrumentation for infrared spectroscopy has been increased accessibility of dedicated high-speed computers, which has led to the proliferation of Fourier transform infrared spectrometers.
   Although…produced 为让步状语从句，which…spectrometers 为非限制性定语从句，修饰主句。

2. The two general classes of infrared detectors now in use are：（a）photon detectors, which are based on the photoconductive effect that occurs in certain semiconductor materials; and (b) thermal detectors, in which absorption of infrared radiation produces a heating effect, which in turn alters a physical property of the detector, such as its resistance.
   (a) photon detectors 和 (b) thermal detectors 均为表语。which…materials 为非限制性定语从句修饰（a）photon detectors，其中 that…materials 为限制性定语从句修饰 effect。in which…resistance 为非限制性定语从句修饰（b）thermal detectors，其中 which…resistance 为非限制性定语从句修饰 effect。

3. The thermocouple, the most widely used infrared detector, is composed of a small piece of blackened gold foil (the surface for absorbing the incident radiation) welded to two fine wires made of dissimilar metals.
   the most widely used infrared detector 为 The thermocouple 的同位语，welded…metals 为过去分词短语作定语修饰 foil。

4. The heat is transmitted to the gas, which expands and causes a flexible silvered diaphragm affixed to the other end of the tube to bulge outward.
   which…outward 为非限制性定语从句修饰 gas，affixed…tube 为过去分词作定语修饰 diaphragm，to bulge outward 是不定式短语作 diaphragm 的宾语补足语。

Exercises

Ⅰ．Translate the following into English
1. 背景吸收
2. 电阻温度系数
3. 出口狭缝
4. 傅里叶变换红外光谱仪
5. 入射辐射线
6. 锗化铟

7. 能斯特灯

8. 参考比色皿

9. 扇形旋转反射镜

10. 碳化硅棒

Ⅱ. Translate the paragraph into Chinese

WQF-300 FTIR Spectrometer

Features

(1) The WQF-300 uses wedge refractive scanning TRANSEPT-Ⅲ interferometer instead of the common Michlson interferometer.

(2) The WQF-300 structure employs building blocks mode which can be assembled in many ways to suit your specific needs.

(3) Data processing CPU 80486, rich software and various national special used FTIR spectrum library.

(4) Motional mechanism comprised of electromagnetic driver and precision mechanical guiding improve the requirement of operating environment for avoiding inconvenience caused by air-bearing.

Specifications

(1) Spectral Range: 4400—400cm^{-1}

(2) Resolution: 1.5cm^{-1}

(3) Wavenumber precision: ±0.01

(4) Scanning speed: automatically optimized for resolution and detector type 0.2—1.5cm/s

(5) Signal to RMS noise: Better than 10000 : 1

(6) Detector: DTGS standard, MCT optional

(7) IR source: High-efficiency reflex sphere source is standard

(8) FTIR Accessories: GC/IF interface, ATR, Diffuse/specular reflectance and micro cell etc.

Ⅲ. Translate the passage into Chinese

Spectrum 100 FTIR Spectrometer

Product details

The PerkinElmer Spectrum^{TM} 100 FT-IR spectrometer is the gold standard for research, materials testing and academia. The system's high sensitivity, sampling speed, and stability, backed by PerkinElmer's knowledge, experience and responsive service and support, enable laboratories to achieve the highest quality and reproducible results with ease. Nowhere else will you receive the same confidence in an Infrared system than with the PerkinElmer Spectrum 100 FT-IR system.

Technical Specifications

PerkinElmer FT-IR spectrometers are built to the highest manufacturing standards. Our technical specifications document presents confirmed performance specifications based on 100% product factory testing. All instruments will meet or achieve better than the confirmed specifications, under normal conditions of use as described in the user manual.

Features/Benefits

Exclusive source design for accurate, repeatable measurements

Go button and LCD display for increased productivity and ease-of-use

Smart, zero-alignment, modular accessories for quick, predictable and reproducible sampling

Intuitive software ensures easy and consistent operation

Atmospheric Vapor Compensation (AVC) enhances accuracy and precision

Absolute Virtual Instrument (AVI) standardizes the instrument's wavenumber scale to a far higher accuracy than can be achieved with conventional calibration methods

Spectrum software provides intuitive user operation and helps ensure consistent results, day-to-day, user-to-user

FTIR & FT-NIR Spectrometers

Defining the standards for FTIR technology for over 60 years, PerkinElmer is an experienced and knowledgeable supplier of FT-IR and FT-NIR spectrometers for laboratories worldwide. By taking a comprehensive quality approach — from product design, development and manufacturing through to customer service and support -PerkinElmer provides the highest quality FT-IR and FT-NIR systems, along with the most accurate and reproducible results in the industry.

Reading Materials

Water Pollution and Pollutants

Micororganisms（微生物） Wherever there is suitable food, sufficient moisture, and an appropriate temperature, microorganisms will thrive. Sewage（污水）provides an ideal environment for a vast array of microbes（微生物）, primarily bacteria（细菌）, plus some viruses（病毒）and protozoa（原生动物）. Most of these microorganisms in wastewater are harmless and can be employed in biological processes to convert organic matter to stable end products. However, sewage may also contain pathogens（病原体）from the excreta（排泄物）of people with infectious diseases that can be transmitted by contaminated（污染的）water. Waterborne（水上的）bacterial diseases such as cholera（霍乱）, typhoid（伤寒）, and tuberculosis（肺结核）, viral（过滤性毒菌引起的）diseases such as infectious hepatitis（肝炎）, and the protozoan-caused dysentery（痢疾）, while seldom a problem now in developed countries, are still a threat where properly treated water is not available for public use. Tests for the few pathogens that might be present are difficult and time consuming, and standard practice is to test for other more plentiful organisms that are always present (in the billions) in the intestines（肠）of warm-blooded animals, including humans.

Solids The total solids (organic plus inorganic) in wastewater are, by definition, the residues（残渣）after the liquid portion has been evaporated and the remainder dried to a constant weight at 103℃. Differentiation（区别）between dissolved solids and undissolved, that is, suspended solids is accomplished by evaporating filtered and unfiltered wastewater samples. The difference in weight between the two dried samples indicates the suspended solids content. To further categorize the residues, they are held at 550℃ for 15 minutes. The ash remaining is considered to represent inorganic solids and the loss of volatile matter to be a measure of the organic content.

Suspended solids (SS) and volatile suspended solids (VSS) are the most useful. SS and BOD (biochemical oxygen demand) are used as measures of wastewater strength (废水浓度) and process performance (处理结果). VSS can be an indicator of the organic content of raw wastes and can also provide a measure of the active microbial population (活性微生物群体) in biological processes.

Inorganic constituents　　The common inorganic constituents of wastewater include:

1. Chlorides and sulphates. Normally present in water and in wastes from humans.

2. Nitrogen and phosphorous (磷). In their various forms (organic and inorganic) in wastes from humans, with additional phosphorous from detergents (洗涤剂).

3. Carbonates (碳酸盐) and bicarbonates (碳酸氢盐). Normally present in water and wastes as calcium (钙) and magnesium (镁) salts.

4. Toxic substances. Arsenic (砷), cyanide (氰化物), and heavy metals such as Cd, Cr, Cu, Hg, Pb, and Zn are toxic inorganics which may be found in industrial wastes.

In addition to these chemical constituents, the concentration of dissolved gases, especially oxygen, and the hydrogen ion concentration expressed as pH are other parameters (参数) of interest in wastewater.

Organic matter　　Proteins and carbohydrates (碳水化合物) constitute 90 percent of the organic matter in domestic sewage. The sources of these biodegradable (生物能够分解的) contaminants include excreta (排泄物) and urine (尿) from humans; food wastes from sinks; soil and dirt from bathing, washing, and laundering (洗烫); plus various soaps, detergents, and other cleaning products.

Unit 15　Mass Spectrometer

The basic principle

If something is moving and you subject it to a sideways force, instead of moving in a straight line, it will move in a curve - deflected out of its original path by the sideways force[1].

The amount of deflection you will get for a given sideways force depends on the mass of the ball. If you knew the speed of the ball and the size of the force, you could calculate the mass of the ball if you knew what sort of curved path it was deflected through[2]. The less the deflection, the heavier the ball.

You can apply exactly the same principle to atomic sized particles.

An outline of what happens in a mass spectrometer

Atoms can be deflected by magnetic fields - provided the atom is first turned into an ion. Electrically charged particles are affected by a magnetic field although electrically neutral ones aren't.

The sequence is as follows.

Stage 1: Ionization

The atom is ionized by knocking one or more electrons off to give a positive ion. This is true even for things which you would normally expect to form negative ions (chlorine, for example) or never form ions at all (argon, for example). Mass spectrometers always work with positive ions.

Stage 2: Acceleration

The ions are accelerated so that they all have the same kinetic energy.

Stage 3: Deflection

The ions are then deflected by a magnetic field according to their masses. The lighter

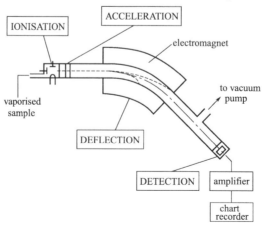

Figure 15-1　A full diagram of a mass spectrometer

they are, the more they are deflected.

The amount of deflection also depends on the number of positive charges on the ion—in other words, on how many electrons were knocked off in the first stage[3]. The more the ion is charged, the more it gets deflected.

Stage 4: Detection

The beam of ions passing through the machine is detected electrically.

A full diagram of a mass spectrometer is illustrated in Figure 15-1.

Understanding what's going on

The need for a vacuum

It's important that the ions produced in the ionization chamber have a free run through the machine without hitting air molecules.

Ionization

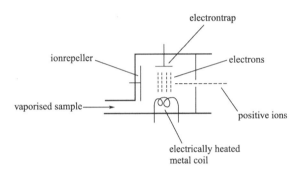

Figure 15-2 A diagram of ionization

A diagram of ionization is illustrated in Figure 15-2. The vaporized sample passes into the ionization chamber. The electrically heated metal coil gives off electrons which are attracted to the electron trap which is a positively charged plate[4].

The particles in the sample (atoms or molecules) are therefore bombarded with a stream of electrons, and some of the collisions are energetic enough to knock one or more electrons out of the sample particles to make positive ions.

Most of the positive ions formed will carry a charge of $^+1$ because it is much more difficult to remove further electrons from an already positive ion.

These positive ions are persuaded out into the rest of the machine by the ion repeller which is another metal plate carrying a slight positive charge.

Acceleration

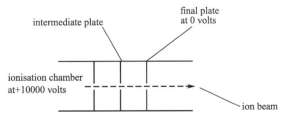

Figure 15-3 A diagram of acceleration

A diagram of acceleration is illustrated in Figure 15-3. The positive ions are repelled away from the very positive ionization chamber and pass through three slits, the final one of which is at 0 volts. The middle slit carries some intermediate voltage. All the ions are accelerated into a finely focused beam.

Deflection

Different ions are deflected by the magnetic field by different amounts. The amount of deflection depends on:

(1) the mass of the ion. Lighter ions are deflected more than heavier ones.

(2) the charge on the ion. Ions with 2 (or more) positive charges are deflected more than ones with only 1 positive charge.

These two factors are combined into the *mass/charge ratio*. Mass/charge ratio is given the symbol m/z (or sometimes m/e).

For example, if an ion had a mass of 28 and a charge of 1^+, its mass/charge ratio would be 28. An ion with a mass of 56 and a charge of 2^+ would also have a mass/charge ratio of 28.

In the Figure 15-4, ion stream A is most deflected - it will contain ions with the smallest mass/charge ratio. Ion stream C is the least deflected - it contains ions with the greatest mass/charge ratio.

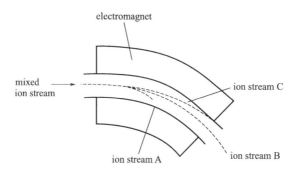

Figure 15-4 A diagram of deflection

It makes it simpler to talk about this if we assume that the charge on all the ions is 1^+. Most of the ions passing through the mass spectrometer will have a charge of 1^+, so that the mass/charge ratio will be the same as the mass of the ion[5].

Assuming 1^+ ions stream A has the lightest ions, stream B the next lightest and stream C the heaviest. Lighter ions are going to be more deflected than heavy ones.

Detection

Only ion stream B makes it right through the machine to the ion detector. The other ions collide with the walls where they will pick up electrons and be neutralized. Eventually, they get removed from the mass spectrometer by the vacuum pump.

When an ion hits the metal box, its charge is neutralized by an electron jumping from the metal on to the ion (as shown in Figure 15-5). That leaves a space amongst the electrons in the metal, and the electrons in the wire shuffle along to fill it.

A flow of electrons in the wire is detected as an electric current which can be amplified and recorded. The more ions arrives, the greater the current.

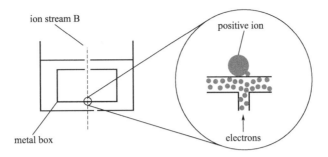

Figure 15-5　A diagram of detection

Detecting the other ions

How might the other ions be detected - those in streams A and C which have been lost in the machine?

Remember that stream A was most deflected - it has the smallest value of m/z (the lightest ions if the charge is 1^+). To bring them on to the detector, you would need to deflect them less - by using a smaller magnetic field (a smaller sideways force).

To bring those with a larger m/z value (the heavier ions if the charge is $+1$) on to the detector you would have to deflect them more by using a larger magnetic field.

What the mass spectrometer output looks like

The output from the chart recorder is usually simplified into a "stick diagram". This shows the relative current produced by ions of varying mass/charge ratio.

The "stick diagram" for molybdenum is shown is Figure 15-6.

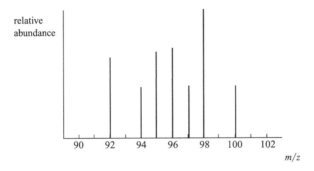

Figure 15-6　The "stick diagram" for molybdenum

You may find diagrams in which the vertical axis is labeled as either "relative abundance" or "relative intensity". Whichever is used, it means the same thing. The vertical scale is related to the current received by the chart recorder - and so to the number of ions arriving at the detector: the greater the current, the more abundant the ion.

As you will see from the diagram, the commonest ion has a mass/charge ratio of 98. Other ions have mass/charge ratios of 92, 94, 95, 96, 97 and 100.

That means that molybdenum consists of 7 different isotopes. Assuming that the ions all have a charge of 1^+, which means that the masses of the 7 isotopes on the carbon-12 scale are 92, 94, 95, 96, 97, 98 and 100.

New Words and Phrases

acceleration [ækˌseləˈreiʃən] *n.* 加速度，加速
bombard [ˈbɔmbɑːd] *vt.* 炮轰，轰击
calculate [ˈkælkjuleit] *v.* 计算，推算
collision [kəˈliʒən] *n.* 碰撞，冲突
curve [kəːv] *n.* 曲线，曲线图表 *vt.* 弯，使弯曲
deflect [diˈflekt] *v.* （使）偏斜，（使）偏转
deflection [diˈflekʃən] *n.* 偏斜，偏转，偏差
isotope [ˈaisəutəup] *n.* 同位素
label [ˈleibl] *n.* 标签，商标 *vt.* 贴标签于，分类，标注
molybdenum [məˈlibdinəm] *n.* 钼
neutral [ˈnjuːtrəl] *n.* 中立者 *adj.* 中性的
neutralize [ˈnjuːtrəlaiz；(US) nuː-] *v.* 中和，使中和
outline [ˈəutlain] *n.* 大纲，轮廓，略图
provided [prəːˈvaidid] *conj.* 倘若
repeller [riˈpel] *n.* 排斥
shuffle [ˈʃʌfl] *n.* 改变位置，移动
sideway [ˈsaidwei] *n.* 小路，人行道 *adj.* 侧面，旁边
subject [ˈsʌbdʒikt] *vt.* 使屈从于……，使隶属
trap [træp] *n.* 陷阱

bombard with   用……轰炸
charged particle   带电粒子
chart recorder   绘图仪
collide with   同……发生冲突
deflect out of   偏离
electron trap   电子捕获
in other words   换句话说
ionization chamber   电离室
kinetic energy   动能
knock...off   除掉，消除
mass spectrometer   质谱仪
mass/charge ratio   质荷比
negative ion   负离子
positively charged plate   正极
relative abundance   相对丰度
relative intensity   相对强度
sideways force   侧向力
stick diagram   棒图
straight line   直线
subject...to   使……服从，使……遭受
vacuum pump   真空泵
work with   与……共事，与……合作，对……起作用

Notes

1. If something is moving and you subject it to a sideways force, instead of moving in a straight line, it will move in a curve - deflected out of its original path by the sideways force.
   本句为真实条件句,条件句为并列句。deflected...force 补充说明主句 it will move in a curve。

2. If you knew the speed of the ball and the size of the force, you could calculate the mass of the ball if you knew what sort of curved path it was deflected through.
   本句为双条件虚拟句。

3. The amount of deflection also depends on the number of positive charges on the ion—in other words, on how many electrons were knocked off in the first stage.
   on how...stage 省略了前一句的主谓部分 The amount of deflection also depends。

4. The electrically heated metal coil gives off electrons which are attracted to the electron trap which is a positively charged plate.
   which...trap 定语从句修饰 electrons,而 which...plate 为定语从句修饰前一定语从句中的 trap。

5. Most of the ions passing through the mass spectrometer will have a charge of 1^+, so that the mass/charge ratio will be the same as the mass of the ion.
   passing...spectrometer 现在分词短语作定语修饰 ions,so that...ion 为结果状语从句。

Exercises

Ⅰ. Translate the following into English
1. 带电粒子
2. 电子捕获
3. 电离室
4. 质谱仪
5. 质荷比
6. 正极
7. 相对丰度
8. 侧向力
9. 棒图
10. 真空泵

Ⅱ. Translate the paragraph into Chinese

GC/MS

A mass spectrometer creates charged particles (ions) from molecules. It then analyzes those ions to provide information about the molecular weight of the compound and its chemical structure. There are many types of mass spectrometers and sample introduction techniques which allow a wide range of analyses. This discussion will focus on mass spectrometry as it's used in the powerful and widely used method of coupling Gas Chromatography (GC) with Mass Spectrometry (MS). A mixture of compounds to be analyzed is initially injected into the GC where the mixture is vaporized in a heated chamber. The gas mixture travels through a GC column, where the compounds become separated as they interact with the column.

Reading Materials

Types of Solid Wastes

Food Wastes　Food wastes are the animal, fruit, or vegetable residues resulting from the handling, preparation, cooking, and eating of foods (also called garbage). The most important characteristic of these wastes is that they are highly putrescible (易腐烂的) and will decompose rapidly, especially in warm weather. Often, decomposition will lead to the development of offensive odors (刺鼻的气味). In many locations, the putrescible nature of these wastes will significantly influence the design and operation of the solid waste collection system. In addition to the amounts of food wastes generated at residences, considerable amounts are generated at cafeterias (自助餐厅) and restaurants, large institutional facilities (组织机构) such as hospitals and prisons, and facilities associated with the marketing of foods, including wholesale and retail (批发和零售) stores and markets.

Rubbish　Rubbish consists of combustible and noncombustible solid wastes of household, institutions, commercial activities, etc., excluding food wastes or other highly putrescible material. Typically, combustible rubbish consists of materials such as paper, cardboard, plastics, textiles, rubber, leather, wood, furniture, and garden trimmings (清理下来的东西). Noncombustible rubbish consists of items such as glass, crockery (陶瓷), tin cans, aluminum cans, ferrous and other nonferrous metals, and dirt.

Ashes and residues　Materials remaining from the burning of wood, coal, coke, and other combustible wastes in homes, stores, institutions, and industrial and municipal facilities for purposes of heating, cooking, and disposing of combustible wastes are categorized as ashes and residues. Residues from power plants normally are not included in this category. Ashes and residues are normally composed of fine, powdery materials, cinders (灰烬), clinkers (炉渣), and small amounts of burned and partially burned materials. Glass, crockery, and various metals are also found in the residues from municipal incinerators (焚化炉).

Demolition and construction Wastes　Wastes from razed (拆毁) buildings and other structures are classified as demolition (破坏) wastes. Wastes from the construction, remodeling (改造), and repairing of individual residences, commercial buildings, and other structures are classified as construction wastes. These wastes are often classified as rubbish. The quantities produced are difficult to estimate and variable in composition, but may include dirt, stones, concrete, bricks, plaster, lumber, shingles (屋顶板), and plumbing (铅管), heating, and electrical parts.

Hazardous Wastes　Chemical, biological, flammable, explosive, or radioactive wastes that pose a substantial danger, immediately or over time, to human, plant, or animal life are classified as hazardous. Typically, these wastes occur as liquids, but they are often found in the form of gases, solids, or sludges (污泥). In all cases, these wastes must be handled and disposed of with great care and caution.

Unit 16　Nuclear Magnetic Resonance Spectrometry

Introduction

Nuclear magnetic resonance spectrometry (NMR) involves measuring the absorption of radiofrequency radiation by a sample material that is placed in a strong magnetic field[1]. The radiation used is in the 100 MHz range. The magnetic fields are large; the most sophisticated instruments use some of the largest constant magnetic fields that can be generated.

The nuclei of many atoms possess a magnetic moment. This means that they act like small bar magnets—magnetic dipoles. The radiofrequency radiation is absorbed by the nuclear magnets which are thereby raised from their ground states to their excited states. As illustrated in Figure 16-1, the ground state is the energy level of the nucleus when the magnetic dipole is aligned along the magnetic field, and the excited state is the energy level when the magnetic dipole is aligned against the magnetic field[2]. Nuclei, such as those of hydrogen or C, behave as if they can be oriented in only these two ways. The orientation of a nuclear dipole is quantized.

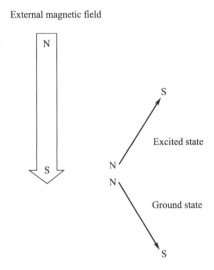

Figure 16-1　The spectroscopic transition for nuclear magnetic resonance

As in other spectrometries, the energy of the transition is determined by molecular and atomic properties, but in NMR spectroscopy, the energy also depends on the magnetic field. Also, as in other spectrometries, the magnitude of the power absorbed is proportional to the concentration of the absorbing species. Thus, for a sample containing protons, if we excite the proton nuclei, the signal that is measured is proportional to the number of protons in the sample. This is the basis of the measurement in the NMR application.

The nuclei are sitting in the middle of the electron clouds of their atoms. It may seem surprising, but as far as the nuclear magnet is concerned, this is an isolated environment. Once the radiofrequency energy excites the nuclei from the ground to the excited state, they stay in the excited state for a relatively long time: up to seconds. When we measure the number of nuclei returning to the ground state in an experiment, the signal looks like a change in concentration with first-order kinetics. The characteristic time associated with this first-order rate process is called the relaxation time. For more advanced techniques in NMR, this is an extremely important quantity.

NMR Instruments and Samples

The NMR signal from a sample has approximately the same magnitude as random noise generated by the sample itself in the instrument. Obtaining routine NMR spectra requires sophisticated electronics. The methods of construction and optimization of NMR instrument response is a topic of advanced study.

More sophisticated NMR instruments use pulses of radiofrequency radiation to excite the protons in the sample. Then they collect data of the type illustrated in the application. The NMR spectrum is constructed from these data. The mathematical relationship between the output over time and the output displayed with frequency/ field is called a Fourier transform. Instruments of this latter type are called *Fourier transrorm NMR spectrometers*, abbreviated FT-NMR. The type of NMR spectrometer described below is called a continuous wave spectrometer, abbreviated CW-NMR. CW-NMR instruments are still quite widely used.

The major features of an NMR instrument are illustrated in Figure 16-2. The instrument consists of a radiofrequency source that is extremely stable in both frequency and power, a highly sensitive radiofrequency receiver, and a magnet that produces a steady, strong field[3]. Of course, a method of recording the spectrum is required. This is usually a recorder, which is used to plot the energy absorbed versus the chemical shift.

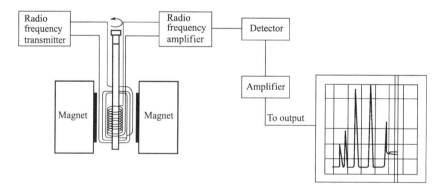

Figure 16-2 A general NMR machine.

The sample in a common NMR experiment consists of a relatively concentrated solution of the solid or liquid being investigated. If the sample is a liquid, it is best to use the pure liquid. The most sensitive CW instruments can obtain a spectrum in a few minutes with a mg of sample, close to the lower limit for CW ^{1}H-NMR. The more commonly available instruments require 10 mg of sample for proton NMR. The sample is placed in the bottom of a precisely cylindrical tube 5 mm in diameter to a depth of 2—3 cm. Standard tubes are 20—25 cm long (If the tube is not precise in its shape, the spinning side-bands are enhanced and may even be larger than the absorption peaks). This tube is spun around its long axis in the sample compartment. The reason for spinning the sample is to average out some of the imperfections in the constant magnetic field. This is critical because the resolution of the spectrum depends on the quality (the homogeneity) of the magnetic field.

To obtain an NMR spectrum, either the field can be scanned at a constant radiofrequency or the frequency can be scanned with a fixed field value[4]. In most contemporary instruments, the frequency is varied, and the output is plotted as if the field were scanned. This scanning frequency is generated by using a second oscillator that operates at about 1 kHz—in the region of audiofrequencies. The outputs from the audiofrequency oscillator and the locked-in radiofrequency oscillators are mixed to produce a sum of the two frequencies (the details of frequency mixing can be found in more advanced references). In this way, a very stable and precisely measurable frequency can be generated to obtain precise measurements of relative chemical shifts. The audiofrequency oscillator can be scanned over a wide enough range to obtain a spectrum. For ^1H, this is, as you have seen, about 1000 Hz.

The radiofequency radiant energy is transmitted to the sample through a coil surrounding the sample tube, as shown in Figure 16-2. In essence, the energy is absorbed and reradiated by the sample. This radiation is detected and amplified by sophisticated noise-rejecting amplifiers and put out as the output signal. When an NMR absorption is reached, less power is reradiated by the sample, and the difference shows up as a peak (which is really a dip) in the spectrum output. The power is lost through a nonradiative process, as is the case in other spectral regions. For the best results, the magnet, transmitter coil, and detector coil are perpendicular to each other.

General application and principle of NMR Spectrometry

In fact, the most customary application of NMR is determining organic molecule structures. For such studies, spectra of radiofrequency-energy absorption are measured and not the time dependence of the signal.

The frequency at which the absorption of energy occurs in an NMR experiment depends on two factors:

1. The identity of the nucleus;
2. The magnetic field strength.

New words and Phrases

align [əˈlain] *vi.* 排列 *vt.* 使成一行
audiofrequency [ˌɔːdiəˈfriːkwənsi] *n.* 音频
compartment [kəmˈpɑːtmənt] *n.* 舱,室,(分隔)间,箱
dip [dip] *n.* 俯角,倾向,偏角
dipole [ˈdaipəul] *n.* 偶极
essence [ˈesns] *n.* 本质,要素,特性

homogeneity [ˌhɔməudʒeˈniːiti]   *n.* 同种，同质，均匀性
imperfection [ˌimpəˈfekʃən]   *n.* 不完整性，不足，缺点，缺陷
moment [ˈməumənt]   *n.* 力矩
nonradiative [ˈnɔnˈreidieitiv]   *adj.* 非辐射的，不辐射的
nuclei [ˈnjuːkliai]   nucleus 的复数形   *n.* 原子核，核子
orientation [ˌɔ(ː)rienˈteiʃən]   *n.* 方向，方位，倾向性
oscillator [ˈɔsileitə]   *n.* 振荡器
perpendicular [ˌpəːpənˈdikjulə]   *adj.* 垂直的，正交的
proton [ˈprəutɔn]   *n.* 质子
quantize [ˈkwɔntaiz]   *v.* 使量子化
random [ˈrændəm]   *adj.* 任意的，随便的
relaxation [ˌriːlækˈseiʃən]   *n.* 松弛，放宽，娱乐
resonance [ˈrezənəns]   *n.* 反响，谐振，共振
sophisticated [səˈfistikeitid]   *adj.* 复杂的，精致的
spectroscopic [ˌspektrəˈskɔpik]   *adj.* 分光镜的
absorption peak   吸收峰
as far as...is concerned   就……而言
be perpendicular to   与……垂直
chemical shift   化学位移
constant radiofrequency   恒定射频
excited state   激发态
fixed field value   固定磁场值
Fourier transform NMR spectrometer   傅里叶变换光谱仪
ground state   基态
in essence   本质上，大体上，其实
locked-in   *adj.* 牢固的，固定的
magnetic dipole   磁偶极
magnetic field   磁场
magnetic moment   磁矩
noise-rejecting   抗噪声
nuclear magnet   核磁体
nuclear magnetic resonance spectrometry   核磁共振光谱法
radiant energy   辐射能
radiofrequency oscillator   射频振荡器
radiofrequency radiation   射频辐射
relaxation time   松弛时间，弛豫时间
spinning side-band   旋转边频

Notes

1. Nuclear magnetic resonance spectrometry (NMR) involves measuring the absorption of radiofrequency radiation by a sample material that is placed in a strong magnetic field. measuring...material 动名词短语作动词 involves 的宾语，that...field 为定语从句修饰 material。

2. As illustrated in Figure16-1, the ground state is the energy level of the nucleus when the magnetic dipole is aligned along the magnetic field, and the excited state is the energy level when the magnetic dipole is aligned against the magnetic field.

此句为并列复合句,两个 when...field 从句分别为第一分句和第二分句的时间状语。

3. The instrument consists of a radiofrequency source that is extremely stable in both frequency and power, a highly sensitive radiofrequency receiver, and a magnet that produces a steady, strong field.

consists of 的并列宾语为 source, receiver 和 magnet, that...power 为定语从句修饰 source, 定语从句 that...field 修饰 magnet。

4. To obtain an NMR spectrum, either the field can be scanned at a constant radiofrequency or the frequency can be scanned with a fixed field value.

either...or...引导两个并列分句, either...or...意思为:"要么……,要么……"

Exercises

I. Translate the following into English
1. 化学位移
2. 恒定射频
3. 激发态
4. 基态
5. 磁偶极
6. 磁矩
7. 核磁体
8. 辐射能
9. 射频振荡器
10. 射频辐射

II. Translate the paragraph into Chinese

Nuclear Magnetic Resonance Spectrometer

The nuclei of certain isotopes behave as though they are bar magnets. Two of the more relevant nuclei are hydrogen-1 and carbon-13. When compounds containing these isotopes are placed in a strong external magnetic field, the nuclear magnets orient parallel to the external field. Irradiating them with electromagnetic energy in the radio part of the spectrum causes them to flip in the opposite direction. When they return to the lower energy orientation, the added energy is emitted as a photon. The energy of the photon is characteristic of the environment of the nucleus being observed. An instrument known as a Nuclear Magnetic Resonance (NMR) Spectrometer is designed to allow the observation of the nuclei as they relax from resonance. The NMR spectrometer excites the nuclei and then observes the signal as the energy of the nuclei decays back to the ground state.

Reading Materials

POPs Problems in the World (I)

Although the terms POPs and Persistent Organic Pollutants were not coined (invent use) until years later, Rachel Carson's 1962 classic *Silent Spring* described the deleterious effects（害处）of a number of pesticides（杀虫剂，农药）that were later shown to be POPs, including DDT, aldrin［艾氏剂：一种剧毒杀虫剂，根据德国化学家 K. Alder (1902—1958) 的姓命名］and dieldrin（狄氏剂，杀虫剂）. Several toxic（有毒的）and persistent（残留，作用持久地）pesticides eventually recognized as POPs were banned by industrialized countries in the 1960s and 70s. It was thought at the time that such national measures would effectively limit or abolish（消除）the problem associated with these chemicals. However, environmental monitoring programmes gradually made it clear that, after an initial decline, concentrations in the environment were not declining further. It also became clear that some populations, such as the Inuit Eskimos（因纽特人）, are at particular risk because there are high concentrations of some POPs in their traditional staple foods（主要食物）.

What are POPs and why they can cause serious problems?

POPs stands for Persistent Organic Pollutants（残留有机污染物）that is, poisonous substances that persist or hang about in the environment. They come mostly from fertilisers（化肥）, pesticides and industrial waste. Problems arise because they are taken in by plants and animals, which we, or other animals, eat.

Some human populations, such as the Inuit who eat salmon（大麻哈鱼）and seal（海豹）, receive more than the Tolerable Daily Intake established by the World Health Organization（WHO）. One single meal may contain as much as 100 times the acceptable daily intake. Breast-fed infants may also easily exceed the acceptable intake. The effects of consuming POPs can be serious, including harmful effects on fertility（生育能力）and embryo development（胚胎发育）, damage to the nervous system（神经系统）and cancer.

The problems

Persistent organic pollutants are among the most dangerous chemicals ever created by humans. POPs chemicals include many pesticides, industrial chemicals and chemical byproducts（化学副产品）. Despite their different uses and origins, all POPs share basic characteristics that make them an urgent global environmental health problem.

POPs break down（浓度降低）very slowly in soil, air, water and living organisms（生物）, and persist in the environment for long periods of time.

POPs concentrate in（聚集在）the food chain（食物链）, building up to high levels in the tissues（肌体组织）of all living creatures, including humans.

POPs travel long distances in global air and water currents, and concentrate in high-latitude（高纬度地区）, low-temperature regions of the globe.

POPs are linked with serious health effects in humans and other species, including reproductive（生殖）and developmental（生长发育）illnesses, immune suppression（免疫功能紊乱）, nervous system disorders, cancers and hormone disruption（激素分泌紊乱）.

(Continued on page 122)

PART THREE INTRODUCTION OF CHEMICAL EQUIPMENT

Unit 17 Crystallization Equipment

Commercial crystallizers may operate either continuously or batch-wise. Except for special applications, continuous operation is preferred. The first requirement of any crystallizer is to create a supersaturated solution, because crystallization cannot occur without supersaturation. Three methods are used to produce supersaturation, depending primarily on the nature of the solubility curve of the solute. (1) Solutes like potassium nitrate and sodium sulfite are much less soluble at low temperatures than at high temperatures, so supersaturation can be produced simply by cooling. (2) When the solubility is almost independent of temperature, as with common salt, or diminishes as the temperature is raised, supersaturation is developed by evaporation. (3) In intermediate cases a combination of evaporation and cooling is effective. Sodium nitrate, for example, may be satisfactorily crystallized by cooling without evaporation, evaporation without cooling, or a combination of cooling and evaporation.

Vacuum crystallizers

Most modern crystallizers fall in the category of vacuum units in which adiabatic evaporative cooling is used to create supersaturation. In its original and simplest form, such a crystallizer is a closed vessel in which a vacuum is maintained by a condenser usually with the help of a steam-jet vacuum pump, or booster, placed between the crystallizer and the condenser[1]. A warm saturated solution at a temperature well above the boiling point at the pressure in the crystallizer is fed to the vessel. A magma volume is maintained by controlling the level of the liquid and crystallizing solid in the vessel, and the space above the magma is used for release of vapor and elimination of entrainment. The feed solution cools spontaneously to the equilibrium temperature; since both the enthalpy of cooling and the enthalpy of crystallization appear as enthalpy of vaporization, a portion of the solvent evaporates. The supersaturation generated by both cooling and evaporation causes nucleation and growth. Product magma is drawn from the bottom of the crystallizer. The theoretical yield of crystals is proportional to the difference between the concentration of the feed and the solubility of the solute at equilibrium temperature.

Figure 17-1 shows a continuous vacuum crystallizer with the conventional auxiliary units for feeding the unit and processing the product magma. The essential action of a single body is much like that of a single-effect evaporator, and in fact these units can be operated in multiple effect. The magma circulates from the cone bottom of the crystallizer body through a downpipe to a low-speed low-head circulating pump, passes upward through a vertical tubular heater with condensing steam in the shell, and thence into the body[2]. The heated stream enters through a tangential inlet just below the level of the magma surface. This imparts a swirling motion to the magma, which facilitates flash evaporation and equilibrates the magma with the vapor through the action of an adiabatic flash. The supersaturation thus generated provides the driving potential for nucleation and growth. The volume of the magma divided by the volumetric flow rate of magma through the slurry pump gives the average residence time.

Feed solution enters the downpipe before the suction of the circulating pump.

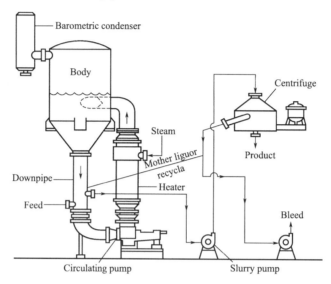

Figure 17-1　A continuous vacuum crystallizer

Mother liquor and crystals are drawn off through a discharge pipe upstream from the feed inlet in the downpipe. Mother liquor is separated from the crystals in a continuous centrifuge; the crystals are taken off as a product or for further processing, and the mother liquor is recycled to the downpipe. Some of the mother liquor is bled from the system by a pump to prevent accumulation of impurities.

The simple form of vacuum crystallizer has serious limitations from the stand-point of crystallization. Under the low pressure existing in the unit, the effect of static head on the boiling point is important; for example, water at 7℃ has a vapor pressure of 7.6 mmHg, which is a pressure easily obtainable by steam-jet boosters[3]. A static head of 300mm increases the absolute pressure to 30mmHg, where the boiling point of water is 29℃. Feed at this temperature would not flash if admitted at any level more than 300mm below the surface of the magma. Admission of the feed at a point where it does not flash, as in Figure 17-1, is advantageous in controlling nucleation.

Because of the effect of static head, evaporation and cooling occur only in the liquid layer near the magma surface, and concentration and temperature gradients near the surface are formed. Also crystals tend to settle to the bottom of the crystallizer, where there may be little or no supersaturation. The crystallizer will not operate satisfactorily unless the magma is well agitated, to equalize concentration and temperature gradients and suspend the crystals. The simple vacuum crystallizer provides no good method for nucleation control, for classification, or for removal of excess nuclei and very small crystals.

Draft tube-baffle crystallizer

A more versatile and effective equipment is the draft tube-baffle (DTB) crystallizer. The crystallizer body is equipped with a draft tube, which also acts as a baffle to control the circulation of the magma, and an upward-directed propeller agitator to provide a controllable circulation within the crystallizer. An additional circulation system, outside the crystallizer body and driven by a circulation pump, contains the heater and feed inlet. Product slurry is removed through an outlet near the bottom of the conical lower section of the crystallizer body. For a given feed rate, both the internal and external circulations are independently variable and provide controllable variables for obtaining the required CSD.

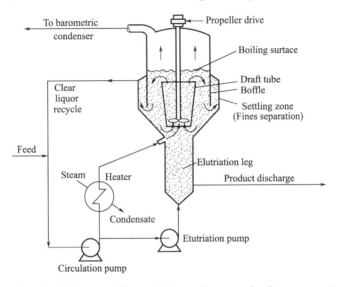

Figure 17-2 Draft tube-baffle crystallizer with internal system for fines separation and removal

Draft tube-baffle crystallizers can be equipped with an elutriation leg below the body to classify the crystals by size and may also be equipped with a baffled settling zone for fines removal. An example of such a unit is shown in Figure 17-2. Part of the circulating liquor is pumped to the leg and used as a hydraulic sorting fluid to carry small crystals back into the crystallizing zone for further growth. The discharge slurry is withdrawn from the lower part of the elutriation leg and sent to a filter or centrifuge, and the mother liquor is returned to the crystallizer.

Unwanted nuclei are removed by providing an annular space, or jacket, by enlarging the cone bottom and using the lower wall of the crystallizer body as a baffle. The annular space provides a settling zone, in which hydraulic classification separates fine crystals from larger ones by floating them in an upward-flowing stream of mother liquor, which is withdrawn from the top of the settling zone. The fine crystals so withdrawn are 60-mesh in size or smaller, and although their number is huge, their mass is small, so that the stream from the jacket is nearly solids free. When this stream, called the clear liquor recycle, is mixed with the fresh feed and pumped through a steam heater, the solution becomes unsaturated and most of the tiny crystals dissolve. The liquor, now essentially clear, is rapidly mixed with the slurry circulating in the main body of the crystallizer.

By removing a large fraction of the mother liquor from the jacket in this fashion, the magma density is sharply increased. Magma densities of 30 to 50 percent, based on the ratio of the volume of settled crystals to that of the total magma, are achieved.

New Words and Phrases

adiabatic [ˌædiəˈbætik] *adj.* 绝热的，隔热的
baffle [ˈbæfl] *n.* 挡板
centrifuge [ˈsentrifjuːdʒ] *n.* 离心分离机
crystallization [ˈkristəlaiˈzeiʃən] *n.* 结晶化
crystallizer [ˈkristəlaizə] *n.* 结晶器
diminish [diˈminiʃ] *vt.* （使）减少，（使）变小
downpipe [ˈdaunpaip] *n.* 下流管
draft [drɑːft] *n.* 气流
elutriation [iˌluːtriˈeiʃən] *n.* 淘析，析出
feed [fiːd] *n.* 进料
hydraulic [haiˈdrɔːlik] *adj.* 水力的，水压的，液压的
intermediate [ˌintəˈmiːdjət] *adj.* 中间的 *n.* 媒介
liquor [ˈlikə] *n.* 液体
nucleation [ˌnjuːkliˈeiʃən] *n.* 成核现象，晶核形成
residence [ˈrezidəns] *n.* 滞留
slurry [ˈsləːri] *n.* 泥浆，浆
soluble [ˈsɔljubl] *adj.* 可溶的，可溶解的
static [ˈstætik] *adj.* 静态的，静止的
supersaturate [sjuːpəˈsætʃəreit] *vt.* 使过度饱和
supersaturation [ˈsjuːpəˌsætʃəˈreiʃən] *n.* 过度饱和
tangential [tænˈdʒenʃ(ə)l] *adj.* 切线的
upstream [ˈʌpˈstriːm] *adv.* 向上游，溯流，逆流地
volumetric [vɔljuˈmetrik] *adj.* 测定体积的
adiabatic flash　绝热闪蒸
average residence time　平均滞留时间
baffled settling zone　挡板沉降区
be proportional to　与……成正比
circulating pump　循环泵
crystallization equipment　结晶设备
draft tube-baffle crystallizer　导流管板结晶器
elutriation leg　析出段
feed inlet　进料口
hydraulic sorting fluid　液压分流
low-head circulating pump　低压头循环泵
mother liquor　母液
multiple effect　多效
single-effect　单效

slurry pump　浆液泵
solubility curve　溶解度曲线
stand-point　观点
static head　静压头
steam-jet　蒸汽喷嘴
tangential inlet　切向进口
vacuum crystallizer　真空结晶器
volumetric flow rate　体积流速

Notes

1. In its original and simplest form, such a crystallizer is a closed vessel in which a vacuum is maintained by a condenser usually with the help of a steam-jet vacuum pump, or booster, placed between the crystallizer and the condenser.
in which...condenser 定语从句修饰 vessel，其中 with...booster 为状语说明方式，placed...condenser 过去分词短语作定语修饰 vacuum pump, or booster。

2. The magma circulates from the cone bottom of the crystallizer body through a downpipe to a low-speed low-head circulating pump, passes upward through a vertical tubular heater with condensing steam in the shell, and thence into the body.
本句为简单句，主语为 The magma，并列谓语为 circulates，passes 和 passes into，只不过为了避免 pass 重复，passes into 中省略了 passes。

3. Under the low pressure existing in the unit, the effect of static head on the boiling point is important; for example, water at 7℃ has a vapor pressure of 7.6 mmHg, which is a pressure easily obtainable by steam-jet boosters
主句为 the effect...is important。which...boosters 非限制性定语从句修饰 7.6 mmHg。

Exercises

Ⅰ. Translate the following into English

1. 绝热闪蒸
2. 平均滞留时间
3. 导流管板结晶器
4. 进料口
5. 低压头循环泵
6. 母液
7. 浆液泵
8. 静压头
9. 真空结晶器
10. 体积流速

Ⅱ. Translate the paragraph into Chinese

Crystallization Systems & Crystallizers

In this activity, our work focuses on the crystallization of solutions and not on the melt crystallization. Our expertise covers the three types of crystallization process:

by concentration

by cooling (under vacuum or with a heat exchanger)

by reaction or equilibrium displacement

We possess the know-how and expertise for all types of crystallization equipment: with total or partial classification, involving the recirculation of the magma, with or without settling zones.

Different types of Crystallizers from GEA Evaporation Technologies (GEA Kestner): Forced Circulation Crystallizer, Oslo Type Crystallizer (classified-suspension crystallizer), DTB crystallizer (draft-tube-baffle crystallizer), Induced Circulation Crystallizer.

Reading Materials

(Continued from page 116)

POPs Problems in the World (Ⅱ)

In a few short decades, POPs have spread throughout the environment to threaten human health and damage land and water ecosystems (生态系统) all over the world. Every living organism on earth now carries measurable levels of POPs chemicals in its tissues.

Because POPs migrate to and build up (聚集) in colder climates, peoples and ecosystems of the Arctic and Antarctic face especially high risks from POPs.

There is strong evidence that exposure to even tiny amounts of POPs at critical periods (敏感期) can cause irreversible damage (无法恢复的伤害). The effects of such exposures can take years to appear and may be very subtle (隐秘的,难以发现的). Sometimes they first appear in the offspring (子女) of exposed parents. In mammals, exposure to POPs begins before birth, as POPs move across the mother's placenta (胎盘) to the developing fetus (胎儿,胚胎). After birth, more POPs are transferred into the tiny newborn's body through its mother's milk.

Because of their particular characteristics, production or use of POPs chemicals anywhere threatens people and the environment everywhere. Coordinated local, national and international efforts are urgently needed to eliminate POPs chemicals, reduce current levels of POPs contamination (污染) and protect future generations from ever greater harm (不断加剧的危害).

The Developing Country Situation

There is a genuine (确实的) lack of knowledge about POPs sources and releases in many developing countries. However, existing data from wildlife in Africa and other regions show concentrations of POPs equal to or higher than those in temperate (气候温暖) or cold regions. There are also occupational health problems (职业健康问题) related to the use of POPs in developing countries. Thus, POPs problems also occur in the countries or regions where they are used.

Border (边境) controls are sometimes ineffective, which can lead to illegal trade in banned POPs. The infrastructure (基础设施) for chemical management and enforcement is often weak and compliance with regulations limited. Pesticide POPs often become a cheap and quick alternative for subsistence (维持生计的) farmers with low levels of education and no modern equipment.

Indeed, many POPs pesticides are easy to use. They are not acutely toxic and thus do not appear overtly (公开的) hazardous. They do not require special knowledge or equipment. They only need to be applied once during a crop's growth cycle and the effect is immediate, visible and persisting. To persuade poor subsistence farmers to stop using these 'benefactors (帮他们拯救庄稼的恩人),' intimate (详细的) knowledge of local conditions and effective means of communicating information are needed. Economic measures such as subsidizing (给予补贴) the price of alternatives and offering training in new techniques are important.

Unit 18 Distillation Equipment

Distillation may be carried out by either of two principal methods. The first method is based on the production of a vapor by boiling the liquid mixture to be separated and condensing the vapors without allowing any liquid to return to the still[1]. There is then no reflux. The second method is based on the return of part of the condensate to the still under such conditions that this returning liquid is brought into intimate contact with the vapors on their way to the condenser[2].

Flash Distillation Plant

Flash distillation consists of vaporizing a definite fraction of liquid in such a way that the evolved vapor is in equilibrium with the residual liquid, separating the vapor from the liquid, and condensing the vapor[3]. Flash distillation is used most for separating components that boil at widely different temperatures. It is not effective in separating components of comparable volatility, which requires the use of distillation with reflux. Figure18-1 shows the elements of flash distillation plant. Feed is pumped by pump a through heater b, and the pressure is reduced through valve c. An intimate mixture of vapor and liquid enters the vapor separator d, in which sufficient time is allowed for the vapor and liquid portion to separate. Because of the intimacy of contact of liquid and vapor before separation, the separated streams are in equilibrium. Vapor leaves through line e and liquid through line g.

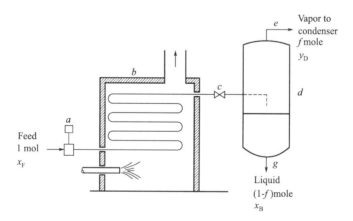

Figure 18-1 Plant for flash distillation

Flash distillation plant is a simple distillation equipment. It is used extensively in petroleum refining, in which petroleum fractions are heated in pipe stills and the heated fluid is flashed into vapor and residual liquid streams, each containing many components[4]. Liquid from an absorber is often flashed to recover some of the solute; liquid from a high-pressure reactor may be flashed to a lower pressure, causing some vapor to be evolved[5].

Distillation Tower

Distillation tower is used for continuous distillation to produce nearly pure products at both the top and bottom of the distillation tower. The feed is admitted to a plate in the central portion of the tower. If the feed is liquid, it flows down the tower to the reboiler and is stripped of component A by the vapor rising from the reboiler. By this means a bottom product can be produced which is nearly pure.

A distillation tower equipped with the necessary auxiliaries and containing rectifying and stripping sections is shown in Figure18-2[6]. Tower A is fed near its center with a steady flow of feed of definite concentration. Assume that the feed is a liquid at its boiling point. The action in the tower is not dependent on this assumption, and other conditions of the feed will be discussed. The plate on which the feed enters is called the feed plate. All plates above the feed plate constitute the rectifying section, all plates below the feed, including the feed plate itself, constitute the stripping section. The feed flows down the stripping section to the bottom of the tower, in which a definite level of liquid is maintained. Liquid flows by gravity to reboiler B, This is a steam-heated vaporizer that generates vapor and returns it to the bottom of the tower. The vapor passes up the entire tower. At one end of the reboiler is a weir. The bottom product is withdrawn from the pool of liquid on the downstream side of the weir and flows through the cooler G. This cooler also preheated the feed by heat exchange with the hot bottoms.

The vapors rising through the rectifying section are completely condensed in condenser

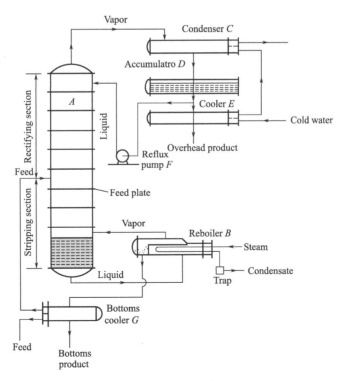

Figure 18-2 Continuous fractionating tower with rectifying and stripping sections

C, and the condensate is collected in accumulator D, in which a definite liquid level is maintained. Reflux pump F takes liquid from the accumulator and delivers it to the top plate of the power. This liquid stream is called reflux. It provides the downflow liquid in the rectifying section that is needed to act on the upflow vapor. Without the reflux, no rectification would occur in the rectifying section, and the concentration of the overhead product would be no greater than that of the vapor rising from the feed plate. Condensate not picked up by the reflux pump is cooled in heat exchanger E, called the product cooler, and withdrawn as the overhead product. If no azeotropes are encountered, both overhead and bottom products may be obtained in any desired purity if enough plates and adequate reflux are provided.

The plant shown in Figure18-2 is often simplified for small installations. In place of the reboiler, a heating coil may be placed in the bottom of the tower to generate vapor from the pool of liquid there. The condenser is sometimes placed above the top of the tower, and the reflux pump and accumulator are omitted. Reflux then returns to the top plate by gravity. A special valve, called a reflux splitter, may be used to control the rate of reflux return. The remainder of the condensate forms the overhead product.

New Words and Phrases

absorber [əb'sɔːbə] *n.* 吸收者，吸收器
accumulator [əˈkjuːmjuleitə] *n.* 蓄电池，收集器
azeotrope [əˈziːətrəup] *n.* 共沸混合物，恒沸物
comparable [ˈkɔmpərəbl] *adj.* 可比较的，比得上的
condensate [kɔnˈdenseit] *n.* 冷凝物
cooler [ˈkuːlə] *n.* 冷却器
distillation [ˌdistiˈleiʃən] *n.* 蒸馏，蒸馏法，蒸馏物
downflow [ˈdaunfləu] *n.* 向下流动，溢流管
flash [flæʃ] *n.* 闪光，闪现 *v.* 闪光，闪现，反射，使迅速传遍
fractionate [ˈfrækʃəneit] *vt.* 使分馏
intimacy [ˈintiməsi] *n.* 亲密
intimate [ˈintimit] *adj.* 亲密的，密切的
reboiler [riˈbɔilə] *n.* 再沸器
rectification [ˌrektifiˈkeiʃən] *n.* 精馏
rectify [ˈrektifai] *vt.* 精馏
reflux [ˈriːflʌks] *n.* 回流，逆流，退潮
remainder [riˈmeində] *n.* 残余，剩余物
residual [riˈzidjuəl] *adj.* 剩余的，残留的
still [stil] *n.* 蒸馏器，蒸馏釜
strip [strip] *vt.* 除去，剥去
upflow [ˈʌpfləu] *vi.* 向上流 *n.* 向上流动
weir [wiə] *n.* 堰，回流堰
a fraction of 一小部分
be flashed into 闪蒸为
be in equilibrium with 与……保持平衡

central portion 中部
continuous fractionating tower 连续精馏塔
distillation equipment 蒸馏设备
distillation tower 蒸馏塔
downflow liquid 下流液
feed plate 进料板
flash distillation 闪蒸
flash distillation plant 闪蒸设备
heating coil 蛇形加热管
high-pressure reactor 高压反应器
petroleum refining 炼油
pipe still 管式蒸馏釜
pool of liquid 蓄液池
rate of reflux return 回流液回流速度
rectifying section 精馏段
reflux pump 回流泵
reflux splitter 回流分配器
residual liquid 剩余液体
stripping section 提馏段
upflow vapor 上升蒸汽

Notes

1. The first method is based on the production of a vapor by boiling the liquid mixture to be separated and condensing the vapors without allowing any liquid to return to the still.
   名词短语 the production...separated 和动名词短语 condensing...still 分别作介词 on 的宾语。

2. The second method is based on the return of part of the condensate to the still under such conditions that this returning liquid is brought into intimate contact with the vapors on their way to the condenser.
   under such conditions 为主句的方式状语，that...condenser 为定语从句修饰 conditions。

3. Flash distillation consists of vaporizing a definite fraction of liquid in such a way that the evolved vapor is in equilibrium with the residual liquid, separating the vapor from the liquid, and condensing the vapor.
   动名词短语 vaporizing...liquid, separating...liquid 和 condensing the vapor 同为介词 of 的宾语。定语从句 that...liquid 修饰方式状语 in such a way 中的 way。

4. It is used extensively in petroleum refining, in which petroleum fractions are heated in pipe stills and the heated fluid is flashed into vapor and residual liquid streams, each containing many components.
   in which...streams 为非限制性定语从句修饰 petroleum refining，现在分词短语 each containing many components 则作状语说明 vapor 和 residual liquid streams。

5. Liquid from an absorber is often flashed to recover some of the solute; liquid from a high-pressure reactor may be flashed to a lower pressure, causing some vapor to be evolved.

本句为并列句,现在分词短语 causing...evolved 为伴随状语说明第二分句。

6. A distillation tower equipped with the necessary auxiliaries and containing rectifying and stripping sections is shown in Figure18-2.

过去分词短语 equipped...auxiliaries 和现在分词短语 containing...sections 同为定语修饰 A distillation tower。

Exercises

Ⅰ. Translate the following into English
1. 连续精馏塔
2. 进料板
3. 闪蒸
4. 蛇形加热管
5. 高压反应器
6. 管式蒸馏釜
7. 精馏段
8. 回流泵
9. 回流分配器
10. 提馏段

Ⅱ. Translate the paragraph into Chinese

Batch Distillation Column

Self-contained sieve plate distillation column unit including reboiler, condenser and reflux tank, suitable for use with flammable solvents and fully instrumented for batch operation.

Temperatures throughout the process including those on each and every sieve plate are monitored and displayed on a bench mounted control console, which also houses controls for the power supplied to the reboiler heater and for reflux ratio settings between 0 and 100%.

The front panel connections allow the use of standard laboratory recorders and data loggers and of industry-standard PID and PLC controllers.

A U-tube manometer is incorporated to measure pressure drop over the distillation column height.

The 50mm diameter sieve plate column may be readily interchanged with a packed column supplied as an alternative. A vacuum pump is included for reduced pressure operation. The unit is supplied completely assembled including lagging, and a comprehensive instruction manual describes commissioning, maintenance and instructional assignment.

Process Unit
Height: 2.25m
Width: 0.85m
Depth: 0.80m

Control Console
Height: 0.30m

Width: 0.52m
Depth: 0.40m

Ⅲ. Translate the passage into Chinese

Distillation

Distillation is a widely used method for separating mixtures based on differences in the conditions required to change the phase of components of the mixture. To separate a mixture of liquids, the liquid can be heated to force components, which have different boiling points, into the gas phase. The gas is then condensed back into liquid form and collected. Repeating the process on the collected liquid to improve the purity of the product is called double distillation. Although the term is most commonly applied to liquids, the reverse process can be used to separate gases by liquefying components using changes in temperature and/or pressure.

Distillation is used for many commercial processes, such as production of gasoline, distilled water, xylene, alcohol, paraffin, kerosene, and many other liquids.

Types of distillation include simple distillation (described here), fractional distillation (different volatile "fractions" are collected as they are produced), and destructive distillation (usually, a material is heated so that it decomposes into compounds for collection).

Applications

The chemical, pharmaceutical and food industries and also the field of environmental technology all use and handle a wide range of solvents and volatile compounds in quite differing ways.

Whether concentrating, cleaning or recovering, working with these solvents requires a high level of practical experience and a theoretical understanding of the chemical engineering principles underlying the processes of distillation, evaporation, stripping and rectification.

GEA Evaporation Technologies (GEA Wiegand) employs the latest computer programs and the most modern data banks in its design and planning, thereby simulating the plants in operation and achieving the best layout.

Our distillation Research and Development Center enables complex plant systems to be designed and optimum operating conditions to be established when handling less familiar materials or compounds.

GEA Evaporation Technologies can meet individual needs in finding the distillation solution to specific problems and can even supply a turnkey distillation plant with complete processing lines (e. g. for the manufacture of alcohol) including the required control installations with either conventional controls or the most up-to-date process control engineering. The individual units required in the product area of distillation technology are selected on the strength of many years' experience with vastly differing types of apparatus.

In addition to such well know types of evaporators as falling film, circulation, and stirrer, we use all proven column systems including packed columns, sieve, bubble cup, tunnel or valve trays.

Reading Materials

Chemical Weapons and Protective Measures

What You Need To Know

CWAs(Chemical Warfare Agents(化学试剂)are dangerous chemicals because they have very toxic(有毒有害的)or incapacitating(致残的)effects,and humans are their specific target. For example,some nerve agents(神经剂)are designed to kill in a very short time,while blister agents(水泡剂)are not quite as lethal(致死的). However,a positive aspect of most CWAs is that they live for only a very short time in the environment. They rapidly degrade(毒性降低)into relatively innocuous(无毒的)materials,especially in an aqueous(含水的)environment.

The Basics of Chemical Weaponry

A chemical weapon utilizes a manufactured chemical to incapacitate(致残),harm,or kill people. Strictly speaking,a chemical weapon relies on the physiological effects of a chemical. Although certain chemical weapons can be used to kill large numbers of people, other weapons are designed to injure or terrorize(恐吓)people. In addition to having potentially horrific(令人恐惧的)effects,chemical weapons are of great concern because they are cheaper and easier to manufacture and deliver than nuclear or biological weapons.

Types of Weapons

During World War Ⅰ,chlorine gas(氯气)was used as a chemical weapon,released in massive clouds by the German army to cause lung damage and terror downwind of its release. Modern chemical weapons include the following types of agents:Choking(令人窒息的)Agents,Blister(皮肤水泡)Agents,Nerve Agents.

How Chemical Weapons Work

Chemical agents may be released as tiny droplets(微粒),similar to the action of a bug bomb used to release insecticide(杀虫剂). For a chemical weapon to cause harm,it must come in contact with the skin or mucous membranes(黏膜),be inhaled(吸入),or be ingested(咽下). The activity of the chemical agent depends on its concentration(浓度).

In other words,below a certain level of exposure,the agent won't kill. Below a certain level of exposure,the agent won't cause harm.

Protective Measures

The best protective measure you can take against chemical weapons is to become educated about them. Most of us don't have gas masks or atropine(阿托品)(an injectible used in cases of nerve agent exposure)and won't be on a battlefield,so the recommendations presented here are intended for the general public.

1. Don't Panic

Yes,chemical weapons are more likely to be used in a terrorist scenario(恐怖方案), than nuclear or biological weapons. However,there are several steps you can take to minimize exposure and protect yourself in the event you encounter a chemical agent. Realistically speaking,you are more likely to witness an accidental chemical spill(释放,溢出)than a chemical attack. Your best defense is to face the situation with a level head(保持头脑冷静).

2. Seek High Ground

Chemical agents are more dense (浓度高) than air. They sink to low-lying areas and will follow wind/weather patterns. Seek the highest store of a building or the top of a natural land formation.

3. Seek Open Spaces or Seek a Self-Contained Air Supply

From the point of view of a terrorist, a heavily populated area is a more attractive target than a sparsely populated (人烟稀少) region. Therefore, the threat of a chemical attack is lessened in rural areas.

In the event of an attack, there is some sense in isolating (使……隔离) your air supply. Most chemical agents disperse (散开) after a certain amount of time, so refraining from (控制, 忍住) contacting exposed air may be a good protective measure.

4. Use Your Senses

How do you know if you have been exposed to a chemical agent? You may not be able to see or smell one. In their pure forms, most chemical weapon agents are clear liquids. Impure chemicals may be yellowish liquids. Most are odorless (无嗅的) and tasteless, but some have a slightly sweet or fruity smell. Skin irritation (皮肤刺激), respiratory distress (呼吸困难), and gastrointestinal upset (胃肠不适) all may signal exposure to a chemical agent. However, if you don't die within minutes, you probably won't die at all. Therefore, if you believe you have been exposed to a chemical agent, wait until you feel secure before seeking out medical attention (but do seek it out).

Unit 19 Drying Equipment

Of the many types of commercial dryers available, only a small number of important types are considered here. The first and larger group comprises dryers for solids and semisolid pastes; the second group consists of dryers that can accept slurry or liquid feeds.

Dryers for Solids and Pastes

Typical dryers for solids and pastes include tray and screen-conveyor dryers for materials that cannot be agitated and tower, rotary, screen-conveyor, fluid-bed, and flash dryers where agitation is permissible[1]. In the following treatment these types are ordered, as far as possible, according to the degree of agitation and the method of exposing the solid to the gas or contacting it with a hot surface. The ordering is complicated, however, by the fact that some types of dryers may be either adiabatic or nonadiabatic or a combination of both[2].

Tower dryers

A tower dryer contains a series of circular trays mounted one above the other on a central rotating shaft. Solid feed dropped on the topmost tray is exposed to a stream of hot air or gas that passes across the tray. The solid is then scraped off and dropped to the tray below. It travels in this way through the dryer, discharging as dry product from the bottom of the tower. The flow of solids and gas may be either parallel or countercurrent.

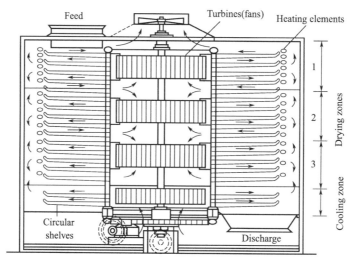

Figure 19-1 Turbodryer

The turbodryer illustrated in Figure19-1 is a tower dryer with internal recirculation of the heating gas. Turbine fans circulate the air or gas outward between some of the trays, over heating elements, and inward between other trays. Gas velocities are commonly 0.6 to

2.4 m/s (2 to 8 ft/s). The bottom two trays of the dryer shown in Figure 19-1 constitute a cooling section for dry solids. Preheated air is usually drawn in the bottom of the tower and discharged from the top, giving countercurrent flow. A turbodryer functions partly by cross-circulation drying, as in a tray dryer, and partly by showering the particles through the hot gas as they tumble from one tray to another[3].

Rotary dryers

A rotary dryer consists of a revolving cylindrical shell, horizontal or slightly inclined toward the outlet. Wet feed enters one end of the cylinder; dry material discharges from the other. As the shell rotates, internal flights lift the solids and shower them down through the interior of the shell. Rotary dryers are heated by direct contact of gas with the solids, by hot gas passing through an external jacket, or by steam condensing in a set of longitudinal tubes mounted on the inner surface of the shell[4]. The last of these types is called a steam-tube rotary dryer. In a direct-indirect rotary dryer, hot gas first passes through the jacket and then through the shell, where it comes into contact with the solids.

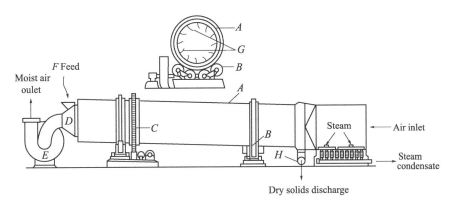

Figure 19-2 Rotary dryers

A typical adiabatic countercurrent air-heated rotary dryer is shown in Figure. 19-2. A rotating shell A made of sheet steel is supported on two sets of rollers B and driven by a gear pinion C. At the upper end is a hood D, which connects through fan E to a stack and a spout F, which brings in wet material from the feed hopper[5]. Flights G, which lift the material being dried and shower it down through the current of hot air, are welded inside the shell. At the lower end the dried product discharges into a screen conveyor H. Just beyond the screen conveyor is a set of steam-heated extended-surface pipes that preheat the air. The air is moved through the dryer by a fan, which may, if desired, discharge into the air heater so that the whole system is under a positive pressure. Alternatively, the fan may be placed in the stack as shown, so that it draws air through the dryer and keeps the system under a slight vacuum. This is desirable when the material tends to dust. Rotary dryers of this kind are widely used for salt, sugar, and all kinds of granular and crystalline materials that must be kept clean and may not be directly exposed to very hot flue gases.

Dryers for Solutions and Slurries

A few types of dryers evaporate solutions and slurries entirely to dryness by thermal means. Typical examples are spray dryers, thin-film dryers, and drum dryers.

Spray dryers

In a spray dryer, a slurry or liquid solution is dispersed into a stream of hot gas in the form of a mist of fine droplets. Moisture is rapidly vaporized from the droplets, leaving residual particles of dry solid, which are then separated from the gas stream. The flow of liquid and gas may be cocurrent, countercurrent, or a combination of both in the same unit.

Droplets are formed inside a cylindrical drying chamber by pressure nozzles, two-fluid nozzles, or, in large dryers, high-speed spray disks. In all cases it is essential to prevent the droplets or wet particles of solid from striking solid surfaces before drying has taken place, so that drying chambers are necessarily large. Diameters of 2.5 to 9 m (8 to 30 ft) are common.

In the typical spray dryer shown in Figure19-3, the chamber is cylinder with a short conical bottom. Liquid feed is pumped into a spray-disk atomizer set in the roof of the chamber. In this dryer the spray disk is about 300mm (12 in) in diameter and rotates at 5,000 to 10,000 rpm. It atomizes the liquid into tiny drops, which are thrown radially into a stream of hot gas entering near the top of the chamber. Cooled gas is drawn by an exhaust fan through a horizontal discharge line set in the side of the chamber at the bottom of the cylindrical sec-

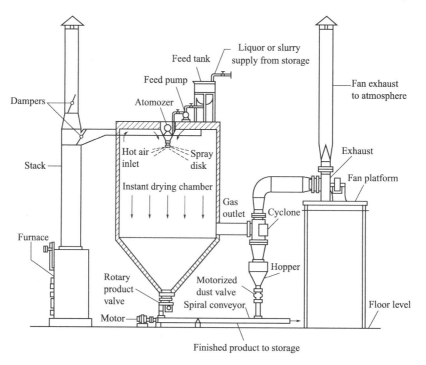

Figure 19-3 Spray dryer with parallel flow

tion. The gas passes through a cyclone separator where any entrained particles of solid are removed. Much of the dry solid settles out of the gas into the bottom of the drying chamber, from which it is removed by a rotary valve and screen conveyor and combined with any solid collected in the cyclone[6].

New Words and Phrases

alternatively [ɔːlˈtəːnətivli]　*adv.* 做为选择，二者择一地
circular [ˈsəːkjulə]　*adj.* 圆形的，循环的
cocurrent [kəˈkʌrənt]　*n.* 并流，同向
conical [ˈkɔnikəl]　*adj.* 圆锥的，圆锥形的
conveyor [kənˈveiə]　*n.* 输送机
countercurrent [ˈkauntəˌkʌrənt]　*n.* 逆流　*adj.* 逆流的
cyclone [ˈsaikləun]　*n.* 旋风，气旋
disk [disk]　*n.* (=disc) 圆板，圆盘
droplet [ˈdrɔplit]　*n.* 小滴
drum [drʌm]　*n.* 鼓，鼓形圆桶
dryer [ˈdraiə]　*n.* 干燥机，干燥器
entrain [inˈtrein]　*vt.* 产生，导致，带走
flight [flait]　*n.* 刮板
flue [fluː]　*n.* 烟洞，烟道，暖气管
gear [giə]　*n.* 齿轮，传动装置
hood [hud]　*n.* 防护罩
hopper [ˈhɔpə]　*n.* 漏斗，料斗
inclined [inˈklaind]　*adj.* 倾斜的，成斜坡的
inward [ˈinwəd]　*adv.* 向内，在内　*adj.* 向内的，内在的
longitudinal [lɔndʒiˈtjuːdinl]　*adj.* 经度的，纵向的
nonadiabatic [ˈnɔnˌædiəˈbætik]　*adj.* 非绝热的
nozzle [ˈnɔzl]　*n.* 管口，喷嘴
ordered [ˈɔːdəd]　*adj.* 规则的，有序的
outward [ˈautwəd]　*adj.* 外面的，向外的　*adv.* 向外
parallel [ˈpærəlel]　*adj.* 平行的，相同的
paste [peist]　*n.* 糊剂，糊状混合物
permissible [pə(ː)ˈmisəbl]　*adj.* 可允许的
pinion [ˈpinjən]　*n.* 小齿轮
radially [ˈreidjəli]　*adv.* 径向地，放射性地
recirculation [ˌriːˈsəːkjuˈleiʃən]　*n.* 再通行，再流通
roller [ˈrəulə]　*n.* 滚柱，托辊
rpm = revolutions per minute 转数/分
screen [skriːn]　*n.* 屏，筛子
semisolid [ˌsemiˈsɔlid, ˌsemai-]　*n.* 半固体　*adj.* 半固体的
shaft [ʃɑːft]　*n.* 轴，支柱
shower [ˈʃauə]　*n.* 淋浴，喷淋管

spout [spaut] *n.* 喷管，喷口
stack [stæk] *n.* 烟囱，烟道
topmost ['təpməust] *adj.* 最高的，顶端的
tumble ['tʌmbl] *vt.* 使摔倒，使滚翻，
turbodryer ['tə:bəu'draiə] *n.* 涡轮干燥机
circular tray   圆形淋盘，圆形塔板
countercurrent flow   逆流
cross-circulation   交叉循环
cyclone separator   旋风分离器
drum dryer   转鼓式干燥器
drying chamber   干燥室
extended-surface   展开面
feed hopper   进料斗
flash dryer   急剧（闪速，气流）干燥机
flue gas   烟道气
fluid-bed dryer   流化床干燥器
gear pinion   小齿轮
longitudinal tube   长管
one above the other   逐个
rotary dryer   转筒干燥器
rotary valve   旋转阀
rotating shaft   旋转轴
screen-conveyor dryer   筛网干燥器
spray disk   喷雾盘
spray dryer   喷雾干燥器
steam-heated   汽热的
steam-tube   蒸汽管
thin-film dryer   薄膜干燥器
tower dryer   塔式干燥器
tray dryer   厢式干燥器
turbine fan   涡轮鼓风机
two-fluid nozzle   气动雾化喷嘴

Notes

1. Typical dryers for solids and pastes include tray and screen-conveyor dryers for materials that cannot be agitated and tower, rotary, screen-conveyor, fluid-bed, and flash dryers where agitation is permissible.
本句并列宾语为 tray and screen-conveyor dryers 和 tower, rotary, screen-conveyor, fluid-bed, and flash dryers, 其中 that cannot be agitated 为定语从句修饰 materials, where agitation is permissible 为定语从句修饰 dryers。

2. The ordering is complicated, however, by the fact that some types of dryers may be either adiabatic or nonadiabatic or a combination of both.

that...both 为同位语从句说明 fact。

3. A turbodryer functions partly by cross-circulation drying, as in a tray dryer, and partly by showering the particles through the hot gas as they tumble from one tray to another.
they 指 solids，as they tumble from one tray to another 为时间状语，表示"当……时候"。

4. Rotary dryers are heated by direct contact of gas with the solids, by hot gas passing through an external jacket, or by steam condensing in a set of longitudinal tubes mounted on the inner surface of the shell.
三个由 by 介词短语引导的方式状语，mounted...shell 过去分词短语作定语修饰 tubes。

5. At the upper end is a hood D, which connects through fan E to a stack and a spout F, which brings in wet material from the feed hopper.
At the upper end is a hood D 是倒装句，which...spout F 非限制性定语从句修饰主语 hood D。which...feed hopper 作定语修饰上一个定语从句中的 s a stack and a spout F。

6. Much of the dry solid settles out of the gas into the bottom of the drying chamber, from which it is removed by a rotary valve and screen conveyor and combined with any solid collected in the cyclone.
from which...cyclone 非限制性定语从句修饰 chamber，其中并列谓语 is combined 中的 is 被省略。

Exercises

Ⅰ. Translate the following into English
1. 旋风分离器
2. 转鼓式干燥器
3. 急剧干燥机
4. 流化床干燥器
5. 转筒干燥器
6. 筛网干燥器
7. 喷雾干燥器
8. 薄膜干燥器
9. 塔式干燥器
10. 厢式干燥器

Ⅱ. Translate the passage into Chinese

Drying Equipment

We have a broad range of Drying Equipment manufacturers, exporters and suppliers source and trade services, which can be searched by this comprehensive vertical web portal. We are dedicated to helping worldwide Drying Equipment buyers purchasing from China Drying Equipment manufacturers, suppliers and exporters. Enquiries are welcome from global agents, importers, chain stores, distributors and wholesalers etc...

Drying Equipment — YZG or FZG Round-shaped, Square-shaped Vacuum
Product Description:
1. Under constant temperature, improving vacuum degree, it can accelerate drying speed.
2. Under constant vacuum degree, improving heating temperature, it can accelerate dr-

ying speed.

3. Factory/Manufacturer: Jiangyin Tongda Machine Equipment Co., Ltd.

(We are the manufacturer & supplier of pharmacy, drying, chemistry industry, rubber pulverizer.)

Drying Equipment - XF Series Negative-voltage Boilling Drying Machine

Product Description: This machine is applicable for drying medicine, chemical raw materials, food and feed, such as drying or removing moisture of raw medicine, tablet granules, Chinese medicine dose, food drink.

Factory/Manufacturer: Jiangyin Tongda Machine Equipment Co., Ltd

Drying Equipment—RXH-Type Oven Series

Product Description: It's suitable for pharmaceutical, chemical, foodstuff, light industry, heavy industry etc., such as original medicines, raw medicine dose, packing bottles, drying vegetables, foodstuffs, plastic resin.

Factory/Manufacturer: Jiangyin Tongda Machine Equipment Co., Ltd

Drying Equipment—FLUID-BED DRYER/GRANULATOR

Factory/Manufacturer: HSIN HUNG TA MACHINERY WORKS CO., LTD.

(Founded as a manufacturer and supplier of professional products including soft calcium carbonate grinding machine, fodder machine, canned machine for food and wine, stainless barrel and pipe project, a whole set of centrifuge project.)

Drying Equipment—Convyer, Shaking Drier

Product Description: food drying

Factory/Manufacturer: JIUH TOONG ENTERPRISE CO., LTD.

(Chemical Machine, Dryer, Filter Machine, Heat Exchange Machine, Conveyer, Reservoir Response Tank.)

Reading Materials

What Is Biochemistry (生物化学)?

Biochemistry is the application of chemistry to the study of biological processes at the cellular (细胞的) and molecular (分子的) level. It emerged as a distinct discipline (学科) around the beginning of the 20th century when scientists combined chemistry, physiology (生理学) and biology (生物学) to investigate the chemistry of living systems.

The study of life in its chemical processes Biochemistry is both a life science and a chemical science - it explores the chemistry of living organisms (生命有机体) and the molecular basis for the changes occurring in living cells (生物细胞). It uses the methods of chemistry, "Biochemistry has become the foundation for understanding all biological processes. It has provided explanations for the causes of many diseases in humans, animals and plants."

Physics, molecular biology and immunology (免疫学) to study the structure and behaviour of the complex molecules are found in biological material and the ways these molecules interact to form cells, tissues and whole organisms.

Biochemists are interested, for example, in mechanisms of brain function, cellular multiplication and differentiation (细胞繁殖和分化), communication within and between cells and organs, and the chemical bases of inheritance (遗传) and disease. The biochemist seeks to determine how specific molecules such as proteins (蛋白质), nucleic acids (核酸), lipids (脂肪), vitamins (维生素) and hormones (激素) function in such processes. Particular emphasis is placed on regulation of chemical reactions in living cells.

An essential science Biochemistry has become the foundation for understanding all biological processes. It has provided explanations for the causes of many diseases in humans, animals and plants. It can frequently suggest ways by which such diseases may be treated or cured.

Because biochemistry seeks to unravel (弄清楚) the complex chemical reactions that occur in a wide variety of life forms, it provides the basis for practical advances in medicine, veterinary (兽医的) medicine, agriculture and biotechnology. It underlies and includes such exciting new fields as molecular genetics (基因学) and bioengineering.

The knowledge and methods developed by biochemists are applied to in all fields of medicine, in agriculture and in many chemical and health related industries. Biochemistry is also unique in providing teaching and research in both protein structure/function and genetic engineering, the two basic components of the rapidly expanding field of biotechnology.

As the broadest of the basic sciences, biochemistry includes many subspecialties (附属专业) such as neurochemistry (神经化学), bioorganic (生物有机) chemistry, clinical (临床) biochemistry, physical biochemistry, molecular genetics, biochemical pharmacology (药理学) and immunochemistry (免疫学).

Recent advances in these areas have created links among technology, chemical engineering and biochemistry.

Unit 20   Reactors

The reactor is the heart of a chemical process. It is the only place in the process where raw materials are converted into products, and reactor design is a vital step in the overall design of the process[1].

The design of an industrial chemical reactor must satisfy the following requirements.

1. The chemical factors: the kinetics of the reaction. The design must provide sufficient residence time for the desired reaction to proceed to the required degree of conversion.

2. The mass transfer factors: with heterogeneous reactions the reaction rate may be controlled by the rates of diffusion of the reacting species; rather than the chemical kinetics.

3. The heat transfer factors: the removal, or addition, of the heat of reaction.

4. The safety factors: the confinement of hazardous reactants and products, and the control of the reaction and the process conditions.

The need to satisfy these interrelated and often contradictory factors, makes reactor design a complex and difficult task. However, in many instances one of the factors will predominate and will determine the choice of reactor type and the design method.

Principal types of reactor

The following characteristics are normally used to classify reactor designs.
1. Mode of operation: batch or continuous.
2. Phases present: homogeneous or heterogeneous.
3. Reactor geometry: flow pattern and manner of contacting the phases.
(1) stirred tank reactor;
(2) tubular reactor;
(3) packed bed, fixed and moving;
(4) fluidized bed.

Stirred tank reactors

Stirred tank (agitated) reactors consist of a tank fitted with a mechanical agitator and a cooling jacket or coils. They are operated as batch reactors or continuously. Several reactors may be used in series.

The stirred tank reactor can be considered the basic chemical reactor, modeling on a large scale the conventional laboratory flask. Tank sizes range from a few liters to several thousand liters. They are used for homogeneous and heterogeneous liquid-liquid and liquid-gas reactions, and for reactions that involve finely suspended solids, which are held in suspension by the agitation[2]. As the degree of agitation is under the designer's control, stirred tank reactors are particularly suitable for reactions where good mass transfer or heat transfer is required.

When operated as a continuous process the composition in the reactor is constant and the same as the product stream, and, except for very rapid reactions, this will limit the conversion that can be obtained in one stage[3].

The power requirements for agitation will depend on the degree of agitation required and will range from about 0.2 kW/m³ for moderate mixing to 2 kW/m³ for intense mixing.

Tubular reactors

Tubular reactors are generally used for gaseous reactions, but are also suitable for some liquid-phase reactions.

If high heat-transfer rates are required, small-diameter tubes are used to increase the surface area to volume ratio. Several tubes may be arranged in parallel, connected to a manifold or fitted into a tube sheet in a similar arrangement to a shell and tube heat exchanger[4]. For high-temperature reactions the tubes may be arranged in a furnace.

The pressure-drop and heat-transfer coefficients in empty tube reactors can be calculated using the methods for flow in pipes.

Packed bed reactors

There are two basic types of packed-bed reactor: those in which the solid is a reactant, and those in which the solid is a catalyst. Many examples of the first type can be found in the extractive metallurgical industries.

In the chemical process industries the designer will normally be concerned with the second type: catalytic reactors. Industrial packed-bed catalytic reactors range in size from small tubes, a few centimeters diameter, to large diameter packed beds. Packed-bed reactors are used for gas and gas-liquid reactions. Heat-transfer rates in large diameter packed beds are poor and where high heat-transfer rates are required fluidized beds should be considered.

Fluidized bed reactors

The essential feature of a fluidized bed reactor is that the solids are held in suspension by the upward flow of the reacting fluid; this promotes high mass and heat-transfer rates and good mixing. Heat-transfer coefficients in the order of 200 W/m² · ℃ typically obtained. The solids may be a catalyst; a reactant in fluidized combustion processes; or an inert powder, added to promote heat transfer.

Though the principal advantage of a fluidized bed over a fixed bed is the higher heat-transfer rate, fluidized beds are also useful where it is necessary to transport a large quantities of solids as part of the reaction processes, such as where catalysts are transferred to another vessel for regeneration[5].

Fluidization can only be used with relative small particle, sized particles, $<300\mu m$ with gases.

A great deal of research and development work has been done on fluidized bed reactors in recent years, but the design and scale up of large diameter reactors is still an uncertain process and design methods are largely empirical.

New Words and Phrases

coil [kɔil] n. 螺旋管
confinement [kənˈfainmənt] n. 限制，约束
contradictory [ˌkɔntrəˈdiktəri] adj. 矛盾的
diffusion [diˈfjuːʒən] n. 扩散，传播，漫射
empirical [emˈpirikəl] adj. 经验的 n. 实验式
extractive [iksˈtræktiv] adj. 抽取的，萃取的
fluidization [ˌfluːidaiˈzeiʃən] n. 液化，流化
geometry [dʒiˈɔmitri] n. 几何学，表面形状
hazardous [ˈhæzədəs] adj. 危险的，冒险的
heterogeneous [ˌhetərəuˈdʒiːniəs] adj. 不均匀的，多相的
homogeneous [ˌhɔməuˈdʒiːnjəs] adj. 均一的，均匀的
interrelated [ˌintəriˈleitid] adj. 相关的
kinetics [kaiˈnetiks] n. 动力学
liter [ˈliːtə] n. 公升
manifold [ˈmænifəuld] n. 歧管，多支管，复式管头
metallurgical [ˌmetəˈləːdʒikəl] adj. 冶金学的
power [ˈpauə] n. 功率
predominate [priˈdɔmineit] vt. 掌握，控制，支配
reactor [ri(ː)ˈæktə] n. 反应堆，反应器
regeneration [riˌdʒenəˈreiʃən] n. 再生，重建，回收
catalytic reactor 催化反应器
chemical factor 化学因素
cooling jacket 冷却夹层
design method 设计方法
extractive metallurgical industries 萃取冶金工业
fixed bed 固定床
fluidized bed 流化床
gaseous reaction 气相反应
hazardous reactants and products 危险反应物和产物
heat transfer factor 传热因素
heat-transfer coefficient 传热系数
heat-transfer rate 传热速率
in parallel 平行
liquid-phase reaction 液相反应
mode of operation 操作模式
packed bed 填充床
pressure-drop 压力降
reaction rate 反应速率

reactor geometry　反应器形状
safety factor　安全因素
scale up　按比例增加
shell and tube heat exchanger　管壳式换热器
stirred tank reactor　搅拌釜式反应器
surface area to volume ratio　表面积与体积比
tube sheet　管板
tubular reactor　管式反应器

Notes

1. It is the only place in the process where raw materials are converted into products, and reactor design is a vital step in the overall design of the process.
   本句为并列句，where…products 为定语从句修饰第一个分句中的 process。

2. They are used for homogeneous and heterogeneous liquid-liquid and liquid-gas reactions, and for reactions that involve finely suspended solids, which are held in suspension by the agitation.
   that…solids 为定语从句修饰 reactions，which…agitation 是定语从句的定语从句，用来修饰 solids。

3. When operated as a continuous process the composition in the reactor is constant and the same as the product stream, and, except for very rapid reactions, this will limit the conversion that can be obtained in one stage.
   本句为并列复合句，第一并列分句的时间状语 When operated as a continuous process 省略了 it is，it 指 reactor。that…stage 为第二并列分句的定语从句修饰 conversion。

4. Several tubes may be arranged in parallel, connected to a manifold or fitted into a tube sheet in a similar arrangement to a shell and tube heat exchanger.
   connected 和 fitted 为并列谓语，省略了 may be。

5. Though the principal advantage of a fluidized bed over a fixed bed is the higher heat-transfer rate, fluidized beds are also useful where it is necessary to transport a large quantities of solids as part of the reaction processes, such as where catalysts are transferred to another vessel for regeneration.
   Though…rate 为让步状语从句，where…processes 为主句主语的定语从句。such as where…regeneration 做定语从句修饰 reaction processes。这部分可以改写成 "…such reaction processes as where catalysts are transferred to another vessel for regeneration."

Exercises

Ⅰ. Translate the following into English
1. 催化反应器
2. 固定床
3. 流化床
4. 传热系数
5. 填充床
6. 反应器形状

7. 管壳式换热器
8. 搅拌釜式反应器
9. 管板
10. 管式反应器

Ⅱ. Translate the paragraph into Chinese

Operational Mode

Chemical reactors may be operated in batch, semibatch, or continuous modes. When a reactor is operated in a batch mode, the reactants are charged, and the vessel is closed and brought to the desired temperature and pressure. These conditions are maintained for the time needed to achieve the desired conversion and selectivity, that is, the required quantity and quality of product. At the end of the reaction cycle, the entire mass is discharged and another cycle is begun. Batch operation is labor-intensive and therefore is commonly used only in industries involved in limited production of fine chemicals, such as pharmaceuticals. In a semibatch reactor operation, one or more reactants are in the batch mode, while the coreactant is fed and withdrawn continuously. In a chemical reactor designed for continuous operation, there is continuous addition to, and withdrawal of reactants and products from, the reactor system.

Reading Materials

The Brief Introduction of Chemical Abstracts

35-CHEMISTRY OF SYNTHETIC HIGH POLYMERS(高聚物)

This section includes the chemical transformations（变化）of synthetic high polymers, synthesis and reactions of polymers, related monomers（单体）, and polymer models; reaction kinetics（动力学）, thermodynamics（热力学）, and mechanisms of these transformations. Studies of polymers prepared for a specific use or of a specific class are contained in the section（类别）encompassing（包括）the use or class; e.g., polypeptides（多肽）in Section 34; plastics in Sections 37 or 38; elastomers（弹性体）in Section 39; fibers in Section 40; coatings（涂料）in Section 42.

38-PLASTICS FABRICATION（制造）**AND USES**

This section includes end-product（成品）fabrication of plastics, fabricating processes or techniques of chemical and chemical engineering interest, and plastics reclamation（回收）. Fabrication of resins（树脂）of some specific classes or for some specific uses are included in the section encompassing the class or use: e.g., elastomers are placed in Section 39; fibers in Section 40; waxes（蜡）in Section 45; prosthetic devices（修复器械）in Section 63.

40-TEXTILES AND FIBERS

This section includes analysis, preparation, manufacture, testing, processing and composition of natural and synthetic fibers and the chemicals used in their manufacture and processing. Fibers for use as reinforcing agents（增强剂）are included in the appropriate section encompassing the materials being reinforced. Dye synthesis and color-structure relationship are included in Section 41. Dry cleaning and laundering（洗烫）are included in Section

46. Preparation and processing of inorganic fibrous materials by methods unrelated to textile processing are included in the appropriate inorganic section.

42-COATINGS, INKS, AND RELATED PRODUCTS

This section includes the manufacture and use of decorative, finishing, and protective coatings (装饰、修复和保护性涂料) and the materials used in their manufacture. Coatings of a specific class or for a specific use are included in the section encompassing the class or use: e.g., fiber coatings in Section 40; paper coating in Section 43; vitreous (玻璃质的) coatings in Section 57; cosmetic enamels (化妆用油彩) in Section 62; dental coatings in Section 63; electrode oxide (电极氧化物) coatings in Section 72; photographic coatings in Section 74.

47-APPARATUS AND PLANT EQUIPMENT

This section includes laboratory apparatus for research and development, industrial apparatus and equipment for carrying out any of the unit operations (involving physical change) and unit processes (involving chemical change), when the equipment has a multipurpose (多用途的) application. Apparatus and equipment having a singular use, identifiable with (适用于) a specific section, are placed in that appropriate section. Included also in this section are high-and low-temperature apparatus [e.g., furnaces, Dewars (冷凝器)], material-handling (处理原料) apparatus (e.g., conveyors, vessels), and general construction materials for the equipment. Apparatus and equipment undefinable as to (未限定) specific area of application or for multiple areas of application are placed here.

Key to the exercises

Unit 1

Ⅱ. Translate the following expressions into English
1. gravitational force
2. the mass of the body
3. mathematical formula
4. the states of matter
5. the structure and composition of matter
6. melting point
7. boiling point
8. the law of conservation of mass and energy
9. the chemical and physical properties
10. kinetic and potential energy

Ⅲ. Translate the passage into Chinese

一切物质均有质量。化学家对物体的质量感兴趣，因为他们要知道需要用多少材料才能制备一定数量的产品。

物体的质量就是测量其在静止或运动状态时反抗变化的量。

物体的质量也决定其重量。某物体的重量仅是该物体被地球所吸引的力的量度。这个力取决于物体的质量，地球的质量和物体在地球表面的位置，特别是物体离地球中心的距离。因为地球的两极是稍微扁平的，所以南北两极表面离地球中心的距离比赤道表面离地球中心的距离要小。因此，当用一个测量力的弹簧秤测量一个物体的重量时，在北极或南极所测得的物体重量较在赤道所测得的更重。例如，如果用弹簧秤测得你的重量在赤道是 150 磅，那么在同一弹簧秤上，在北极则是 150.8 磅，几乎重了 1 磅。然而，你的质量却是相同的。

Unit 2

Ⅱ. Translate the following expressions into English
1. Water solutions
2. degrees of ionization
3. nitric acid, hydrochloric acid, sulfuric acid and phosphoric acid
4. oxidizing agents
5. change the color of indicators
6. litmus and phenolphthalein indicators
7. basic solution, acid solution and neutral solution
8. neutralization of acid and base
9. potassium hydroxide, sodium hydroxide and ammonium hydroxide
10. acid concentration expressed as pH

Ⅲ. Translate the passage into Chinese

酸具有以下通性：它们有酸味，能使蓝色石蕊试纸变成红色，能与活泼的金属作用而释放出氢气，能与碳酸盐作用释放出二氧化碳，并能中和碱。这些性质是氢离子（H^+）在酸的水溶液中所具有的性质。

碱具有在溶液中能电离出氢氧根离子的特性。它能够中和酸。具有明显碱性的物质叫碱。

盐可以通过中和作用，金属加酸，金属氧化物加酸，金属碳酸盐加酸，以及一些特殊的方法来制备。盐类的溶解度已概括在溶解度规律中。

有些化学反应是可逆的。在可逆反应中，在一系列特定的浓度、温度和压力条件下，两个相对的化学反应产生了平衡。

化学反应的速率受温度、压力（假如反应物或生成物中有气体的话），催化剂及浓度的影响。

质量作用的原理是：可以通过增加一种反应物质的浓度或减少一种生成物的浓度，使可逆平衡反应接近几乎完全的反应。

Unit 3

Ⅱ. Translate the following expressions into English

1. Hydrochloric acid
2. Hydrobromic acid
3. Nitric acid
4. Hypochlorous acid
5. Chlorous acid
6. Chloric acid
7. Perchloric acid
8. Sulfuric acid
9. Ferrous hydroxide
10. Ferric hydroxide

Ⅲ. Translate the passage into Chinese

当我们接触到不太常用但却比较复杂的化合物时，通俗名称的运用就让位于更有规则的命名法。如果化合物中只有两种元素，习惯上把金属性较大的元素的名词放在前面，而把金属性较小的即电负性较大的元素放在后面，并加上后缀"-ide"。例如：

| KCl | 氯化钾 | NaBr | 溴化钠 | CaO | 氧化钙 |
| HI | 碘化氢 | BaS | 硫化钡 | | |

仅含有两种元素，但含有两个以上原子的化合物必须加上前缀，一、二、三等。氮的氧化物就是这类化合物的一些例子。这类化合物的另一些例子是氯的氧化物。因为氯像氮一样，电负性比氧少校，所以把氯这个词置于前面。

Cl_2O	一氧化二氯	ClO_3	三氧化氯
ClO	一氧化氯	Cl_2O_7	七氧化二氯
ClO_2	二氧化氯	ClO_4	四氧化氯

假如不引起混淆，前缀"mono-"和"di-"有时可以省略。

Unit 4

Ⅲ. Translate the passage into Chinese

卤代烃（烷基卤化物）

虽然 IUPAC 命名法把化合物视为卤代烃，并且越来越多的人使用这种方法。但是，今天普通命名法和 IUPAC 命名法都在普遍使用。

分子式	IUPAC 命名法	普通命名法
CH_3Cl	氯甲烷	甲基氯
CH_3CH_2Br	溴乙烷	乙基溴

CH₃CHICH₃	2-碘丙烷	异丙基碘
CH₃CF(CH₃)₂	2-氟-2-甲基丙烷	叔丁基氟
C₆H₅CH₂Cl	氯甲基苯	苄基氯

芳基卤化物

芳烃通常是使用标明芳环上取代基位置的号码来命名。

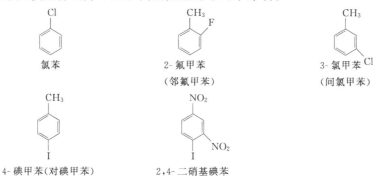

脂族胺

脂肪族胺是通过指明连接氮原子上的烷基，然后加上后缀"胺"来命名的。

分子式	名称	分子式	名称
CH₃NH₂	甲基胺	(CH₃)₂CHNH₂	1-甲基乙基胺（异丙基胺）
CH₃CH₂NH₂	乙基胺	CH₃CH₂NHCH₃	甲基乙基胺
(CH₃)₂NH	二甲基胺	(CH₃)₃N	三甲基胺
CH₃CH₂CH₂NH₂	丙基胺	(CH₃)₃CNH₂	1,1-二甲基乙胺（叔丁基胺）

具有不同烷基更为复杂的叔胺可以视为最长碳链的衍生物，斜体字 *N* 插在每一个取代基的名称前面。

   *N*-乙基-*N*-甲基丙胺

含有四价氮的化合物称为季铵化合物，通过变后缀"胺"为"铵"来命名。

(CH₃)₄N⁺I⁻   四甲基碘化铵

芳 胺

芳胺中最简单的是苯胺，其他化合物大都命名为苯胺的衍生物。

甲基苯胺也称为甲苯胺。

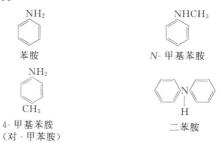

脂肪族或芳香族胺都可以把"胺"作为烷烃或其他相应烃的后缀来命名。
这种命名法很少用于简单的胺，但广泛适用于像 1,6-己二胺和 1,3-苯二胺这样的化合物。

Unit 5

Ⅱ. Translate the following into English

1. 2,3-dihydroxybutanedioic (tartaric) acid

2. 2-hydroxybutanedioic (malic) acid
3. 2-hydroxypropane-1,2,3-tricarboxylic (citric) acid
4. 2-hydroxypropanoic (lactic) acid
5. 3,4,5-trihydroxybenzenecarboxylic (gallic) acid
6. ammonium cyanate
7. carbon tetrachloride
8. ethanedioic (oxalic) acid
9. ethanoic (acetic) acid
10. uric acid

Ⅲ．Translate the passage into Chinese

醇

尽管普通命名法采用的方法是说明适当的烷烃并加上单词"醇"，而且这种方法仍然用于简单的化合物，例如：甲醇，异丙醇和苯甲醇等。但是，IUPAC 命名法普遍适用于大多数醇。

IUPAC 命名法通常是去掉相应烷烃的后缀"-ane"，并用后缀"-ol"替代。羟基的位置是通过在名称的前面插入相应的数字来表示。

分子式	IUPAC 命名法	普通命名法
CH_3OH	甲醇	甲醇
CH_3CH_2OH	乙醇	乙醇
$CH_3CH_2CH_2OH$	1-丙醇	正丙醇
$CH_3CHOHCH_3$	2-丙醇	异丙醇
$CH_3COH(CH_3)_2$	2-甲基-2-丙醇	叔丁醇
$C_6H_5CH_2OH$	苯甲醇	苯甲醇
$C_6H_5CH_2CH_2OH$	2-苯基乙醇	苯乙醇

酚

苯酚是羟基直接连接到芳环上的化合物，其通式为 ArOH。像醇一样，根据酚所含的羟基数目可将其分为一元酚或多元酚。酚家族中最简单和最重要的成员就是苯酚。

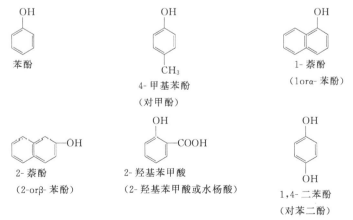

苯酚

4-甲基苯酚
（对甲酚）

1-萘酚
（1 or α-萘酚）

2-萘酚
（2-or β-萘酚）

2-羟基苯甲酸
（2-羟基苯甲酸或水杨酸）

1,4-二苯酚
（对苯二酚）

醚

普通命名法特别指出连接到氧原子上的烷基或芳基，然后再加上单词"醚"。某些烷基芳基醚的名称不能指明它们的结构，例如：茴香醚（苯甲醚）和苯乙醚（苯乙醚）。

IUPAC 命名法把醚视为烷烃的烷氧基的取代物或芳环的烷氧基取代物。

例如： CH₃CH₂CHCH₃   2-甲氧基丁烷
              |
              OCH₃

分子式	IUPAC 命名法	普通命名法
CH₃OCH₃	甲氧基甲烷	甲醚
CH₃OCH₂CH₃	甲氧基乙烷	甲乙醚
CH₃CH₂OCH₂CH₃	乙氧基乙烷	乙醚
C₆H₅OCH₃	甲氧基苯	苯甲醚（茴香醚）
C₆H₅OCH₂CH₃	乙氧基苯	苯乙醚
C₆H₅OC₆H₅	苯氧基苯	二苯醚

Unit 6

Ⅲ. Translate the passage into Chinese

醛

醛的命名起源于使醇脱氢得到的化合物的名称。

普通命名法是通过将相应的羧酸的后缀"-ic"变成"-aldehyde"来命名。

IUPAC 命名法是通过将相应的烷烃的后缀"-e"用"-al"代替来命名。

由于羰基只能连接一个烷基，所以羰基必须在碳链的一端。

分子式	IUPAC 命名法	普通命名法
HCHO	甲醛	蚁醛
CH₃CHO	乙醛	醋醛
CH₃CH₂CHO	丙醛	丙醛
CH₃(CH₂)₂CHO	正丁醛	丁醛
C₆H₅CH₂CHO	苯乙醛	苯乙醛

最简单的芳醛是苯甲醛（安息香醛）C₆H₅CHO。

酮

普通命名法是通过专门指定每一个连接到羰基上的烃基，然后加上"酮"来命名的。

IUPAC 命名法源自相应烷烃的主干名称，并用后缀"one"替换"-e"。羰基的位置用常用的方法来指示，羰基碳原子包含在直链序列内。

分子式	IUPAC 命名法	普通命名法
CH₃COCH₃	丙酮	二甲酮
CH₃COCH₂CH₃	丁酮	甲乙酮
CH₃CO(CH₂)₂CH₃	2-戊酮	甲丙酮
CH₃CH₂COCH₂CH₃	3-戊酮	二乙酮

羰基直接连接到苯环上的酮称为相应脂肪族羰基化合物的苯衍生物。这些化合物以前统称为苯酮。

苯乙酮（乙酰苯）   二苯甲酮（苯酰苯）

羧 酸

普通命名法一般是根据羧酸来源的拉丁名称或希腊名称来命名的。

虽然蚁酸也存在于刺荨麻和某些其他植物中，但是蚁酸的名称还是来源于蒸馏捣碎的蚂蚁得到的酸的名称。

如果酒精含量比较少的甜葡萄酒暴露在空气中，他就常常会变酸，用于受到通常称为醋

蝇的细菌的侵袭而转变成醋。这种微生物不是把糖转变成酒精,而是将它转变成醋酸。其他一些普通名称的语源:

名称	来源	语源
丙酸	植物和动物产品	希腊字:proto 第一,pion 脂肪
丁酸	腐臭的黄油	拉丁字:butyrum 黄油
己酸	山羊奶	拉丁字:Caper 山羊

烃链上取代基的位置可用希腊字母 α,β,γ 等来表示。

例如: $\overset{\gamma}{CH_3}\overset{\beta}{CH_2}\overset{\alpha}{CH}CH_2COOH$ β-甲基戊酸
      $\quad\quad\quad\quad\quad |$
      $\quad\quad\quad\quad CH_3$

IUPAC 命名法是通过使用相应烷烃的名称并将后缀"-e"换为"-oic"来命名。取代基的位置是按照含有羧基的最长直链上的数字来表示的。

分子式	IUPAC命名法	普通命名法
HCOOH	甲酸	蚁酸
CH_3COOH	乙酸	醋酸
CH_3CH_2COOH	丙酸	丙酸
$CH_3(CH_2)_2COOH$	丁酸	正丁酸
$(CH_3)_2CHCOOH$	2-甲基丙酸	异丁酸
$CH_3(CH_2)_3COOH$	戊酸	正戊酸
$CH_3(CH_2)_{14}COOH$	十六酸	棕榈酸(软脂酸)
$CH_3(CH_2)_{16}COOH$	十八酸	硬脂酸
$C_6H_5CH_2COOH$	2-苯基乙酸	苯乙酸

芳香族酸的名称常常是与相应的烃有关,例如:苯甲酸(安息香酸)和甲基苯甲酸(甲苯甲酸)或者像脂肪族化合物都是从它们的天然来源物质的名称得到的。

苯甲酸   　　　　　　　3-甲基苯甲酸
(安息香酸) 　　　　　(间-甲基苯甲酸)

Unit 7

Exercises

Ⅲ. Translate the following into Chinese

酰 基 氯

每一脂肪族化合物都可以通过从相应羧酸的 IUPAC 命名法或普通命名法去掉后缀"-ic"换上"-yl",然后使用"氯化物"来命名。

分子式	IUPAC命名法	普通命名法
CH_3COCl	乙基酰氯	乙基酰氯
CH_3CH_2COCl	丙基酰氯	丙基酰氯

芳香酰基氯化物可以视为芳香族羰基的氯化物,像脂肪族化合物一样,它可以通过将系统命名法或普通命名法名称的后缀"-ic"换上"-yl",然后加上"氯化物"来命名。

例如:C_6H_5COCl　　苯基酰氯(苯甲酰氯)

酸 酐

简单化合物使用含有相同酰基的羧酸 IUPAC 命名法或普通命名法,并将酸换成酸酐。对于混合酸酐,分别命名每一个酰基。

分子式	IUPAC 命名法	普通命名法
$(CH_3CO)_2O$	乙酐	醋酸酐
$(CH_3CO)O(COCH_2CH_3)$	乙丙酐	乙丙酐

芳香族酐命名方法相似于其母体酸，例如：$(C_6H_5CO)_2O$ 称为苯酐或苯甲酸酐。

酰 胺

酰胺是氨的单酰基衍生物，根据连接到氮原子上的烷基或芳基的数目，可将酰胺分为伯酰胺，仲酰胺和叔酰胺。

每一化合物都可通过将 IUPAC 命名法的后缀"-oic 酸"或普通命名法的"-ic 酸"换上后缀"-amide"来命名。

分子式	IUPAC 命名法	普通命名法
CH_3CONH_2	乙酰胺	乙酰胺
$CH_3CONHCH_3$	N-甲基乙酰胺	N-甲基乙酰胺

由苯甲酸形成的最简单的酰胺就是苯甲酰胺（$C_6H_5CONH_2$）。

Unit 8

Ⅲ．Translate the passage into Chinese

酯

酯可以通过母体羧酸的 IUPAC 命名法或普通命名法的名称并用后缀"-ate"替换"-ic"来命名，相应醇的烷基和酚的芳基名称放在酯的名称前面。

分子式	IUPAC 命名法	普通命名法
$HCOOCH_3$	甲酸甲酯	甲基甲酸盐
$CH_3COOCH_2CH_3$	乙酸乙酯	乙基乙酸盐
$CH_3COOC_6H_5$	乙酸苯酯	苯基乙酸盐

由苯甲酸得到的最简单的酯是苯甲酸甲酯。

磺 酸

芳香族磺酸是极性化合物，比相应的脂肪族酸重要得多。在磺酸中，磺酸基的硫原子直接连接到芳环上。

磺酸的命名是把后缀磺酸放到磺酸基取代的化合物后面。

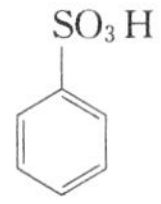

苯磺酸

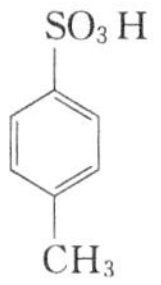

4-甲基苯磺酸
（对甲基苯磺酸）

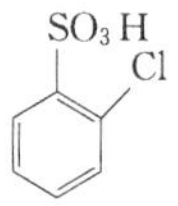

2-氯苯磺酸

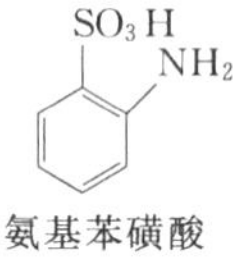

2-氨基苯磺酸
邻氨基苯磺酸

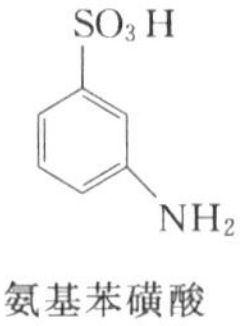

3-氨基苯磺酸
间氨基苯磺酸

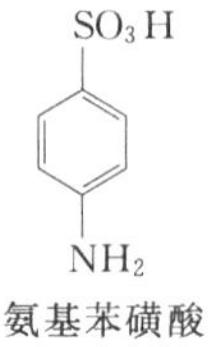

4-氨基苯磺酸
对氨基苯磺酸

氨 基 酸

氨基酸使用系统命名法是把它们视为羧酸的氨基衍生物。然而，许多氨基酸使用原始名称来命名的，这种命名法一般不能说明它们的酸性，但能较好地说明与氨的关系。这些名称都使用后缀"-ine"。

$$NH_2CH_2COOH \qquad\qquad CH_3\underset{\underset{NH_2}{|}}{C}HCOOH$$

氨基乙酸甘氨酸   2-氨基丙酸丙氨酸

在普通命名法的一般规律之外还存在着酸性氨基酸。

$$HOOCCH_2\underset{\underset{NH_2}{|}}{C}HCOOH \qquad\qquad HOOC(CH_2)_2\underset{\underset{NH_2}{|}}{C}HCOOH$$

氨基丁二酸天门冬氨酸   2-氨基戊二酸谷氨酸

Unit 9

Ⅱ．Translate the following into Chinese by checking up the dictionary：

1. 单糖
2. 二糖
3. 多醣
4. 葡萄糖
5. 果糖
6. 麦芽糖
7. 乳糖
8. 淀粉
9. 纤维素
10. 蔗糖

Ⅲ．Translate the passage into Chinese

聚合物是一种高分子量的物质，其大小远远超出迄今所提到的各种化合物。对于把一个物质归类为聚合物应具有的最小分子量，并无一致的意见，但实用的最小分子量为 1000 左右。许多商品聚合物的分子量在 10000～50000 之间，虽然某些商品聚合物的分子量要高得多。聚合物是许多低分子量分子通过化合成高分子量化合物的反应所生成的。能生成聚合物的化合物，如能生成聚乙烯的乙烯，成为单体（mono，单一；mer，单元）。可见，聚合物是由许多单元组成的分子，而生成聚合物分子所涉及的过程就成为聚合。

加聚物是由许多分子量超过 1000 的单体自我结合形成的。然而，凝聚过程可以产生凝聚物。在凝聚过程中，存在消除副产物，但不存在自我加成反应。

Unit 10

Ⅱ．Translate the following into Chinese

1. 活化能
2. 胶水
3. 化学药品和日用化学品
4. 铁氰化铁
5. 精细化学品
6. 食品和饲料添加剂
7. 高纯化学药品
8. 信息化学品
9. 普鲁士蓝
10. 氧化钒

Ⅲ．Translate the passage into Chinese

表面活性剂是化学化合物，当它们溶解在水或其他溶剂中的时候，就分散在液固相，液液相和液气相之间，并改变界面的性质。随着发泡，乳状液，悬浮液和气溶胶的形成，界面发生变化。

这一定义显得很专业化，实际上，生产肥皂（一种主要的表面活性剂）就是最古老的化学工业分支。最近一项有关工业过程的调查表明，在化学工业和联合产品生产企业中，表面活性剂是应用最广泛的一组化合物。表面活性剂不仅在其主要用途的清洗剂（肥皂，洗涤剂等）方面很重要，而且在稳定乳状液（例如，在食品和化妆品），作为塑料工业、矿物浮选和石油钻井的脱膜剂，以及其他许多方面的应用中也有很重要的作用。

化学上，根据表面活性剂的生色基团是阴离子、阳离子、非离子或两性离子给表面活性剂分类。用于清洁剂中的表面活性剂通常要与各种添加剂混合，以改变它们的性能。洗涤剂就是这样配制的。肥皂是一种阴离子表面活性剂，但是由于历史的原因，长期以来肥皂与合成洗涤剂分隔开来。因此，我们总是说它们是肥皂和洗涤剂。

Unit 11

Ⅱ．Translate the paragraph into Chinese

岛津是能够把微软视窗软件融入每一个软件产品的几家制造商之一。在用户友好界面的视窗环境下工作，使你马上就能操作。即使你不常使用分光光度计，在你繁忙的工作中，当你走到仪器旁的时候，你也能很快地得到分析结果。在视窗条件下操作，工作既快又直接了当。视窗很容易将实验室网络连接起来，并且支持很多的外围设备。对于经验丰富的分光光度计操作者而言，岛津个人光谱软件可以为你提供意想不到的灵活性和更为广泛的分析范围。

Ⅲ．Translate the passage into Chinese

723型可见分光光度计

这种物美价廉的可见分光光度计是为了满足日常严格的定量和定性分析要求而设计的。把独立的微处理机嵌入723型分光光度计中，它就具备了只能在其他更为复杂的仪器上才能看到的许多功能。它已经广泛地用在医药卫生，临床检验，生物化学，石油化学，环境保护和各种生产线质量控制领域。

特点

1. 723分光光度计配有先进的微处理器控制技术。它提供了"0"和"100"自动调节功能，直接消除比色皿不匹配的误差。

2. 出色的测量准确度，重复性和稳定性。

3. 具有直接浓度读出，线性衰减，同步测绘和波长扫描功能。按照用户要求，可以增加特殊功能。

4. 广泛的可选附件可用于扩大系统功能，诸如：传统的比色皿和半微量比色皿，微量恒温自动样品附件，积分球附件等。

5. 处理容易，自动化程度高，操作可靠。

结构

1. 绘图器：可选择四种颜色（黑，蓝，绿和红）。光谱曲线和直角坐标图可以清楚打印。各种参数和确定数据也可打印。

2. 发光二极管数字显示器：四位发光二极管数字显示器可以显示仪器确定的数据和波长。

3. 发光二极管状态显示器：显示工作模式和四个比色皿架的位置。

4. 样品室：有足够的空间容纳全部的附件。

5. 单色器：由微机控制，除了样品室以外，不需要手动控制。

6. 键盘：有许多功能键和数字键。所有功能都可通过软触键操作。塑料薄膜操作键盘保护仪器设备不受尘土污染。

规格

波长	330～800nm
波长读出器	4位二级发光管显示器
波长可读性	0.1nm
波长准确性	±0.1nm
波长再现性	0.5nm
单色器	单光束，利特罗装置 光栅1200g/mm
带宽	6nm

杂散光	≤1％（T）(360nm)
光源	卤素钨灯 12V 35W
分光光度计读数范围	0～100％（T）0～2A
分光光度计读数准确性	±0.5％（T）
分光光度计读数再现性	0.4％（T）
绘图器	4种颜色绘图器
T-A 转换精确度	≤±0.002 A（0.5A）
	≤±0.004 A（1A）
稳定性	≤±0.004 A/1h
电力消耗	80W
用电要求	220V±10％，50～60Hz
体积	560mm×400mm×260mm
重量	25kg

标准配置

723型可见分光光度计	1件
电源线	1条
10mm 玻璃比色皿	4个
10mm 玻璃比色皿架	1个
50mm 销售架	1个
钬过滤器（用于波长校正）1件	
卤钨灯 12V 30W	1个（备用）
换灯标准扳手	1件
保险丝	1件（备用）
记录纸	1卷（备用）
四色记录比	1套（备用）
防尘罩	1个
操作手册	1本

可选附件

半微量熔融石英比色皿
7521自动样品装置
7522恒温比色皿架
7524φ60mm 积分球附件
7523微型自动样品装置
7221微型自动样品装置
10mm 熔融石英比色皿
10mm 密封熔融石英比色皿
10mm 玻璃比色皿
20mm 玻璃比色皿
30mm 玻璃比色皿
50mm 玻璃比色皿

上海进出口办公室第三分析仪器厂
地址：中国，上海，汾阳路77号

邮编：200031

电话：(021) 43754601

传真：(021) 47187721

电报：5157（上海）

Unit 12

Ⅱ．Translate the passage into Chinese

岛津 GC-14B 系列气相色谱

GC-14B 系列气相色谱仪是由高性能柱箱，可变的样品注入系统，独立的流动控制装置，高灵敏度的检测器，检测器控制装置，可移动灵巧键盘装置和其他装置组成。每一装置设计简单，但性能很高。

1. 流量控制装置

各种流量控制器，诸如：单柱流水线，双柱流水线，适用于开口或非开口样品注射器。

2. 检测器控制装置

可从热传导检测器，火焰离子检测器，电导检测器，火焰光度检测器和火焰热离子检测器中，最多选择三个控制器装配在一起。增加一个可选控制器箱可同时安装四个控制器。

3. 柱箱

柱箱具有弯曲的内表面（与已知性能的 GC-15A 和 GC-16A 相同）以保证保留时间的异常再现。这类柱箱最适合于毛细管柱气相色谱。它是垂直型的，可使从注射器端口和检测箱辐射的热量降低到最小程度。在柱箱后面安装的计算机控制风扇可使温度编程控制的冷却区的空气进行交换。

4. 灵活的样品注入端口系统

（每一样品注入端口装置是独立温控的装置。）样品注入装置是弹药筒形的，从下列装置中最多选择四个安装在一起。

（1）裂口或非裂口装置

（2）用于单柱的玻璃衬垫系统装置

（3）用于双柱的玻璃衬垫系统装置

（4）柱上冷却系统装置

（5）移动针头系统装置

5. 检测器

最多四个检测器可以安装在一起。

(1) 高灵敏度火焰离子检测器。

(2) 高灵敏度，具有保护辐射源的恒电流电子捕获检测器。

(3) 高灵敏度恒电流电子捕获检测器。

(4) 高灵敏度火焰热离子检测器。

(5) 高灵敏度和高稳定性火焰光度检测器。

(6) 易操作热传导性检测器。

6. 键盘装置

控制系统的设计是为了保证操作非常容易。当这种键盘拆下的时候，GC-14B 系列气相色谱仪可根据事先设置好的仪器参数进行操作。

当 GC-14B 系列气相色谱仪有外部计算机（诸如：另一台气相色谱仪，数据处理器，个人计算机或主机）控制时，就不需要这种键盘装置了。这一特点使得 GC-14B 系列气相色谱仪特别适合于实验室自动化操作。

（键盘装置具有和岛津 GC-9A 系列气相色谱仪相似的键排布。）

Unit 13

Ⅱ．Translate the passage into Chinese

北京瑞利分析仪器公司（原北京第二光学仪器厂）是机械电子工业部规划定点的国内规模最大的光谱仪器制造公司。公司固定资产总值 3200 万元，占地面积 60000 平方米，现有职工 900 余人，其中工程技术人员 200 余人，高级职称的工程技术人员 30 余人。

公司已有超过 25 年生产光谱仪器经验，现研制生产六大系列 20 多个品种产品：原子吸收系列、发射光谱系列、紫外/可见光系列、傅里叶红外系列、生化系列及光栅单色仪系列的光谱分析仪器，其中，原子吸收国内市场占有率超过 50%。

公司成功地从法国、日本、瑞士和美国引进先进技术，包括原子吸收制造技术，紫外/可见光制造技术和傅里叶红外制造技术等。仪器设备的质量和性能达到国际水平。公司的成功不仅使得瑞利产品多次在国际上中标，而且出口到美国、韩国、东南亚和欧洲等。

公司还从国外引进了加工中心，数控压弯机，数控冲床等高精度自动化机械加工设备，并具备光学加工、光栅刻化、光栅复制等尖端制造技术，用于仪器检验的高低温实验室，耐高电压实验，振动试验等检测手段，为实现仪器的优良品质，提供了可靠的保证。

北京瑞利分析仪器公司，中国光谱分析仪器制造业的骄傲。

Unit 14

Ⅱ．Translate the paragraph into Chinese

WQF-300 傅里叶变换红外光谱仪

特点

（1）WQF-300 使用 TRANSEPT-Ⅲ型楔形折射扫描干涉仪，代替普通的麦克尔逊干涉仪。

（2）WQF-300 为积木式结构，可以自由组装以适合用户的特殊需求。

（3）数据处理 CPU 80486，丰富的软件和傅里叶变换红外光谱仪国内专用红外光谱数据库。

（4）由电磁驱动装置和精密机械导轨构成的运动部件，改善了对使用环境的要求，避免了使用空气轴承带来的不便。

规格

（1）光谱范围：4400～400 cm^{-1}

（2）分辨率：1.5 cm^{-1}

（3）波数精度：±0.01

（4）扫描速度：0.2～1.5cm/s 自动优化分辨率和检测器

（5）信噪比：优于 10000∶1

（6）检测器：标准配置 DTGS，用户任选 MCT 检测器

（7）红外光源：标准高强度反射球形光源

（8）附件：GC/IF 接口，ATR，漫反射和微量样品器

Ⅲ．Translate the passage into Chinese

Spectrum 100 傅里叶变换红外光谱仪

产品详细资料

PerkinElmer Spectrum™100 傅里叶变换红外光谱仪为科学研究、材料检验和高等教育建立了最高标准。由于 PerkinElmer 公司的知识、经验、快速服务和技术支持，本系统具有高灵敏度、快速取样和高稳定性特点，在实验室可以容易地获得高质量和可再现的分析结

果。无论在何处,你都会最信任 PerkinElmer Spectrum 100 傅里叶变换红外光谱系统。

技术规格

  PerkinElmer 傅里叶变换红外光谱仪是按照最高的生产标准制造的。我们公布的技术规格是经过产品生产企业 100% 检验确认的。在用户手册规定的正常使用条件下,全部仪器将达到或超过验证的技术规格。

特点

  为准确测量和重复测量而设计的独特光源
  为提高检测效率和易于操作而设计的按钮和液晶显示器
  为快速取样,提前取样和重复取样提供精密配件、调零配件和标准配件
  直观软件确保操作简单和前后一致
  空气水蒸气补偿器保证分析结果的准确性和精密度
  绝对虚拟仪器使得仪器波数刻度的标准化程度远远高于传统刻度校正方法
  光谱软件为用户提供直观操作,有助于不同时间和不同用户的分析结果保持一致

傅里叶变换红外及近红外光谱仪

  60 多年来,PerkinElmer 一直制定傅里叶变换红外光谱技术标准,它具有丰富的经验和渊博的知识,它是全球实验室傅里叶变换红外及近红外光谱仪的供应商。通过采用全面质量监控方法——从产品的设计,开发和制造到客户服务和技术支持,PerkinElmer 公司提供了最高质量的傅里叶变换红外和近红外光谱系统。在工业上,该系统可获得最高准确度和可再现的分析结果。

Unit 15

  II．Translate the paragraph into Chinese

气相色谱与质谱

  质谱仪可从分子中产生带电粒子(离子)。然后对这些离子进行分析,提供有关化合物分子量和化合物分子结构的信息。有很多类型的质谱仪和能够进行广泛的分析样品引入技术。本文将集中讨论的是:在具有强大和广泛用途的气相色谱和质谱连用中的质谱仪。待分析的混合物首先注入气相色谱,混合物在加热室汽化。气体混合物通过色谱柱,随着它与色谱柱的相互作用,将化合物分离开来。

Unit 16

  II．Translate the paragraph into Chinese

核磁共振光谱仪

  某些同位素原子核的作用就像条形磁铁似的。相关性比较大的两个原子核是氢(质量数为 1)和碳(质量数为 13)。当含有这些同位素的化合物放在外界强磁场的时候,核磁体就顺着外磁场平行排列。使用光谱无线电部分的电磁能量照射样品,就会使核磁体转向相反的方向。当它们返回到较低的能量方位时,多余的能量就以光子的形式发射。光子能量是观察到的核子环境的特性。核磁共振光谱仪就是为了观察原子核由于共振而出现松弛现象而设计的。核磁共振光谱仪是原子核激发,然后,观察原子核能量衰减到基态时的信号。

Unit 17

  II．Translate the paragraph into Chinese

结晶系统和结晶器

  在结晶操作中,我们工作的重点是溶液的结晶,而不是熔融液的结晶。我们的专业技术包括了三类结晶操作过程:

  浓缩结晶

冷却结晶（在真空条件下或使用热交换器）

反应置换或平衡置换结晶

我们拥有各种类型结晶设备的实际经验和专业知识：全分级或部分分级，晶浆循环，有沉降区或无沉降区设备。

使用 GEA 蒸发技术（GEA 凯斯特纳）的不同类型的结晶器：强制循环结晶器，奥斯陆型结晶器（分级悬浮结晶器），DTB 结晶器（导流管板结晶器），诱导循环结晶器。

Unit 18

Ⅱ．Translate the paragraph into Chinese

间歇蒸馏塔

完备的筛板蒸馏塔装置，包括再沸器、冷凝器和回流罐，适用于易燃溶剂和全仪表间歇操作。

监控全过程的温度（包括每一块塔板的温度），并在装有控制台的操作台上进行显示。控制台还装有给再沸加热起供电的控制装置，并可在 0～100％之间设定回流比。

前仪表板连接点可以接入标准记录仪和数据自动分析记录仪，并可接入工业标准的比例积分微分控制器和可编程逻辑控制器。

装置的 U 型管压力计可以测量整个蒸馏塔高度范围的压力降。

装置包括了填料塔配件，直径 50mm 的筛板蒸馏塔很容易与填料塔互换。真空泵用于减压操作。装置完全组装（包括绝缘层材料），综合说明手册描述了试车、保养和教学任务。

过程装置

高：2.25m

宽：0.85m

长：0.80m

控制台

高：0.30m

宽：0.52m

长：0.40m

Ⅲ．Translate the passage into Chinese

蒸　　馏

蒸馏广泛用于分离混合物，它是根据将混合物组分变成气相所需的条件不同而对混合物进行分离。为了分离液体混合物，可以加热液体使具有不同沸点的组分转变成气体。然后，气体冷凝成液态并回收。为了提高产品的纯度，重复蒸馏收集的液体，这就叫做双蒸馏。尽管蒸馏最常用于液体，但是，通过组分在一定的温度和（或）压力下的变化来液化组分，可以使用蒸馏的逆过程来分离气体。

蒸馏适用于许多工业过程，例如：生产汽油、蒸馏水、二甲苯、乙醇、石蜡、煤油和许多其他液体。

蒸馏包括简单蒸馏（刚刚描述过的），分馏（产生不同挥发度馏分，并回收）和分解蒸馏（通常，一种物质被加热，然后收集分解的化合物）。

应　　用

化学工业，制药工业和环境技术领域都以不同的方法使用和处理大量的溶剂和挥发性化合物。

无论是浓缩，清洗或回收，处理这些溶剂都需要丰富的实践经验和充分掌握化工原理理论知识，这是蒸馏、蒸发、提馏和精馏操作的基础。

在规划设计中，GEA 蒸发技术使用了最新计算机程序和最现代的数据库，因此，它可以模拟工厂操作，并达到最佳布局。

我们的蒸馏研发中心能够设计复杂的工厂系统。当处理不同的物料或化合物时，能够使需要设定的操作条件最优化。

在寻找特殊问题的蒸馏解决方案方面，GEA 蒸馏技术（GEA Wiegand）可以满足个别需要。它甚至可以提供具有全部控制流程（比如，乙醇的制造）的交钥匙蒸馏工厂。工厂配有必需的控制装置，既可用传统控制方法，又可使用最新过程控制工程。凭借着我们具有的大量不同类型设备的多年经验，可以选择蒸馏技术生产领域所需某一装置。

除了众所周知的降膜蒸发器、循环蒸发器和搅拌蒸发器以外，我们使用所有著名的蒸馏塔系统，包括填料塔、筛板塔、泡罩塔、隧道塔或浮阀塔。

Unit 19

Ⅱ．Translate the passage into Chinese

干 燥 设 备

我们拥有丰富的干燥设备制造商、出口商、供应商和贸易服务部门的资源，通过这个综合垂直网络入口可以进行搜索。我们竭尽全力帮助全球干燥设备的购买者购买中国生产商、供货商和出口商提供的干燥设备。欢迎全球的代理商、进口商、连锁商、分销商和批发商垂询。

干燥设备——YZG/FZG 圆筒真空干燥器，方形真空干燥器

产品描述：

1. 恒温下，提高真空度，加快干燥速度。
2. 恒真空度条件下，改进加热温度，加快干燥速度。
3. 工厂/制造商：江阴通达机械设备有限公司

（我们生产和销售制药、干燥、化学工业和橡胶磨粒设备。）

干燥设备——XF 系列负电压沸腾干燥机

产品描述：本设备适用于干燥药品、化工原料和食品饲料，例如，从原料药、片粒、中药制剂和食品饮料中除湿和干燥。

工厂/制造商：江阴通达机械设备有限公司

干燥设备——RXH 型烤箱系列

产品描述：本产品适用于制药、化工、食品、轻工和重工等领域。例如：原药、原料药剂、包装瓶、干燥蔬菜、食品和塑料树脂等。

工厂/制造商：江阴通达机械设备有限公司

干燥设备——流化床干燥器/制粒机

工厂/制造商：新弘大机器厂有限公司

（这是一家专业产品的制造商和供应商，产品包括：软碳酸钙研磨机、饲料机、食品和酒类装罐机，不锈钢桶和管道，全套离心机装置。）

干燥设备——输送震动干燥机

产品描述：食品干燥

工厂/制造商：JIUH TOONG 企业股份有限公司

（化工机械、干燥器、过滤机、热交换机、运输机和压缩空气备用罐。）

Unit 20

Ⅱ．Translate the paragraph into Chinese

操 作 方 式

化学反应器可以是间歇操作、半间歇操作或连续式操作。当反应器是间歇操作时，要放入反应物，封闭反应器，使反应达到所需的温度和压力。这些条件要保持足够长的时间，以到达所需的转化率和选择性，也就是获得所需产品的数量和质量。在每一反应周期结束之后，全部物料要排放出去，开始另一反应周期。间歇操作是劳动密集型工作，因此，通常只用于生产有限精细化工产品的产业上，比如医药制品。在半间歇式反应器操作中，有一种或一种以上的反应物处于间歇操作方式，而其余反应物则是连续进料和连续排放。如果化学反应器是为连续操作而设计的，那么反应系统就存在反应物和产物的连续添加和连续排放。

Translation

第 1 部分　无机和有机化学基本知识

第 1 单元　无机化学的基本概念

物　　质

物质的定义

我们把物质定义为具有体积和质量的任何东西。质量是物质所具有的量，并且由于作用其上的重力使质量具有了重量单位。尽管重量是可以变化的，但是，物体的质量是不变的，物体的质量可以用它抗拒位置变化（或运动）来测量。抗拒位置变化（或运动）的质量的性质称之为惯性。因为物质确实占有体积，我们就可以把占有确定单位体积的各种物质的质量进行比较。质量与单位体积的关系叫做物质的密度。密度可以用数学公式表示为 $D=\dfrac{m}{V}$。化学上，质量（m）的基本单位是克（g），体积（V）是立方厘米（cm^3）或毫升（mL）。

物质的状态

物质以气态、液态和固态三种状态存在。固体具有一定的体积和形状。液体具有一定的体积，但形状取决于它的容器，气体既没有一定的形状也没有一定的体积。由于增加热量，物质的这三种状态常常能够转变。例如：冰转变为液态的水，最后变成水蒸气就是一个很好的实例。

物质的组成

物质可以再进一步划分为两种普通类型：纯物质和混合物。纯物质要么是单质，要么是化合物。如果物质仅仅是由一种原子组成的，就称之为单质。然而，如果物质是由两种或两种以上的原子按照一定的组成结合在一起，就把它划分为化合物。我们把化合物总是以一定的组成存在的现象称之为定比定组成定律。以水为例，它总是以两个氢原子对一个氧原子的关系生成化合物水。然而，混合物的组成是千变万化的。

物质的化学性质和物理性质

物质的物理性质通常是指那些用我们的感官能够感知到的物质的特性。是指在物质的最基本结构不发生变化的情况下所观察到的那些特性。如：物质的颜色、气味、水溶解性、密度、熔点、味道、沸点和硬度等。

判定物质的化学性质是根据一种物质能否与其他物质发生化学反应来决定。一些常见的物质化学特性如：铁在潮湿空气中生锈，氮不燃烧，金不生锈，钠与水反应，银不与水反应，而水可以通电流分解等。

物质的化学变化和物理变化

物质的变化要么是物理变化，要么是化学变化。一般地讲，物理变化改变的是物质的物理性质，但物质的结构不发生变化。常见的物理变化是形状和状态，例如：打碎玻璃，锯掉木头，融化冰，使一块金属磁化。某些情况下，物理变化是很容易逆转的，我们可以让发生物理变化的物质恢复原状。

化学变化总是物质的组成和结构上的变化。化学变化总是伴随着能量的变化。当生成一种新的结构时所释放出的能量超过原物质的化学能量时，通常能量会以热量或光，或热量和光的形式释放出来，这种反应就叫做放热反应。然而，如果新结构需要吸收的热量比从反应物那里得到的更多的话，我们就称之为吸热反应。这种反应是可以用曲线来表示的。

质量守恒

当普通化学反应发生时，反应物的质量等于产物的质量。换句话说，就是在化学变化过程中，物质既不能创造也不能毁灭，只能从一种形式变为另一种形式。这可以称之为质量守恒定律。这一定律与爱因斯坦的质量和能量关系式是矛盾的，爱因斯坦的质量和能量关系式表明质量和能量是可以相互转变的。

能　　量

能量的定义

能量通常被定义为做功的能力。

能量的形式

能量可以各种各样的形式存在。通常，在化学反应中以热能形式存在。其他一些形式的能量是：光能、声能、机械能、电能和化学能。能量可以从一种形式转变为另一种形式。例如，燃烧煤生成的热量可以使水变为水蒸气，水蒸气推动涡轮机的轮子产生机械能，涡轮机驱动发电机的转子发电，然后，我们可以在家中用电来照明、取暖，并用电来驱动许多家用电器。能量分为势能和动能。势能是由于位置具有的能量，动能是由于运动所具有的能量。势能和动能之间的差异可以用位于山坡上的一块巨石来说明。巨石在峡谷的上方时，它具有高的势能。然而，如果它落下来的话，势能就变成了动能。这一描述非常类似于原子模型中的电子跑到低能级上的情况。

能量守恒

实验表明在物理或化学变化中，能量既不能得到也不能失去。这一原理叫做能量守恒定律，常常叙述如下：在普通的物理和化学变化中，能量既不能创造也不能消灭。

质量和能量守恒

由于原子理论的引入和人们对物质和能量的本质的更彻底地理解，人们发现了这两个概念间存在的关系。爱因斯坦建立了质量和能量守恒定律。这一定律说明物质和能量在特定的条件下是可以互相转变的。这种条件已经在原子核反应器和加速器中建立起来，这一定律也得到了验证。这一关系式可用爱因斯坦著名的方程式表示如下：$E=mc^2$

能量＝质量×光速的平方

第 2 单元　酸、碱、盐

酸

判定酸的特性方法有很多，其中最重要的有如下。

1. 酸的水溶液导电。这种导电性取决于电离的程度。有些酸几乎完全电离，而有些酸仅仅轻微电离。下表说明了一些酸和它们的电离程度。

酸		
完全或几乎完全电离	中等电离	轻微电离
硝酸		氢氟酸
盐酸	草酸	醋酸
硫酸	磷酸	碳酸
氢碘酸	亚硫酸	氢硫酸
氢溴酸		（大多数其他的酸）

2. 酸与比氢离子更活泼的金属反应放出氢气（有些酸是强氧化剂，不会释放出氢气。比较浓的硝酸就是这样的一种酸）。

3. 酸能够改变指示剂的颜色。常用的指示剂有石蕊和酚酞。石蕊是从植物中提取的一种染料。当石蕊加到一种酸性溶液或含有石蕊溶液的试纸浸到酸性溶液中的时候，表示中性的紫色就会变成粉红色。酚酞在碱性溶液中呈红色，在中性或酸性溶液中变成无色。

4. 酸与碱发生反应，两者各自失去原有的特性，生成盐和水。这种反应叫做中和反应。通式如下：酸＋碱＝盐＋水

举例：$Mg(OH)_2 + H_2SO_4 \longrightarrow MgSO_4 + 2H_2O$

5. 如果知道是弱酸溶液，你就可以尝一下，会品到酸味。

6. 酸与碳酸盐反应时，放出二氧化碳。例如：

$$CaCO_3 + 2HCl \longrightarrow CaCl_2 + H_2CO_3 （不稳定并分解）$$
$$\longrightarrow H_2O + CO_2$$

第一年化学课程使用的最普通的理论是阿仑尼乌斯理论，它说明酸是在水溶液中产生氢离子的一种物质。尽管我们陈述了水溶液中的氢离子，但是它们实际上不是单个的氢离子而是与极性水分子上的氧结合生成 H_3O^+ 离子（水合氢离子）。实际上我们所关注的是酸溶液中的这种水合氢离子。

碱

碱也可以用建立在实验观察基础上的一些可操作的说明来定义。一些重要的碱如下。

碱	
完全电离或几乎完全电离	轻微电离
氢氧化钾	
氢氧化钠	
氢氧化钡	氨水
氢氧化锶	（所有其他的碱）
氢氧化钙	

1. 碱在水溶液中导电。碱的导电程度取决于它们的电离程度。见上表普通的碱及其电离程度。

2. 碱会使指示剂发生颜色变化。石蕊在碱性溶液中由红变蓝，酚酞由无色变成粉红色。

3. 碱与酸反应相互中和并生成盐和水。

4. 碱与脂肪反应生成一类被称之为肥皂的化合物。早期的人们使用这种方法制造肥皂。

5. 碱的水溶液摸着感到滑腻，强碱对皮肤具有很强的腐蚀性。

盐

盐是一种离子化合物,它含有除氢离子以外的正离子和除氢氧根离子以外的负离子。制备一种特殊盐的常用方法是通过中和适当的酸和碱生成盐和水。

用 pH 表示酸的浓度

酸和碱的浓度常用 pH 来表示。pH 可定义为 $-\lg[H^+]$,$[H^+]$ 是用每升摩尔来表示的氢离子的浓度。以 10 为底的对数是求底数为 10 的指数幂。

求 pH 举例:求 0.1 摩尔/升 HCl 的 pH。

第一步 因为 HCl 几乎完全电离为 H^+ and Cl^-,$[H^+]$ = 0.1 摩尔/升。

第二步 由定义得

$pH = -\lg[H^+]$,$pH = -\lg 10^{-1}$

第三步 10^{-1} 的以 10 为底的对数等于 -1

所以 $pH = -(-1)$

第四步 $pH = 1$。

由于水分子的轻微电离,通常水的氢离子的浓度为 10^{-7} 摩尔/升,水的 pH=7,这时它既不呈酸性也不呈碱性。通常长 pH 范围是 1~14。

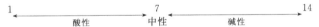

第 3 单元 无机化合物的命名

写 分 子 式

根据人们对氧化数和化合价的认识以及对原子结构的理解,现在就能够写出化学式。表 3-1 是在大学一年级经常遇到的氧化数表。

表 3-1 氧化数表

分 类	一价(Ⅰ)	二价(Ⅱ)	三价(Ⅲ)	四价(Ⅳ)	五价(Ⅴ)
金属阳离子(+)	氢 H 钾 K 钠 Na 银 Ag 汞 Hg 铜 Cu 金 Au ① 铵根(NH_4)	钡 Ba 钙 Ca 钴 Co 镁 Mg 铅 Pb 锌 Zn 汞 Hg 铜 Cu 铁 Fe 锰 Mn 锡 Sn	铝 Al 金 Au 砷 As 铬 Cr 铁 Fe 磷 P 锑 Sb 铋 Bi	碳 C 硅 Si 锰 Mn 锡 Sn 铂 Pt 硫 S	砷 As 磷 P 锑 Sb 铋 Bi
非金属阴离子(-)	氟 F 氯 Cl 溴 Br 碘 I	氧 O 硫 S	氮 N 磷 P	碳 C	
	非金属的最后音节在二元化合物中变成-ide。				

续表

分类	一价（Ⅰ）	二价（Ⅱ）	三价（Ⅲ）	四价（Ⅳ）	五价（Ⅴ）
根（一）	氢氧根（OH） 碳酸氢根（HCO$_3$） 亚硝酸根（NO$_2$） 硝酸根（NO$_3$） 次氯酸根（ClO） 氯酸根（ClO$_3$） 亚氯酸根（ClO$_2$） 高氯酸根（ClO$_4$） 醋酸根（C$_2$H$_3$O$_2$） 高锰酸根（MnO$_4$） 硫酸氢根（HSO$_4$）	碳酸根（CO$_3$） 亚硫酸根（SO$_3$） 硫酸根（SO$_4$） 四硼酸根（B$_4$O$_7$） 硅酸根（SiO$_3$） 铬酸根（CrO$_4$） 草酸根（C$_2$O$_4$）	硼酸根（BO$_3$） 磷酸根（PO$_4$） 亚磷酸根（PO$_3$） 亚铁氰酸根[Fe(CN)$_6$]	铁氰酸根 [Fe(CN)$_6$]	

注：① 根。

一 般 观 察

金属符号具有＋号，而除了铵离子以外，非金属和所有的根都具有－号。

当一种元素显示出两种可能的氧化态时，低氧化态可以用后缀-ous来表示，而高氧化态用-ic来表示。表示这种差异的另一种方法就是在元素名称后面的括号里使用罗马数字表示氧化态。例如：＋2氧化态的铁表示为亚铁或铁（Ⅱ）。

根是一组元素，在化合物的构成中它的作用就像单一的原子一样。这些根内的化学键主要是共价键，但是总的来说，当元素化合时，原子基团具有过多的电子，因此原子基团是负电子。

当你写一个分子式的时候，了解它是否存在是很重要的。例如，你可以轻而易举地写出硝酸碳的分子式，但是还没有化学家制备出这种化合物。用三个例子，通过每一步骤来说明书写分子式的基本规律。

1. 先表示正部分的组成符号，再表示负部分的组成符号。

　　卤化钠　　　　　　氧化钙　　　　　　硫酸铵
　　NaCl　　　　　　　CaO　　　　　　　(NH$_4$)SO$_4$

2. 在每一个元素的右上角写出各自的氧化数（暂时将根放在括号内）。

　　Na^{1+}Cl^{1-}　　　　　Ca^{2+}O^{2-}　　　　　(NH$_4$)$^{1+}$SO$_4^{2-}$

3. 写下等于另一个元素或根的氧化数的下标数。这同机械十字法一样，因为正氧化数显示了失去或共用的电子数，而负氧化数显示了获得或共用的电子数，所以你有多少失去的电子（或共用中部分失去的电子）就有多少获得的电子（或共用中部分获得的电子）。

　　Na$_1^{1+}$Cl$_1^{1-}$　　　　　Ca^{2+}O^{2-}　　　　　(NH$_4$)$_2^{1+}$(SO$_4$)$_1^{2-}$

4. 重写化学式，省略下标1，省略具有下标1的括号，省略正号和负号。

　　NaCl　　　　　　　CaO　　　　　　　(NH$_4$)$_2$SO$_4$

5. 一般地说，最后的化学式下标数要降至最低值。然而，却有些例外，例如，过氧化氢（H$_2$O$_2$）和乙炔（C$_2$H$_2$）。除了这些例外，你必须要了解有关化合物的更特殊的信息。

要想熟练地书写化学式，唯一的方法就是要记住常见元素的氧化数（或学会使用周期表的族数），并要练习写化学式。

命名化合物

二元化合物是由两种元素组成的。化合物的名称也是由两种元素组成的，把第二个元素名称的结尾变成-ide，例如，NaCl＝sodium chloride（氯化钠），AgCl＝silver chloride（氯化银）。如果金属有两种不同的氧化数，低氧化数就可以用后缀-ous 来表示，高氧化数就可以用-ic 来表示。更现代化的方法就是用罗马数字放在名称的后面来表示氧化数。

例如：

$FeCl_2$ = ferrous chloride 氯化亚铁 or iron（Ⅱ）chloride 或氯化铁（Ⅱ）。

$FeCl_3$ = ferric chloride 氯化铁 or iron（Ⅲ）chloride 或氯化铁（Ⅲ）。

如果元素化合发生组成变化的，那么就生成两种或两种以上组成的化合物，第二个元素的名称前面可以放上一个前缀，如一、三和五。例如：二氧化碳 CO_2，一氧化碳 CO，三氧化二磷 P_2O_3 和五氧化二磷 P_2O_5。请注意，当使用这些前缀时，就没有必要指明名称里第一个元素的氧化态，因为第二个元素的前缀已经做了说明。

由三种元素组成的三元化合物，通常是由一种元素和一个根组成的。要命名它们，你只要按照前面正部分和后面负部分的顺序命名每一个部分即可。

二元酸在词干的前面或是非金属元素全名前面使用 hydro-并加上后缀-ic（氢……的）。例如，氢氯酸（HCl）和氢硫酸（H_2S）。

三元酸通常包含氢、非金属和氧。因为氧的含量经常变化，在这个系列中最常见酸的形式仅仅是由非金属的词干加上后缀-ic 组成。比最常见的酸少一个氧原子的酸具有后缀-ous。

比最常见的酸多一个氧原子的酸应具有前缀 per-和后缀-ic。比具有-ous 后缀的酸少一个氧原子的酸应具有前缀 hypo-和后缀-ous。

通过了解下列简单的规律，你能记住常见的酸及其盐的名称。

规律	举例
-ic 算生成-ate 盐	硫酸生成硫酸盐
-ous 算生成-ite 盐	亚硫酸生成亚硫酸盐
hydro-（词干）-ic 酸生成-ide 盐	氢氯酸生成氯化物的盐

三元酸名称具有前缀 hypo-或 per-，前缀仍然保留在盐的名称前面（次氯酸＝次氯酸钠）。表 3-2 为常见酸和碱的化学式。

表 3-2　常见酸和碱的化学式

酸（二元）		酸（三元）	
名　　称	化学式	名　　称	化学式
氢氟酸	HF	硝酸	HNO_3
氢氯酸	HCl	亚硝酸	HNO_2
氢溴酸	HBr	次氯酸	HClO
氢碘酸	HI	亚氯酸	$HClO_2$
氢硫酸	H_2S	氯酸	$HClO_3$
碱		高氯酸	$HClO_4$
名　　称	化学式	硫酸	H_2SO_4
氢氧化钠	NaOH	亚硫酸	H_2SO_3
氢氧化钾	KOH	磷酸	H_3PO_4
氨水	$NH_3·H_2O$	亚磷酸	H_3PO_3
氢氧化钙	$Ca(OH)_2$	碳酸	H_2CO_3
氢氧化镁	$Mg(OH)_2$	乙酸	$HC_2H_3O_2$
氢氧化钡	$Ba(OH)_2$	草酸	$H_2C_2O_4$
氢氧化铝	$Al(OH)_3$	硼酸	H_3BO_3
氢氧化亚铁	$Fe(OH)_2$	硅酸	H_2SiO_3
氢氧化铁	$Fe(OH)_3$		
氢氧化锌	$Zn(OH)_2$		
氢氧化锂	LiOH		

第4单元 有机化合物命名

现代命名脂肪族化合物系统是以烷烃名称为基础的,所以首先解决烷烃化合物的命名是符合逻辑的。

除了烷烃系列的前四个化合物,甲烷、乙烷、丙烷和丁烷以外,分子中原子的数目可以用表示特定数字的希腊字母前缀加上字母 "-ane" 来表示。

烷 烃 名 称

碳原子数	名称	分子式	碳原子数	名称	分子式
1	甲烷	CH_4	6	己烷	C_6H_{14}
2	乙烷	C_2H_6	7	庚烷	C_7H_{16}
3	丙烷	C_3H_8	8	辛烷	C_8H_{18}
4	丁烷	C_4H_{10}	9	壬烷	C_9H_{20}
5	戊烷	C_5H_{12}	10	癸烷	$C_{10}H_{22}$

不同的习惯用不同的方法使用这些化合物的名称。最为通用和系统的方法是由国际纯粹和应用化学联合会任命的委员会设计的命名方法,人们把它称之为 IUPAC 命名法。IUPAC 命名法甚至为最复杂的分子提供了方便和相对简单的命名方法,它还具有把同种原理应用到每一系列化合物的优点。

有时为了命名许多更为简单的各种同系物化合物的名称,仍然使用普通命名法或半系统命名法。但是对于较为复杂的分子来说,人们一般更多的使用 IUPAC 命名法。

普通命名法或半系统命名法

许多简单的化合物是根据它们的官能团或来源命名的,尽管有人试图说服化学家普遍采用 IUPAC 命名法来命名所有的化合物,但是他们仍然广泛地使用普通命名法。

在某些方面,即使是对于复杂的结构来说,普通命名法也确实具有某些优点。因为尽管 IUPAC 命名法可以更清楚地确定结构,但是在某些情况下,特别是在将来必须重复使用时更为麻烦。当然,人们反过来会说,在很多情况下,普通命名法并没有说明任何结构问题。

你可能认为化学家更感兴趣的是化合物如何反应而不是如何命名化合物,但是,目前要解决适用于所有类型化合物的标准化命名法还需很长的时间。本书里采用的首选命名法是与科学教育协会出版物推荐的命名法相一致的,该出版物为《教育科学适用的化学命名法、化学符号和化学术语》。

IUPAC 系统命名法(日内瓦系统命名法)

下面概括了使用的系统命名法原则的要点。

(1) 选择最长的连续碳链为母烃,并根据母烃来命名。

(2) 给链上的碳原子编号,以便指明链上任何取代基的位置。选择编号碳链的起始端,使其号码为最低值。例如:

$$\overset{1}{CH_3}-\overset{2}{CH_2}-\overset{3}{CH_2}-\overset{4}{CH_2}-\overset{5}{CH_3}$$

(3) 取代基的名称按照阿拉伯字母顺序放在母烃的名称前面,取代基的位置放在整个名称的前面。

（4）选择的官能团上的序号要尽可能小，官能团的序号要放在名称的前面。编写官能团序号要优于其他取代基。例如：请看下列醇的命名。简单的醇是通过去掉母烃名称末端的"e"并加上后缀"-ol"来命名的。

CH_3CH_2OH　　　　　　　乙醇　　　　　　（母烃为乙烷）

$\overset{3}{C}H_3\overset{2}{C}H\overset{1}{C}H_2OH$　　　　2-甲基-1-丙醇　　　（母烃为丙烷）
　|
　CH_3

随着以后章节对化合物的介绍，我们还会涉及具有其他官能团化合物的命名方法。

第5单元　有机化合物的性质

引　言

化学是研究元素和元素如何一起反应生成化合物的科学。有机化学仅仅是与碳化合物相关的化学，大多数情况下，有机化合物也包括氢元素。最初，在人们认识含碳和氢的化合物数量超过其他元素全部化合物总数几倍，并且这个数量每年都在增加之前，人们很难认识到这个庞大的研究领域。

有机化合物这一术语容易让人对根据化合物的来源把它们分成有机物和无机物两大类产生误解。有机化合物源于生物，例如蔬菜和动物质，而无机化合物是从矿物质获得的。

史前人们就知道了有机物。尽管人们除了有机物的作用和来源以外，并不知道其他方面的事情，但是有机化合物还是在一些方面得到了应用。水果中的糖可用于甜化目的，并且可以用来酿制葡萄酒。由蔬菜和动物质获得的油和脂肪可以用来制造肥皂，而像靛青和茜素这样的蔬菜色素可用于给织物染色。

直到16和17世纪，人们在分离有机物方面才取得了真正重大的进展。在这一时期，像甲醇、丙酮和乙酸这样的化合物才从木醋酸中提取出来，木醋酸是通过木材干馏得到的。到18世纪末，随着溶剂萃取方法广泛用于植物质和动物质，在已有的有机化合物中又增加了一些新的化合物。正是在这一时期，瑞典化学家席勒成功地从柠檬中提取了2-羟基丙烷-1,2,3-三羧酸（柠檬酸），后来，其他的化学家又从葡萄中分离了2,3-二羟基丁二酸（酒石酸），从苹果中分离出了2-羟基丁酸（苹果酸），从酸奶中分离出了2-羟基丙酸（乳酸），从尿中分离出了尿酸，从核果瘤中分离出了3,4,5-三羟基苯甲酸（五倍子酸）和从酢浆草分离出了乙二酸（草酸）。在1772年和1777年之间，拉瓦锡做了一系列的燃烧实验，正是在这些实验中，由于这些有机物分别产生了产物二氧化碳和水，拉瓦锡确定有机化合物中含有碳和氢。此外，他还通过把二氧化碳溶解在氢氧化钾溶液中计算出产生的二氧化碳的数量。

渐渐地，化学家了解到大多数有机物一般也含有其他元素氧、氮和硫，并且第一次知道了它们的化学性质。

19世纪初期，随着发现的元素越来越多，很显然，与从生物中得到的化合物相关的元素仅仅限于几种，并且这些化合物易于燃烧。

1828年，德国化学家维勒成为了在实验室中有目的地合成有机化合物的第一人。在偶然看到氰酸铵蒸发后产生尿素后，他重复做了几次实验证实了这一结论。

今天，制备技术和制备原理都非常得清楚，使得制备有机物几乎和无机物一样容易。

有机化合物的特性

有机化合物一般是气体、挥发性液体或低熔点固体，如果不含有极性基团，例如：羟基、羧基和磺酸基等，它们不易溶于水。但是，它们通常溶于非极性有机溶剂中，例如：四氯化碳、二乙醚、苯等。在氧气过量下燃烧，有机化合物产生二氧化碳和水（除非当化合物不含氢元，这种情况相对少见）。烃（也就是只含有碳和氢的化合物）的完全燃烧，只产生二氧化碳和水。

与许多无机反应相比，有机反应一般比较慢，并且常常需要能量，通常是热能。有机化学反应很少能进行到底，因此，必须仔细纯化才能分离出理想的高纯产品。这与许多瞬间进行到底的无机化学反应，特别是那些在极性介质中发生的化学反应形成非常鲜明的对比。

同分异构现象在有机化学中是普遍现象。同分异构现象是某些化合物具有的能力，也就是具有相同分子式，但是却由于原子的排列结构不同，存在的形式不同。例如，分子式C_2H_6O表示两种完全不同的化合物，乙醇和甲醚，它们具有完全不同的性质。

要理解化合物的分子是如何从它们的组成元素形成的，我们必须至少要对这些元素的原子结构有一个定性的了解，然后再考虑把这些原子结合起来的化学键的类型。

第6单元 烃

烷 烃

除了本系列前四个化合物，即甲烷、乙烷、丙烷和丁烷以外，直链烷烃是通过使用与碳原子数相对应的希腊字母前缀和加上后缀"-ane"来命名的。

对于支链烷烃，选择最长的碳原子直链并据此命名。烷基取代剂的名称放在主链名称前面，取代剂的位置用适当的序号表示出来。

$$CH_3-CH_2-CH_2-CH_3$$
丁烷

$$CH_3-CH_2-CH_2-CH_2-CH_3$$
戊烷

$$CH_3-\underset{\underset{CH_3}{|}}{CH}-CH_2-CH_3$$
2-甲基丁烷（异戊烷）

$$CH_3-\underset{\underset{CH_3}{|}}{CH}-CH_2-CH_2-CH_3$$
2-甲基戊烷（异己烷）

$$CH_3-\underset{\underset{CH_3}{|}}{\overset{\overset{CH_3}{|}}{C}}-CH_3$$
2,2-二甲基丙烷（新戊烷）

乙 烯

按照 IUPAC 命名法，烯烃是通过去掉对应烷烃的后缀"-ane"并换上后缀"-ene"来命名的。在需要的地方，用相应的数字放在烯烃名称前面来指示双键的位置。有时，乙烯和丙烯仍然分别使用普通命名法。

分子式	IUPAC 命名法	普通命名法
$CH_2=CH_2$	乙烯	乙烯
$CH_3-CH=CH_2$	丙烯	丙烯
$CH_3-CH_2-CH=CH_2$	1-丁烯	1-丁烯
$CH_3-CH=CH-CH_3$	2-丁烯	2-丁烯
$CH_3-CH_2-\underset{\underset{C_6H_5}{\mid}}{CH}-CH=CH_2$	3-苯基-1-戊烯	—

乙 炔

炔烃的 IUPAC 命名法是以与相对烷烃词干为主体,用后缀 "-yne" 取代 "-ane" 来命名的。把对应的数字放在炔烃名称前面指示三键的位置。

分子式	IUPAC 命名法	普通命名法
$CH\equiv CH$	乙炔	乙炔
$CH_3C\equiv CH$	丙炔	甲基乙炔
$CH_3CH_2C\equiv CH$	1-丁炔	乙基乙炔
$CH_3C\equiv CCH_3$	2-丁炔	二甲基乙炔
$CH_3CH_2\underset{\underset{C_6H_5}{\mid}}{CH}C\equiv CH$	3-苯基-1-戊炔	—

石油的分馏

原油被分馏,馏分在一定的沸点范围内收集。

每一馏分碳原子的含量基本上确定在一定的范围内最先蒸馏出来的是分子量较小和挥发性较大的组分。然而,由于一定比例具有相对较高分子量的、更易挥发的支链化合物的存在,较轻馏分的碳原子含量增加。实际上,这并不重要。因为每一馏分的用途基本上与它们的挥发度和黏度有关,而与它们各自的组分无关。

馏分	蒸馏温度范围/℃	近似碳的含量
气体	20℃以下	$C_1\sim C_4$
石油醚	20~60	$C_5\sim C_6$
(石油醚)	60~100	$C_6\sim C_7$
汽油	40~205	$C_5\sim C_{12}$(环烷烃)
煤油	175~325	$C_{12}\sim C_{18}$(芳香烃)
柴油	275~400	$C_{12}\sim C_{25}$
润滑油	不挥发性液体	—
沥青	残渣	—

馏分的用途

较易挥发组分通常用作燃料。

馏分	用途
气体	加热
石油醚	有机溶剂
(石油醚)	有机溶剂

汽油	需要挥发性液体的内燃机燃料
煤油	加热燃料，发动机所需挥发性较小的液体，例如：拖拉机，喷气式发动机
柴油	加热燃料，用于柴油发动机
润滑油	润滑剂
沥青	道路建设和屋顶

润滑油馏分常常含有高熔点的长链烷烃（$C_{20} \sim C_{34}$），当遇冷时，它们就形成蜡。如果这些组分存在于馏分当中，特别是在寒冷季节，它们就容易堵塞炼油厂的管道。然而，通过冷凝和过滤可以分离这些组分。这种固体叫做固体石蜡（熔点 50～55℃）可用来制造凡士林。

石油馏分可以为制备其他的化工产品提供有用的化合物，并且含有 5 个碳原子更易挥发的馏分可以为大规模生产脂肪族化合物提供重要的原材料。

第 7 单元　芳烃性质和苯的命名

根据两种常见的有机化合物类型：脂肪族化合物和芳香族化合物，可以方便地对有机化合物进行分类。今天，脂肪族化合物和芳香族化合物的字面含意几乎没有什么意义。因为，有机化合物可以根据它们的分子结构和性质进行更精确的分类。

脂肪族化合物就是那些具有开链碳原子的化合物或是结构和性质类似于这种开链化合物的环状化合物。

芳香族化合物就是那些具有苯环结构的化合物或是电子结构和化学作用类似于苯的其他化合物。有许多化合物，开始它们的外表一点不像苯，但是它们的电子结构却基本相似。

无论如何，目前根据苯环结构可以方便地解释芳烃的性质。因为，芳烃的定义涵盖了大多数常见的芳香族化合物。

苯分子结构的历史发展

凯库勒于 1858 年第一个确定了四价碳原子。自那以后，他就多次尝试着写出苯分子的结构。芳香族化合物含碳的量相对比较大，最初人们尝试着写出如下难以让人接受的线性分子结构。

$$CH_3-C\equiv C-C\equiv C-CH_3$$
$$CH_2=CH-C\equiv C-CH=CH_2$$
$$CH\equiv C-CH-CH-C\equiv CH$$

这样的化合物应该容易在不饱和键上进行加成反应，然而，苯却没有显示出进行这类反应的倾向。另外，这种线性分子应该有几个同分异构体，但是，实际上苯却没有同分异构体。

当人们认识到一元取代衍生物（C_6H_5Y）没有结构异构体时，这就意味着所有碳原子可能都是同样地以环形排列。

人们已经观察到苯的二元取代基衍生物的三种异构体，这为支持苯的环状结构提供了进一步的证据。

1865 年，凯库勒第一次提出了让人能够接受的苯的环状结构：

$$\begin{array}{c} H \\ | \\ C \\ H-C \diagup \diagdown C-H \\ \| \| \\ H-C \diagdown \diagup C-H \\ C \\ | \\ H \end{array}$$

它可以更方便地写为：

命名取代苯衍生物

一个氢原子被一个原子或原子团取代的苯分子称之为一元取代衍生物。

甲苯

氯苯

硝基苯

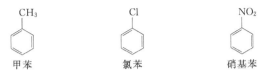

对于每一个二取代衍生物，根据取代基在苯环上的位置，有三种不同的同分异构体。当两个取代基位于苯环上两个相邻的碳原子上时，异构体称之为邻位衍生物。当两个取代基位于相隔位置时，称之为间位衍生物。当两个取代基处于相对位置时，称之为对位衍生物。通过给环上的碳原子标号，并且选择最小和的数值来确定取代基的位置。

例如，请看三个二溴代苯的同分异构体。

1,2-二溴苯

1,3-二溴苯

1,4-二溴苯

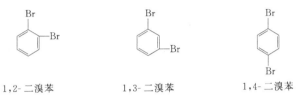

每一个三取代基苯的衍生物都有三个同分异构体。

1,2,3-三氯苯

1,2,4-三氯苯

1,2,5-三氯苯

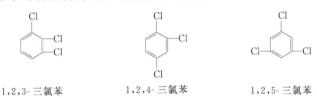

如果存在的一个取代基形成特定名称的化合物，那么就只涉及两个取代基的位置。

2,6-二硝基苯甲酸

2-氯-4-硝基苯酚

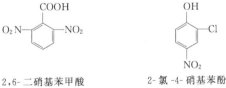

一元取代苯衍生物的 C_6H_5— 部分称之为苯基，它类似于脂肪族中的烃基。为了方便起见，特别是书写复杂的结构式时，苯基常常缩写为“Ph”。

苯基和取代苯基同样都可统称为芳基，并且可以缩写为“Ar”。

除了芳基的普通芳香性以外，当芳基的确切性质对特定的反应并不具有特别的重要性时，通常我们把芳基视为一个芳基系统。

C_6H_5— 苯基

C_6H_5—
C_6H_4Y—
C_6H_3YZ—
etc.

} 统称为芳基

第8单元 聚合物的性质

尽管从最广泛的意义上来看,聚合常常用来表示像乙炔、甲醛和乙醛那样相对简单的环化过程(正如已经看到的),但是术语聚合物一般用来描述至少由几百个重复单元组成的化合物,它们的相对分子量超过 5000。

不同的教科书使用各种方法来划分聚合物,两个更受人们喜欢的方法是按照它们形成的化学方式或按照它们的物理性质和形态来分类。

术语弹性体通常是用来指橡胶或橡胶状的材料,它们具有确定的弹性,也就是在施加压力的情况下变形,在除去压力的情况下恢复原状。尽管聚乙烯可以伸展,但是它不能恢复原状,因此,它不属于弹性体。

划分为纤维的聚合物通常可以抽成线,并进行纺织。

塑料是能够塑造的固体化合物,而树脂是固体或半固体。树脂通常是透明或半透明的物质,且具有光泽,但不能铸塑。

因为聚合物术语常常互换,所以聚合物的分类并不是严格按照定义来划分的。主要基于这一原因,也为了有助于避免不必要的模糊概念,本章聚合物的分类是根据生成聚合物的化学加工类型来分类的。

从化学上讲,聚合反应基本上有两种模式:加聚和缩聚。在加聚反应中,聚合产品理论上是单体反应分子的整数倍。因此,具有同样的百分比组成,例如,聚乙烯和聚苯乙烯。缩聚反应发生在两种不同的单体间,或是至少发生在同一组内作用不同的官能团之间,也就是每一个反应分子至少包含两个相同的官能团,它们通常位于端点,例如:尼龙 66 和聚酯(涤纶)。如果其中的一种反应物具有两种以上的不同作用的官能团,聚合反应在三维空间发生,并形成大型交联结构。

缩聚通常导致共聚物的产生。

有机硅聚合物(硅树脂)提供了一种不同但是重要的缩聚聚合物类型,这会在本章的后面讨论。

聚合物中链的类型

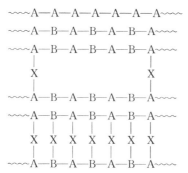

在上述交联聚合物中,相邻基团 A、B 和 X 可以是相同也可以是不同的基团。而且,X 代表的单位数可以变化,也可以是无数的。

除了生成线性交替共聚物以外,有时,共聚作用生成任意共聚物和块状聚合物。

~~~A—B—A—A—B—B—A~~~　　任意共聚物

~~~A—A—A—A—B—B—B~~~　　块状聚合物

由于加成反应形成共聚物，例如：丁苯橡胶，或者缩聚反应生成尼龙-66。

两种不同类型单体之间的共聚作用形成加成聚合物，常常导致形成一种材料，这种材料显示了两种单体聚合物的优异性质，例如：维荣，它是氯乙烯和醋酸乙烯的共聚物。

交联作用对物理性质的影响

尽管线性聚合物和共聚物可能具有许多支链，但是，它们不含有单链的连接。因此，一旦加热，每个链之间的距离可以显著的增加，引起聚合物软化，并且更易变形。因为聚合物链之间的结合力是分子间弱吸引力，它只需要很小的温度变化就能克服结合力并使之软化。一旦冷却，就发生可逆过程。这种类型的聚合物叫做热塑性塑料，例如：聚乙烯和聚氯乙烯。

实际上，因为单个链相互连接，交联聚合物不是很容易软化。通常当提供足够的热量使交联断裂的时候，整个聚合物分子已经分解了。这类化合物被称之为热固性塑料，例如：脲醛树脂和酚醛树脂，它们需要强热才能引发任何形式的化学变化。

尽管具有小型交联的聚合物经常显示出线性结构和大型交联结构之间中间体的热性质，但是，具有大型交联结构的聚合物实际上是不能软化的。

天然聚合物和合成聚合物

尽管某些天然产品，像橡胶、羊毛、棉花和丝绸实际上都是利用天然材料，并且更多的是通过使用许维茨试剂（一种氢氧化铜的氨溶液）处理，由棉花和羊毛、木头、麦秆和甘蔗渣等原料再生。但是，今天人们能够合成大量不同类型的聚合物。纤维素的碱溶液通过细喷雾器喷到稀硫酸中，破坏四氨合铜络合物，使纤维素沉淀，抽成线，纺成人造丝。

用醋酸处理上述纤维素产品时，纤维素中的羟基可以被羧基取代，并且生成不燃烧的材料。它具有光泽的外表和低吸水率。不同形式的这种聚合物有电影胶片和特列塞尔。

在英国和美国，比使用四氨合铜络离子更好的技术是纤维胶工艺。在这种工艺中，纤维素的钠盐用二硫化碳处理生成磺酸盐，磺酸盐在稀碱溶液中生成黏稠的、胶状的溶液。经过络合反应的一段时间以后，用稀酸处理再生纤维素。我们就可以得到这种聚合物的丝或片（玻璃片）。用丙三醇溶液处理后，玻璃片会变得柔软。

我们可以从纤维素中获得更多的合成纤维、人造丝绸、漆和塑料等材料。纤维衍生物包括硝化纤维清漆、纤维酯、硝化纤维塑料和纤维醚。

聚 合 条 件

商业上生产许多材料，确切的生产条件只有生产者知道，对外是严格保密的。特别是对于所用催化剂性质的详情更是如此。所以，对于每一生产过程不会说明准确的信息。

某些生产技术原理基本上是简单的，但是需要苛刻的生产条件。例如，低密度聚乙烯需要 3000 个大气压。因此在实验室中很难模拟出这样的情况。然而，许多其他的生产过程在原理和生产上相对来说是简单的。并且在通常或相对温和的温度和压力条件下就可操作。例如：生产尼龙-66、尼龙-610、酚醛树脂和脲醛树脂。

为了控制重复单位的数量，支链程度或链之间的交叉程度，反应过程的条件常可用来控制特制聚合物，以满足其应用目的。例如，我们可以生产各种尼龙，纤维或块状固体。并且还可以得到高密度、坚硬和晶体状的聚乙烯或密度更低和更柔软的材料。

现在有很多不同种类的聚合物可以使用，要研究比较多的聚合物是不可能的。本章试图概括制备某些更重要和更常见材料的生产技术。

第9单元 橡胶与塑料

天 然 橡 胶

生橡胶是从自然界广泛分布的乳胶得到的。乳胶是白色流体的胶状溶液，通过简单地加入醋酸，生橡胶就会从乳胶中凝结出来。商业上大量使用的乳胶都是从橡胶树上得到的，巴西三叶胶树，它生长于巴西亚马逊河地区，但是，现在它生长在世界上不同地区的种植园里，例如，斯里兰卡和马来西亚。

天然橡胶是一类称之为多萜烯的碳氢化合物，$(C_5H_8)_n$，主要以两种异构体形式存在。顺式异构体具有很大的弹性，而反式异构体，有名的古塔胶（反式-聚-甲基-1,3-丁二烯）没有弹性，当它加热到100℃以上的时候，就会软化成塑料样的东西。古塔胶可以用作水下电缆和高尔夫球的外皮。

天然橡胶的原材料在每一聚合物链之间只含有限的交联，同样，天然橡胶也显示出热塑性，也就是，一旦加热它就变软变黏。一冷却，它就变硬变脆。

这些问题在很大程度上通过硫化来克服。硫化技术首先是在1838年由查尔斯·古德伊尔发现并引入的。这一技术只需要把生橡胶与8%的硫共同加热，使之在聚合物链之间形成交联。冷硫化过程使用2.5%的二氯化二硫和二硫化碳。

硫化催化剂可以是有机物或无机物，它们可用来增加化合速率并使反应在较低的温度下进行。

硫化橡胶在宽的温度范围内具有较高的张力、耐久力和弹性。

橡胶制品通过加入其他的添加剂可以大大地延长寿命，众所周知的抗氧化剂就能延缓自氧化过程。某种醛和苯胺的聚合产物可用于这种目的，它还具有加速反应的另一优点。

合 成 橡 胶

最早在市场上销售的合成橡胶（美国，1932年）是聚-2-氯-1,3-丁二烯（氯丁橡胶）。不幸的是这种橡胶遇到了挫折，即使是今天，生产这种橡胶仍然比天然橡胶贵得多，因此，它一般不适用于生产像轮胎这样的用品。由于它具有很强的抗化学品和自氧化能力，它确实具有某种特殊用途。这种聚合物是从乙炔获得的。

获得最廉价的1,3-丁二烯的商业来源是对丁烷，1-丁烯和2-丁烯进行气相催化脱氢。

1,3-丁二烯生成一些有用的共聚物，其中的两个共聚物如下所述。

丁钠橡胶是在1927~1933年期间在德国开发出来的，并且是第一个制造出来的相对较高分子质量的1,3-丁二烯橡胶。生产过程中使用了钠作为聚合催化剂，而实际上，丁钠橡胶的名称由单体和催化剂的名称，1,3-丁二烯和钠得来。

毫无疑问，丁苯橡胶（GRS，Buna S or Cold Rubber）是一种最为有用的多用途橡胶。它是通过70%的1,3-丁二烯和30%苯乙烯的自由基共聚合反应得到的。它在第二次世界大战期间开发出来，以取代难以得到的天然橡胶。

这种产物用与天然橡胶相同的方法进行硫化，它就具有了比大多数其他合成橡胶更好的耐久性，商业上用它制造轮胎。

较硬的橡胶可以通过增加苯乙烯的百分比来得到。

塑　　料

简单的烯烃聚合就能够生成一类长链的加成聚合物。这些聚合物是强度高和柔韧性强的固体，从表面上看，它具有无限的家庭和商业用途。

聚乙烯可通过一些不同的技术来生产，每一种方法生产的聚合物都具有些微的差异。早期的生产过程多利用非常高的压力和温度，压力范围为 1000～3000 大气压，温度范围为 200～400℃。

帝国化学工业公司使用的高压生产过程需要含有微量氧的乙烷，氧作为自由基引发剂。这个过程要在 1500 大气压以上和大约 200℃ 的条件下进行。有机过氧化合物的热分解也可以用来引发反应。

用这种过程生产的材料含有比较多的支链甲基，它可以称之为低密度聚乙烯（$0.92g/cm^3$）。

齐格勒过程需要更为温和的条件，温度 50～75℃，压力 2～7 大气压。乙烯通入烃介质中，其中氯化钛和三乙基氯悬浮液作为催化剂。当反应完成时，催化剂用稀酸分解，而聚合物通过过滤分离。

菲利浦过程也使用烃介质，但是在这种情况下，催化剂三氧化二铬是通过 90% 的二氧化硅和 10% 的氧化铝发挥作用。生产条件为 150～180℃ 和 30～35 大气压，比齐格勒过程的条件要更高一些。尽管聚合物的链要比高压技术生成的链少很多，但是，它还是包含了很多的支链甲基。

齐格勒和菲利浦产品叫作高密度聚乙烯（$0.945～0.96g/cm^3$），其聚合物分子排列更规则和更紧密，形成更坚硬和晶体结构更好的材料，并且具有更强的张力。除此之外，这两种材料比低密度聚乙烯都具有更高的软化温度，齐格勒聚合物的软化温度为 120～128℃，而菲利普聚合物软化温度为 130～136℃。

商业上，四氟乙烯是通过二氟甲烷高温分解得到的，像其他的甲烷和乙烷的氯氟衍生物一样，四氟乙烯也是很有价值的制冷剂，它被称之为氟利昂-22。

聚四氟乙烯的聚合需要有过氧化物引发剂和 45～50 大气压的条件。

尽管聚四氟乙烯是一种热塑性塑料，但是它具有 327℃ 的高温软化温度，当温度超过 400℃ 时，还能保持相对的稳定性。此外，这种聚合物还具有很高的抗化学物质的能力，并且具有极低的摩擦系数，它特别适合于用来制造不粘锅厨具。

苯为商业上获得苯乙烯提供了有用的原材料。苯与乙烷进行弗里德克尔-克拉夫茨烷基化反应生成乙苯，然后乙苯分解为苯乙烯。

通过过氧化二苯甲酰引发剂使苯乙烯在 85～100℃ 发生聚合反应。

这样产生的热塑料可溶解于苯。然而，少量二乙基苯（$CH_2=CHC_6H_4CH=CH_2$）的存在可引发高度交联，并且不再生成热塑性塑料，这种材料也不溶于苯。

第 10 单元　精细化学品

精细化工企业是生产精细化学品的企业。精细化工产品和特殊化工产品都称之为精细化学品。精细化学品可以分为 11 类：农药，染料，涂料（包括油漆和墨水），颜料，试剂，高纯化学品，信息化学品（包括光感材料和磁性记录材料），食品和饲料添加剂，胶黏剂，催化剂和助剂，化学药品和日用化学品。

农　药

农药是生物试剂，物理试剂和化学试剂，它用来杀死对人类有害的植物或动物。实际上，农药这一术语常常只用于化学试剂。人们把各种农药都视为杀虫剂，杀线虫剂，杀真菌剂，除草剂和灭鼠剂，也就是分别对昆虫类，线虫类（或者蛔虫），真菌，杂草和啮齿动物起主要作用的试剂。

农药可以源于植物（例如，除虫菊酯，印度楝树油）或矿物，它们已可以用化学方法来制造（例如，滴滴涕）。也可以使用食肉动物或其他生物方法制造。寄生虫和食肉动物靠吃有害物生存，在生物试剂中，病源使它们生病，生化信息素干扰昆虫交配。还有基因工程农药，例如，产生毒素的细菌株用于防治蛾幼虫。

化学农药通常是接触毒药，胃毒药或熏剂毒药。接触性毒药与有害物进行物理接触后，会立即产生效果或延缓产生效果。熏剂最初可以是固态，液态或气态，但是杀死有害物都是在气体状态下。

某些杀虫剂和杀真菌剂都可以吸收，也就是说，通过有农药的植物部分传给植物的其他部分，这里农药仅对吃这种植物的害虫起作用。非选择性的农药既可以影响目标有害物，也可以影响其他有机物；选择性农药只影响目标有害物。持久性农药就是那些在环境中保持很长时间的农药。

染　料

染料是天然物质或合成物质，用于给各种材料染色，特别是纺织品，皮革和食品。天然染料之所以这样称呼，是因为它们是由植物获得（例如，茜素，儿茶，靛青和洋苏木心材），由动物获得（例如，胭脂虫，干燥雌体和提尔紫）和由某些天然存在的矿石（例如，赭土和普鲁士蓝）。在现代染色工艺中，它们完全可以用合成染料来替代。大多数合成染料是由煤焦油制备的，煤焦油是由像苯这样的芳香烃组成的，由苯可以制备靛青或蒽，蒽产生茜素。虽然某些材料，例如，丝绸和羊毛可以简单地放到染料里浸泡就可染色（这样使用的染料常常叫做直接染料），但是，包括棉的其他材料通常需要使用媒染剂。茜素就是一种媒染料，它产生的颜色取决于使用的媒染剂。染料还可以根据在染色过程中需要的介质分为酸性染料或碱性染料。靛青之所以称之为染缸染料，也是由于它的使用方法。靛青首先经过化学处理使之溶解，然后用于染缸中浸染的材料。当材料浸满了染料的时候，把它们取出，在空气中晾干，靛青又恢复到原来不溶的状态。现在人们还不完全清楚染料附着在材料上并使之染色的过程是什么。一种理论认为在染料和被处理的纤维之间发生化学反应，另一种理论认为染料被纤维吸收。

颜　料

颜料是把颜色传给其他材料的物质。在油漆中，颜料是一种粉状物质，当它与液体介质混合后，就把颜色留给了着色表面。油漆中使用的颜料几乎都是金属化合物，但是也使用有机化合物。大多数黑色颜料都是有机化合物，例如，骨炭（兽炭或炭黑）和灯烟。有些金属颜料是天然存在的。世界上某些地方鲜艳、漂亮的岩石和土壤，例如，黄赭土，黄土和棕土都是铁的氧化物。一氧化铅是一种黄色的铅的化合物。红铅也是铅的氧化物。铬酸铅或铬黄也是一种重要的黄色颜料。白铅或碱性碳酸铅也是一种长期使用的颜料，它与氧化锌混合着色更牢。镉黄是硫化镉。天青石是一种重要的蓝色染料，也叫做普鲁士蓝（铁氰化铁）。绿色染料是由普鲁士蓝和铬黄混合制成的。朱砂（硫化汞）是红色的。颜料存在于植物和动物体内。例如，植物漂亮的颜色就是由于叶绿素和黄色色素这两种物质存在的结果，动物中也存在着这两种色素。在其他植物中还存在胡萝卜素和花青素，胡萝卜素的存在使胡萝卜和其他的蔬菜变黄，花青素使花变蓝，变红和变紫。血色是从红细胞球中的血色素得到的。人皮肤颜色的形成也是由于色素存在的结果造成的。

试　剂

试剂或反应物是用于引发化学反应的一种材料。例如，盐酸就是化学试剂，它能够引起碳酸钙释放二氧化碳。同样，盐酸是一种化学试剂，它与锌反应产生氢气，但现象不明显，即使如此，氢气是由酸产生，而不是由金属产生。要把涉及化学反应的化学药品分为"试剂"的话，这主要是一个习惯和看法的问题。

从术语的另一用途来看，当购买和制备化学药品的时候，"试剂"指的是：在化学分析，化学反应和物理实验中，具有足够纯度化学药品。试剂的纯度标准由国际美国材料实验协会制定。例如，试剂级的水必须含有极少量诸如钠离子和氯离子，硅和细菌的杂质，还要具有很高的电阻系数。

胶 黏 剂

胶黏剂是能够粘到其他物质的表面，并能使它们相互粘到一起的物质。特别是指合成胶黏剂的时候，胶水有时用来代替胶黏剂。动物胶，一种用动物的皮，蹄或骨制成的白明胶可能史前时期人们就已经知晓了，直到20世纪它一直就是主要的胶黏剂。现在制作家具时常使用这种胶。动物胶可以固态销售（既可以是沉淀，也可以是片状物。在有水夹层的胶壶中熔化，当它变热时即可使用），也可以液态胶水（一种酸性溶液）销售。由植物得到的胶黏剂也是重要的，它们包括天然树胶和树脂，植物黏液，淀粉及淀粉衍生物。它们通常用来给纸和纺织品上浆，为标签，密封和制造纸制品涂胶。其他由动物和植物来源得到的胶黏剂包括血胶，鱼胶，酪素胶，橡胶胶黏剂和纤维素衍生物。由合成树脂可以制备具有特殊性质的胶黏剂。某些合成树脂，比如，环氧树脂，其强度大到可以用来替代焊接或铆接的建筑结构。胶带具有一层压敏胶黏剂。

催 化 剂

催化剂是能够引起化学反应速率发生变化，而本身在反应中不被消耗的物质。加快反应速率的物质叫做正催化剂，简单地说，是催化剂。而减小反应速率的物质叫做负催化剂，或者叫做抑制剂。

酶就是自然界最常见、最有效的催化剂。大多数人体或其他生物内发生的化学反应都是高能量反应，如果根本没有酶催化剂存在的话，反应速率很慢。例如，在没有催化剂的情况况下，淀粉水解成为葡萄糖需要几周的时间，人的唾液中存在的痕量的唾液淀粉酶能够加速反应，使淀粉得到消化。某些酶能够使反应速率提高10亿倍以上。酶一般是专门的催化剂，也就是，它们只催化一种特定反应物（称之为基质）的反应。通常，酶和其基质具有互补的结构，由于酶中存在的官能团，它们可以结合在一起生成更容易反应的络合物，酶可以稳定反应的转变状态或降低活化能。某些物质的毒性作用（例如，一氧化碳和神经气体）就是由于它们阻碍了人体内维持生命的催化反应。

催化剂在化学实验室和化学工业上也是非常重要的。某些反应在少量酸或碱存在的情况况，反应速率快得多，我们就说酸是催化剂或碱是催化剂。例如，酯的水解是在少量碱的存在下被催化的。在这一反应中，是氢氧根离子与酯进行反应，由于碱的存在，氢氧根的浓度大大超过纯水中氢氧根的浓度。虽然由碱提供的某些氢氧根离子在第一步反应中全部消耗掉，它们在随后的反应中又从水中产生出来，存在的氢氧根离子净含量在反应开始和反应结束时没有发生变化，所以碱是催化剂，而不是反应物。

　　细颗粒金属常常被用作催化剂，它们吸收反应物到其表面，反应在这里更容易发生。例如，氢和氧混合而不反应生成水，但是如果有少量的粉末铂加入到气体混合物的话，气体很容易反应。加氢反应，例如，由植物油生成硬煮脂肪就是以细颗粒金属或金属氧化物作催化剂的。商业上生产硫酸和硝酸也依靠表面催化剂。除了铂以外，其他常用的表面催化剂是铜，铁，镍，钯，铑，钌，硅胶（二氧化硅）和氧化钒。

第 2 部分 分析仪器介绍

第 11 单元 紫外可见分光光度计

光度分析法也许是所有光谱分析法中应用最广泛的方法,而且在定量分析中具有重要意义。溶液吸收的可见光量或其他辐射能量是可以测量的,因为它取决于吸收物质的浓度,所以能够对存在的物质数量进行定量分析。

比色法是根据物质吸收可见光的能力来鉴定物质。可见比色法是将未知浓度的有色溶液与一种或一种以上已知浓度的有色溶液进行比较。在分光光度法中,通过光电池这样的检测器,在特定的波长下测量发射光强度和输出光强度的比值。

吸收光谱还可以提供指纹对吸收物质进行定性分析。

分光光度计的组成

在紫外可见光区有几种光源可以使用。人们已经把汞蒸气灯用作光源,但是,由于这些灯释放热量,就需要进行热绝缘或冷却。通常多用于可见和近红外光区的是钨丝白炽灯。这些是热光源或"黑体光源",固体灯丝材料在高温下产生辐射,这与灯丝的实际化学性质没有太大的关系。这些光源提供了大约 320~3000nm 的辐射,不幸的是,其中大部分辐射处于近红外区。通常在 3000K 的操作温度下,只有大约全部辐射能的 15% 位于可见光区,而在 2000K 时,只有 1%。使操作温度高于 3000K 以上会大大提高总能量输出,并且使最大强度波长移向短波。但是,灯的使用寿命会大大缩短。在紫外光区产生大量的辐射需要高温,这会很不方便。在灯中加入低压碘蒸气或溴蒸气,钨丝灯的寿命会大大的延长。如果给钨丝灯加上熔融硅灯罩,它就成为受欢迎的光源。目前这种灯就叫做石英卤素灯。紫外光区的大部分鉴定工作都使用氢或氘放电灯,通常在低压直流电下操作(气压大约 5mm,电压 40V)。这些灯可以提供连续辐射,最短波长大约为 160nm,但是窗口材料一般会限制短波光的发射(石英大约可发射光的波长是 200nm,而使用熔融硅可发射光的波长 185nm)。大约在 360nm 以上,氢放射线形成连续光谱,因此,白炽灯一般用于较长波长下的测量。氘灯价格更贵,但是,与相同构造和瓦数的氢灯相比较,氘灯的光谱强度和寿命是氢灯的 2~5 倍。

光源发射出的连续辐射用单色器进行分散。

目前使用的检测器主要有三种类型。图 11-1 所示的叫做叠层电池或光电电池。这种

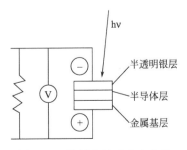

图 11-1 叠层电池或光电电池

装置通过测量在半导体层上产生的电压，来测量光量子的强度。半导体上的光子产生被银层吸收的电子。电压的大小决定于撞击检测器的光子的数量。第二类检测器是光电检测器或叫作真空光电管，如图 11-2 所示。这种检测器是由一种涂铯光电阴极组成的真空管。具有足够能量的光子撞击在阴极产生电子，电子在阳极被收集。通过系统中的电流测量光通量。真空光电管类型的检测器需要进一步放大才能正常使用。最后一种常用的检测器如图 11-3 所示。这种检测器是由发光阴极管组成的，发光阴极管是由一系列光电倍增电极组成的，它也称为光电倍增器。由光电阴极产生的初级电子在电场的作用下加速，使其撞击在面积不大的第一个光电倍增电极上。撞击电子具有足够的能量产生 2～5 个次级电子，次级电子加速撞击第二个光电倍增器会产生更多的电子。这样产生瀑布效应，最后全部电子在阳极被收集。典型情况下，光电倍增管有 9～16 级，每一辐射光子可获得 10^6～10^9 个电子。

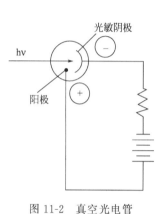

图 11-2　真空光电管

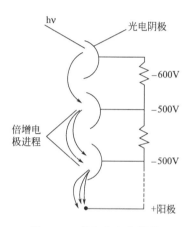

图 11-3　真空光电倍增管

单光束和双光束分光光度计

测量紫外可见辐射吸收是测量相对性质。测量者必须不断地把样品的吸收和分析参考样品的吸收或空白溶液的吸收进行比较，以确保测量的可靠性。样品和参比样品的比率取决于仪器的构造。在单光束仪器中，在光源和检测器之间只有一个光源或一条光路。这通常意味着在每次读数之后，把样品从光路移开，并换上参比样品。因此，在测量之间通常会存在几秒钟的间隔。

然而在双光束仪器中，样品和参比样品在一秒钟内可进行多次的比较。光源产生的光通过单色器分解成两束独立的光——一束用于样品，另一束用于参考样品。图 11-4 显示了两种类型的双光束分光光度计。测量样品和参考样品的吸收可以在空间分割开来，如图 11-4A 所示，然而，这种测量需要两个完全匹配的检测器。或者，样品和参考样品的测量可以在时间上分割开来，如图 11-4B 所示，这种技术使用快速旋转的反光镜或"斩光器"快速转换来自于样品和参考样品的光束。这种方法仅需要一个检测器，可能是这两种方法中更好的一种。

双光束操作法与单光束操作法相比主要有两个优点。快速检测样品和参考样品有助于消除由于光源强度的飘移、电子的不稳定性和光路系统的任何变化引起的误差。双光束操作也容易实现自动化：光谱可用纸带记录仪记录。

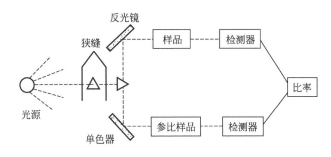

图 11-4A 双光束空间结构

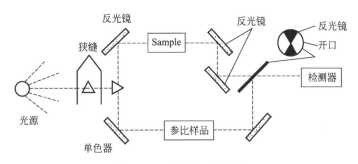

图 11-4B 双光束时间结构

图 11-4 两类双光束分光光度计示意图

第 12 单元 气相色谱

气相色谱仪

气相色谱仪与用于其他形式的柱色谱仪（见图 12-1）几乎没有什么区别。气相色谱仪是由载气源（在规定范围内，可以将载气流量控制在所需的数量级）；进样口（可以从 25℃ 加热到 500℃）；色谱柱（在空气浴中，恒温在 25~400℃）和检测器（适用于气相样品）组成的。相关溶质的汽化以及使它们处于气态都需要高温。因为分配系数与温度有关，所以温度须控制在±0.1 和±0.01℃之间（这取决于在测量保留时间时所需的精确度）。进样口和检测器温度一般控制在比柱温高 10%（无论如何，对于火焰离子化检测器来说，温度应在 100℃ 以上，见后面的内容），以确保样品快速汽化和防止样品冷凝。通常，柱温至少要设置在比溶质沸点高 25℃ 的位置上（当然，这并不是绝对的，因为我们所需要的是：在操作温度下，物质必须具有适当高的蒸气压）。

气相色谱柱

最常用的色谱柱是由装满大小非常均固体颗粒的管子组成的，固体颗粒表面涂有液体固定相。也许，最常用的载体是海藻（例如，Johns-Manville 红色硅藻土色谱载体）。根据实验对管材进行选择。通常使用铝管和铜管，但是，色谱活性氧化物薄膜和催化反应活性氧化物薄膜可能会使铝和铜不适合敏感化合物（例如，类固醇）；在这样的情况下，可以使用不锈钢管或玻璃管（玻璃管惰性更强，但是操作不方便）。

空心色谱柱是由 25~100m 长，内径为 0.3~0.6mm 的钢管、玻璃管或石英管组成

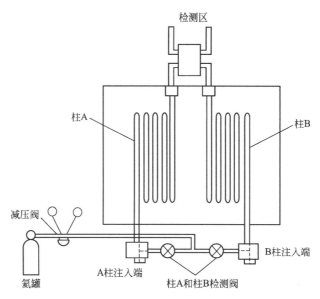

图 12-1 双柱气相色谱结构图

的,其内壁涂有固定相薄膜。这些叫做涂壁空心色谱柱。尽管熔融石英色谱柱不会改变色谱柱的特性,但是,因为熔融石英色谱柱的惰性内表面可以减少较高极性溶质的拖尾现象,也因为它具有很高的机械柔韧性,所以,熔融石英色谱柱受到用户的喜爱。石英色谱柱的机械柔韧性是由于在其外表面涂有一层聚合物,它可以排除湿气,防止水合作用和某些薄壁开裂。在石英色谱柱内涂极性固定相还存在一些问题,但是,通过键合相可以形成涂层。它是适当使用类似化学物质来制备的,这些化学物质用来制备液相色谱柱所用的大量键合固定相。

在气相色谱法的前十年里,就有人提出和论证了毛细管色谱法。直到 20 世纪 70 年代人们才真正认识到毛细管色谱法的重要性。当时毛细管色谱技术已经很成熟,并且人们需要分离越来越复杂的混合物(特别是环境和生物医药研究方面),这些促使人们开发毛细管色谱柱的商业用途。早期工作人员对商品仪器的研究取得了一些进展,但是,没有根本性的进展。大部分变化主要集中在(a)减少样品进口死体积和检测器结构;(b)更好和更均匀的温度控制箱,改进温度编程的线性范围。大量应用毛细管色谱柱主要对注入到较低温度的色谱柱进行温度编程。给低温色谱柱注入样品集中在柱端的注入区,并可减少外进样器对谱带变宽的影响。

毛细管柱与填充柱相比容量有限,也就是固定相较少,绝对保留值较小。因此,许多毛细管气相色谱法只能测定注入溶液的少量成分,不能测定痕量成分(通过样品制备过程,实际分析样品中的痕量组分仍然可以用适当的萃取和浓缩的方法来确定,但是,注射溶液的浓度是比较高的)。因为涂壁空心色谱柱容量低,也因为其他原因,有人建议使用表面涂层空心色谱柱。在使用固定相之前,这些色谱柱管内涂上细微颗粒的金属氧化物,石墨或铝硅酸盐。因为表面积比较大,所以,色谱柱的容量就比较大。

尽管毛细管色谱柱的塔板高度比填装紧密的填充柱要高,但是,毛细管色谱柱的主要优点不在于塔板高度,而在于获得较小压力降的塔板数。例如,如果 20,000 块理论塔板是一根好的填充色谱柱的上限的话,那么,空心色谱柱可以达到 75,000 到 150,000 块理论塔板。毛细管色谱法是对填充柱色谱法的一种技术上的补充。在确定适当分辨率和最大分析数量的时,优先选用填充柱。

色谱法载体材料

色谱法载体的作用是吸附固定相。海藻就是一种有用的载体，它们是微小单细胞藻类的骨架（硅藻类），主要由无定形含水硅和微量金属氧化物杂质组成。这种材料具有多孔和大表面积的优点。各种硅藻土载体的某些性质如表 12-1 所示。例如，红色硅藻土色谱载体 P 是由特级耐火砖制备的，它是粉色的（因此叫做 P）煅烧硅藻土，硬度高且不易粉碎。它主要适用于低极性和中等极性的溶质（例如，烃）。它是比较好的吸附剂，具有相互作用性质。如果根本没有液相的话，载体就用作吸附剂，进行的操作就是气-固色谱。给活性吸附剂涂上液体薄膜的作用是降低气-固活性，而不是消除气-固活性。业已表明即使填充质量百分数为 20% 的液体量，也不能消除这种活性。可以使用几种技术来降低这种活性，例如，酸洗和用二甲基二氯硅烷与活泼硅进行硅烷基化取代氢原子。对于确定的分析任务，选择载体与选择固定相一样重要；例如，如果保留值与固定相溶液和载体的吸附有一定的关系话，那么保留时间将随着样品的数量发生变化。如果选择了不恰当的载体的话，某些化合物（例如，固醇）将会在色谱柱上分解。

表 12-1　某些海藻载体的性质

性　质	红色硅藻土色谱载体			
	A	G	P	W
颜色	粉红	牡蛎白	粉红	白色
类型	熔融煅烧	熔融煅烧	熔融煅烧	煅烧
密度,g/cm^3				
① 疏松质量	0.40	0.47	0.38	0.18
② 填装质量	0.48	0.58	0.47	0.24
表面积,m^2/g	2.7	0.5	4.0	1.0
表面积,m^2/cm^3	1.3	0.29	1.88	0.29
最大液相装载量	25%	5%	30%	15%
pH	7.1	8.5	6.5	8.5
加工特性	好	好	好	较脆

第13单元　原子吸收光谱测定法

最常见的元素分析技术有火焰发射光谱测定法，原子吸收光谱测定法和原子荧光光谱测定法。所有这些技术都是以原子蒸气的放射性辐射，原子蒸气的吸收和原子蒸气的荧光为基础的。任何原子光谱测定法的关键组成部分都是样品产生原子蒸气（气态游离原子或离子）的系统，这就是原子的气化源。可以使用多种原子气化源产生原子蒸气，这些原子气化源包括火焰，直流电弧，交流电火花，电热雾化器，微波等离子体，射频等离子体和激光。最广泛使用的原子化器是火焰和电热原子化器，这些能源子气化源将在本章进行讨论。

原子吸收光谱测定法是用于分析原料和样品元素组成特征的最为重要的技术之一。1955年，沃尔什在题为"原子吸收光谱在化学分析中的应用"的划时代性的论文中把它作为多种用途的分析方法提了出来。在最近的一篇论文中，沃尔什指出在 1955 年以前的几十年里，就应该提出原子吸收概念，这是由于缺乏光电检测，不理解基尔霍夫定律，只考虑连续光源和不想犯错误而出错等原因造成的。沃尔什重要的贡献就是把空心阴极灯作为光源。这一作法提供了光源所需的光谱分辨率，并可以使用非常简单的测量系统。图 13-1 为原子吸收分光光度计结构图。

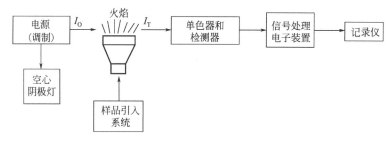

图 13-1　原子吸收分光光度计结构图

当原子吸收光谱测定法作为一种分析方法出现时，选择和开发原子吸收测量方法的合适光源是非常重要的一步。这一要求也许看似简单，因为对于任何吸收测量方法，都需要被样品吸收的放射光源。对于大多数分子光谱吸收测量而言，通过将宽带（连续光源）和单色器结合起来就很容易达到这种目的。然而，原子吸收测量法遇到的问题是需要火焰中非常窄的原子吸收谱线轮廓（波长范围为 0.001～0.005 nm）。因此，当使用连续光源的时候，就需要使用分辨率高和价格昂贵的单色器来达到这样的通带，造成光的通过量降低，使得吸收测量所用光的强度很低。1955 年，沃尔什提出使用特定元素线性光源进行测量，从而诞生了作为多种分析技术的原子吸收光谱测定法。他建议使用的最初光源就是空心阴极灯。

空心阴极灯示意图如图 13-2 所示。灯的阴极通常是由单一元素（或相关元素的合金）构成的，灯发射出的光谱是元素和充入的气体的光谱，最常充入的气是氖。请看皮勒撰写的有关空心阴极放电的论文。如果元素的一条重要谱线被充入的气体氖所重叠，就可以把氖气更换为氩气。灯的操作电流为几毫安，这就要求灯与 5～10kΩ 的电阻串联起来，应用的电压为 100～300V。当灯在低电流（大约 3mA）操作时，原子放射的谱线宽度大约等于（或小于）火焰中自由原子的吸收谱线轮廓。因此，空心阴极灯为原子吸收测量方法提供了一种非常理想的光源，其波长完全与被分析物的波长相匹配，并且带宽非常适合于火焰中的原子。

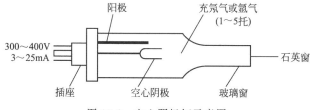

图 13-2　空心阴极灯示意图

然而，应该提到是，如果使用具有高分辨率光栅和高强度连续光源的分光光度计，也可以进行非常好的原子吸收测定。

第 14 单元　红外分光光度计

红外光谱仪器

红外光谱法是一种吸收类型的光谱法。虽然光源、检测器和用于制造光学元件的材料不同，但是色散型红外分光光度计与用于可见和紫外放射吸收研究的仪器具有基本相同的组成。尽管人们今天正在使用高质量色散仪，而且将来还会继续生产这种仪器，但是人们在红外光谱仪方面取得的最重要的发展就是增加了专用高速计算机，计算机可以使傅里叶变换红外分光光度计得到普遍的应用。

光　　源

红外光源是嵌入的固体，用电加热到大约 2000K 并产生强度与波长相对应的黑体辐射光源特征曲线。波数在 $5000cm^{-1}$ 处光强度最大，在 $500cm^{-1}$ 处光强逐渐降低到最大光强的 1%。

能斯特灯可能是应用最广的一种红外光源。它通常是由稀土金属氧化物组成的一个圆柱体，直径约 2mm，长约 20mm。操作温度可高达 1800K。由于它的电阻温度系数为负值，所以开始必须给能斯特灯进行外部加热，以保证通过足够的电流来维持所需的温度。同样，因为它的这种性质就需要采取某种方法来控制电流，以便光源不因过热而烧毁。

另一种光源，格罗巴碳化硅电阻加热元件，是直径约为 5mm，长度约为 50mm 的碳硅棒。它的操作温度要比能斯特灯低（大约 1600K），所以可以避免空气氧化。在 $1500cm^{-1}$ 以下的波数范围内，碳硅棒产生的输出要比能斯特灯更高。

第三种光源是紧密缠绕的镍铬铁合金线圈，用电加热后产生白炽光。这种光源在红外光区的强度低于前两者，但其使用寿命较长。

检　测　器

由于可以使用的红外光源一般强度较低，并且红外光子的能量也相对较低，所以，检测红外线辐射要比可见和紫外线更难。因为光子不具有足够的能量使电子产生光电效应，所以普通的光电管不能用于红外光区。

目前使用的红外检测器一般有两种类型：(a) 光子检测器，其工作原理依据某种半导体材料产生的光电效应；(b) 热检测器，其工作原理为红外辐射光线被吸收后产生热效应，热效应再转换为检测器的物理性质，例如，电阻。

光子检测器是由一薄层半导体材料组成的，诸如，硫化铅、碲化铅、锑化铟或锗与铜或汞混合，使其附着在不导电的玻璃上，密封在真空套内，防止半导体与空气发生反应。半导体材料吸收具有足够能量的光子，使得不传导状态下束缚的电子跃迁到传导状态，最终材料的电阻变小。这些束缚的电子被激发需要具有高于某一最小值的能量。因此，这些检测器对于远红外谱线都有确定的断点。硫化铅检测器能够检测到波长 $1\sim3\mu m$ 的辐射，响应时间为 $10\mu s$。当用其他材料制备的检测器冷却到液态氮或液态氦的温度时，灵敏度向更长的波长方向移动，响应时间快至 20ns。

热检测器可以根据材料的性质分为四类。热电偶是最广泛使用的红外检测器，它是由一小块黑金箔（其表面用来吸收入射辐射）焊接到由两条不同金属细丝而组成的。热电偶的两个接点之间产生低电压。其中一个接点（参比接点）连接到热阱上，小心防止入射辐射，这样，它就可保持在相对稳定的温度上。因为阻断了入射辐射，只有温度变化是重要的因素。为了使传导热量损失降低到最小程度，所有部件密封在具有红外发射窗口的真空容器内。热电堆是指由几个热电偶串联组成的检测器，其输出值可以叠加。这些检测器具有大约 100ms 的响应时间，并且具有相对稳定的频率响应。

第二类检测器是热敏电阻或测辐射热计，当它受到红外线照射时，电阻就会发生变化。两个匹配的感应元件用作惠斯登电桥的双臂，一个不受红外线辐射，另一个直接受到红外线的辐射，表面涂有增加吸收的涂层。两个元件之间的温度差按比例产生电压差。热敏电阻就是由钴或镍这样的金属氧化物组成的，它们具有很高的电阻温度系数，大约是 0.4%/℃。

戈雷检测器或气动检测器是以限定惰性气体压力随温度增加为基础的。红外射线被密封在小金属管一端的涂黑硬金属板吸收。热量传给气体，气体膨胀使得连接在小管另一端容易变形的镀银隔板向外膨胀。薄金属隔板的变形既可通过使其成为光学系统的一部分来测量（在光学系统中，由隔板反射的光束照射到光电管上），或者通过使其成为动力平行板电容器的一块板来测量。相对于固定板，易变形隔板的变化会使普通板发生变化，因此，使其电容发生变化。戈雷检测器与热电偶检测器具有大约相等的灵敏度，它适用于近红外和中红外辐射区，但并不经常使用。它更适用于 $200cm^{-1}$ 以下的光区，可用于远红外光区的仪器。

最近开发的红外线检测仪是热电检测仪。某些晶体，如：硫酸三甘氨酸，重氢硫酸三甘氨酸，锂钽铁矿和其他晶体都具有内在电极化，它发生在电偶极距序列形成的轴上。由于吸收红外线辐射引发晶格空间的热变化，导致电极化变化。如果把晶体放在由金属平板组成的电极之间，电极与外电路相连，为了平衡电荷重新分配，电路中就会产生电流。热电效应与温度变化率有关，与温度的绝对值无关。因此，它只对调制的辐射做出反应，而对缓慢变化的背景辐射没有反应。所以，热电检测器的操作响应很快，并且广泛应用于傅里叶变换红外光谱法中。

色散型红外光谱仪

到目前为止，红外光谱仪最普通的用途就是对化合物进行定性分析。然而，由于红外光谱的复杂性，大多数商用仪器都是双光束记录型仪器，它可以消除大气中 CO_2 和 H_2O 造成的背景吸收。

由光源发射出的光线被分为两束，一束通过样品池，另一束通过参比池。旋转式扇形反光镜交替反射样品光束和参比光束到反光镜上，通过反光镜和进口狭缝进入单色器。这样，样品光束和参比光束交替脉冲通过单色器。每一脉冲通过光栅被分散，通过出口狭缝发射并聚焦在检测器上。

第15单元　质　谱　仪

基 本 原 理

如果某物体处于运动之中，给它施加侧力，它就不会沿着直线运动，而改为曲线运动，也就是说：由于侧力的作用，使其偏离了原来的运动路径。

确定侧力产生的偏转与球的质量有关。如果知道球的速度和体积，又知道它通过何种弯曲路径产生偏转，就能计算出球的质量。球越重，偏转越小。

同样的原理完全可以应用到原子大小的颗粒上。

质谱仪概要

倘若原子首先转变成离子的话，原子受磁场的影响能够产生偏转。尽管原子是电中性的，但是，带电粒子会受到磁场的影响。

原子的变化顺序如下。

步骤1：电离

通过原子失去一个或更多的电子可以使原子电离，从而产生正离子。即使人们通常认为生成负离子的物质（例如，氯）或根本不能生成离子的物质（例如，氩），也能失去电子生成正离子。质谱仪总是对正离子起作用。

步骤 2：加速

离子被加速，结果使所有离子具有同样的动能。

步骤 3：偏转

根据离子的质量，然后，离子在磁场的作用下发生偏转。离子的质量越小，偏转越大。

偏转的程度还与离子的电荷数有关，换句话说，与在第一步中失去的电子数有关。离子电荷越多，粒子偏转越大。

步骤 4：检测

通过仪器的离子束可以用电学手段来检测。

质谱仪全图见图 15-1。

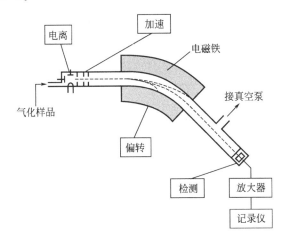

图 15-1　质谱仪全图

理解操作步骤

获得真空

在电离室产生的离子不会碰撞空气分子自由通过仪器，这是重要的。

电离

电离示意图如图 15-2 所示。气化样品进入电离室。电加热金属螺旋线圈产生的电子被电子捕获器吸收，电子捕获器是正极。

因此，样品中的粒子（原子或分子）被电子流轰击，其中某些具有足够能量的碰撞使样品离子失去一个或几个电子，从而产生正离子。

因为再从正离子中去掉电子会变得更困难，所以生成的正离子大多数具有 1 个正电荷。

这些正离子被离子排除器挤到仪器的其他地方，离子排除器是另一块略带正电荷的金属板。

加速

加速示意图如图 15-3 所示。正离子从很正的电离室排出，并通过三个狭缝，最终狭缝电压为 0 伏。中间的狭缝具有中等电压。全部离子被加速成为非常细的聚焦离子流。

偏转

不同的离子在磁场的作用下受不同程度的影响产生偏转。偏转程度与下列因素有关：

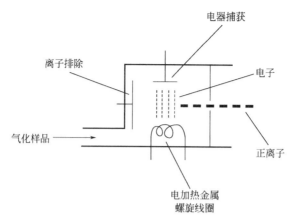

图 15-2　电离示意图

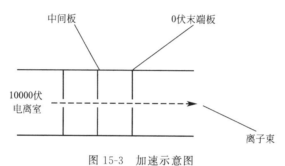

图 15-3　加速示意图

（1）离子的质量。质量小的离子比质量大的离子偏转程度大。

（2）离子的电荷。带 2 个或更多正电荷的离子比带 1 个正电荷的离子偏转程度大。

把这两个因素合并成质荷比。质荷比的符号为 m/z（或 m/e）。

例如，如果一个离子质量为 28，电荷为 1^+，那么它的质核比为 28。一个离子的质量为 56，电荷为 2^+，质核比也为 28。

在图 15-4 中，离子流 A 偏转最大，它包含的离子质荷比最小。离子流 C 偏转最小，它含的离子质荷比最大。

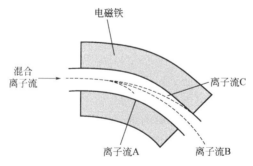

图 15-4　偏转示意图

如果我们假设所有离子的电荷为 1^+，那么讨论质荷比就简单多了。大多数通过质谱仪的离子具有 1^+ 电荷，所以，质荷比就等于质子的质量。

假若 1^+ 离子流 C 质量最轻，离子流 B 质量较重，离子流 C 质量最重。那么，轻离子比重离子偏转程度大。

检测

只有离子流 B 恰好通过仪器进入离子检测器。其他的离子与仪器壁碰撞，并与电子中和。最终，这些离子通过真空泵离开质谱仪。

当离子撞击金属盒时，接触离子的金属产生电子，并中和离子电荷（如图 15-5 所示）。金属的电子中就留下空缺，导线输入电子进行补充。

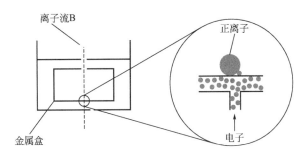

图 15-5 检测示意图

导线的电子流是以放大的电流被检测和记录的。传递的离子越多，电流越大。

检测其他离子

其他离子怎样检测？离子流 A 和 C 就在仪器中消失了吗？

请记住离子流 A 偏转最大，它具有最小的质荷比（如果电荷数为 1^+，离子最轻）。为了使它们进入检测器，通过使用较小的磁场（较小的侧力），使它们发生较小偏转。

为了使那些具有较大质荷比（如果电荷为 +1，质量较重的离子）到达检测器，就必须使用较大的磁场使它们发生更大的偏转。

质谱仪输出式样

记录仪上的输出通常简化为"棒图"。它显示了质荷比发生变化的离子所产生的相对电流。

金属钼的"棒图"见图 15-6。

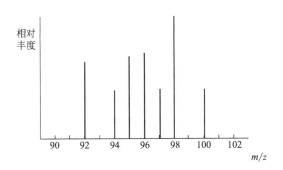

图 15-6 金属钼的"棒图"

从图中可以看到，纵轴为"相对丰度"或"相对强度"。无论使用哪一个术语，它表示的含义都是一样的。纵轴的刻度与记录仪接受的电流有关，也就是与到达检测器的离子数量有关：电流越强，离子的丰度越大。

正如你从这张图所看到的，最普通离子的质荷比为 98。其他离子的质荷比分别为 92，94，95，96，97 和 100。

这就说明金属钼是由 7 种同位素组成的。假设所有离子都具有电荷数 1^+，按照碳-12 标准，7 种同位素的质量就分别为 92，94，95，96，97，98 和 100。

第16单元 核子共振光谱测定法

介 绍

核磁共振光谱测定法（简称 NMR）就是测量置于强磁场的样品对射频放射线吸收的程度。所用放射线的频率在 100MHz 范围以内。磁场强度很大，最复杂的仪器使用了某些可以产生的最大的恒磁场。

许多原子核都具有磁矩。这就意味着它们很像具有磁偶极的小磁棒一样。射频辐射被核磁体吸收，因此核磁体从基态跃迁到激发态。如图 16-1 所示，基态是磁矩顺着磁场排列的能级，而激发态是磁矩反着磁场排列的能级。例如，氢和碳的原子核好像只有这两种排列方式。核偶极的定向排列是量子化的。

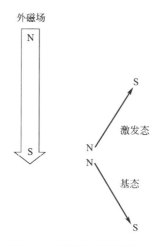

图 16-1 核磁共振光谱传输

虽然在其他光谱测定法中，能量的传递由分子和原子特性决定。但是，在核子共振光谱测定法中，能量还与磁场有关。而且，正像其他光谱测定法一样，吸收能量的大小与吸收核素的浓度成正比。因此，对于含有质子的样品而言，如果我们激发质子，测量的信号就与样品中质子的数量成正比。这就是应用核磁共振测量法的基础。

原子核位于原子电子云的中心。这可能使人感到吃惊，但是就核磁体而言，这却是孤立的环境。一旦射频能量使原子核从基态跃迁到激发态，它们就在激发态保持比较长的时间（最长几秒钟）。当我们在实验中测量返回到基态的原子核数量时，信号看起来就像是浓度随着一级动力学变化似的。与一级速率过程相关的特征时间叫做弛豫时间。对于核磁共振光谱法中更为先进的技术而言，这是一个非常重要的量。

核磁共振仪器和样品

样品产生的核磁共振光谱信号与仪器中样品产生的随机噪声信号大约相等。要获得常规的核磁共振光谱需要精深的电子学知识。制造仪器的方法和优化核磁共振光谱仪器的响应是深入研究的主题。

大多数复杂的核磁共振光谱仪使用射频辐射脉冲，激发样品中的质子。然后，在应用中收集典型插图数据。核磁共振光谱就是由这些数据构成的。时间输出和频率（或场）显示输出之间的数学关系时称之为傅里叶变换。这类仪器就叫作傅里叶转换核磁共振光谱仪，缩写为 FT-NMR。下面所讲的核磁共振光谱仪叫做连续光谱仪，缩写为 CW-NMR。CW-NMR 仪器仍然被广泛使用。

图 16-2 说明了核磁共振光谱仪的主要特点。仪器是由产生非常稳定频率和能量的射频源、高灵敏度的射频接收器和产生稳定强磁场的磁铁组成的。当然，需要记录光谱图。记录光谱图通常使用记录仪，它用来绘制吸收能量与化学位移的关系曲线。

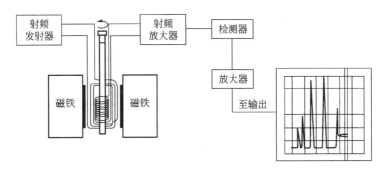

图 16-2　普通核磁共振光谱仪

普通核磁共振实验使用的样品是由待测较浓的固体溶液或液体组成的。如果样品是液体，最好选择纯液体。最灵敏的 CW 仪器可以在几分钟内得到 1mg 样品（接近 CW^{1}H-NMR 的样品下限）的光谱图。使用更普通的仪器需要 10 毫克的样品产生核磁共振所需的质子。样品放置在直径为 5mm，深度为 2~3cm 的精密圆管的底部。标准管的长度为 20~25cm（如果样品管形状不精确，旋转的边频就会放大，甚至超过吸收峰值）。样品管在样品室中绕着长轴旋转。在恒磁场中，旋转样品的原因是使某些缺陷达到平均化。因为光谱的分辨率取决于磁场的质量（均匀性），所以这是至关重要的。

为了得到核磁共振光谱，要么用恒定的射频扫描磁场，要么用固定的磁场值扫描频率。大多数当代仪器频率是变化的，记录输出就好像磁场被扫描一样。扫描频率是由二次振荡器产生的。二次振荡器的操作频率大约为音频范围的 1kHz。音频振荡器和固定射频振荡器产生的输出是两种频率的混合产物（混合频率的详细内容可参阅更高级的参考资料）。用这种方法，可以产生非常稳定和可以精密测量的波长，从而能够精密测量相对化学位移。在很宽的频率范围内扫描音频振荡器可以得到光谱。正像你所看到的，^{1}H 的音频大约为 1000 Hz。

如图 16-2 所示，射频辐射能通过缠绕在样品管上的线圈传给样品。实际上，样品吸收能量，然后又释放能量。释放的能量通过复杂的抗噪声放大器检测和放大，并作为输出信号输出。当形成核磁共振吸收时，样品不再释放多少能量，这种能量释放差异在输出的谱图上以峰来（实际上是一种倾向）显示。正如其他光谱区域一样，通过非辐射过程，能量消失。为了得到最佳结果，磁铁、发射机线圈和检测器线圈必须相互垂直。

核磁共振仪的一般应用及原理

实际上，核磁共振光谱测定法最常见的应用是测定有机物的分子结构。对于这样的研究工作，测量的是射频能量吸收光谱，而不是时间与信号的关系。

在核磁共振实验中，产生能量吸收的频率与两个因素有关：

1. 原子核的一致性；
2. 磁场的强度。

第3部分 化工设备介绍

第17单元 结晶设备

　　商业上既可以使用连续性操作结晶器，也可以使用间歇性操作结晶器。除了有特殊应用之外，优先选用连续性操作。任何结晶器的首要任务都是产生过饱和溶液，因为没有过饱和状态，就不可能产生结晶。根据溶质溶解度曲线的性质，主要可以用三种方法产生过饱和溶液。(1) 当溶质溶解度在低温比高温小很多时，例如：硝酸钾和亚硫酸钠，可以通过简单地冷却产生过饱和溶液。(2) 当溶液的溶解度几乎与温度无关，例如食盐，或溶液的溶解度随温度升高而减小，那么通过蒸发产生过饱和溶液。(3) 在中间状态下，联合使用蒸发和冷却效果更好。例如硝酸钠，只通过冷却或蒸发就能得到所需的结晶，或者联合使用冷却和蒸发手段同样可以得到所需的结晶。

真空结晶器

　　大多数现代结晶器都属于真空装置，它使用绝热真空冷却方式产生过饱和溶液。最初结晶器的样式简单，它只是一个密闭容器。容器中是通过在结晶器和冷凝器之间安装蒸气喷嘴真空泵或增压器来维持真空。在结晶器的压力下，高于沸点的热饱和溶液倒入这种容器中。晶浆的体积通过控制容器中溶液液面和结晶的固体来调节，晶浆上方的空间用来释放蒸汽和消除泡沫夹带现象。原料液自发冷却到平衡温度，因为冷却焓和结晶焓的和约等于部分溶液的蒸发焓。由冷却和蒸发产生的过饱和溶液引起晶核形成和成长。产品晶浆从结晶器底部引出。在平衡温度下，晶体的理论产率与进料浓度和溶质的溶解度的差值成正比。

　　图17-1显示的是一个连续真空结晶器，带有传统的辅助装置用于进料和处理晶浆产品。单釜结晶器的作用更像一台单效蒸发器，而实际上这些装置可以进行多效操作。晶浆从结晶器锥底通过下流管进入慢速低压头循环泵，使晶浆向上流动并通过管状加热器，加热器壳内充满冷凝水蒸气，然后进入结晶器。热蒸汽通过晶浆表面下方的切向进口输入。这就把涡流运动传给了晶浆，晶浆加速了闪蒸，并且通过绝热闪蒸作用使得晶浆和水蒸气保持平衡状态。这样产生的过饱和溶液就为晶核的形成和生长提供了推动力。通过料浆泵的晶浆体积流速来区分晶浆体积可以得到平均滞留时间。

　　原料液在循环泵抽吸前进入下流管。母液和晶体从下流管的原料入口通过排放管向上排放。母液和晶体在连续离心分离机中得到分离；晶体作为产品取出或者做进一步加工处理，而母液则循环给下流管。为了防止杂质的积累，有些母液通过泵在系统中循环。

　　从结晶的角度来看，形式简单的结晶器具有严重的局限性。在装置具有的低压情况下，有关沸点的静压头作用是很重要的，例如，水在7℃具有蒸气压7.6 mmHg，这一压力很容易通过蒸汽喷嘴式调压器获得。300mm的静压头可使绝对压力增加到30mmHg。在这一压力下，水的沸点是29℃。如果料液在比晶浆液面高300mm的任意水平面上，在这一温度下，料液不会闪蒸。如图17-1所示，在料液不会发生闪蒸的这一点进料非常有利于控制晶核的形成。

　　由于静压头效应，蒸发和冷却仅仅在晶浆表面附近的液层出现。并且在晶浆表面附近形

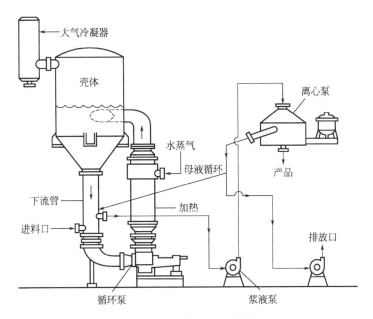

图 17-1　连续真空结晶器

成浓度梯度和温度梯度。而且由于结晶沉淀在结晶器底部，那里不会出现过饱和现象。为了使浓度梯度和温度梯度相同，并使晶体在晶浆中悬浮起来，只有充分搅拌才能使结晶器的操作令人满意。简单真空结晶器不能为控制晶核形成、分粒或除去过多的晶核和很小的晶体提供好的办法。

导流管板结晶器

导流管板结晶器是一种用途更广和效率更高的设备。结晶器壳体上装有导流管，它可以用作管板控制晶浆循环。它还装有垂直向上的螺旋桨式搅拌器，以控制结晶器内的晶浆循环。在结晶器壳体外有一附加循环系统，它由循环泵驱动，包括加热器和进料口。产品浆液通过结晶器壳体锥底旁的出口排除。对于确定的进料流速，内外循环都是独立变化的，并可为获得所需的定速驱动提供可控变量。

为了按体积划分晶体，气流管板式结晶器可在壳体下面安装一个析出段。为了去除细小晶体也可安装一个挡板沉降区。这种装置如图 17-2 所示。部分循环母液泵入析出段，它被用作液压分流使小晶体返回到结晶器继续生长。流出的浆液从析出段下面排放，并送至过滤器或离心分离机。母液返回到结晶器。

通过提供的环隙和扩大结晶器锥底，并使用结晶器的下部作为挡板可将多余的晶核除去。环隙提供了沉降区，在沉降区，通过使细小晶体漂浮在向上流动的母液上，液压分粒使得细小晶体从大晶体中分离出来。母液在沉降区上部分离出来。这样分离出来的细小晶体小于或等于 60 目。虽然它们数量很多，但质量很小，所以从环系流出的液体几乎不含固体颗粒。我们把这种流出液称为循环清液，当它与新的料液混合并泵入蒸气加热器时，溶液变成不饱和状态，大多数细小晶体溶解。现在人们已经知道，这种液体与结晶器主体中循环料浆快速混合。

用这种方法从环隙中除去大部分母液，晶浆密度迅速提高。按照沉淀晶体与全部晶浆体积比计算，晶浆密度可以达到 30%～50%。

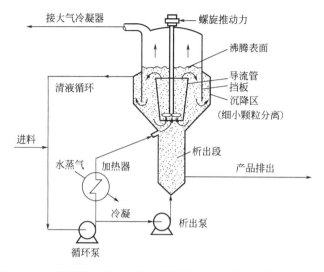

图 17-2 导流管板结晶器（具有精密分离和排放作用的内在系统）

第 18 单元　蒸馏设备

蒸馏可通过两种主要方法中的一种来实现。第一种方法是将欲分离的液体混合物加热沸腾产生蒸汽，并使蒸气冷凝，但是，没有任何液体返回到蒸馏釜。也就是没有回流。第二种方法是部分冷凝液返回到蒸馏釜，在这种情况下，返回的液体与向上运动的蒸气进行充分接触。

闪 蒸 设 备

闪蒸是蒸发一定量的液体，将蒸气与液体分离，并将蒸气冷凝而组成的操作过程。在液体蒸发过程中，产生的蒸汽与剩余的液体保持平衡。闪蒸主要用于分离沸点相差很大的组分。它在分离挥发度相差不大的组分时效果不好，在这种情况下，需要使用有回流的蒸馏。图 18-1 显示了闪蒸设备的组成部分。泵 a 将进料打入加热器 b，通过阀门 c 使压力降低。气液混合物进入到蒸汽分离管 d，在分离管 d 中，有足够的时间使气液分离。由于分离前气液密切接触，分离的流体处于平衡状态。蒸气通过管 e 排出，而液体通过管 g 排出。

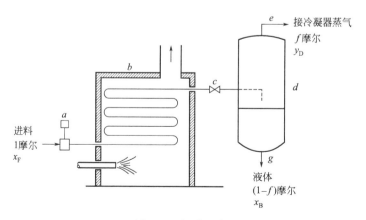

图 18-1　闪蒸设备

闪蒸设备是一种简单的蒸馏装置，广泛用于炼油。石油馏分在管式蒸馏釜中加热，受热流体闪蒸产生蒸汽和剩余液体，每一流体都含有多种组分。从吸收器得到的液体常常闪蒸以回收某些溶质。从高压反应器得到的液体也可以闪蒸恢复低压，产生某些蒸气。

蒸 馏 塔

蒸馏塔用于连续生产，在塔顶和塔底几乎可以产生纯粹的产品。进料在蒸馏塔中间塔板进入。如果进料是液体，它就会沿着塔向下流入再沸器，通过再沸器上升蒸气提馏组分 A。使用这种方法，几乎可以得到纯的塔底产品。

如图 18-2 所示，蒸馏塔需要配备附属设备，并包括精馏段和提馏段。塔 A 要在塔的中部位置以一定浓度稳流液体进料。假设进料是处于沸点的液体。塔的作用与这种假设无关，其他进料条件将在后面讨论。物料进入的塔板叫做进料板。进料板以上所有塔板构成了精馏段，进料板以下所有的塔板（包括进料板）构成提馏段。进料沿着提馏段向下流到塔底，塔底保持一定的液面。液体在重力的作用下流向再沸器 B。再沸器 B 是蒸气加热器，它可以产生蒸气，并使蒸气返回到塔底。蒸气沿塔向上运动。再沸器的一端有一个回流堰。从回流堰下面的蓄液池可以获得塔底产品，它流入塔底冷凝器 G。通过与塔底进行热交换，冷凝器也可以预热进料。

由精馏段上升的蒸气全部在冷凝器 C 中冷凝，冷凝物收集在收集器 D 中。收集器维持一定的液面。回流泵 F 从收集器中提取液体，并将它输送到塔的顶层塔板。这一液流称为回流。它提供了精馏段所需的回流液，回流液与上升蒸气发生作用。没有回流，精馏段就不会发生精馏作用，塔顶产品浓度就不会高于进料板处蒸气的浓度。由回流泵聚集的冷凝物在热交换器（产品冷凝器）E 中冷却，并作为产品提取出来。如果不形成共沸物，并且有足够多的塔板和适当的回流比，我们就可以得到任何所需纯度的塔顶产品和塔底产品。

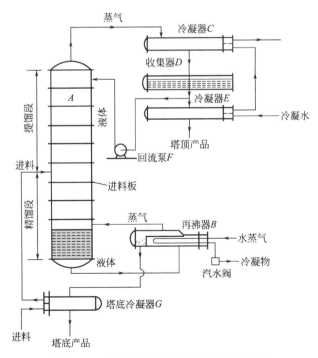

图 18-2 有提馏段和精馏段的连续精馏塔

图 18-2 所示的设备在小型装置中常被简化。在塔底可以用加热管替换再沸器，代替蓄液池产生蒸汽。有时冷凝器放在塔顶的上方，省去回流泵和收集器。这样，回流液就可以在重力的作用下流回到塔顶。一种叫做回流分配器的特殊阀门可以控制返回的回流比。剩下的冷凝物就形成了塔顶产品。

第19单元　干燥设备

工业上使用的干燥器有很多种，本文只介绍少数几种重要的干燥器。第一组也是较大的一组，由处理固体和半固体糊状物干燥器组成。第二组由可以处理晶浆或液体进料的干燥器组成。

固体和糊剂干燥器

典型的固体和糊剂干燥器包括不使用搅拌的厢式干燥器和筛网干燥器，以及带搅拌的塔式干燥器、旋转干燥器、筛网干燥器、流化床干燥器和急剧干燥器。在下列操作中，要尽可能根据搅拌程度，固体处于气体中的方式或固体与加热面接触境况来订购搅拌器。可是，由于某些类型的干燥器可能是绝热的、非绝热的或者是绝热或非绝热相结合，所以选购干燥器相当复杂。

塔式干燥器

塔式干燥器包括一组逐个安装在中心旋转轴上的圆形塔盘。顶盘落下的固体物料从塔盘的热气流中通过。然后固体被刮下落入下一块塔盘。物料就这样通过干燥器，干燥产品从塔底排除。固体和气体的流动既可采用并流，也可采用逆流。

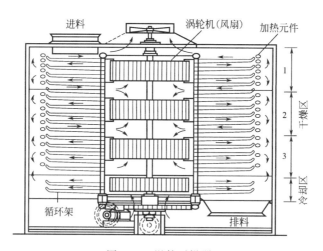

图 19-1　涡轮干燥器

图 19-1 所示的涡轮干燥器是具有热气内循环的塔式干燥器。涡流鼓风机使加热器上方的塔盘间气体向外循环，而其他塔盘间的气体向内循环。气流速度一般为 0.6~2.4m/s（2~8 英尺/秒）。图 19-1 所示干燥器底部的两块塔盘构成了干燥固体的冷却区。预热空气采用逆流方式从塔底进入，从塔顶排出。例如在箱式干燥器中，涡轮干燥器一部分是交叉循环干燥。另一部分是当物料从一块塔盘进入到另一块塔盘时，把物料颗粒喷入到热气中。

转筒干燥器

转筒式干燥器由一个旋转的圆筒壳体组成，水平放置或稍微向出口倾斜。湿物料从圆筒一端输入，干物料从另一端排出。随着筒体的旋转，内刮板铲起固体，并在筒内大量向前输送。转筒式干燥器可以通过气体与固体直接接触加热，使气体通过转筒外夹层加热，也可使水蒸气通过一组安装在筒体内壁的长管冷凝来加热物料。这三类干燥器的最后一类叫做蒸汽管转筒式干燥器。在直接-间接转筒干燥器中，热气气首先是通过夹层，然后通过筒体与固体物料接触。

如图 19-2 所示，它是一种典型的绝热逆流空气加热转筒干燥器。薄钢板制作的旋转壳体 A 由两组托轮 B 支撑，并通过齿轮 C 旋转。转筒上端有一个机罩 D，通过风机 E 将烟囱和喷口 F 连接起来，喷口 F 从加料斗获取湿物料。挡板 G 焊接在筒内，将待干燥的物料刮起并分散于热空气流中。在转筒的低端，干燥产品被输出到筛网输送机 H 上。就在筛网输送机旁有一套预热空气的气热展开管。空气靠鼓风机穿过干燥器，如果需要的话，鼓风机可以将空气输送到加热器，以便整个系统保持正压。或者，鼓风机装在如图所示的烟囱处，以便抽出干燥器中的空气，并使系统保持在微真空状态下。对于物料要成为粉末，使用微真空操作系统是理想的。这类转筒干燥器广泛用于盐、糖和各种粒状物料和晶体物料，物料必须保持清洁，不能直接置于烟道气中。

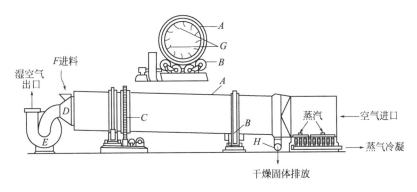

图 19-2 转筒式干燥器

溶液和晶浆干燥器

有些干燥器通过加热方式完全干燥溶液和晶浆。典型干燥器有喷雾干燥器、薄膜干燥器和转鼓干燥器。

喷雾干燥器

在喷雾干燥器中，晶浆或液体溶液以细小的雾滴形式分散到热气流中。雾滴中的水分很快被蒸发，剩下干燥的固体颗粒，然后将固体颗粒与气流进行分离。在同一装置中，可以采用液气并流、液气逆流或既有并流又有逆流。

在圆柱形干燥室内，通过使用压力喷嘴、气动雾化喷嘴产生雾滴。在大型干燥器中，也可使用高速喷雾盘形成雾滴。无论如何，干燥前必须防止雾滴或潮湿的固体颗粒撞击固体表面，因此干燥室的面积要足够大。通常干燥室的直径为 2.5～9m（8～30 英尺）。

在图 19-3 所示的典型喷雾干燥器中，干燥室是由一个带短锥底的圆筒组成的。液体进料泵入干燥室顶部的喷雾盘雾化器。在这种干燥器中，喷雾盘直径大约 300mm（12 英寸），转速 5000～10000 转/每分钟。干燥器将液体雾化成微小雾滴，雾滴喷入从干燥室顶部进入的热气流

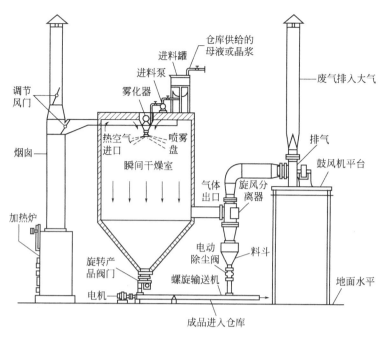

图 19-3 并流喷雾干燥器

中。冷却空气通过水平排气管用排气扇排除,排气管安装在干燥室侧面靠近圆桶底部的地方。气体通过旋风分离器除去固体颗粒。大多数干燥固体从气体中沉降到干燥室底部,干燥的固体颗粒用旋转阀和筛网传送器分离出来,并与用旋风方法收集的固体颗粒集中在一起。

第 20 单元 反 应 器

反应器是化工过程的核心。在化工过程中,它是唯一将原料转化为产物的装置。在整个设计过程中,设计反应器是最重要的一步。

设计工业化学反应器的必须满足以下要求。

1. 化学因素:反应动力学。设计必须为所需的反应提供足够的停留时间,以保证反应达到所需的转化率。

2. 质量传递因素:对于均相反应,反应速率受到反应物扩散速率的限制,而不受化学动力学的限制。

3. 热量传递因素:反应热的移出和加入。

4. 安全因素:限制危险反应物的使用和危险产物的生成,控制反应和反应条件。

为了满足这些相互关联的、而又常常矛盾的因素,使得反应器的设计复杂而又困难。然而,在许多情况下,某一个因素占据支配地位,它决定了反应器类型的选择和设计方法。

反应器的主要类型

以下特点通常用于区分反应器的设计。

1. 操作方式:间歇式和连续式。

2. 相态:均相或多相。

3. 反应器的几何形状:流动型态和相接触方式。

(1) 搅拌釜式反应器;

(2) 管式反应器；
(3) 填充床，固定或流动；
(4) 流化床。

搅拌釜式反应器

搅拌釜式反应器是由装有机械搅拌器的反应釜和冷却夹层或螺旋管组成的。它们可以作为间歇式反应釜来使用，也可作为连续性反应釜来使用。还可以把几个反应器串联起来使用。

釜式反应器被视为基本的化学反应器，它是根据通常实验室使用的烧瓶放大仿制的。反应釜的体积可以是几升到几千升。它们可以用于均相反应和多相液-液和液-气反应，也适用于具有细小悬浮固体颗粒的反应，固体悬浮颗粒是通过搅拌悬浮起来的。因为设计人员可以控制搅拌程度，所以，搅拌釜式反应器特别适用于需要良好传质或传热的反应。

当反应器连续操作时，反应器中物质的组成不变，产品流也不变。除非反应速率很快，才会限制单段反应达到的转化率。

搅拌功率与需要搅拌的程度有关，中等混合需要的功率为 $0.2 kW/m^3$，而强烈混合需要的功率为 $2 kW/m^3$。

管式反应器

管式反应器通常适用于气相反应，但有时也适用于某些液相反应。

如果要求很高的传热速率，使用小直径的管道来提高表面积与体积比。可以把几个管子平行排列安装在复式接头上，或者采取类似于管壳式换热器的方法，把管子固定在管壳上。对于高温反应，管子可以排放在燃烧炉内。

在空管反应器中，压力降和热传递系数可以使用管路流程法进行计算。

填充床反应器

填充床反应器有两种基本类型，一种是固体为反应物的反应器，另一种是固体为催化剂的反应器。第一种类型的反应器可以在很多萃取冶金工业中看到。

在化工生产中设计者通常关注的是第二种反应器：催化反应器。工业上的填充床催化反应器，体积可以从直径几厘米的小管到大直径的填充床。填充床反应器适用于气体反应和气-液反应。大直径填充床的传热速率低，而需要高传热速率的填充床时，应该考虑流化床。

流化床反应器

流化床的基本特点就是由于反应流体向上流动使得固体悬浮起来。这样有利于提高传质和传热速率，并使混合作用更充分。对于夹层和内螺旋管来说，传热系数是可以达到 $200 W/m^2 \cdot ℃$ 的。固体可以是催化剂、硫化燃烧过程中的反应物或者是为了提高传热效率而加入的惰性粉末。

虽然流化床优于固定床的主要优点是传热速率比较高，但是，作为反应过程的一部分，流化床也适用于传送大量的固体，例如，需要将催化剂传给另一容器再生的过程。

流化只用于相对较小的颗粒，与气体混合在一起的颗粒直径小于 $300 \mu m$。

近年来对流化床反应器进行了大量的研发，但是，大直径反应器的设计和按比例放大仍然是没有把握的，设计方法主要是靠经验。

Vocabulary

New Words

A

absorber [əb'sɔːbə] n. 吸收者，吸收器 (18)
acceleration [ækˌseləˈreiʃən] n. 加速度，加速 (15)
accessibility [ˌæksesiˈbiliti] n. 易接近，可到达的 (14)
accompany [əˈkʌmpəni] vt. 陪伴，伴奏 (1)
accumulator [əˈkjuːmjuleitə] n. 蓄电池，收集器 (18)
acetate [ˈæsiˌteit] n. 醋酸盐，醋酸纤维素及其制成的产品 (3)
acetic [əˈsiːtik] adj. 醋的，乙酸的 (2)
acetone [ˈæsiˌtəun] n. 丙酮 (5)
acetylene [əˈsetiliːn] n. 乙炔，电石气 (3)
achievable [əˈtʃiːvəbl] adj. 做得成的，可完成的，可有成就的 (12)
acidic [əˈsidik] adj. 酸的，酸性的 (2)
additive [ˈæditiv] n. 添加剂 (10)
adhesive [ədˈhiːsiv] n. 胶黏剂 (10)
adiabatic [ˌædiəˈbætik] adj. 绝热的，隔热的 (17)
adsorbent [ædˈsɔːbənt] adj. 吸附的 n. 吸附剂 (12)
agents [ˈeidʒənt] n. 手段，工具，剂 (2)
alcohol [ˈælkəhɔl] n. 酒精，酒 (4)
algae [ˈældʒiː] n. 藻类，海藻 (12)
align [əˈlain] vi. 排列 vt. 使成一行 (16)
alignment [əˈlainmənt] n. 列队，成直线 (14)
aliphatic [ˌæliˈfætik] adj. 脂肪族的，脂肪质的 (4)
alizarin [əˈlizərin] n. 茜素 (5)
alkanes [ˈælkein] n. 链烷，烷烃 (4)
alkyl [ˈælkil] n. 烷基，烃基 adj. 烷基的，烃基的 (6)
alphabetically [ˌælfəˈbetikəl] adv. 依字母顺序地，字母地 (4)
alternatively [ɔːlˈtəːnətivli] adv. 做为选择，二者择一地 (19)
alumino-silicate [əˌljuːmənəuˈsilikeit] n. 铝硅酸盐 (12)
aluminum [əˈljuːminəm] n. 铝 (3)
ambiguity [ˌæmbiˈgjuːiti] n. 含糊，不明确 (8)
ammoniacal [əˈməuniækəl] adj. 氨的，氨性的 (8)
ammonium [əˈməunjəm] n. 铵 (2)
amorphous [əˈmɔːfəs] adj. 无定形的，无组织的 (12)

aniline [ˈænili:n]　*n.* 苯胺　*adj.* 苯胺的　　　　　　　　　　　　　　　　　　　(9)
anions [ˈænaiən]　*n.* 阴离子　　　　　　　　　　　　　　　　　　　　　　　　(3)
anode [ˈænəud]　*n.* 阳极，正极　　　　　　　　　　　　　　　　　　　　　　(11)
anthocyanin [ˌænθəˈsaiənin]　*n.* 花青素，花色醣苷　　　　　　　　　　　　　(10)
anthracene [ˈænθrəsi:n]　*n.* 蒽　　　　　　　　　　　　　　　　　　　　　　(10)
antimonic [ˌæntiˈməunik]　*adj.* 锑的，含锑的　　　　　　　　　　　　　　　　(3)
antimonide [ˈæntiˌmənaid]　*n.* 锑化物　　　　　　　　　　　　　　　　　　　(14)
antimonous [ˈæntiˌməunəs]　*adj.* 有锑的，似锑的　　　　　　　　　　　　　　(3)
antimony [ˈæntiməni]　*n.* 锑　　　　　　　　　　　　　　　　　　　　　　　(3)
appliance [əˈplaiəns]　*n.* 用具，器具　　　　　　　　　　　　　　　　　　　(1)
aqueous [ˈeikwiəs]　*adj.* 水的，水成的　　　　　　　　　　　　　　　　　　(2)
argon [ˈɑ:gɔn]　*n.* 氩　　　　　　　　　　　　　　　　　　　　　　　　　　(13)
armature [ˈɑ:mətjuə(r)]　*n.* （电动机、发电机的）转子，电枢　　　　　　　(1)
aromatic [ˌærəuˈmætik]　*adj.* 芳香族的　　　　　　　　　　　　　　　　　　(6)
aromaticity [ˌærəməˈtisiti]　*n.* 芳香族化合物的结构（特性）　　　　　　　　(7)
arsenic [ˈɑ:sənik]　*n.* 砷，砒霜　　　　　　　　　　　　　　　　　　　　　(3)
arsenious [ɑ:ˈsi:niəs]　*adj.* 含砒素的，含砷的　　　　　　　　　　　　　　(3)
asphalt [ˈæsfælt]　*n.* 沥青　　　　　　　　　　　　　　　　　　　　　　　　(6)
assign [əˈsain]　*vt.* 分配，指派　　　　　　　　　　　　　　　　　　　　　(1)
atomic [əˈtɔmik]　*adj.* 原子的，原子能的　　　　　　　　　　　　　　　　　(1)
atomizer [ˈætəmaizə]　*n.* 雾化器，原子化器　　　　　　　　　　　　　　　　(13)
audiofrequency [ˌɔ:diəˈfri:kwənsi]　*n.* 音频　　　　　　　　　　　　　　　(16)
auric [ˈɔ:rik]　*adj.* 金的，正金的，三价金的　　　　　　　　　　　　　　　(3)
aurous [ˈɔ:rəs]　*adj.* 亚金的，一价金的，金的，含金的　　　　　　　　　　(3)
autoxidation [ɔ:ˌtɔksiˈdeiʃən]　*n.* 自然氧化　　　　　　　　　　　　　　　(9)
auxiliary [ɔ:gˈziljəri]　*n.* 助剂　　　　　　　　　　　　　　　　　　　　　(10)
azeotrope [əˈzi:ətrəup]　*n.* 共沸混合物，恒沸物　　　　　　　　　　　　　　(18)

B

bacillus [bəˈsiləs]　*n.* 杆状菌，细菌　　　　　　　　　　　　　　　　　　　(10)
baffle [ˈbæfl]　*n.* 挡板　　　　　　　　　　　　　　　　　　　　　　　　　(17)
bandpass [bændpɑ:s]　*n.* （光谱）通带　　　　　　　　　　　　　　　　　　(13)
barium [ˈbɛəriəm]　*n.* 钡　　　　　　　　　　　　　　　　　　　　　　　　(2)
base [beis]　*n.* 底部，基础，底数，碱　　　　　　　　　　　　　　　　　　(2)
basic [ˈbeisik]　*adj.* 基本的，碱性的　　　　　　　　　　　　　　　　　　　(2)
benzene [ˈbenzi:n, benˈzi:n]　*n.* 苯　　　　　　　　　　　　　　　　　　　(5)
benzenecarboxylic [ˈbenzi:nˌkɑ:bɔkˈsilik]　*adj.* 苯羧基的　　　　　　　　(5)
bicarbonate [baiˈkɑ:bənit]　*n.* 重碳酸盐　　　　　　　　　　　　　　　　　(3)
bifunctional [ˌbaiˈfʌŋkʃnl]　*adj.* 有双功能基团或结合点的　　　　　　　　　(8)
biomedical [ˌbaiəuˈmedikəl]　*adj.* 生物（学和）医学的　　　　　　　　　　(12)
bismuth [ˈbizməθ]　*n.* 铋　　　　　　　　　　　　　　　　　　　　　　　　(3)
bismuthic [ˈbizməθik, bizˈmju:θik]　*adj.* 铋的，含五价铋的　　　　　　　　(3)
bismuthous [ˈbizməθəs]　*adj.* 亚铋的，含三价铋的　　　　　　　　　　　　　(3)
bisulfate [baiˈsʌlfeit]　*n.* 硫酸氢盐　　　　　　　　　　　　　　　　　　　(3)
bitumen [ˈbitjumin]　*n.* 沥青　　　　　　　　　　　　　　　　　　　　　　(6)
bivalent [ˈbaiˌveilənt]　*adj.* 二价的　　　　　　　　　　　　　　　　　　　(3)

body ['bɔdi] *n.* 身体，人，主要部分，物体 (1)
bolometer [bəu'lɔmitə] *n.* 测辐射热仪 (14)
bombard ['bɔmbɑːd] *vt.* 炮轰，轰击 (15)
bond [bɔnd] *n.* 结合（物），胶黏（剂），债券，合同 *v.* 结合 (3)
borate ['bɔːreit] *n.* 硼酸盐 *vt.* 使与硼酸混合 (3)
boric ['bɔːrik] *adj.* 硼的 (3)
boulder ['bəuldə] *n.* 大石头，漂石 (1)
bromine ['brəumiːn] *n.* 溴 (3)
butane ['bjuːtein] *n.* 丁烷 (4)
butene ['bjuːtiːn] *n.* 丁烯 (6)
butylene ['bjuːtiliːn] *n.* 丁烯 (6)
butyne ['bjutain] *n.* 丁炔 (6)

C

cabinetmaking ['kæbinit,meikiŋ] *n.* 细木工艺 (10)
cadmium ['kædmiəm] *n.* 镉 (10)
calcine ['kælsain] *v.* 烧成石灰，煅烧 (12)
calcium ['kælsiəm] *n.* 钙 (2)
calculate ['kælkjuleit] *v.* 计算，推算 (15)
capillary [kə'piləri] *n.* 毛细管 *adj.* 毛状的，毛细作用的 (12)
carbamide ['kɑːbəmaid] *n.* 尿素 (5)
carbon ['kɑːbən] *n.* 碳，（一张）复写纸 (2)
carbonate ['kɑːbəneit] *n.* 碳酸盐 *vt.* 使变成碳酸盐，使充满二氧化碳 (2)
carbonic [kɑː'bɔnik] *adj.* 碳的，由碳得到的 (2)
carotene ['kærətiːn] *n.* 胡萝卜素 (10)
carrier ['kæriə] *n.* 载体，吸收剂 (12)
cascade [kæs'keid] *n.* 小瀑布，喷流 *vi.* 成瀑布落下 (1)
casein ['keisiːin] *n.* 干酪素，酪蛋白 (10)
catechu ['kætitʃuː] *n.* 儿茶 (10)
category ['kætigəri] *n.* 种类，别，范畴 (1)
cathode ['kæθəud] *n.* 阴极 (11)
cation ['kætaiən] *n.* 阳离子 (3)
caustic ['kɔːstik] *adj.* 腐蚀性的，刻薄的 (2)
cellophane ['seləfein] *n.* 玻璃纸 (8)
cellulose ['seljuləus] *n.* 纤维素 (8)
cement [si'ment] *n.* 水泥，接合剂 (10)
centimeter ['senti,miːtər] *n.* 厘米 (1)
centrifuge ['sentrifjuːdʒ] *n.* 离心分离机 (17)
cesium ['siːzjəm] *n.* 铯 (11)
Ceylon [si'lɔn] *n.* 锡兰（Srilanka，首都为科伦坡 Colombo） (9)
characterization [,kæriktərai'zeiʃən] *n.* 特性 (13)
charcoal ['tʃɑːkəul] *n.* 木炭 (10)
Charles Goodyear [tʃɑːlz'gudjiə] *n.* 查尔斯·古德伊尔 （1800—1860，发明硬橡皮制造法的美国人） (9)
chemical ['kemikəl] *adj.* 化学的 *n.* 化学制品，化学药品 (1)
chemistry ['kemistri] *n.* 化学 (1)

chlorate ['klɔːrit] n. 氯酸盐 (3)
chloric ['klɔːrik] adj. 氯的，含氯的 (3)
chlorine ['klɔːriːn] n. 氯 (3)
chlorite ['klɔːrait] n. 亚氯酸盐，绿泥石 (3)
chlorobenzene [ˌklɔːrə'benziːn] n. 氯苯 (7)
chlorodifluoromethane ['klɔːrəudaiˌfluːərə'meθein] n. 氯二氟甲烷 (9)
chloroethene [ˌklɔːrəu'eθiːn] n. 氯乙烯 (8)
chlorophyll ['klɔːrəfil] n. 叶绿素 (10)
chlorous ['klɔːrəs] adj. 亚氯酸的，与氯化合的 (3)
chopper ['tʃɔpə] n. 断路器，斩光器 (11)
chromate ['krəumeit] n. 铬酸盐 (3)
chromatograph [ˌkrəu'mætəgrɑːf] n. 色谱仪，用色谱（法）分析 (12)
chromatographic [ˌkrəumætə'græfik] adj. 色谱（分析）的，色谱法的 (12)
chromatography [ˌkrəumə'tɔgrəfi] n. 色谱法 (12)
chrome [krəum] n. 铬，铬合金 (10)
chromium ['krəumjəm] n. 铬 (3)
chromosorb ['krəuməsɔːb] n. 红色硅藻土色谱载体 (12)
cine ['sini] n. 电影，电影院 (8)
circular ['səːkjulə] adj. 圆形的，循环的 (19)
citric ['sitrik] adj. 柠檬的，采自柠檬的 (5)
classification [ˌklæsifi'keiʃən] n. 分类，分级 (1)
clumsy ['klʌmzi] adj. 笨拙的 (4)
coating ['kəutiŋ] n. 被覆，衣料 (10)
cobalt [kə'bɔːlt, 'kəubɔːlt] n. 钴 (3)
cochineal ['kɔtʃiniːl] n. 胭脂虫（由胭脂虫制成的）洋红 (10)
cocurrent [kə'kʌrənt] n. 并流，同向 (19)
coefficient [ˌkəui'fiʃənt] n. 系数 (12)
coil [kɔil] n. 螺旋管 (20)
collectively [kə'lektivli] adv. 全体地，共同地 (7)
collision [kə'liʒən] n. 碰撞，冲突 (15)
colorimetry [ˌkʌlə'rimitri] n. 比色法 (11)
comparable ['kɔmpərəbl] adj. 可比较的，比得上的 (18)
compartment [kəm'pɑːtmənt] n. 舱，室，（分隔）间，箱 (16)
component [kəm'pəunənt] n. 成分 adj. 组成的，构成的 (1)
composition [ˌkɔmpə'ziʃən] n. 作文，组成，成分，合成物 (1)
compound ['kɔmpaund] n. 混合物，化合物 adj. 复合的 v. 混合，配合 (1)
concentration [ˌkɔnsen'treiʃən] n. 浓缩，浓度 (11)
condensate [kɔn'denseit] n. 冷凝物 (18)
condensation [ˌkɔnden'seiʃən] n. 浓缩 (9)
conduct ['kɔndʌkt, -dəkt] n. 行为，操作 v. 引导，管理，传导 (2)
conduction [kən'dʌkʃən] n. 传导 (2)
confinement [kən'fainmənt] n. 限制，约束 (20)
conical ['kɔnikəl] adj. 圆锥的，圆锥形的 (19)
conservation [ˌkɔnsə(ː)'veiʃən] n. 保存，保持，守恒 (1)
constant ['kɔnstənt] n. 常数，恒量 adj. 不变的，持续的 (1)
container [kən'teinə] n. 容器，集装箱 (1)

continuum [kən'tinjuəm] n. 连续统一体，连续光谱 (11)
contradictory [ˌkɔntrə'diktəri] adj. 矛盾的 (20)
conventions [kən'venʃən] n. 大会，协定，习俗，惯例 (4)
convert [kən'və:t] vt. 使转变，转换…… (1)
conveyor [kən'veiə] n. 输送机 (19)
cooler ['ku:lə] n. 冷却器 (18)
copolymer [kəu'pɔlimə] n. 共聚物 (8)
copolymerization [kəuˌpɔliməraiˈzeiʃən] n. 共聚合（作用） (8)
copper ['kɔpə] n. 铜，警察 (3)
corpuscle ['kɔ:pʌs(ə)l] n. 血球，微粒 (10)
countercurrent ['kauntəˌkʌrənt] n. 逆流 adj. 逆流的 (19)
covalent [kəu'veilənt] adj. 共有原子价的，共价的 (3)
crystalline ['kristəlain] adj. 水晶的，晶体的 (8)
crystallization ['kristəlai'zeiʃən] n. 结晶化 (17)
crystallizer ['kristəlaizə] n. 结晶器 (17)
cuprammonium ['kju:prə'məunjəm] n. 铜铵 (8)
cupric ['kju:prik] adj. 二价铜的 (3)
cuprous ['kju:prəs] adj. 亚铜的，一价铜的 (3)
curve [kə:v] n. 曲线，曲线图表 vt. 弯，使弯曲 (15)
cutoff ['kʌtɔ:f] n. 切（断）开，关（闭，停）车，停电 (14)
cuvette [kju:'vet] n. 小玻璃管，透明小容器，试管 (11)
cyanate ['saiəneit] n. 氰酸盐 (5)
cyclization [ˌsaikli'zeiʃən] n. 环化（作用） (8)
cycloalkane [ˌsaikləu'ælkein] n. 环烷烃 (6)
cyclone ['saikləun] n. 旋风，气旋 (19)

D

decane ['dekein] n. 癸烷 (4)
decompose [ˌdi:kəm'pəuz] v. 分解，（使）腐烂 (1)
dedicated ['dedikeitid] adj. 专用的 (14)
deflect [di'flekt] v. （使）偏斜，（使）偏转 (15)
deflection [di'flekʃən] n. 偏斜，偏转，偏差 (15)
deliberately [di'libərətli] adv. 故意地 (5)
density ['densiti] n. 密度 (1)
deposite [di'pɔzit] vt. 沉积 (14)
derivative [di'rivətiv] n. 衍生物 (7)
detector [di'tektə] n. 检测器 (11)
deuterated ['dju:təreitid] adj. 含重氢的 (14)
deuterium [dju:'tiəriəm] n. 氘 (11)
diaphragm ['daiəfræm] n. 膈，隔膜，隔板
diatomite [dai'ætəmait] n. 硅藻土 (12)
diatoms ['daiətəm] n. 硅藻属 (12)
dibenzenecarboxy ['dai 'benzi:nkɑ:'bɔksi] n. 二苯羧基 (9)
dibenzoyl [dai'benzəuil] n. 联苯甲酰 (9)
dibromobenzene [dai'brəuməu'benzi:n] n. 二溴苯 (7)
diethenylbenzene [dai'eθinil'benzi:n] n. 二乙烯基苯 (9)

diethyl [daiˈeθil] adj. 二乙基的 (5)
diffusion [diˈfjuːʒən] n. 扩散，传播，漫射 (20)
dihydroxybutanedioic [dihaiˈdrɔksibjuːtæniˈdaiəic] adj. 二羟基丁酸的 (5)
dimethyl [ˌdaiˈmeθil] adj. 二甲基的 (6)
dimethyldichlorosilane [daiˈmeθiˌdaiklɔːrəlˈdaiklɔːrə] n. 二甲基二氯硅烷 (12)
dimethylpropane [ˌdaiˈmeθilˈprəupein] n. 二甲基丙烷 (6)
diminish [diˈminiʃ] vt. （使）减少，（使）变小 (17)
dioxide [daiˈɔksaid] n. 二氧化物 (2)
dip [dip] n. 俯角，倾向，偏角 (16)
dipole [ˈdaipəul] n. 偶极 (16)
disk [disk] n. (＝disc) 圆板，圆盘 (19)
dislodge [disˈlɔdʒ] vt. -lodged, -lodging 驱逐，移出，移走 (11)
distillation [ˌdistiˈleiʃən] n. 蒸馏，蒸馏法，蒸馏物 (18)
distinct [disˈtiŋkt] adj. 清楚的，明显的，截然不同的，独特的 (1)
disubstituted [daiˈsʌbstitjuːtid] adj. 二基取代的 (7)
divinylbenzene [daiˈvainilˈbenziːn] n. 二乙烯基苯 (9)
dope [dəup] vt. 向……内掺入 (14)
downflow [ˈdaunfləu] n. 向下流动，溢流管 (18)
downpipe [ˈdaunpaip] n. 下流管 (17)
draft [drɑːft] n. 气流 (17)
droplet [ˈdrɔplit] n. 小滴 (19)
drum [drʌm] n. 鼓，鼓形圆桶 (19)
dryer [ˈdraiə] n. 干燥机，干燥器 (19)
dyestuff [ˈdaistʌf] n. 染料 (2)
dynode [ˈdainəud] n. 倍增器电极 (11)

E

echelle [eiˈʃel] n. 阶梯（分级）光栅 (13)
elastomer [iˈlæstəmə(r)] n. 弹性体，人造橡胶 (8)
element [ˈelimənt] n. 要素，元素，成分 (1)
elutriation [iˌljuːtriˈeiʃən] n. 淘析，析出 (17)
empirical [emˈpirikəl] adj. 经验的 n. 实验式 (20)
endothermic [ˌendəuˈθɔːmik] adj. 吸热（性）的 (1)
entrain [inˈtrein] vt. 产生，导致，带走 (19)
epoxy [eˈpɔksi] adj. 环氧的 (10)
essence [ˈesns] n. 本质，要素，特性 (16)
ethanal [ˈeθənæl] n. 乙醛 (8)
ethane [ˈeθein] n. 乙烷 (4)
ethanedioic [ˈeθeindiəic] n. 乙二酸的 (5)
ethanoic [ˈiːθənic] n. 醋酸的 (5)
ethanol [ˈeθənɔːl, -nəul] n. 乙醇，酒精 (4)
ethene [ˈeθiːn] n. 乙烯 (6)
ethenyl [ˈeθinil] n 乙烯基 (8)
ether [ˈiːθə] n. 醚 (5)
ethoxyethane [eˈθɔksiˈeθein] n. 乙氧基乙烷 (5)
ethyl [ˈeθil, ˈiːθail] n. 乙烷基 (6)

ethylbenzene [ˌeθil'benziːn] *n.* 乙苯 (9)
ethylene ['eθiliːn] *n.* 乙烯，乙烯基 (6)
ethyne ['eθain] *n.* 乙炔 (6)
evacuate [i'vækjueit] *vt.* 抽真空 (14)
exception [ik'sepʃən] *n.* 除外，例外，反对，异议 (3)
excitation [ˌeksi'teiʃən] *n.* 刺激，激发 (14)
exothermic [ˌeksəu'θɔːmik] *adj.* 发热的，放出热量的 (1)
experiment [iks'perimənt] *n.* 实验，试验 *vi.* 进行实验，做试验 (1)
exploitation [ˌeksplɔi'teiʃən] *n.* 开发，开采，剥削 (12)
exponent [eks'pəunənt] *n.* 说明者，代表者，典型，指数 (2)
extractive [iks'træktiv] *adj.* 抽取的，萃取的 (20)

F

fatty ['fæti] *adj.* 脂肪的，含脂肪的 (7)
feed [fiːd] *n.* 进料 (17)
ferric ['ferik] *adj.* （正）铁的，三价铁的 (3)
ferricyanide [ˌferi'saiənaid] *n.* 铁氰化物 (3)
ferrocyanide [ˌferəu'saiənaid, -nid] *n.* 氰亚铁酸盐，亚铁氰化物 (10)
ferrous ['ferəs] *adj.* 铁的，含铁的，亚铁的 (3)
fiber ['faibə] *n.* 纤维 (=fibre) (8)
filler ['filə] *n.* 填充剂，漏斗 (13)
firebrick [faiəbrik] *n.* 耐火砖 (12)
flash [flæʃ] *n.* 闪光，闪现 *v.* 闪光，闪现，反射，使迅速传遍 (18)
flight [flait] *n.* 刮板 (19)
flue [fluː] *n.* 烟洞，烟道，暖气管 (19)
fluidization [ˌfluːidai'zeiʃən] *n.* 液化，流化 (20)
fluorescence [fluə'resns] *n.* 荧光，荧光性 (13)
fluorine ['flu(ː)əriːn] *n.* 氟 (3)
flux [flʌks] *n.* 流量，通量，助溶剂，焊接 (11)
formula ['fɔːmjulə] *n.* 公式，规则 (1)
fractionate ['frækʃəneit] *vt.* 使分馏 (18)
fragrant ['freigrənt] *adj.* 芬芳的，香的 (7)
freon-22 ['friːɔn] *n.* 氟里昂，二氯二氟（氟三氯）甲烷 (9)
friable ['fraiəbl] *adj.* 易碎的，脆的 (12)
fumigant ['fjuːmigənt] *n.* 熏剂 (10)
fundamentally [ˌfʌndə'mentəli] *adv.* 基础地，根本地 (8)
fungi ['fʌndʒai, 'fʌŋgai] *n.* 真菌类 (10)
fungicides ['fʌndʒisaid] *n.* 杀真菌剂 (10)

G

gallic ['gælik] *adj.* 五倍子的 (5)
gasoline ['gæsəliːn] *n.* 汽油 (6)
gear [giə] *n.* 齿轮，传动装置 (19)
gel [dʒel] *n.* 凝胶体 (10)
gelatin ['dʒelətin, 'dʒelə'tiːn] *n.* 凝胶，白明胶 (10)

generator ['dʒenəreitə]　*n.* 发电机，发生器 (1)
Geneva [dʒi'ni:və]　*n.* 日内瓦城（瑞士西南部城市） (4)
geometry [dʒi'ɔmitri]　*n.* 几何学，表面形状 (20)
germanium [dʒə:'meiniəm]　*n.* 锗 (14)
Globar ['gləu'bɑ:]　*n.* 格罗巴碳化硅电阻加热元件，碳硅棒 (14)
glower ['gləuə]　*n.* 炽热体，灯丝 (14)
glue [glu:]　*n.* 胶，胶水 (10)
glycerol ['glisərɔl]　*n.* 甘油，丙三醇 (8)
grapes [greip]　*n.* 葡萄，葡萄树 (5)
graphically ['græfikəl]　*adj.* 绘成图画似的，绘画的 (1)
grating ['greiti]　*n.* 光栅 (14)
gravitational [,grævi'teiʃnl]　*adj.* 重力的 (1)
grouping ['gru:piŋ]　*n.* 分组 (1)

H

hardness ['hɑ:dnis]　*n.* 硬，硬度，艰难 (1)
hazardous ['hæzədəs]　*adj.* 危险的，冒险的 (20)
hemoglobin [,hi:məu'gləubin]　*n.* 血色素 (10)
heptane ['heptein]　*n.* 庚烷 (4)
herbicide ['hə:bisaid]　*n.* 除草剂 (10)
heterogeneous [,hetərəu'dʒi:niəs]　*adj.* 不均匀的，多相的 (20)
hevea ['hi:viə]　*n.* 三叶胶树（大戟科树木） (9)
hexane [hek'sein]　*n.* （正）己烷 (4)
hides [haid]　*n.* 兽皮，皮革 (10)
homogeneity [,hɔməudʒe'ni:iti]　*n.* 同种，同质，均匀性 (16)
homogeneous [,hɔməu'dʒi:njəs]　*adj.* 均一的，均匀的 (20)
hood [hud]　*n.* 防护罩 (19)
hoof [hu:f]　复数 hooves　*n.* 蹄 (10)
hopper ['hɔpə]　*n.* 漏斗，料斗 (19)
hydrated ['haidreitid]　*adj.* 含水的，与水结合的 (12)
hydraulic [hai'drɔ:lik]　*adj.* 水力的，水压的，液压的 (17)
hydriodic [,haidri'ɔdik]　*adj.* 碘氢的 (2)
hydrobromic ['haidrəu'brəumik]　*adj.* 氢溴酸的，溴化氢的 (2)
hydrocarbon ['haidrəu'kɑ:bən]　*n.* 烃，碳氢化合物 (5)
hydrocarbon ['haidrəu'kɑ:bən]　*n.* 烃，碳氢化合物 (6)
hydrochloric [,haidrəu'klɔ:rik]　*adj.* 氯化氢的，盐酸的 (2)
hydrofluoric ['haidrəflu(:)'ɔrik]　*adj.* 含氟化氢的，含氟化氢的氢氟酸的 (2)
hydrogen ['haidrəudʒən]　*n.* 氢 (1)
hydrogenation [,haidrədʒə'neiʃən]　*n.* 加氢，氢化（作用） (10)
hydronium [hai'drəuniəm]　*n.* 水合氢，离子 (2)
hydrosulfuric [hai'drəusʌl'fjuərik]　*adj.* 含氢及硫的 (2)
hydroxide [hai'drɔksaid, -sid]　*n.* 氢氧化物，羟化物 (2)
hydroxybutanedioic [hai'drɔksibju:tæni'daiəic]　*adj.* 羟基丁酸的 (5)
hydroxypropane [hai'drɔksi'prəupein]　*n.* 羟基丙烷，丙醇 (5)
hydroxypropanoic [hai'drɔksi'prəupeinic]　*adj.* 羟基丙酸的 (5)
hypochlorite [,haipəu'klɔ:rait]　*n.* 次氯酸盐 (3)

hypochlorous [ˌhaipəu'klɔːrəs]　n. 次氯酸　(3)

I

i. d. = inside dimensions 内尺寸　(12)
illuminate [i'ljuːmineit]　vt. 照明，照亮　vi. 照亮　(14)
impart [im'pɑːt]　vt. 分给，授予　(10)
imperfection [ˌimpə'fekʃən]　n. 不完整性，不足，缺点，缺陷　(16)
impinging [im'pindʒiŋ]　n. 碰撞　(11)
impregnate ['impregneit]　vt. 使怀孕，使充满，注入　adj. 怀孕的，充满的　(2)
incandescence [ˌinkæn'desəns]　n. 白热，炽热　(14)
incandescent [ˌinkæn'desnt]　adj. 遇热发光的，白炽的　(11)
inclined [in'klaind]　adj. 倾斜的，成斜坡的　(19)
indicator ['indikeitə]　n. 指示器，指示剂　(2)
indigo ['indigəu]　n. 靛，靛青　(5)
indium ['indiəm]　n. 铟　(14)
inertia [i'nəːʃjə]　n. 惯性，惯量　(1)
inertness [i'nəːtnis]　n. 不活泼　(12)
infrared ['infrə'red]　adj. 红外线的　(14)
inhibitor [in'hibitə(r)]　n. 抑制剂　(10)
initiator [i'niʃieitə]　n. 引发剂　(9)
inlet ['inlet]　n. 进口，入口　(12)
insecticide [in'sektisaid]　n. 杀虫剂　(10)
instantaneously [ˌinstən'teinjəsli]　adv. 瞬间地，即刻地，即时地　(5)
interchangeable [intə'tʃeindʒəb(ə)l]　adj. 可互换的　(1)
intermediate [ˌintə'miːdjət]　adj. 中间的　n. 媒介　(17)
interrelated [intəri'leitid]　adj. 相关的　(20)
intimacy ['intiməsi]　n. 亲密　(18)
intimate ['intimit]　adj. 亲密的，密切的　(18)
inward ['inwəd]　adv. 向内，在内　adj. 向内的，内在的　(19)
iodine ['aiədiːn；(US) 'aiədain]　n. 碘，碘酒　(3)
ion ['aiən]　n. 离子　(2)
ionization [ˌaiənai'zeiʃən]　n. 电离，离子化（作用）　(2)
ionize ['aiənaiz]　vt. 使离子化　vi. 电离电离，离子化　(2)
iron ['aiən]　n. 铁，熨斗　vt. 烫平，熨　(1)
isohexane [ˌaisə'heksein]　n. 异己烷　(6)
isomerism [ai'səmərizm]　n. 同分异构现象　(5)
isopentane [ˌaisəu'pentein]　n. 异戊烷，2-甲基丁烷　(6)
isotope ['aisəutəup]　n. 同位素　(15)

J

junction ['dʒʌŋkʃən]　n. 接头　(14)

K

Kekule 凯库勒（1829—1896，德国化学家，有机结构理论奠基人）　(7)

kermes ['kə:miz]　*n.* 胭脂，干燥雌体（取出作胭脂染料） (10)
kerosene ['kerəsi:n]　*n.* 煤油，火油 (6)
kinetic [kai'netik]　*adj.* 动的，动力（学）的 (1)
kinetics [kai'netiks]　*n.* 动力学 (20)

L

label ['leibl]　*n.* 标签，商标　*vt.* 贴标签于，分类，标注 (15)
lacquer ['lækə]　*n.* 漆，漆器 (8)
lactic ['læktik]　*adj.* 乳的，乳汁的 (5)
lampblack *n.* 灯烟，灯黑 (10)
landmark ['lændmɑ:k]　*n.* （航海）陆标，里程碑，划时代的事 (13)
larvae ['lɑ:və]　*n.* 幼虫 (10)
Lavoisier　拉瓦锡（1743—1794，法国化学家，氧发现者） (5)
lead [li:d]　*n.* 领导，铅，石墨 (3)
linkage ['liŋkidʒ]　*n.* 连接 (3)
liquor ['likə]　*n.* 液体 (17)
liter ['li:tə]　*n.* 公升 (20)
litharge ['liθɑ:dʒ, li'θɑ:dʒ]　*n.* 一氧化铅，铅黄 (10)
lithium ['liθiəm]　*n.* 锂 (3)
litmus ['litməs]　*n.* 石蕊 (2)
logarithm ['lɔgəriθm]　*n.* 对数 (2)
logwood ['lɔgwud]　*n.* 洋苏木树，洋苏木的心材（供作染料用） (10)
longitudinal [lɔndʒi'tju:dinl]　*adj.* 经度的，纵向的 (19)
lubricant ['lu:brikənt]　*n.* 滑润剂 (6)
lucid ['lu:sid]　*adj.* 明晰的 (5)
luster ['lʌstə]　*n.* 光彩，光泽 (8)

M

magnesium [mæg'ni:zjəm]　*n.* 镁 (3)
magnetize ['mægnitaiz]　*vt.* 使磁化，吸引　*vi.* 受磁 (1)
malic ['mælik, 'mei-]　*adj.* 苹果的，由苹果取得的 (5)
manganese [ˌmæŋgə'ni:z, 'mæŋgəni:z]　*n.* 锰 (3)
manganic [mæŋ'gænik]　*adj.* 锰的，得自锰的 (3)
manganous ['mæŋgənəs]　*adj.* （亚）锰的，二价锰的 (3)
manifold ['mænifəuld]　*n.* 歧管，多支管，复式管头 (20)
mass [mæs]　*n.* 质量，群众　*adj.* 群众的，大规模的　*vt.* 使集合　*vi.* 聚集 (1)
mathematical [ˌmæθi'mætikəl]　*adj.* 数学的，精确的 (1)
maturation [ˌmætju'reiʃən]　*n.* 成熟 (12)
mercuric [mə:'kjuərik]　*adj.* 汞的，含二价汞的 (3)
mercurous ['mə:kjurəs]　*adj.* 亚汞的，含水银的，一价汞的 (3)
mercury ['mə:kjuri]　*n.* 水银，汞 (14)
mercury ['mə:kjuri]　*n.* 水银，汞 (3)
meta ['metə]　*adj.* 邻位的 (7)
metallurgical [ˌmetə'lə:dʒikəl]　*adj.* 冶金学的 (20)
methanal ['meθənæl]　*n.* 甲醛 (8)

methane ['meθein] n. 甲烷，沼气 (4)
methanol ['meθənɔl, -nəul] n. 甲醇 (5)
methoxymethane [mə'θɔksi'meθein] n. 甲氧基甲烷 (5)
methylacetylene ['meθilə'setiliːn] n. 甲基乙炔 (6)
methylbenzene [ˌmeθil'benziːn, -ben'ziːn] n. 甲苯 (7)
2-methylbutane ['meθil'bjuːtein] n. 2-甲基丁烷 (6)
2-methylpentane ['meθil'pentein] n. 2-甲基戊烷 (6)
milliampere [ˌmili'æmpɛə] n. 毫安培 (13)
milliliter ['mililiːtə (r)] n. 千分之一公升，毫升 (1)
misinterpretation ['misinˌtəːpri'teiʃən] n. 误译，曲解 (13)
mixture ['mikstʃə] n. 混合，混合物，混合剂 (1)
molar ['məulə] adj. 质量的，摩尔的 n. 臼齿，磨牙 (2)
molybdenum [mə'libdinəm] n. 钼 (15)
moment ['məumənt] n. 力矩 (16)
monochromator [mɔnəu'krəumeitə] n. 单色器，单色仪，单色光镜 (11)
monomer ['mɔnəmə] n. 单体 (8)
monomeric [ˌmɔnə'merik] adj. 单节显性的 (8)
monosubstituted ['mɔnə'sʌbstitjuːtid] adj. 一元取代的 (7)
monovalent [ˌmɔnəu'veilənt] adj. 单价的 (3)
mordant ['mɔːdənt] n. 媒染，媒染剂，金属腐蚀剂，金属箔黏合剂 (10)
moth [mɔθ] n. 蛾，蛀虫 (10)
mucilage ['mjuːsilidʒ] n. （植物的）黏液，胶水 (10)
multielement ['mʌltiˌelimənt] n. 多元素，多元件 (13)

N

nematicide [ni'mætisaid] n. 杀线虫剂（＝nematocide） (10)
nematode ['nemətəud] n. 线虫类 (10)
neon ['niːən] n. 氖 (13)
neopentane [ˌniːəu'pentein] n. 新戊烷，季戊烷 (6)
neoprene ['ni (ː) əupriːn] n. 氯丁（二烯）橡胶 (9)
neutral ['njuːtrəl] n. 中立者，中立国 adj. 中立的，中立国的，中性的 (2)
neutral ['njuːtrəl] n. 中立者 adj. 中性的 (15)
neutralization [ˌnjuːtrəlai'zeiʃən] n. 中立化，中立状态，中和 (2)
neutralize ['njuːtrəlaiz；(US) nuː-] v. 中和，使中和 (15)
nichrome ['nikrəum] n. 镍铬铁合金，镍铬耐热合金 (14)
nickel ['nikl] n. 镍 (14)
nitrate ['naitreit] n. 硝酸盐，硝酸钾 (3)
nitric ['naitrik] adj. 氮的，含氮的，硝石的 (2)
nitrite ['naitrait] n. 亚硝酸盐 (3)
nitrobenzene [ˌnaitrəu'benziːn] n. 硝基苯 (7)
nitrogen ['naitrədʒən] n. 氮 (1)
nitrous ['naitrəs] adj. 含有三价氮的，亚硝（酸）的 (3)
nomenclature [nəu'menklətʃə] n. 命名法，术语 (4)
nonadiabatic ['nɔnˌædiə'bætik] adj. 非绝热的 (19)
nonane ['nɔnein] n. 壬烷 (4)
nonconducting ['nɔnkən'dʌktiŋ] adj. 不传导的 (14)

212

non-flammable [nɔn'flæməbl]　　*adj.* 不易燃的　　(8)
nonradiative ['nɔn'reidieitiv]　　*adj.* 非辐射的，不辐射的　　(16)
nozzle ['nɔzl]　　*n.* 管口，喷嘴　　(19)
nucleation [ˌnjuːkli'eiʃən]　　*n.* 成核现象，晶核形成　　(17)
nuclei ['njuːkliai]　　nucleus 的复数形　　*n.* 原子核，核子　　(16)
nylon ['nailən]　　*n.* 尼龙　　(8)

O

ocher ['əukə(r)]　　*n.* 黄土，赭土　　(10)
octane ['ɔktein]　　*n.* 辛烷　　(4)
olefins ['əuləfin]　　*n.* 石蜡　　(6)
operational [ˌɔpə'reiʃənl]　　*adj.* 操作的，运作的　　(2)
ordered ['ɔːdəd]　　*adj.* 规则的，有序的　　(19)
organosilicon [ˌɔːɡənəu'silikən]　　*adj.* 有机硅（化合物）的　　(8)
orientation [ˌɔ(ː)rien'teiʃən]　　*n.* 方向，方位，倾向性　　(16)
ortho ['ɔːθə]　　*adj.* 间位的　　(7)
oscillator ['ɔsileitə]　　*n.* 振荡器　　(16)
outline ['əutlain]　　*n.* 大纲，轮廓，略图　　(15)
outward ['autwəd]　　*adj.* 外面的，向外的　　*adv.* 向外　　(19)
overlap [ˌəuvə'læp]　　*vt.* （与……）交迭　　(13)
oxalate ['ɔksəleit]　　*n.* 盐　　(3)
oxalic [ɔk'sælik]　　*adj.* 草酸的，乙二酸的　　(2)
oxide ['ɔksaid]　　*n.* 氧化物　　(3)
oxidizing ['ɔksiˌdaiz]　　*v.* （使）氧化　　(2)
oxygen ['ɔksidʒən]　　*n.* 氧　　(1)
oyster ['ɔistə]　　*n.* 牡蛎，蚝　　(12)

P

palladium [pə'leidiəm]　　*n.* 钯　　(10)
para ['pɑːrə]　　*adj.* 对位的　　(7)
paraffins ['pærəfin, -fiːn]　　*n.* 石蜡　　(6)
parallel ['pærəlel]　　*adj.* 平行的，相同的　　(19)
parasite ['pærəsait]　　*n.* 寄生虫，食客　　(10)
parentheses [pə'renθisis]　　*n.* 圆括号，插入语，插曲　　(3)
paste [peist]　　*n.* 糊剂，糊状混合物　　(19)
pathogen ['pæθədʒ(ə)n]　　*n.* 病菌，病原体　　(10)
pentane ['pentein]　　*n.* 戊烷　　(4)
pentane ['pentein]　　*n.* 戊烷　　(6)
perchlorate [pə'klɔːreit]　　*n.* 高氯酸盐（或酯）　　(3)
perchloric [pə'klɔːrik]　　*adj.* （含）高氯的　　(3)
permanganate [pəː'mæŋɡənit, -neit]　　*n.* 高锰酸　　(3)
permissible [pə(ː)'misəbl]　　*adj.* 可允许的　　(19)
peroxide ['ɔksaid]　　*n.* 氧化物　　(3)
peroxide [pə'rɔksaid]　　*n.* 过氧化物，过氧化氢　　(9)
perpendicular [ˌpəːpən'dikjulə]　　*adj.* 垂直的，正交的　　(16)

pest [pest] *n.* 有害物 (10)
pesticide ['pestisaid] *n.* 杀虫剂 (10)
petrol ['petrəl] *n.* （英）汽油 ［=（美）gasoline］ (6)
petroleum [pi'trəuliəm] *n.* 石油 (6)
phenolmethanal ['fi:nəl'meθænæl] *n.* 酚醛 (8)
phenolphthalein [ˌfinəl'fθæli:n] *n.* 酚酞 (2)
phenylethene [ˌfenəl'eθil] *n.* 苯乙基 (8)
pheromone ['ferəməun] *n.* ［生化］信息素 (10)
phosphate ['fɔsfeit] *n.* 磷酸盐 (3)
phosphite ['fɔsfait] *n.* 亚磷酸盐 (3)
phosphoric [fɔs'fɔrik] *adj.* 磷的（尤指含五价磷的），含磷的 (2)
phosphorous ['fɔsfərəs] *adj.* （亚）磷的 (3)
phosphorus ['fɔsfərəs] *n.* 磷 (3)
photocathode [ˌfəutəu'kæθəud] *n.* 光电阴极 (11)
photocell ['fəutəsel] *n.* 光电池 (11)
photodetector [ˌfəutəudi'tektə] *n.* 光电探测器 (11)
photoemissive [ˌfəutəui'misiv] *adj.* 光电发射的 (11)
photomultiply [ˌfəutəu'mʌltipli] *adj.* 光电倍增的 (11)
photon ['fəutən] *n.* 光子 (11)
photosensitive ['fəutəu'sensitiv] *adj.* 光敏的 (10)
phototube ['fəutəutju:b] *n.* 光电器 (11)
photovoltaic [ˌfəutəuvɔl'teiik] *adj.* 光电的 (11)
physical ['fizikəl] *adj.* 身体的，物质的，自然的，物理的 (1)
pigment ['pigmənt] *n.* 色素，颜料 (10)
pillow ['piləu] *n.* 枕头，枕垫 (13)
pinion ['pinjən] *n.* 小齿轮 (19)
plantation [plæn'teiʃən] *n.* 种植园 (9)
plasma ['plæzmə] *n.* 等离子体，等离子区 (13)
platinum ['plætinəm] *n.* 白金，铂 (3)
pliable ['plaiəbl] *adj.* 易曲折的，柔软的，圆滑的，柔韧的 (8)
pneumatic [nju(:)'mætik] *adj.* 汽动的 (14)
polar ['pəulə] *adj.* 两极的，极地的，极性的 *n.* 极线，极面 (2)
polyethene [ˌpɔli'eθi:n] *n.* 聚乙烯 (8)
polyester ['pɔliestə] *n.* 聚酯 (8)
polymer ['pɔlimə] *n.* 聚合体 (8)
polymerization [ˌpɔliməraɪ'zeiʃən] *n.* 聚合 (8)
polystyrene [ˌpɔli'staiəri:n] *n.* 聚苯乙烯 (8)
polyvinyl [ˌpɔli'vainil] *adj.* 乙烯聚合物的 (8)
positive ['pɔzətiv] *adj.* 正的，阳的，正电的 (3)
potassium [pə'tæsjəm] *n.* 钾， (2)
potential [pə'tenʃ(ə)l] *adj.* 潜在的，可能的，位的 *n.* 潜能，潜力，电压 (1)
power ['pauə] *n.* 功率 (20)
predator ['predətə] *n.* 掠夺者，食肉动物 (10)
predominantly [pri'dɔminənt] *adj.* 卓越的，支配的，主要的 (3)
predominate [pri'dɔmineit] *vt.* 掌握，控制，支配 (20)
preferred [pri'fə:d] *adj.* 首选的 (4)

· 214 ·

prefix ['pri:fiks] *n.* 前缀 (4)
principle ['prinsəpl] *n.* 法则，原则，原理 (1)
product ['prɔdəkt] *n.* 产品，产物，乘积 (1)
proficient [prə'fiʃnt] *n.* 精通 (3)
profile ['prəufail] *n.* 外形，轮廓 (13)
proliferation [prəulifə'reiʃən] *n.* 增殖，扩散 (14)
propane ['prəupein] *n.* 丙烷 (4)
propanone ['prəupənəun] *n.* 丙酮 (5)
propene ['prəupi:n] *n.* 丙烯 (6)
property ['prɔpəti] *n.* 财产，性质，特性 (1)
proportional [prə'pɔ:ʃənl] *adj.* 比例的，成比例的 (14)
propylene ['prəupili:n] *n.* 丙烯 (6)
propyne ['prəupain] *n.* 丙炔 (6)
proton ['prəutɔn] *n.* 质子 (16)
provided [prə'vaidid] *conj.* 倘若 (15)
ptyalin ['taiəlin] *n.* 唾液淀粉酶 (10)
purple ['pə:pl] *adj.* 紫色的 *n.* 紫色 (2)
pyrethrin [pai'ri:θrin] *n.* 除虫菊酯 (10)
pyroelectric [ˌpaiərəui'lektrik, ˌpi-] *adj.* 热电的 (14)
pyroligneous [ˌpaiərəu'ligniəs] *adj.* 焦木的，干馏木材而得 (5)
pyrolysis [ˌpaiə'rɔlisis, ˌpi-] *n.* 高温分解 (9)

Q

qualitative ['kwɔlitətiv] *adj.* 性质上的，定性的 (5)
quantize ['kwɔntaiz] *v.* 使量子化 (16)
quartz [kwɔ:ts] *n.* 石英 (11)

R

radially ['reidjəli] *adv.* 径向地，放射性地 (19)
radical ['rædikəl] *adj.* 根本的，基本的，激进的 (3)
radiofrequency ['reidiəu'fri:kwənsi] *n.* 射频 (13)
random ['rændəm] *adj.* 任意的，随便的 (16)
rayon ['reiən] *n.* 人造丝，人造纤维 (8)
reactant [ri:'æktənt] *n.* 反应物 (1)
reactor [ri(:)'æktə] *n.* 反应堆，反应器 (20)
reagent [ri(:)'eidʒənt] *n.* 反应力，反应物，试剂 (10)
reboiler [ri'bɔilə] *n.* 再沸器 (18)
recirculation [ˌri:sə:kju'leiʃən] *n.* 再通行，再流通 (19)
rectification [ˌrektifi'keiʃən] *n.* 精馏 (18)
rectify ['rektifai] *vt.* 精馏 (18)
reflux ['ri:flʌks] *n.* 回流，逆流，退潮 (18)
refrigerant [ri'fridʒərənt] *adj.* 制冷的 *n.* 制冷剂 (9)
regeneration [riˌdʒenə'reiʃən] *n.* 再生，重建，回收 (20)
relationship [ri'leiʃənʃip] *n.* 关系，关联 (1)
relaxation [ˌri:læk'seiʃən] *n.* 松弛，放宽，娱乐 (16)

remainder [ri'meində] *n.* 残余，剩余物 (18)
render ['rendə] *vt.* 熔解，精炼，通过加热减少 (10)
repeller [ri'pel] *n.* 排斥 (15)
residence ['rezidəns] *n.* 滞留 (17)
residual [ri'zidjuəl] *adj.* 剩余的，残留的 (18)
resin ['rezin] *n.* 树脂 (8)
resistance [ri'zistəns] *n.* 反抗，阻力，电阻 (1)
resistor [ri'zistə] *n.* 电阻，电阻器 (13)
resolution [ˌrezə'ljuːʃən] *n.* 分辨率，解析度 (13)
resonance ['rezənəns] *n.* 反响，谐振，共振 (16)
respective [ris'pektiv] *adj.* 分别的，各自的 (3)
retention [ri'tenʃən] *n.* 保留值 (12)
reverse [ri'vəːs] *n.* 相反，倒退 *adj.* 相反的，颠倒的 *vt.* 颠倒，倒转 (1)
rhodium ['rəudiəm, -djəm] *n.* 铑 (10)
riveting ['rivitiŋ] *n.* 铆接（法） (10)
rodent ['rəudənt] *adj.* 咬的，嚼的 *n.* 啮齿动物 (10)
rodenticide [rəu'dentiˌsaid] *n.* 灭鼠剂 (10)
roller ['rəulə] *n.* 滚柱，托辊 (19)
roundworm [raundwəːm] *n.* 蛔虫 (10)
rpm = revolutions per minute 转数/分 (19)
ruthenium [ruː'θiːniəm] *n.* 钌 (10)

S

Scheele 谢勒（1742—1786，瑞典化学家，第一个从尿结石里分离出尿酸 $C_5H_4N_4O_3$） (5)
schematically [ski'mætikli] *adv.* 图解地，图表地 (11)
screen [skriːn] *n.* 屏，筛子 (19)
semiconductor ['semikən'dʌktə] *n.* 半导体 (14)
semisolid [ˌsemi'sɔlid, ˌsemai-] *n.* 半固体 *adj.* 半固体的 (19)
shaft [ʃɑːft] *n.* 轴，支柱 (19)
shower ['ʃauə] *n.* 淋浴，喷淋管 (19)
shuffle ['ʃʌfl] *n.* 改变位置，移动 (15)
sideway ['saidwei] *n.* 小路，人行道 *adj.* 侧面，旁边 (15)
sienna [si'enə] *n.* （富铁）黄土（用作颜料），赭色 (10)
silanize ['silənaiz] *vt.* 使硅烷化 (12)
silicate ['silikit] *n.* 硅酸盐 (3)
silicon ['silikən] *n.* 硅，硅元素 (3)
silicone ['silikəun] *n.* 硅树脂 (8)
silver ['silvə] *n.* 银，银子 *vt.* 镀银 (3)
slurry ['sləːri] *n.* 泥浆，浆 (17)
sodium ['səudjəm, -diəm] *n.* 钠 (1)
solubility [ˌsɔlju'biliti] *n.* 可解决性，可解释性，溶解性，溶解度 (1)
soluble ['sɔljubl] *adj.* 可溶的，可溶解的 (17)
solute ['sɔljuːt] *n.* 溶解物，溶质 (12)
solutions [sə'ljuːʃən] *n.* 解答，溶解，溶液 (2)
somewhat ['sʌm(h)wɔt] *adv.* 稍微，有点，有些 (2)
sophisticated [sə'fistikeitid] *adj.* 复杂的，精致的 (16)

species ['spiːʃiz] *n.* 种类，（原）核素，物种	(13)
spectra ['spektrə] 复数 spectrum ['spektrəm] *n.* 范围，光谱	(11)
spectral ['spektrəl] *adj.* 光谱的	(11)
spectrophotometer [ˌspektrəufə'tɔmitə] *n.* 分光光度计	(11)
spectroscopic [ˌspektrə'skɔpik] *adj.* 分光镜的	(16)
spout [spaut] *n.* 喷管，喷口	(19)
spur [spəː] *vt.* （spurred；spurring）刺激，鼓舞，鞭策	(12)
squirt [skwəːt] *v.* 喷出	(8)
stack [stæk] *n.* 烟囱，烟道	(19)
stannic ['stænik] *adj.* 锡的，四价锡的	(3)
stannous ['stænəs] *adj.* 锡的，含有锡的，含二价锡的	(3)
state [steit] *n.* 情形，状态 *adj.* 国家的，州的 *vt.* 声明，陈述，规定	(1)
static ['stætik] *adj.* 静态的，静止的	(17)
stem [stem] *n.* 茎，干	(6)
steroid ['stiərɔid] *n.* 类固醇	(12)
still [stil] *n.* 蒸馏器，蒸馏釜	(18)
strain [strein] *n.* 同类，同族	(10)
stringent ['strindʒənt] *adj.* 收缩的，变紧的	(9)
strip [strip] *vt.* 除去，剥去	(18)
strontium ['strɔnʃiəm] *n.* 锶	(2)
structure ['strʌktʃə] *n.* 结构，构造，建筑物 *vt.* 建筑，构成，组织	(1)
subdivide ['sʌbdi'vaid] *v.* 再分，细分	(1)
subject ['sʌbdʒikt] *vt.* 使屈从于……，使隶属	(15)
subscript ['sʌbskript] *adj.* 写在下方的	(3)
substance ['sʌbstəns] *n.* 物质，实质，主旨	(1)
substituent [sʌb'stitjuənt] *n.* 取代，取代基 *adj.* 取代的	(4)
substitution [ˌsʌbsti'tjuːʃən] *n.* 代替	(4)
substrate ['sʌbstreit] *n.* 培养基	(10)
suffix ['sʌfiks] *n.* 后缀，下标 *vt.* 添后缀	(3)
sulfate ['sʌlfeit] *n.* 硫酸盐 *v.* 以硫酸或硫酸盐处理，使变为硫酸盐	(3)
sulfite ['sʌlfait] *n.* 亚硫酸盐	(3)
sulfur ['sʌlfə] *n.* 硫黄 *vt.* 用硫磺处理	(3)
sulfuric [sʌl'fjuərik] *adj.* 硫的，正硫的	(2)
sulfurous ['sʌlfərəs] *adj.* 硫的，含硫的，亚硫的	(2)
supersaturate [sjuːpə'sætʃəreit] *vt.* 使过度饱和	(17)
supersaturation ['sjuːpəˌsætʃə'reiʃən] *n.* 过度饱和	(17)
support [sə'pɔːt] *n.* 载体	(12)
symbol ['simbəl] *n.* 符号，记号，象征	(3)
systemic [sis'temik] *adj.* 系统的，全身的，（农药）散发的，内吸的	(10)

T

table ['teibl] *n.* 桌子，石板，表格	(2)
tangential [tæn'dʒenʃ(ə)l] *adj.* 切线的	(17)
tantalite ['tæntəlait] *n.* 钽铁矿	(14)
tar [tɑː] *n.* 焦油，柏油	(10)
tartaric [tɑː'tærik] *adj.* 酒石的，似酒石的，含有酒石的	(5)

teflon ['teflən]　　*n.* 特氟纶，聚四氟乙烯　　(9)
telluride ['teljuraid]　　*n.* 碲化物　　(14)
terylene ['teriˌliːn]　　*n.* 涤纶　　(8)
tetraborate [ˌtetrə'bɔːreit]　　*n.* 四硼酸盐　　(3)
tetrachloromethane ['tetrəˌklɔːrəu'miːθein, -'me-]　　*n.* 四氯化碳　　(5)
tetrafluoroethene ['tetrə'fluːərə'eθiːn]　　*n.* 四氟乙烯　　(9)
tetravalency ['tetrə'veilənsi]　　*n.* 四价　　(7)
tetravalent [ˌtetrə'veilənt]　　*adj.* 四价的　　(3)
thermistor [θəː'mistə]　　*n.* 热敏电阻　　(14)
thermocouple ['θəːməuˌkʌpl]　　*n.* 热电偶　　(14)
thermopile ['θəːməupail]　　*n.* 热电堆　　(14)
thermoplastics [ˌθəːmə'plæstiks]　　*n.* 热塑性塑料　　(8)
tin [tin]　　*n.* 锡，马口铁，罐　　(3)
titanium [tai'teinjəm, ti-]　　*n.* 钛　　(9)
toluene ['tɔljuiːn]　　*n.* 甲苯　　(7)
topmost ['tɔpməust]　　*adj.* 最高的，顶端的　　(19)
toxin ['tɔksin]　　*n.* 毒素　　(10)
translocate [trænsləu'keit]　　*vt.* 改变……的位置　　(10)
translucent [trænz'ljuːsnt]　　*adj.* 半透明的，透明的　　(8)
transparent [træns'pɛərənt]　　*adj.* 透明的，显然的，明晰的　　(8)
trap [træp]　　*n.* 陷阱　　(15)
tricarboxylic [traiˌkɑːbɔk'silik]　　*adj.* (分子中含有) 二 (个) 羧基的　　(5)
tricel ['trisl]　　*n.* 特列赛尔（三醋酯纤维织物，商标名）　　(8)
trichlorobenzene [ˌtraiklɔːrə'beziːn]　　*n.* 三氯（代）苯　　(7)
triglycine ['triglisain]　　*n.* 次氨基三乙酸　　(14)
trihydroxy [traihai'drɔksi]　　*adj.* 三羟（基）的　　(5)
trisubstituted [trai'sʌbstiˌtjuːtid, -ˌtuːtid]　　*adj.* 三元取代的　　(7)
1,2,3-tripropaneol [trai'prəupeinəl]　　*n.* 1,2,3-丙三醇　　(8)
trivalent [trai'veilənt]　　*adj.* 三价的　　(3)
tumble ['tʌmbl]　　*vt.* 使摔倒，使滚翻　　(19)
tungsten ['tʌŋstən]　　*n.* 钨　　(11)
turbine ['təːbin, -bain]　　*n.* 涡轮　　(1)
turbodryer ['təːbəu'draiə]　　*n.* 涡轮干燥机　　(19)
Tyrian ['tiriən]　　*n.* 提尔人　　(10)

U

Ultramarine [ˌʌltrəmə'riːn]　　*n.* 深蓝色，天青石做成的蓝色颜料　　(10)
ultraviolet ['ʌltrə'vaiəlit]　　*adj.* 紫外线的，紫外的　　(11)
umber ['ʌmbə]　　*n.* 棕土，焦茶色　　(10)
unicellular ['juːni'seljulə]　　*adj.* 单细胞的　　(12)
upflow ['ʌpfləu]　　*vi.* 向上流　*n.* 向上流动　　(18)
upstream ['ʌp'striːm]　　*adv.* 向上游，溯流，逆流地　　(17)
urea ['juəriə]　　*n.* 尿素　　(5)
uric ['juərik]　　*adj.* 尿的，取自尿中的　　(5)
urine ['juərin]　　*n.* 尿　　(5)

V

valence ['veiləns]　　*n.* （化合）价，原子价　　　　　　　　　　　　　　　（3）
vanadium [və'neidiəm，-djəm]　　*n.* 钒，铅矿　　　　　　　　　　　　　（10）
vaporize ['veipəraiz]　　*v.* （使）蒸发　　　　　　　　　　　　　　　　（1）
vat [væt]　　*n.* （装液体的）大桶，大缸（尤指染缸）　　　　　　　　　　（10）
vehicle ['vi:ikl]　　*n.* 媒介物　　　　　　　　　　　　　　　　　　　　（10）
vermilion [və'miljən]　　*n.* 朱砂，朱红色　　　　　　　　　　　　　　　（10）
vinyl ['vainil，'vinil]　　*n.* 乙烯基　　　　　　　　　　　　　　　　　（8）
vinyon ['vinjən]　　*n.* 维荣　　　　　　　　　　　　　　　　　　　　　（8）
virtually ['və:tjuəli]　　*adv.* 事实上，实质上　　　　　　　　　　　　　（8）
viscosity [vis'kɔsiti]　　*n.* 黏质，黏性　　　　　　　　　　　　　　　　（6）
volatility [ˌvɔlə'tiliti]　　*n.* 挥发性　　　　　　　　　　　　　　　　　（6）
volumetric [vɔlju'metrik]　　*adj.* 测定体积的　　　　　　　　　　　　　（17）

W

Walsh [wɔ:lʃ]　　*n.* 沃尔什（姓氏）　　　　　　　　　　　　　　　　　（13）
wattage ['wɔtidʒ]　　*n.* 瓦特数　　　　　　　　　　　　　　　　　　　（11）
weir [wiə]　　*n.* 堰，回流堰　　　　　　　　　　　　　　　　　　　　（18）
whatsoever [wɔtsəu'evə(r)]　　*pron.* 无论什么　　　　　　　　　　　　（4）
Wohler 维勒（1800—1882，德国化学家，第一个在实验室中从氰酸氨制备有机化合物尿素）　　（5）

X

xanthate ['zænθeit]　　*n.* 磺酸盐　　　　　　　　　　　　　　　　　　（8）
xanthophyll ['zænθəˌfil]　　*n.* 黄色色素，叶黄质　　　　　　　　　　　（10）

Y

yarn [jɑ:n]　　*n.* 纱，纱线　　　　　　　　　　　　　　　　　　　　（8）

Z

zinc [ziŋk]　　*n.* 锌　　*vt.* 涂锌于　　　　　　　　　　　　　　　　（3）
Ziegler 齐格勒（1898—1973，德国化学家，曾获得1963年诺贝尔化学奖）　　（9）

Phrases

a factor of one billion or more　十亿倍以上　　　　　　　　　　　　　（10）
a fraction of　一小部分　　　　　　　　　　　　　　　　　　　　　　（18）
absolute retention　绝对保留值　　　　　　　　　　　　　　　　　　　（12）
absorption peak　吸收峰　　　　　　　　　　　　　　　　　　　　　　（16）
acetate process　醋酸纤维法　　　　　　　　　　　　　　　　　　　　（8）
activation energy　活化能　　　　　　　　　　　　　　　　　　　　　（10）
addition polymerization　加聚反应　　　　　　　　　　　　　　　　　（8）

addition reactions　加成反应　(7)
adhere to　黏着　(8)
adhesive cement　胶浆，胶水　(10)
adiabatic flash　绝热闪蒸　(17)
aldehyde-phenylamine (aniline) condensation products　乙醛苯胺浓缩产品　(9)
aliphatic compound　脂肪族化合物　(6)
alkyl group　烷基　(7)
alkyl substituent　烷基（烃基）取代基　(6)
all-purpose　通用的，多用途的　(9)
alternating-current sparks　交流电火花　(13)
ammonium cyanate　氰酸铵　(5)
amorphous hydrated silica　无定形含水硅　(12)
animal black　兽炭黑，骨炭　(10)
animal matter　动物质　(5)
aromatic character　芳香性　(7)
aromatic compound　芳香族化合物　(7)
aryl groups or radical　芳香基，芳基　(7)
as a (general) rule　总体上，通常　(3)
as a whole　总的来说　(3)
as far as…is concerned　就……而言　(16)
as such　同样地，同量地　(9)
assign to　分配　(1)
ASTM International　美国材料实验协会　(10)
at the present time　目前　(4)
at this stage　眼下，暂时　(7)
atomic absorption spectrometer　原子吸收分光光度计　(13)
atomic absorption spectrometry　原子吸收光谱测定法　(13)
atomic fluorescence spectrometry　原子荧光光谱法　(13)
atomic spectrometric method　原子光谱法　(13)
attached to　附着　(2)
average residence time　平均滞留时间　(17)
background absorption　背景吸收　(14)
baffled settling zone　挡板沉降区　(17)
barrier-layer　阻挡层，势垒　(11)
basic lead carbonate　碱性碳酸铅　(10)
be analogous to　类似于……，与……相似　(7)
be attached to　附属于，喜爱　(7)
be based upon　基于　(4)
be classified as　分类为　(1)
be composed of　由……构成　(1)
be concerned with　关心……　(2)
be converted from one form to another　由一种形式转变为另一种形式　(1)
be defined as　定义为　(1)
be expected to　应该……　(7)
be flashed into　闪蒸为　(18)
be in equilibrium with　与……保持平衡　(18)

Term	English	Chinese	Page
be insoluble in	不溶于		(5)
be made up of	由……组成		(1)
be perpendicular to	与……垂直		(16)
is proportional to	与……成正比		(17)
be referred to as	被称为		(1)
be reserved to	保留用……		(8)
be soluble in	溶于		(5)
be subdivided into	被划分为		(1)
bear resemblance to	与……相同		(7)
become impregnated with	充满……		(10)
become proficient at	精通		(3)
blackbody radiation sources	黑体辐射源		(14)
block polymer	嵌段共聚物,成块聚合物		(8)
boiling point	沸点		(1)
bombard with	用……轰炸		(15)
bonded phase	键合固定相		(12)
bone black	骨炭		(10)
branched alkane	支链烷烃		(6)
broad-band	带(频)宽		(13)
buna rubber [ˈbjuːnəˈrʌbə]	丁钠橡胶		(9)
by the presence of	由于……的存在		(9)
capillary column	毛细管柱		(12)
capillary gas chromatography	毛细管气相色谱法		(12)
carbamide-methanal (urea-formaldehyde) resin	脲醛树脂		(8)
carbon tetrachloride	四氯化碳		(5)
carrier gas	载气		(12)
carry through	达到,完成,坚持,保存		(3)
catalytic reactor	催化反应器		(20)
central portion	中部		(18)
cesium-coated photocathode	涂铯光电阴极		(11)
charged particle	带电粒子		(15)
chart recorder	绘图仪		(15)
chemical behaviour	化学作用		(7)
chemical factor	化学因素		(20)
chemical mode	化学模式		(8)
chemical shift	化学位移		(16)
chlorofluoro-derivatives	氯氟衍生物		(9)
2-chloro-4-nitrophenol [ˈklɔːrə] [ˌnaitrəˈfiːnəul]	n. 2-氯-4-硝基苯酚		(7)
chrome yellow	铬黄		(10)
circular tray	圆形淋盘,圆形塔板		(19)
circulating pump	循环泵		(17)
coal tar	煤焦油		(10)
Cold Cure process	冷硫化过程		(9)
collide with	同……发生冲突		(15)
colloidal solution	胶体溶液		(9)
column chromatography	柱色谱法		(12)

column head 柱头	(12)
common (or semi-systematic) name 普通命名（或半系统命名）	(4)
common name 普通命名法	(6)
complementary structure 补充结构	(10)
composed of 由……组成	(8)
condensation polymerization 缩聚合（作用）	(8)
constant radiofrequency 恒定射频	(16)
continuous fractionating tower 连续精馏塔	(18)
cooling jacket 冷却夹层	(20)
countercurrent flow 逆流	(19)
criss-cross ['kriskrɔs] n. 十字形 adj. 十字形的 adv. 十字形地	(3)
cross-circulation 交叉循环	(19)
crude petroleum 原油	(6)
crystallization equipment 结晶设备	(17)
cuprammonium process 铜铵法	(8)
cyclic compounds 环化合物	(7)
cyclone separator 旋风分离器	(19)
DDT [ˌdiːdiːˈtiː] (dichloro-diphenyl-trichloroethane) 二氯二苯三氯乙烷（杀虫剂的一种）	(10)
dead volume 死体积	(12)
deflect out of 偏离	(15)
design method 设计方法	(20)
deuterated trigylcine sulfate (DTGS) 重氢硫酸三甘氨酸	(14)
deuterium electrical-discharge lamps 氘放电灯	(11)
diametrically opposite 直对的	(7)
2,3-dihydroxybutanedioic (tartaric) acid 2,3-二羟基丁酸或酒石酸	(5)
dilute sulphuric (Ⅵ) acid 稀硫酸	(8)
dinitrobenzenecarboxylic acid [dainaitrəuˈbenziːnˌkɑːbˈsilikˈæsid] 二硝基苯甲酸	(7)
2,6-dinitrobenzoic acid [daiˈnaitrəubenˈzəuikˈæsid] 2,6-二硝基苯甲酸	(7)
dip into 把……浸入（液体）中	(2)
direct-current arc 直流电弧	(13)
dispersive-type infrared spectrophotometer 色散型红外光谱仪	(14)
distillation equipment 蒸馏设备	(18)
distillation tower 蒸馏塔	(18)
distribution coefficient 分配系数	(12)
disubstituted derivatives 二取代衍生物	(7)
double bond 双键	(6)
double-beam 双光束	(14)
downflow liquid 下流液	(18)
draft tube-baffle crystallizer 导流管板结晶器	(17)
draw out 抽出，拉长	(8)
drum dryer 转鼓式干燥器	(19)
dry distillation 干馏	(5)
drying chamber 干燥室	(19)
dyeing fabrics 染色织物	(5)
elastic properties 弹性	(9)
electric dipole moment 电偶极矩	(14)

electron trap 电子捕获 (15)
electronic configuration 电子构型，电子排布 (7)
electrothermal atomizer 电热原子化器 (13)
element-specific line source 特定元素线性光源 (13)
elutriation leg 析出段 (17)
entrance slit 进口狭缝 (14)
ethanedioic (oxalic) acid 乙二酸或草酸 (5)
ethanoic (acetic) acid 乙酸或醋酸 (5)
ethenyl ethanoate (vinyl acetate) (8)
excited state 激发态 (16)
exit slit 出口狭缝 (14)
extended-surface 展开面 (19)
extractive metallurgical industries 萃取冶金工业 (20)
far-infrared 远红外 (14)
feed additives 饲料添加剂 (10)
feed hopper 进料斗 (19)
feed inlet 进料口 (17)
feed plate 进料板 (18)
ferric ferrocyanide 铁氰化铁 (10)
filler gas 填充气体 (13)
finely divided 细碎粒（粒状）的 (10)
fixed bed 固定床 (20)
fixed field value 固定磁场值 (16)
flame-ionization detector 火焰离子化检测器 (12)
flash distillation 闪蒸 (18)
flash distillation plant 闪蒸设备 (18)
flash dryer 急剧（闪速，气流）干燥机 (19)
flow rate 流量 (12)
flue gas 烟道气 (19)
fluid-bed dryer 流化床干燥器 (19)
fluidized bed 流化床 (20)
flux-calcined 熔融煅烧 (12)
for the purpose of 为了，因……起见 (13)
for the time being 暂时，目前 (3)
Fourier transform infrared spectrometers 傅里叶变换红外光谱仪 (14)
Fourier transrorm NMR spectrometer 傅里叶变换光谱仪 (16)
free-radical 自由基，游离基 (9)
freon-22 ['friːɔn] 氟里昂，二氟二氯（氟三氯）甲烷 (9)
Friedel-Crafts alkylation reaction 弗里德克尔-克拉夫茨烷基化反应 (9)
functional group 官能团 (4)
fused-silica lamp envelope 熔融适应灯封套 (11)
gas chromatograph 气相色谱 (12)
gas-chromatographic column 气相色谱柱 (12)
gas-chromatographic instrumentation 气相色谱仪 (12)
gaseous reaction 气相反应 (20)
gear pinion 小齿轮 (19)

general-purpose 多种用途的，多方面的	(13)
give birth to 产生	(13)
gives rise to 引起，使发生	(7)
ground state 基态	(16)
handling characteristics 操作特性	(12)
hazardous reactants and products 危险反应物和产物	(20)
heat transfer factor 传热因素	(20)
heating coil 蛇形加热管	(18)
heat-transfer coefficient 传热系数	(20)
heat-transfer rate 传热速率	(20)
high-pressure reactor 高压反应器	(18)
high-resolution echelle 高分辨率光栅	(13)
hollow-cathode lamp 空心阴极灯	(13)
homologous series 同系列	(4)
hydraulic sorting fluid 液压分流	(17)
hydrogenation reaction 氢化反应	(10)
2-hydroxybutanedioic (malic) acid 2-羟基丁酸或苹果酸	(5)
2-hydroxypropane-1,2,3-tricarboxylic (citric) acid 2-羟基丙烷-1,2,3-三甲酸	(5)
2-hydroxypropanoic (lactic) acid 2-羟基丙酸或乳酸	(5)
ICI (Imperial Chemical Industries Ltd) 英国化学工业公司	(9)
in a sense 在某种意义上	(8)
in accordance with 与……一致，依照	(4)
in essence 本质上，大体上，其实	(16)
in excess of 超过，较……为多	(8)
in favour of 参加支持……的活动	(7)
in other words 换句话说	(15)
in parallel 平行	(20)
in place of 代替	(10)
in some instances 在某些情况下	(4)
in some respects 在某些方面	(4)
in terms of 根据，按照，在……方面	(7)
in the emergence of 出现	(13)
in/with regard to 关于	(1)
incident radiation 入射的辐射线	(14)
indium antimonide 锗化铟	(14)
infrared spectrometer 红外光谱仪	(14)
internal combustion engine 内燃机	(6)
ionization chamber 电离室	(15)
IUPAC name 国际命名法	(6)
kinetic energy 动能	(15)
Kirchoff's law 基尔霍夫定律	(13)
knock…off 除掉，消除	(15)
lead chromate 铬酸铅	(10)
lead sulfide 硫化铅	(14)
lead telluride 碲化铅	(14)
life-sustaining 一生的	(10)

linear alternating copolymers 线性交替共聚物 (8)
linear molecule 线性分子 (7)
liquid chromatography 液相色谱法 (12)
liquid stationary phase 液体固定相 (12)
liquid-phase reaction 液相反应 (20)
literal meaning 字面意义 (7)
lithium tantalite 锂钽铁矿 (14)
locked-in 牢固的，固定的 (16)
longitudinal tube 长管 (19)
low water-absorption properties 低吸水性 (8)
low-head circulating pump 低压头循环泵 (17)
magnetic dipole 磁偶极 (16)
magnetic field 磁场 (16)
magnetic moment 磁矩 (16)
magnetic recording materials 磁性记录材料 (10)
marine diatomite 海藻土 (12)
mass spectrometer 质谱仪 (15)
mass/charge ratio 质荷比 (15)
massively cross-linked polymer 大型交联聚合物 (8)
massively cross-linked structure 大型交联结构 (8)
melting point 熔点 (1)
mercuric sulfide 硫化银 (10)
mercury-vapor lamp 汞蒸气灯 (11)
meta (m) derivative 邻位衍生物 (7)
2-Methyl-1-propanol 2-甲基-1-丙醇 (4)
microwave plasma 微波等离子体 (13)
minor cross-linked polymer 小型交联聚合物 (8)
minor-level 少量的 (12)
mode of operation 操作模式 (20)
monosubstituted derivative 一元取代衍生物 (7)
moth larvae 蛾幼虫 (10)
mother liquor 母液 (17)
multiple effect 多效 (17)
narrow absorption profile 窄吸收谱线轮廓 (13)
negative ion 负离子 (15)
Nernst glower 能斯特灯 (14)
next-but-one 间位的 (7)
noise-rejecting 抗噪声 (16)
non-polar 非极化的 (5)
non-stick 东西不粘上的 (9)
nuclear magnet 核磁体 (16)
nuclear magnetic resonance spectrometry 核磁共振光谱法 (16)
nut galls 核果瘤 (5)
on the application of ……方面的应用 (8)
one above the other 逐个 (19)
open tubular column 空心色谱柱 (12)

open-chain compounds 开链化合物	(7)
organic solvent 有机溶剂	(6)
organosilicon polymers 有机硅聚合物	(8)
ortho(o)derivative 间位衍生物	(7)
oxidation number 氧化数	(3)
oyster White 牡蛎白	(12)
packed bed 填充床	(20)
packed column 填充柱	(12)
para(p)derivative 对位衍生物	(7)
parent alkane 母烃	(4)
petroleum ether 石油醚	(6)
petroleum jelly 凡士林，矿油	(6)
petroleum refining 炼油	(18)
phenolmethanal resin 酚醛树脂	(8)
3-Phenyl-1-pentene ['fenə] ['penti:n] n. 3-苯基-1-戊烯	(6)
3-Phenyl-1-pentyne ['fenə] ['pentain] n. 3-苯基-1-戊炔	(6)
phenyl group or radical 苯基	(7)
photoelectric detection 光电检测	(13)
photoemissive cathode 光电发射阴极	(11)
photometric methods 光度测定法	(11)
photon flux 光子通量	(11)
photosensitive material 光敏材料	(10)
pipe still 管式蒸馏釜	(18)
plastic-like 塑料似的	(9)
plate height 塔板高度	(12)
polar groups 极性基	(5)
polar solute 极性溶质	(12)
poly(2-chloro-1,3-butadiene) 聚-2-氯-1,3-丁二烯	(9)
polymerization catalyst 聚合催化剂	(9)
polyvinyl chloride （PVC)聚氯乙烯	(8)
pool of liquid 蓄液池	(18)
positively charged plate 正极	(15)
preparative techniques 制备技术	(5)
pressure drop 压力降	(12)
pressure-drop 压力降	(20)
Prussian blue 普鲁士蓝	(10)
quantitative analysis 定量分析	(11)
quartz-halogen lamp 石英卤素灯	(11)
radiant energy 辐射能	(16)
radiofrequency oscillator 射频振荡器	(16)
radiofrequency plasma 射频等离子体	(13)
radiofrequency radiation 射频辐射	(16)
rare-earth oxides 稀土金属氧化物	(14)
rate of reflux return 回流液回流速度	(18)
rayon fibre 人造纤维	(8)
reaction rate 反应速率	(20)

reactor geometry 反应器形状	(20)
rectifying section 精馏段	(18)
refer to sb. as 称某人为	(4)
reference compartment 参考比色皿	(14)
reflux pump 回流泵	(18)
reflux splitter 回流分配器	(18)
regenerate from 由……重建	(8)
relative abundance 相对丰度	(15)
relative intensity 相对强度	(15)
relative molecular mass 相对分子质量	(8)
relaxation time 松弛时间，弛豫时间	(16)
residual liquid 剩余液体	(18)
rotary dryer 转筒干燥器	(19)
rotary valve 旋转阀	(19)
rotating sector mirror 旋转扇形反射镜	(14)
rotating shaft 旋转轴	(19)
safety factor 安全因素	(20)
sample compartment 样品比色皿	(14)
SBR rubber (Styrene Butadiene Rubber) 丁苯橡胶	(8)
scale up 按比例增加	(20)
schematic diagram 示意图	(13)
Schweitzer's reagent 许维测试剂（铜氨溶液试剂）	(8)
screen-conveyor dryer 筛网干燥器	(19)
shell and tube heat exchanger 管壳式换热器	(20)
sideways force 侧向力	(15)
silicon carbide rod 碳化硅棒	(14)
single-effect 单效	(17)
slow over 慢下来，减缓，减速	(13)
slurry pump 浆液泵	(17)
solubility curve 溶解度曲线	(17)
solvent extraction 溶剂萃取	(5)
sour milk 酸牛奶	(5)
spectral intensity 光谱强度	(11)
spectral narrowness 光谱收缩	(13)
spectrophotometric methods 分光光度法	(11)
spectroscopic methods 光谱分析法	(11)
spinning side-band 旋转边频	(16)
spray disk 喷雾盘	(19)
spray dryer 喷雾干燥器	(19)
stand-point 观点	(17)
static head 静压头	(17)
steam-heated 汽热的	(19)
steam-jet 蒸汽喷嘴	(17)
steam-tube 蒸汽管	(19)
stick diagram 棒图	(15)
stirred tank reactor 搅拌釜式反应器	(20)

straight line　直线　(15)
straight-chain alkane　直链烷烃　(6)
strip-chart recorder　带状纸记录仪　(11)
stripping section　提馏段　(18)
subject…to　使……服从，使……遭受　(15)
substituted benzene derivatives　取代苯衍生物　(7)
surface area to volume ratio　表面积与体积比　(20)
surface-coated open tubular（SCOT）columns　表面涂层空心色谱柱　(12)
tailor-make polymer　特制聚合物　(8)
tangential inlet　切向进口　(17)
temperature coefficients of resistance　电阻温度系数　(14)
tensile strength　张力　(9)
tetramminecopper（Ⅱ）complex　四氨合铜络合物　(8)
the Einstein mass-energy relationship　爱因斯坦的质量能量关系式　(1)
the Law of Conservation of Mass and Energy　质量和能量守恒定律　(1)
the Law of Conservation of Matter　物质守恒定律　(1)
the Law of Definite Composition of Proportion　定比定组成定律　(1)
thermosetting plastics　热固性塑料　(8)
thermostatted air bath　自动调温气浴　(12)
thin-film dryer　薄膜干燥器　(19)
through-put　产量，通过量　(13)
tower dryer　塔式干燥器　(19)
trace-level　痕量的　(12)
tray dryer　厢式干燥器　(19)
triethyl-aluminium［traiˈeθəlˌæljuːˈminjəm］　三乙（烷）基铝　(9)
triglycine sulfate（TGS）　硫酸三甘氨酸　(14)
3,4,5-trihydroxybenzenecarboxylic（gallic）acid　3,4,5-三羟基苯甲酸或五倍子酸　(5)
triple bond　三键　(6)
tube sheet　管板　(20)
tubular reactor　管式反应器　(20)
tungsten-filament "incandescent" lamp　钨丝白炽灯　(11)
turbine fan　涡轮鼓风机　(19)
two-fluid nozzle　气动雾化喷嘴　(19)
type of bonding　键型　(5)
Tyrian purple　提尔紫　(10)
ultraviolet-visible region　紫外可见光区　(11)
unicellular algae　单细胞海藻　(12)
unsaturated bond　不饱和键　(7)
upflow vapor　上升蒸汽　(18)
uric acid　尿酸　(5)
vacuum crystallizer　真空结晶器　(17)
vacuum pump　真空泵　(15)
vinyl chloride　氯乙烯　(8)
volatile liquids　挥发性液体　(5)
volumetric flow rate　体积流速　(17)
vulcanized rubber　硫化橡胶　(8)

wall-coated open tubular (WCOT) columns 涂壁空心色谱柱	(12)
well-packed 填充好的	(12)
Wheatstone bridge 惠斯登电桥	(14)
with the exception of 除……以外	(4)
without doubt 毫无疑问地	(9)
wood sorrel *n.* 酢浆草	(5)
work with 与……共事，与……合作，对……起作用	(15)

Appendixes

Ⅰ 化学化工常用构词

aci-	酸式	-ether	醚
aero-	空气	ferri-	铁
-al	醛	ferro-	亚铁
ald-	醛	fluo-	氟,荧
-aldehyde	醛	fluoro-	氟代,氟(基)
-amide	酰胺	haem-	血的
-amine	胺	halo-	卤
amino-	氨基	hepta-	七,庚
-ane	烷	hetero-	杂,不同
anhydro-	脱水	hexa-	六,己
anti-	反,抗,对,解,阻	homo-	同(型),高
aryl-	芳(香)基	hydro-	氢化的,氢的,水
-ase	酶	-ic anhydride	酸酐
-ate	(词尾)用于由词尾为-ic 的酸所成的盐类或酯类的名称	-ide	一化物
		infra-	在下,较低
auto-	自,自动	inter-	(在)中(间),互相,合一起
benz-	苯基	intra-	内
bi-	二,两个,双	iso-	异,同,等
bio-	生物的	-ketone	酮
bis-	两个,双	-lactone	内酯
-carboxylic acid	羧酸	laevo-	左旋
chemico-	化学的	lipo-	酯的
chemo-	化学	m-(=meta)	间(位)
chlor-	氯	meso-	内消旋;中(间)
chloro-	氯代,氯(基)Cl—	meta-	间(位)(有机系统名用);偏(无机酸用)
chromato-	色谱	mono-	一,单
chromo-	色	multi-	多
cis-	顺式	nitro-	硝基
co-	共,同,相互	non-	不,非,无
counter-	反,逆	nona-	九,壬
cyan-	氰基 CN—	o-(=ortho)	邻(位)
cycl(o)-	环(合,化),(循环)	octa=	八,辛
de-	脱,去,除,解,减,消,反,止	-oic acid	酸
deca-	十,癸	-ol	醇;酚
dehydro-	脱氢	-one	酮
dextro-	右旋的	ortho-	正,原,邻(位)
di-	二,双(指基的数目);联(二)指两个基以一价相联;双(指两个单体接合)	-osc	糖
		-oside	糖苷
dodeca-	十二	over-	过(度),超,在外 oxo- 氧化,氧代,含氧的
electro-	电	p-(=para-)	(位次)对,仲
-en	(词尾)指烯或环型化合物	penta-	五,戊
endo-	内,桥(环内桥接)	per-	高,过,全
-ene	烯	phono-	声,音
epoxy-	环氧	photo-	光,感光的

续表

poly-	多,聚	syn-	同,共,与;顺式
pre-	预,前,先,在上	tauto-	互变(异构)
pyro-	火,热,高温,焦	tetra-	四,丁
radio-	放射,辐射	thio-	硫代
re-	再,重,回,向后;相互,相反	trans-	反(式);超,跨,过,(以)外,后
retro-	向后	tri-	三,丙
rheo-	流	ultra-	超,过,(以)外,极端,异常,过度
stereo-	立体,固(体)	under-	在下,底下,不足,从属
sub-	下,亚,次,副	uni-	单,一
sulf-	(词头)表示有硫存在	-yl	(某)基
sulfo-	硫代,磺基	-ylene	(某)烯
-sulfonic acid	磺酸	-yne	(某)炔
super-	过,超,高于		

Ⅱ 常见有机基团

acetenyl=ethynyl	乙炔基	formyl	甲酰
acetoxy	乙酸基,乙酰氧基	heptyl	庚基
acetyl	乙酰基	hexyl	己基
aldo	(表示有醛基存在)醛(元),氧代	hydroxy(l)	羟基
alkoxy	烷氧基	methane=methylene	亚甲基
amino	氨基	methenyl=methylidyne	次甲基
amyl=pentyl	戊基	methyl	甲基
aniline	苯胺基	naphthyl	萘基
anthaquinonyl	蒽醌基	nitro	硝基
anth yl	蒽基	nitroso	亚硝基
azido	叠氮基	nonyl	壬基
axo-group	偶氮基	octyl	辛基
benzoxy=benzoyloxy	苯甲酸基	pentyl	戊基
butyl	丁基	phenyl	苯基
carbonyl	碳基	propenyl	丙烯基
carboxy(l)	羧基	propyl	丙基
decyl	癸基	sulfo	磺基
diazo	重氮基	thio	硫代
ethyl	乙基	vinyl	乙烯基

Ⅲ 常见有机化合物命名

Common or trivial name	Systematic (or IUPAC) name	Structure
Paraffin	Alkane	$R-CH_3$
Cycloparaffins or Naphthenes	Cycloalkanes	CH_2-CH_2 $\quad\backslash\;/$ $\quad CH_2$
Olefins	Alkenes	$RCH=CH_2$
Acetylenes	Alkynes	$RC\equiv CH$

Common or trivial name	Systematic (or IUPAC) name	Structure
Methacrylates	2-Methylpropenoates	$CH_2=\underset{\underset{CH_3}{\vert}}{C}-CO_2R$
Ethylene	Ethene	$CH_2=CH_2$
Propylene	Propene	$CH_3CH=CH_2$
Styrene	Phenylethene	$C_6H_5-CH=CH_2$
Acetylene	Ethyne	$HC\equiv CH$
Isoprene	2-Methyl-1,3-butadiene	$CH_2=\underset{\underset{CH_3}{\vert}}{C}-CH=CH_2$
Ethylene oxide	Oxirane	$\underset{CH_2-CH_2}{\overset{O}{\triangle}}$
Propylene oxide	1-Methyloxirane	$\underset{CH_2-CH-CH_3}{\overset{O}{\triangle}}$
Methyl iodide	Iodomethane	CH_3I
Methyl chloride	Chloromethane	CH_3Cl
Methylene dichloride	Dichloromethane	CH_2Cl_2
Chloroform	Trichloromethane	$CHCl_3$
Carbon tetrachloride	Tetrachloromethane	CCl_4
Vinyl chloride	Chloroethene	$CH_2=CH-Cl$
Ethylene dichloride	1,2-Dichloroethane	$ClCH_2CH_2Cl$
Allyl chloride	3-Chloroprope	$CH_2=CH-CH_2-Cl$
Chloroprene	2-Chloro-1,3-butadiene	$CH_2=\underset{\underset{Cl}{\vert}}{C}-CH=CH_2$
Epichlorohydrin	1-Chloromethyloxirane	$\underset{ClCH_2CH-CH_2}{\overset{O}{\triangle}}$
Ethylene glycol	1,2-Ethanediol	$HOCH_2CH_2OH$
Propargyl alcohol	Propynol	$H-C\equiv C-CH_2OH$
Allyl alcohol	1-Propen-3-ol	$CH=CH-CH_2OH$
Iso-Propanol	2-Propanol	$\underset{\underset{OH}{\vert}}{CH_3CHCH_3}$
Glycerol	1,2,3-Propanetriol	$HOCH_2-\underset{\underset{OH}{\vert}}{CH}-CH_2OH$
Sec-Butanol	2-Butanol	$\underset{\underset{OH}{\vert}}{CH_3CHCH_2CH_3}$

Common or trivial name	Systematic (or IUPAC) name	Structure
Pentaerythritol	2,2-Di(hydroxymethyl)-1,3-Propanediol	$HOCH_2-\underset{\underset{CH_2OH}{\|}}{\overset{\overset{CH_2OH}{\|}}{C}}-CH_2OH$
Lauryl alcohol	Dodecanol	$CH_3(CH_2)_{10}CH_2OH$
Acetone	Propanone	CH_3COCH_3
Methylisobutyl ketone	4-Methyl-2-pentanone	$CH_3COCH_2\underset{\underset{CH_3}{\|}}{CH}CH_3$
Formaldehyde	Methanal	$HCOH$
Acetaldehyde	Ethanal	CH_3CHO
Chloral	2,2,2-Trichloroethanal	Cl_3CCHO
Propionaldehyde	Propanal	CH_3CH_2CHO
Acrolein	Propenal	$CH_2=CHCHO$
Butyraldehyde	Butanal	$CH_3CH_2CH_2CHO$
Formic acid	Methanoic acid	HCO_2H
Methyl formate	Methyl methanoate	HCO_2CH_3
Acetic acid	Ethanoic acid	CH_3CO_2H
Acetic anhydride	Ethanoic anhydride	$(CH_3CO)_2O$
Peracetic acid	Perathanoic acid	CH_3CO_3H
Vinyl acetate	Ethenyl Ethanoate	$CH_2=CHO_2CCH_3$
Acrylic acid	Propenoic acid	$CH_2=CH-CO_2H$
Dimethyl oxalate	Dimethyl ethanedioate	$\underset{CO_2CH_3}{\overset{CO_2CH_3}{\|}}$
Propionic acid	Propaonic acid	$CH_3CH_2CO_2H$
Methyl methacrylate	Methyl 2-Methylpropenoate	$CH_2=\underset{\underset{CH_3}{\|}}{C}-CO_2CH_3$
Maleic acid	Cis-Butenedoic acid	$\underset{H_2OC}{\overset{H}{\diagdown}}C=C\underset{CO_2H}{\overset{H}{\diagup}}$
Maleic anhydride	Cis-Butenedioic anhydride	(cyclic anhydride structure)
Citric acid	2-Hydroxypropane-1,2,2-Tricarboxylic acid	$HO-\underset{\underset{CH_2CO_2H}{\|}}{\overset{\overset{CH_2CO_2H}{\|}}{C}}-CO_2H$
Methyl laurate	Methyl dodecanoate	$CH_3(CH_2)_{10}CO_2CH_3$
Stearic acid	Octadecanoic acid	$CH_3(CH_2)_{16}CO_2H$
Acrylonnitrile	Propenonitrile	$CH_2=CH-CN$

续表

Common or trivial name	Systematic (or IUPAC) name	Structure
Adiponitrile	Hexane-1,6-dinitrile	$NC-(CH_2)_6-CN$
Urea	Carbamide	H_2NCONH_2
Ketene	Ethenone	$CH_2=C=O$
Toluene	Methyl benzene	C$_6$H$_5$—CH$_3$
Aniline	Phenylamine	C$_6$H$_5$—NH$_2$
Cumene	iso-Propylbenzene	C$_6$H$_5$—CH(CH$_3$)$_2$
Benzyl alcohol	Phenylmethanol	C$_6$H$_5$—CH$_2$OH
o-Xylene	1,2-Dimethylbenzene	1,2-(CH$_3$)$_2$C$_6$H$_4$
m-Xylene	1,3-Dimethylbenzene	1,3-(CH$_3$)$_2$C$_6$H$_4$
p-Xylene	1,4-Dimethylbenzene	1,4-(CH$_3$)$_2$C$_6$H$_4$
Phthalic acid	Benzene-1,2-dicarboxylic acid	1,2-(COOH)$_2$C$_6$H$_4$
Isophthalic acid	Benzene-1,3-dicarboxylic acid	1,3-(COOH)$_2$C$_6$H$_4$
Terephthalic acid	Benzene-1,4-dicarboxylic acid	1,4-(COOH)$_2$C$_6$H$_4$

续表

Common or trivial name	Systematic (or IUPAC) name	Structure
o-Toluic acid	2-Mthylbenzoic acid	COOH, CH₃ (ortho)
p-Toluic acid	4-Methylbenzoic acid	COOH, CH₃ (para)
p-Tolualdehyde	4-Methylbenzaldehyde	CHO, CH₃ (para)
Benzidine	4,4′-Biphenyldiamine	H₂N-C₆H₄-C₆H₄-NH₂
Furfural	2-Formylfuran	(furan)-CHO
HFA134a	1,1,1,2-Tetrafluoroethane	CF_3CH_2F
LTBE	Ethyl t-butyl ether	$CH_3CH_2OC(CH_3)_3$
MTBE	Methyl t-butyl ether	$CH_3OC(CH_3)_3$
TAME	t-Amyl methyl ether	$H_3C-C(CH_3)(CH_2CH_3)-OCH_3$

Ⅳ 元素名称及读法

原子序数	英语名称	读音	元素符号	中文名称	汉语拼音
1	hydrogen	[ˈhaidrəudʒən]	H	氢	qīng
2	helium	[ˈhiːljəm, -liəm]	He	氦	hài
3	lithium	[ˈliθiəm]	Li	锂	lǐ
4	beryllium	[bəˈriljəm]	Be	铍	pí
5	boron	[ˈbɔːrən]	B	硼	péng
6	carbon	[ˈkɑːbən]	C	碳	tàn
7	nitrogen	[ˈnaitrədʒən]	N	氮	dàn
8	oxygen	[ˈɔksidʒən]	O	氧	yǎng
9	fluorine	[ˈfluəriːn]	F	氟	fú
10	neon	[ˈniːən]	Ne	氖	nǎi
11	sodium	[ˈsəudjəm, -diəm]	Na	钠	nà
12	magnesium	[mægˈniːzjəm]	Mg	镁	měi
13	aluminum	[əˈljuːminəm]	Al	铝	lǚ
14	silicon	[ˈsilikən]	Si	硅	guī

续表

原子序数	英语名称	读音	元素符号	中文名称	汉语拼音
15	phosphorous	[ˈfɔsfərəs]	P	磷	lín
16	sulfur	[ˈsʌlfə]	S	硫	liú
17	chlorine	[ˈklɔːriːn]	Cl	氯	lǜ
18	argon	[ˈɑːgɔn]	Ar	氩	yà
19	potassium	[pəˈtæsiəm]	K	钾	jiǎ
20	calcium	[ˈkælsiəm]	Ca	钙	gài
21	scandium	[ˈkændiəm]	Sc	钪	kàng
22	titanium	[taiˈteinjəm, ti-]	Ti	钛	tài
23	vanadium	[vəˈneidiəm,-djəm]	V	钒	fán
24	chromium	[ˈkrəumjəm]	Cr	铬	gè
25	manganese	[ˈmæŋgəniːz]	Mn	锰	měng
26	iron	[ˈaiən]	Fe	铁	tiě
27	cobalt	[kəˈbɔːlt, ˈkəubɔːlt]	Co	钴	gǔ
28	nickel	[ˈnikl]	Ni	镍	niè
29	copper	[ˈkɔpə]	Cu	铜	tóng
30	zinc	[ziŋk]	Zn	锌	xīn
31	gallium	[ˈgæliəm]	Ga	镓	jiā
32	germanium	[dʒəːˈmeiniəm]	Ge	锗	zhě
33	arsenic	[ˈɑːsənik]	As	砷	shēn
34	selenium	[siˈliːniəm,-njəm]	Se	硒	xī
35	bromine	[ˈbrəumiːn]	Br	溴	xiù
36	krypton	[ˈkriptɔn]	Kr	氪	kè
37	rubidium	[ruːˈbidiəm]	Rb	铷	rú
38	strontium	[ˈstrɔnʃiəm]	Sr	锶	sī
39	yttrium	[ˈitriəm]	Y	钇	yǐ
40	zirconium	[zəːˈkəuniəm]	Zr	锆	gào
41	niobium	[naiˈəubiəm]	Nb	铌	ní
42	molybdenum	[məˈlibdinəm]	Mo	钼	mù
43	technetium	[tekˈniːʃəm]	Tc	锝	dé
44	ruthenium	[ruːˈθiːniəm]	Ru	钌	liǎo
45	rhodium	[ˈrəudiəm,-djəm]	Rh	铑	lǎo
46	palladium	[pəˈleidiəm]	Pd	钯	bǎ
47	silver	[ˈsilvə]	Ag	银	yín
48	cadmium	[ˈkædmiəm]	Cd	镉	gé
49	indium	[ˈindiəm]	In	铟	yīn
50	tin	[tin]	Sn	锡	xī
51	antimony	[ˈæntiməni]	Sb	锑	tī
52	tellurium	[teˈljuəriəm]	Te	碲	dì
53	iodine	[ˈaiədiːn]	I	碘	diǎn
54	xenon	[ˈzenɔn]	Xe	氙	xiān
55	cesium	[ˈsiːzjəm]	Cs	铯	sè
56	barium	[ˈbɛəriəm]	Ba	钡	bèi
57	lanthanum	[ˈlænθənəm]	La	镧	lán
58	cerium	[ˈsiəriəm]	Ce	铈	shì

续表

原子序数	英语名称	读音	元素符号	中文名称	汉语拼音
59	praseodymium	[ˌpreiziəu'dimiəm]	Pr	镨	pǔ
60	neodymium	[ni(:)ə'dimiəm]	Nd	钕	nǚ
61	promethium	[prə'mi:θiəm]	Pm	钷	pǒ
62	samarium	[sə'mɛəriəm]	Sm	钐	shān
63	europium	[juə'rəupiəm]	Eu	铕	yǒu
64	gadolinium	[ˌgædə'liniəm]	Gd	钆	gá
65	terbium	['tə:biəm]	Tb	铽	tè
66	dysprosium	[dis'prəusiəm]	Dy	镝	dī
67	holmium	['hɔlmiəm]	Ho	钬	huǒ
68	erbium	['ə:biəm]	Er	铒	ěr
69	thulium	['θju:liəm]	Tm	铥	diū
70	ytterbium	[i'tə:biəm]	Yb	镱	yì
71	lutetium	[lu:'ti:ʃiəm]	Lu	镥	lǔ
72	hafnium	['hæfniəm]	Hf	铪	hā
73	tantalum	['tæntələm]	Ta	钽	tǎn
74	tungsten	['tʌŋstən]	W	钨	wū
75	rhenium	['ri:niəm]	Re	铼	lái
76	osmium	['ɔzmiəm,-mjəm]	Os	锇	é
77	iridium	[i'ridiəm]	Ir	铱	yī
78	platinum	['plætinəm]	Pt	铂	bó
79	gold	[gəuld]	Au	金	jīn
80	mercury	['mə:kjuri]	Hg	汞	gǒng
81	thallium	['θæliəm]	Tl	铊	tā
82	lead	[li:d]	Pb	铅	qiān
83	bismuth	['bizməθ]	Bi	铋	bì
84	polonium	[pə'ləuniəm]	Po	钋	pō
85	astatine	['æstəti:n]	At	砹	ài
86	radon	['reidɔn]	Rn	氡	dōng
87	francium	['frænsiəm]	Fr	钫	fāng
88	radium	['reidjəm]	Ra	镭	léi
89	actinium	[æk'tiniəm]	Ac	锕	ā
90	thorium	['θɔ:riəm]	Th	钍	tǔ
91	protactinium	[ˌprəutæk'tiniəm]	Pa	镤	pú
92	uranium	[juə'reiniəm]	U	铀	yóu
93	neptunium	[nep'tju:niəm]	Np	镎	ná
94	plutonium	[plu:'təuniəm]	Pu	钚	bù
95	americium	[æmə'risjəm]	Am	镅	méi
96	curium	['kjuəriəm]	Cm	锔	jū
97	berkelium	[bə'kliəm]	Bk	锫	péi
98	californium	[kæli'fɔ:niəm]	Cf	锎	kāi
99	einsteinium	[ain'stainiəm]	Es	锿	āi
100	fermium	['fə:miəm]	Fm	镄	fèi
101	mendelevium	[ˌmendə'li:viəm]	Md	钔	mén
102	nobelium	[nəu'beliəm]	No	锘	nuò
103	lawrencium	[lɔː'rensiəm,lɑː-]	Lr	铹	láo

Ⅴ 常用化工产品英文缩写与中文名称对照表

英文缩写	中文名称	英文缩写	中文名称
A		BP	苯甲醇
A/MMA	丙烯腈/甲基丙烯酸甲酯共聚物	BPA	双酚A
AA	丙烯酸	BPBG	邻苯二甲酸丁(乙醇酸乙酯)酯
AAS	丙烯酸酯-丙烯酸酯-苯乙烯共聚物	BPF	双酚F
ABFN	偶氮(二)甲酰胺	BPMC	2-仲丁基苯基-N-甲基氨基酸酯
ABN	偶氮(二)异丁腈	BPO	过氧化苯甲酰
ABPS	壬基苯氧基丙烷磺酸钠	BPP	过氧化特戊酸特丁酯
B		BPPD	过氧化二碳酸二苯氧化酯
BAA	正丁醛苯胺缩合物	BPS	4,4'-硫代双(6-特丁基-3-甲基苯酚)
BAC	碱式氯化铝	BPTP	聚对苯二甲酸丁二醇酯
BACN	新型阻燃剂	BR	丁二烯橡胶
BAD	双水杨酸双酚A酯	BRN	青红光硫化黑
BAL	2,3-巯(基)丙醇	BROC	二溴(代)甲酚环氧丙基醚
BBP	邻苯二甲酸丁苄酯	BS	丁二烯-苯乙烯共聚物
BBS	N-叔丁基-乙-苯并噻唑次磺酰胺	BS-1S	新型密封胶
BC	叶酸	BSH	苯磺酰肼
BCD	β-环糊精	BSU	N,N'-双(三甲基硅烷)脲
BCG	苯顺二醇	BT	聚1-丁烯热塑性塑料
BCNU	氯化亚硝脲	BTA	苯并三唑
BD	丁二烯	BTX	苯-甲苯-二甲苯混合物
BE	丙烯酸乳胶外墙涂料	BX	渗透剂
BEE	苯偶姻乙醚	BXA	己二酸二丁基二甘酯
BFRM	硼纤维增强塑料	BZ	二正丁基二硫代氨基甲酸锌
BG	丁二醇	**C**	
BGE	反应性稀释剂	CA	醋酸纤维素
BHA	特丁基-4-羟基茴香醚	CAB	醋酸-丁酸纤维素
BHT	二丁基羟基甲苯	CAN	醋酸-硝酸纤维素
BL	丁内酯	CAP	醋酸-丙酸纤维素
BLE	丙酮-二苯胺高温缩合物	CBA	化学发泡剂
BLP	粉末涂料流平剂	CDP	磷酸甲酚二苯酯
BMA	甲基丙烯酸丁酯	CF	甲醛-甲酚树脂,碳纤维
BMC	团状模塑料	CFE	氯氟乙烯
BMU	氨基树脂皮革鞣剂	CFM	碳纤维密封填料
BN	氮化硼	CFRP	碳纤维增强塑料
BNE	新型环氧树脂	CLF	含氯纤维
BNS	β-萘磺酸甲醛低缩合物	CMC	羧甲基纤维素
BOA	己二酸辛苄酯	CMCNa	羧甲基纤维素钠
BOP	邻苯二甲酰丁辛酯	CMD	代尼尔纤维
BOPP	双轴向聚丙烯	CMS	羧甲基淀粉

英文缩写	中文名称	英文缩写	中文名称
D		EBM	挤出吹塑模塑
		EC	乙基纤维素
DAF	富马酸二烯丙酯	ECB	乙烯共聚物和沥青的共混物
DAIP	间苯二甲酸二烯丙酯		
DAM	马来酸二烯丙酯	ECD	环氧氯丙烷橡胶
DAP	间苯二甲酸二烯丙酯	ECTEE	聚(乙烯-三氟氯乙烯)
DATBP	四溴邻苯二甲酸二烯丙酯	ED-3	环氧酯
DBA	己二酸二丁酯	EDC	二氯乙烷
DBEP	邻苯二甲酸二丁氧乙酯	EDTA	乙二胺四醋酸
DBP	邻苯二甲酸二丁酯	EEA	乙烯-醋酸丙烯共聚物
DBR	二苯甲酰间苯二酚	EG	乙二醇
DBS	癸二酸二癸酯	2-EH	异辛醇
DCCA	二氯异氰脲酸	EO	环氧乙烷
DCCK	二氯异氰脲酸钾	EOT	聚乙烯硫醚
DCCNa	二氯异氰脲酸钠	EP	环氧树脂
DCHP	邻苯二甲酸二环乙酯	EPI	环氧氯丙烷
DCPD	过氧化二碳酸二环乙酯	EPM	乙烯-丙烯共聚物
DDA	己二酸二癸酯	EPOR	三元乙丙橡胶
DDP	邻苯二甲酸二癸酯	EPR	乙丙橡胶
DEAE	二乙胺基乙基纤维素	EPS	可发性聚苯乙烯
DEP	邻苯二甲酸二乙酯	EPSAN	乙烯-丙烯-苯乙烯-丙烯腈共聚物
DETA	二(1,2)-亚基三胺		
DFA	薄膜胶黏剂	EPT	乙烯丙烯三元共聚物
DHA	己二酸二己酯	EPVC	乳液法聚氯乙烯
DHP	邻苯二甲酸二己酯	EU	聚醚型聚氨酯
DHS	癸二酸二己酯	EVA	乙烯-醋酸乙烯共聚物
DIBA	己二酸二异丁酯	EVE	乙烯基乙基醚
DIDA	己二酸二异癸酯	EXP	醋酸乙烯-乙烯-丙烯酸酯三元共聚乳液
DIDG	戊二酸二异癸酯		
DIDP	邻苯二甲酸二异癸酯	**F**	
DINA	己二酸二异壬酯		
DINP	邻苯二甲酸二异壬酯	F/VAL	乙烯/乙烯醇共聚物
DINZ	壬二酸二异壬酯	F-23	四氟乙烯-偏氯乙烯共聚物
DIOA	己酸二异辛酯	F-30	三氟氯乙烯-乙烯共聚物
E		F-40	四氟氯乙烯-乙烯共聚物
		FDY	丙纶全牵伸丝
E/EA	乙烯/丙烯酸乙酯共聚物	FEP	全氟(乙烯-丙烯)共聚物
E/P	乙烯/丙烯共聚物	FNG	耐水硅胶
E/P/D	乙烯/丙烯/二烯三元共聚物	FPM	氟橡胶
		FRA	纤维增强丙烯酸酯
E/TEE	乙烯/四氟乙烯共聚物	FRC	阻燃粘胶纤维
E/VAC	乙烯/醋酸乙烯酯共聚物	FRP	纤维增强塑料
E/VAL	乙烯/乙烯醇共聚物	FRPA-101	玻璃纤维增强聚癸二酸癸胺(玻璃纤维增强尼龙1010树脂)
EAA	乙烯-丙烯酸共聚物		
EAK	乙基戊丙酮		

英文缩写	中文名称	英文缩写	中文名称
FRPA-610	玻璃纤维增强聚癸二酰乙二胺(玻璃纤维增强尼龙 610 树脂)	IPN	互贯网络聚合物
		IR	异戊二烯橡胶
FWA	荧光增白剂	IVE	异丁基乙烯基醚

G

GF	玻璃纤维		
GFRP	玻璃纤维增强塑料		
GFRTP	玻璃纤维增强热塑性塑料促进剂		
GOF	石英光纤		
GPS	通用聚苯乙烯		
GR-1	异丁橡胶		
GR-N	丁腈橡胶		
GR-S	丁苯橡胶		
GRTP	玻璃纤维增强热塑性塑料		
GUV	紫外光固化硅橡胶涂料		
GX	邻二甲苯		
GY	厌氧胶		

J

JSF	聚乙烯醇缩醛胶
JZ	塑胶胶黏剂

K

KSG	空分硅胶

L

LAS	十二烷基苯磺酸钠
LCM	液态固化剂
LDJ	低毒胶黏剂
LDN	氯丁胶黏剂
LDPE	高压聚乙烯(低密度)
LDR	氯丁橡胶
LF	脲
LGP	液化石油气
LHPC	低替代度羟丙基纤维素
LIM	液体浸渍模塑
LIPN	乳胶互贯网络聚合物
LJ	接体型氯丁橡胶
LLDPE	线性低密度聚乙烯
LM	低甲氧基果胶
LMG	液态甲烷气
LMWPE	低分子量聚乙烯
LN	液态氮
LRM	液态反应模塑
LRMR	增强液体反应模型
LSR	羧基氯丁乳胶

H

H	乌洛托品
HDI	六亚甲基二异氰酸酯
HDPE	低压聚乙烯(高密度)
HEDP	1-羟基-(1,1)-亚乙基-1,1-二膦酸
HFP	六氟丙烯
HIPS	高抗冲聚苯乙烯
HLA	天然聚合物透明质胶
HLD	树脂性氯丁胶
HM	高甲氧基果胶
HMC	高强度模塑料
HMF	非干性密封胶
HOPP	均聚聚丙烯
HPC	羟丙基纤维素
HPMC	羟丙基甲基纤维素
HPMCP	羟丙基甲基纤维素邻苯二甲酸酯
HPT	六甲基磷酸三酰胺
HS	六苯乙烯
HTPS	高冲击聚苯乙烯

M

MA	丙烯酸甲酯
MAA	甲基丙烯酸
MABS	甲基丙烯酸甲酯-丙烯腈-丁二烯-苯乙烯共聚物
MAL	甲基丙烯醛
MBS	甲基丙烯酸甲酯-丁二烯-苯乙烯共聚物
MBTE	甲基叔丁基醚
MC	甲基纤维素
MCA	三聚氰胺氰脲酸盐
MCPA-6	改性聚己内酰胺(铸型尼龙-6)

I

IEN	互贯网络弹性体
IHPN	互贯网络均聚物
IIR	异丁烯-异戊二烯橡胶
IO	离子聚合物
IPA	异丙醇

英文缩写	中文名称	英文缩写	中文名称
MCR	改性氯丁冷黏鞋用胶	ODA	己二酸异辛癸酯
MDI	3,3'-二甲基-4,4'-二氨基二苯甲烷	ODPP	磷酸辛二苯酯
		OIDD	邻苯二甲酸正辛异癸酯
MDI	二苯甲烷二异氰酸酯	OPP	定向聚丙烯(薄膜)
MDPE	中压聚乙烯(高密度)	OPS	定向聚苯乙烯(薄膜)
MEK	丁酮(甲乙酮)	OPVC	正向聚氯乙烯
MEKP	过氧化甲乙酮	OT	气熔胶
MES	脂肪酸甲酯磺酸盐		
MF	三聚氰胺-甲醛树脂	**P**	
M-HIPS	改性高冲聚苯乙烯	PA	聚酰胺(尼龙)
MIBK	甲基异丁基酮	PA-1010	聚癸二酸癸二胺(尼龙-1010)
MMA	甲基丙烯酸甲酯	PA-11	聚十一酰胺(尼龙-11)
MMF	甲基甲酰胺	PA-12	聚十二酰胺(尼龙-12)
MNA	甲基丙烯腈	PA-6	聚己内酰胺(尼龙-6)
MPEG	乙醇酸乙酯	PA-610	聚癸二酸乙二胺(尼龙-610)
MPF	三聚氰胺-酚醛树脂	PA-612	聚十二烷二酰乙二胺(尼龙-612)
MPK	甲基丙基甲酮	PA-66	聚己二酸己二胺(尼龙-66)
M-PP	改性聚丙烯	PA-8	聚辛酰胺(尼龙-8)
MPPO	改性聚苯醚	PA-9	聚(9-氨基壬酸)(尼龙-9)
MPS	改性聚苯乙烯	PAA	聚丙烯酸
MS	苯乙烯-甲基丙烯酸甲酯树脂	PAAS	水质稳定剂
MSO	石油醚	PABM	聚氨基双马来酰亚胺
MTBE	甲基叔丁基醚	PAC	聚氯化铝
MTT	氯丁胶新型交联剂	PAEK	聚芳基醚酮
MWR	旋转模塑	PAI	聚酰胺-酰亚胺
MXD-10/6	醇溶三元共聚尼龙	PAM	聚丙烯酰胺
MXDP	间苯二甲基二胺	PAMBA	抗血纤溶芳酸
		PAMS	聚α-甲基苯乙烯
N		PAN	聚丙烯腈
NBR	丁腈橡胶	PAP	对氨基苯酚
NDI	二异氰酸萘酯	PAPA	聚壬二酐
NDOP	邻苯二甲酸正癸辛酯	PAPI	多亚甲基多苯基异氰酸酯
NHDP	邻苯二甲酸己正癸酯	PAR	聚芳酰胺
NHTM	偏苯三酸正己酯	PAR	聚芳酯(双酚A型)
NINS	癸二酸二异辛酯	PAS	聚芳砜(聚芳基硫醚)
NLS	正硬脂酸铅	PB	聚1,3-丁二烯
NMP	N-甲基吡咯烷酮	PBAN	聚(丁二烯-丙烯腈)
NODA	己二酸正辛正癸酯	PBI	聚苯并咪唑
NODP	邻苯二甲酸正辛正癸酯	PBMA	聚甲基丙烯酸正丁酯
NPE	壬基酚聚氧乙烯醚	PBN	聚萘二酸丁醇酯
NR	天然橡胶	PBR	丙烯-丁二烯橡胶
		PBS	聚(丁二烯-苯乙烯)
O		PBS	聚(丁二烯-苯乙烯)
OBP	邻苯二甲酸辛苄酯	PBT	聚对苯二甲酸丁二醇酯

· 241 ·

英文缩写	中文名称	英文缩写	中文名称
PC	聚碳酸酯	SPP：	间规聚苯乙烯
PC/ABS	聚碳酸酯/ABS树脂共混合金	SPVC	悬浮法聚氯乙烯
PC/PBT	聚碳酸酯/聚对苯二甲酸丁二醇酯弹性体共混合金	SR	合成橡胶
		ST	矿物纤维
PCD	聚羰二酰亚胺		
PCDT	聚(1,4-环己烯二亚甲基对苯二甲酸酯)	**T**	
		TAC	三聚氰酸三烯丙酯
PCE	四氯乙烯	TAME	甲基叔戊基醚
PCMX	对氯间二甲酚	TAP	磷酸三烯丙酯
PCT	聚对苯二甲酸环己烷对二甲醇酯	TBE	四溴乙烷
PCT	聚己内酰胺	TBP	磷酸三丁酯
PCTEE	聚三氟氯乙烯	TCA	三醋酸纤维素
PD	二羟基聚醚	TCCA	三氯异氰脲酸
PDAIP	聚间苯二甲酸二烯丙酯	TCEF	磷酸三氯乙酯
PDAP	聚对苯二甲酸二烯丙酯	TCF	磷酸三甲酚酯
PDMS	聚二甲基硅氧烷	TCPP	磷酸三氯丙酯
PTA	对苯二甲酸	TDI	甲苯二异氰酸酯
		TEA	三乙胺
R		TEAE	三乙氨基乙基纤维素
RE	橡胶胶黏剂	TEDA	三乙二胺
RF	间苯二酚-甲醛树脂	TEFC	三氟氯乙烯
RFL	间苯二酚-甲醛乳胶	TEP	磷酸三乙酯
RP	增强塑料	TFE	四氟乙烯
RP/C	增强复合材料	THF	四氢呋喃
RX	橡胶软化剂	TLCP	热散液晶聚酯
		TMP	三羟甲基丙烷
S		TMPD	三甲基戊二醇
S/MS	苯乙烯-α-甲基苯乙烯共聚物	TMTD	二硫化四甲基秋兰姆(硫化促进剂TT)
SAN	苯乙烯-丙烯腈共聚物		
SAS	仲烷基磺酸钠	TNP	三壬基苯基亚磷酸酯
SB	苯乙烯-丁二烯共聚物	TPA	对苯二甲酸
SBR	丁苯橡胶	TPE	磷酸三苯酯
SBS	苯乙烯-丁二烯-苯乙烯嵌段共聚物	TPS	韧性聚苯乙烯
		TPU	热塑性聚氨酯树脂
SC	硅橡胶气调织物膜	TR	聚硫橡胶
SDDC	N,N-二甲基硫代氨基甲酸钠	TRPP	纤维增强聚丙烯
SE	磺乙基纤维素	TR-RFT	纤维增强聚对苯二甲酸丁二醇酯
SGA	丙烯酸酯胶		
SI	聚硅氧烷	TRTP	纤维增强热塑性塑料
SIS	苯乙烯-异戊二烯-苯乙烯嵌段共聚物	TTP	磷酸二甲苯酯
		U	
SIS/SEBS	苯乙烯-乙烯-丁二烯-苯乙烯共聚物		
		U	脲
		UF	脲甲醛树脂
SM	苯乙烯		
SMA	苯乙烯-顺丁烯二酸酐共聚物	UHMWPE	超高分子量聚乙烯

英文缩写	中文名称	英文缩写	中文名称
UP	不饱和聚酯	VPC	硫化聚乙烯
		VTPS	特种橡胶偶联剂

V

W

VAC	醋酸乙烯酯		
VAE	乙烯-醋酸乙烯共聚物	WF	新型橡塑填料
VAM	醋酸乙烯	WP	织物涂层胶
VAMA	醋酸乙烯-顺丁烯二酐共聚物	WRS	聚苯乙烯球形细粒
VC	氯乙烯		

X

VC/CDC	氯乙烯/偏二氯乙烯共聚物		
VC/E	氯乙烯/乙烯共聚物	XF	二甲苯-甲醛树脂
VC/E/MA	氯乙烯/乙烯/丙烯酸甲酯共聚物	XMC	复合材料

Y

VC/E/VAC	氯乙烯/乙烯/醋酸乙烯酯共聚物		
VC/MA	氯乙烯/丙烯酸甲酯共聚物	YH	改性氯丁胶
VC/MMA	氯乙烯/甲基丙烯酸甲酯共聚物	YM	聚丙烯酸酯压敏胶乳
VC/OA	氯乙烯/丙烯酸辛酯共聚物	YWG	液相色谱无定型微粒硅胶
VC/VAC	氯乙烯/醋酸乙烯酯共聚物		

Z

VCM	氯乙烯（单体）		
VCP	氯乙烯-丙烯共聚物	ZE	玉米纤维
VCS	丙烯腈-氯化聚乙烯-苯乙烯共聚物	ZH	溶剂型氯化天然橡胶胶黏剂
VDC	偏二氯乙烯	ZN	粉状脲醛树脂胶

REFERENCES

[1] Joseph A. Mascetta. Chemistry the Easy Way. Second Edition. New York：Barron's Educational Series, Inc；1989.

[2] Peter R. S. Murray. Principles of Organic Chemistry. Second Edition. London：Heinemann Educational Books，1977.

[3] Gary D. Christian, James E. O'Reilly. Instrumental Analysis. Second Edition. Boston：Allyn and Bacon, Inc；1956.

[4] John A. Miller，E. F. Neuzil. Modern Experimental Organic Chemistry. Lexington：D. C. Heath and Company，1982.

[5] D. H. Williams，I. Fleming. Spectroscopic Methods in Organic Chemistry（有机化学中的光谱方法）. 第2版. 北京：世界图书出版公司北京公司，2004.

[6] 孙凤霞. 仪器分析. 北京：化学工业出版社，2004.

[7] Warren I. Mc Cabe，Julian C. Smith Peter Harriott. Unit Operations of Chemical Engineering. 第6版（化学工程单元操作. 英文影印版）. 北京：化学工业出版社，2006.